3567405

P9-CDD-808

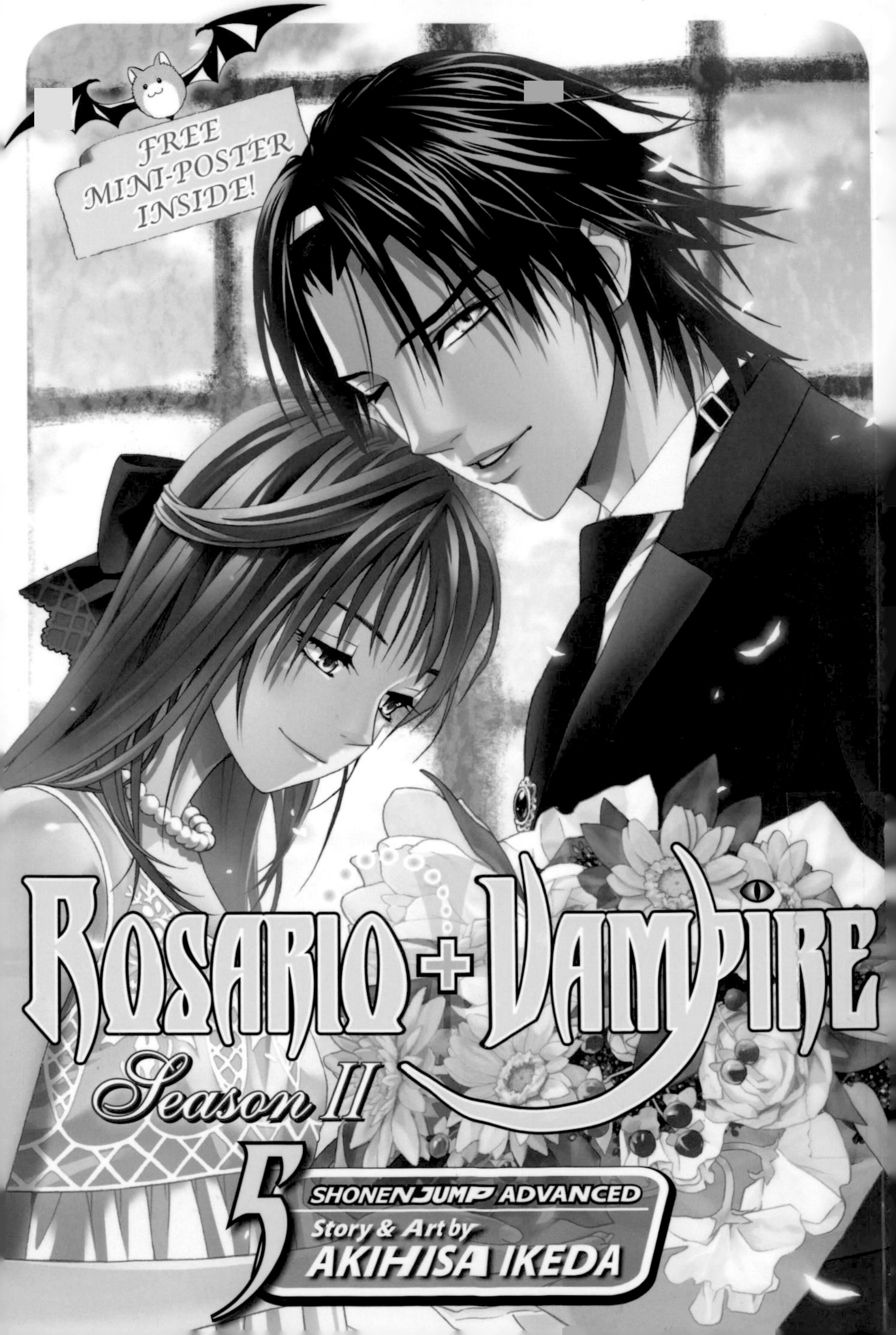
FREE MINI-POSTER INSIDE!
ROSARIO + VAMPIRE
Season II
5
SHONEN JUMP ADVANCED
Story & Art by
AKIHISA IKEDA

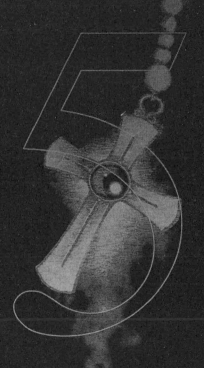

ROSARIO + VAMPIRE

Season II

5

AKIHISA IKEDA

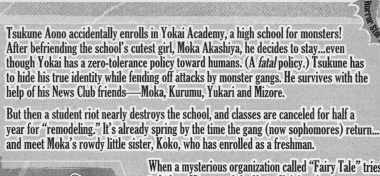

Tsukune Aono accidentally enrolls in Yokai Academy, a high school for monsters! After befriending the school's cutest girl, Moka Akashiya, he decides to stay...even though Yokai has a zero-tolerance policy toward humans. (A *fatal* policy.) Tsukune has to hide his true identity while fending off attacks by monster gangs. He survives with the help of his News Club friends—Moka, Kurumu, Yukari and Mizore.

But then a student riot nearly destroys the school, and classes are canceled for half a year for "remodeling." It's already spring by the time the gang (now sophomores) return... and meet Moka's rowdy little sister, Koko, who has enrolled as a freshman.

When a mysterious organization called "Fairy Tale" tries to kidnap Mizore and the News Club barely manages to save her, Tsukune realizes he lacks the power and technique to protect his friends, so he asks the Headmaster, Ruby, and Inner Moka to train him.

Tsukune Aono

Only his close friends know he's the lone human at Yokai and the only one who can pull off Moka's rosario. Due to repeated infusions of Moka's blood, he sometimes turns into a ghoul.

Moka Akashiya

The school beauty, adored by every boy. Transforms into a powerful vampire when the "rosario" around her neck is removed! Favorite food: Tsukune's blood! ♡

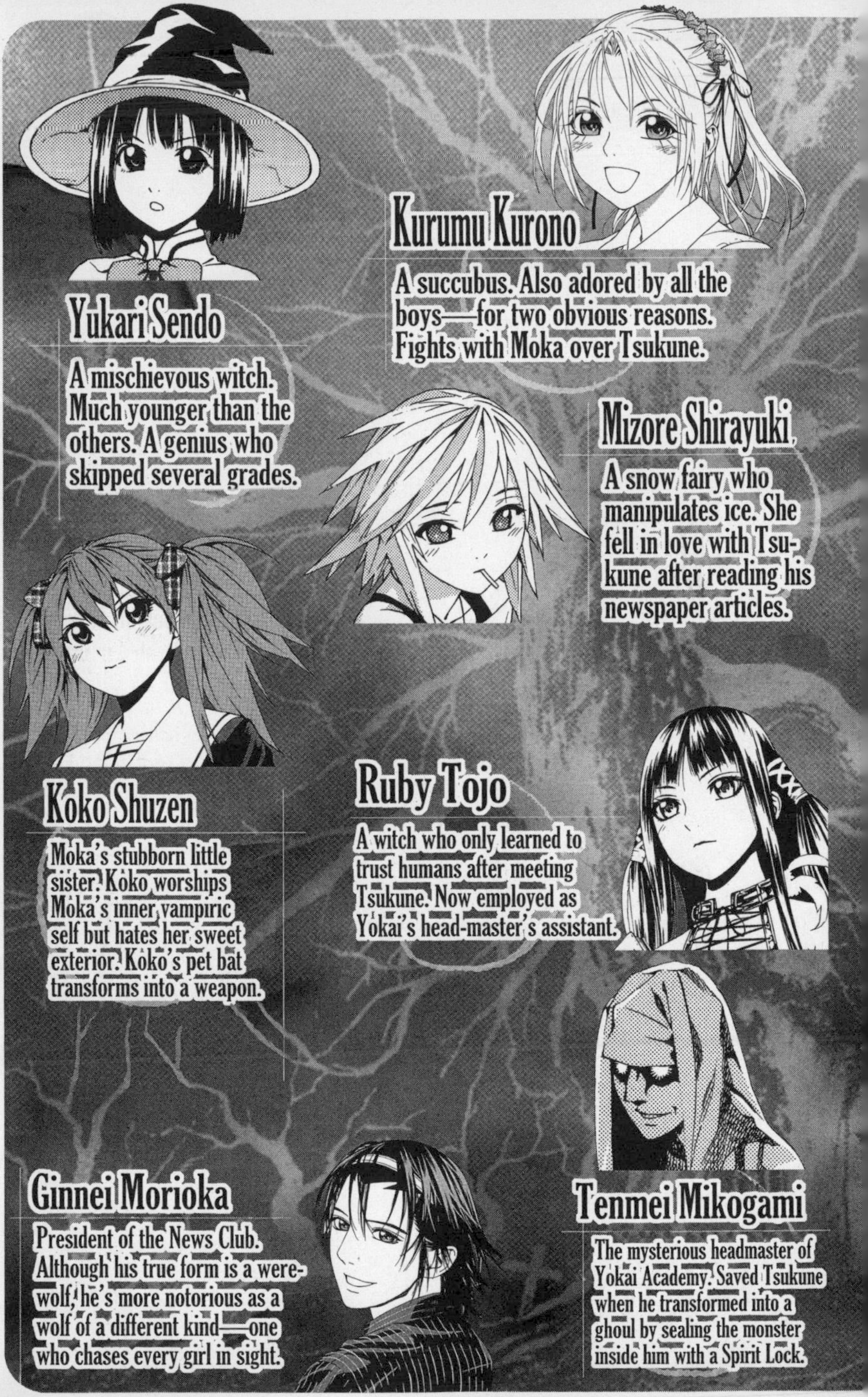
Kurumu Kurono
A succubus. Also adored by all the boys—for two obvious reasons. Fights with Moka over Tsukune.
Yukari Sendo
A mischievous witch. Much younger than the others. A genius who skipped several grades.
Mizore Shirayuki
A snow fairy who manipulates ice. She fell in love with Tsukune after reading his newspaper articles.
Ruby Tojo
A witch who only learned to trust humans after meeting Tsukune. Now employed as Yokai's head-master's assistant.
Koko Shuzen
Moka's stubborn little sister. Koko worships Moka's inner vampiric self but hates her sweet exterior. Koko's pet bat transforms into a weapon.
Tenmei Mikogami
The mysterious headmaster of Yokai Academy. Saved Tsukune when he transformed into a ghoul by sealing the monster inside him with a Spirit Lock.
Ginnei Morioka
President of the News Club. Although his true form is a werewolf, he's more notorious as a wolf of a different kind—one who chases every girl in sight.

ROSARIO+VAMPIRE
season II

5

ontents

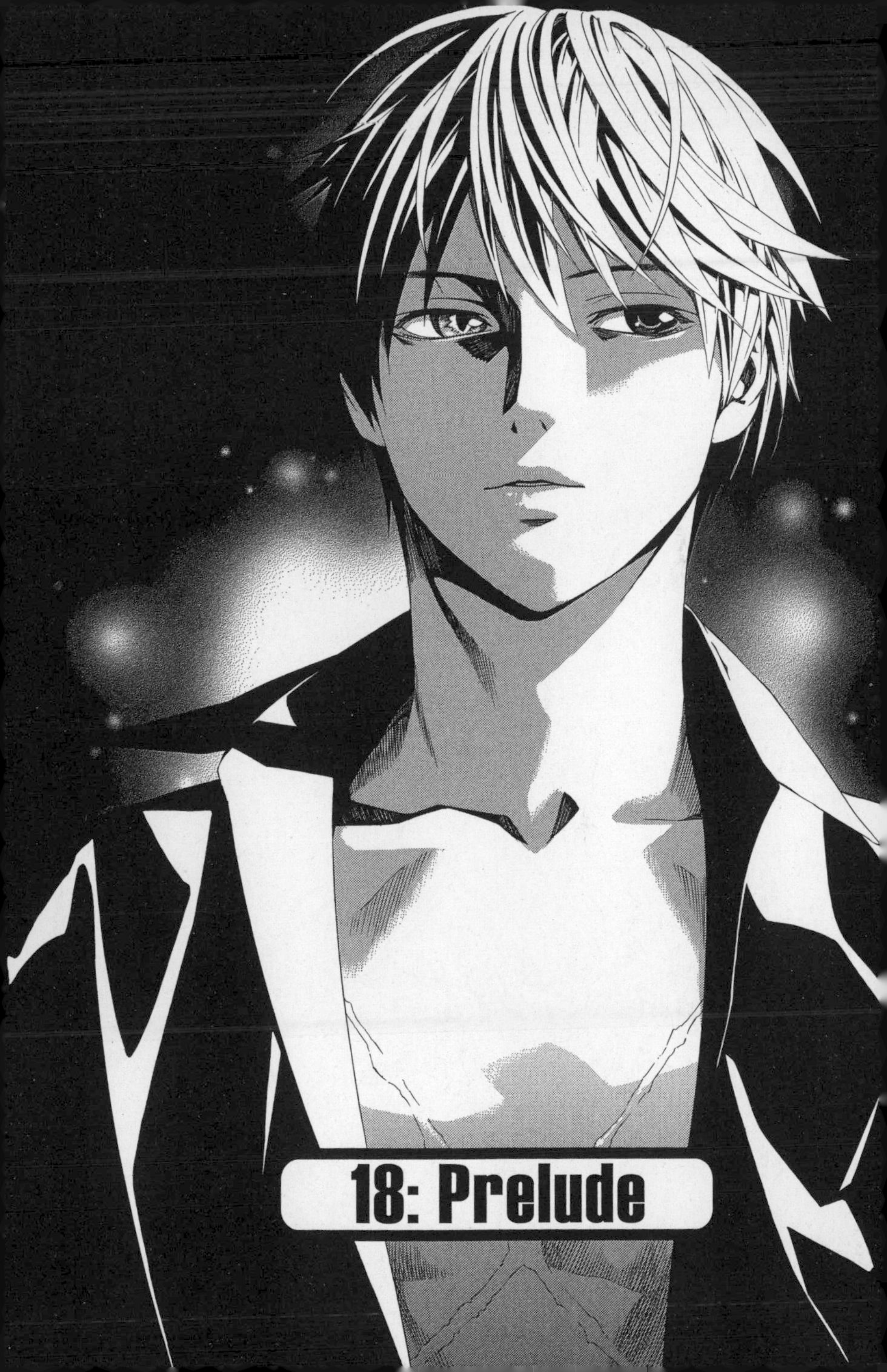
18: Prelude

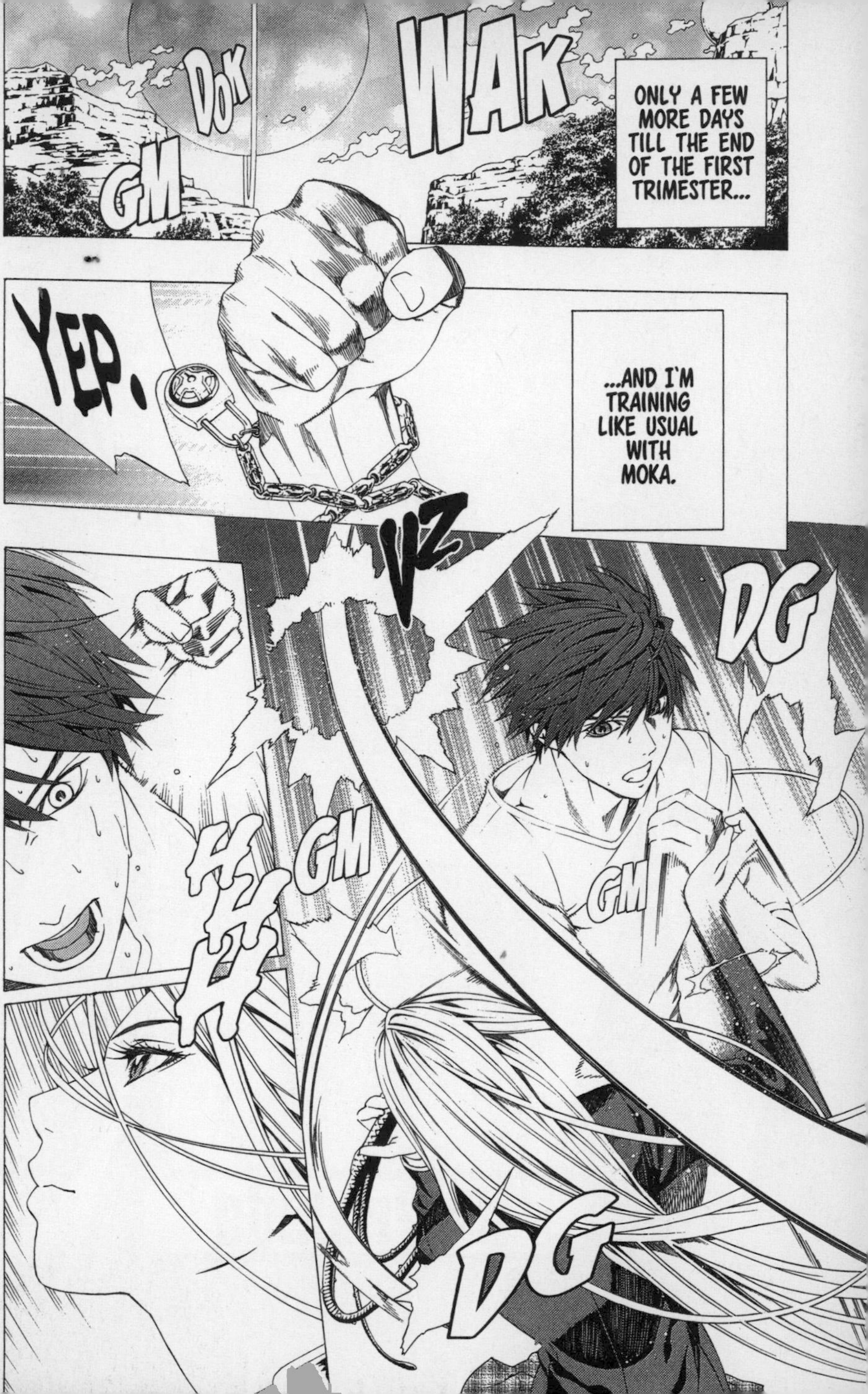
ONLY A FEW MORE DAYS TILL THE END OF THE FIRST TRIMESTER...
WAK
DOK
GM
...AND I'M TRAINING LIKE USUAL WITH MOKA.
YEP.
VZ
DG
GM
GM
DG

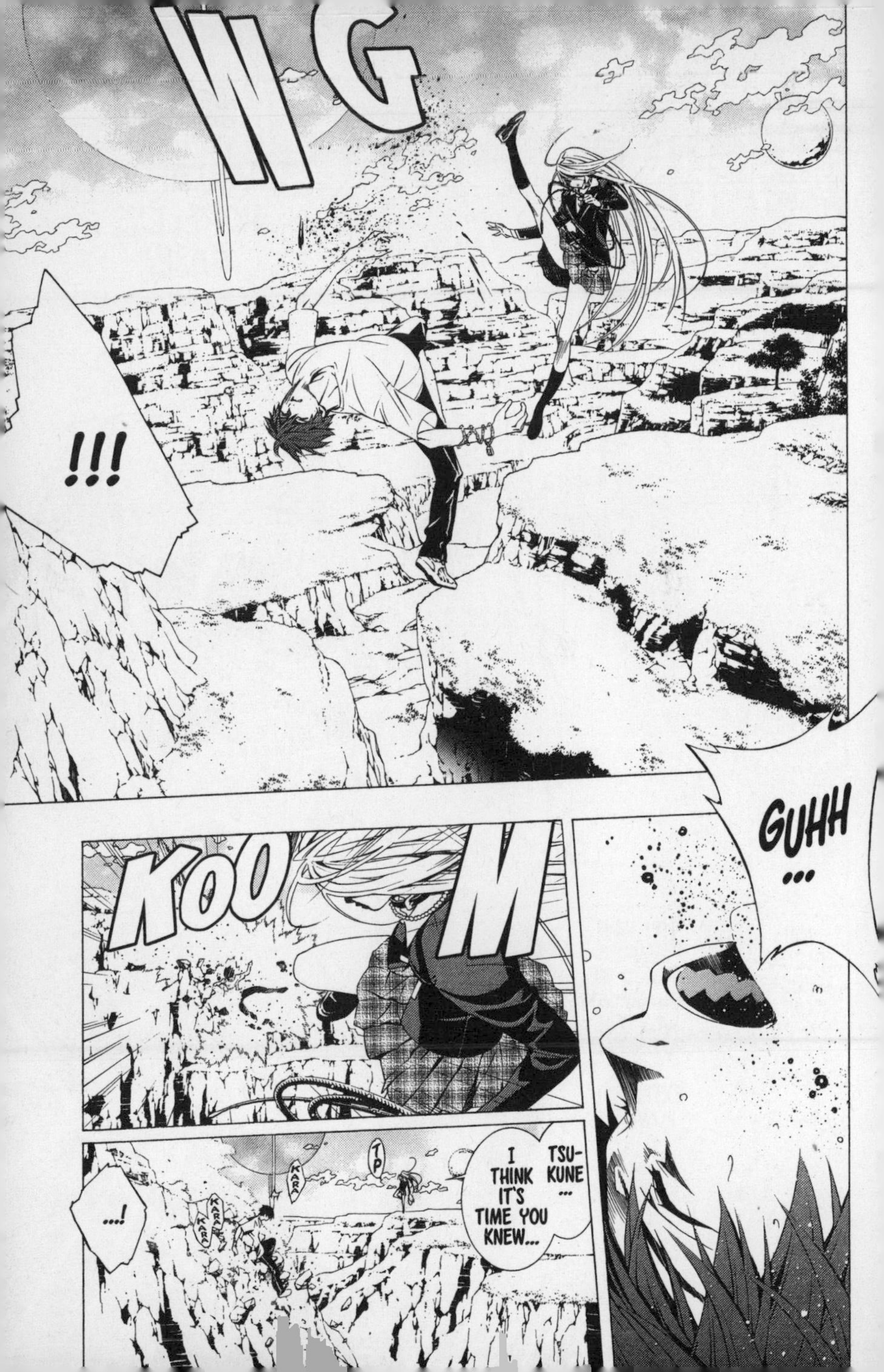
WG
!!!
GUHH ...
TSU-KUNE ...
I THINK IT'S TIME YOU KNEW...
KOOM
TP
KARA
KARA
KARA
...!

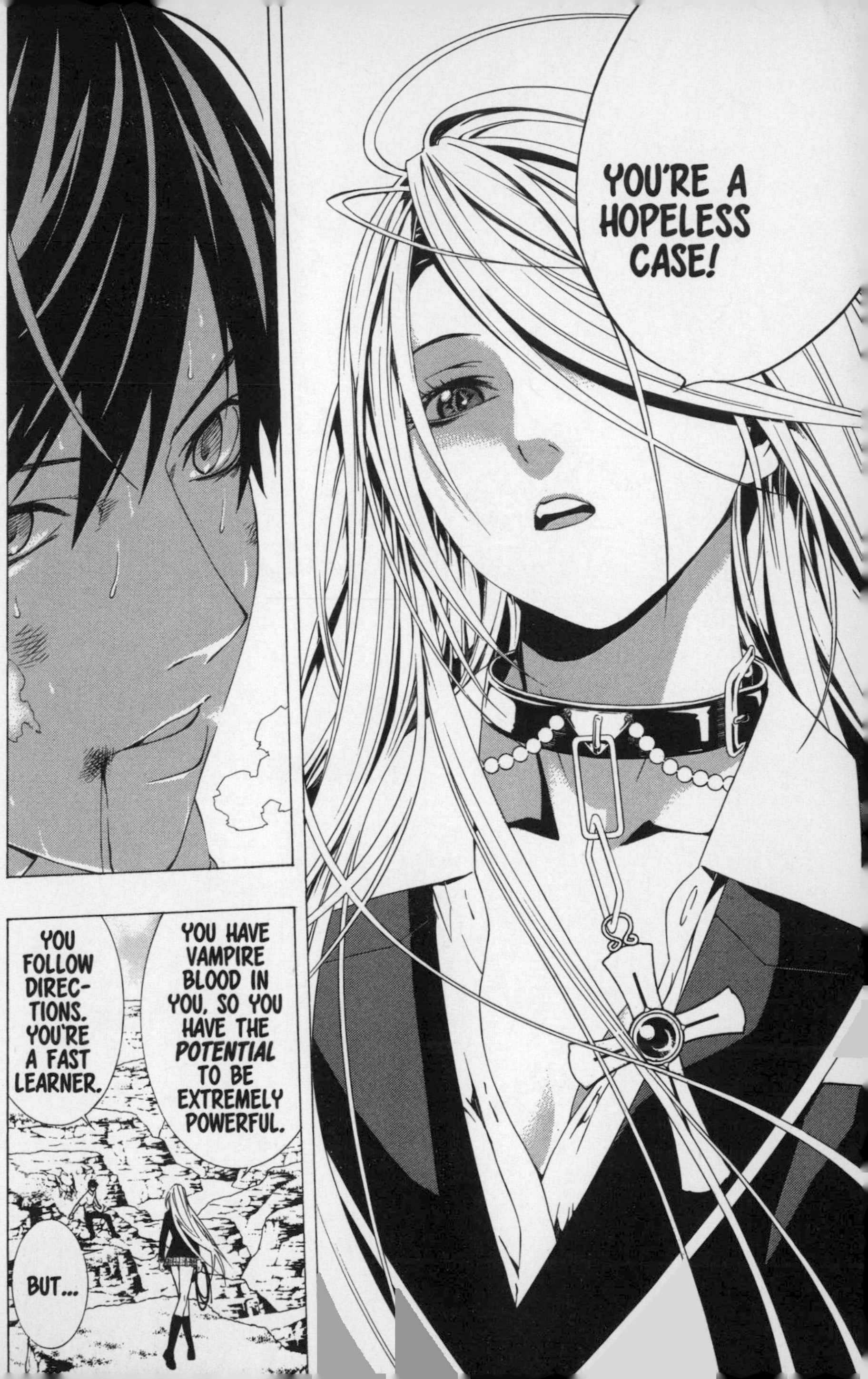
YOU'RE A HOPELESS CASE!
YOU HAVE VAMPIRE BLOOD IN YOU, SO YOU HAVE THE *POTENTIAL* TO BE EXTREMELY POWERFUL.
YOU FOLLOW DIREC-TIONS. YOU'RE A FAST LEARNER.
BUT...

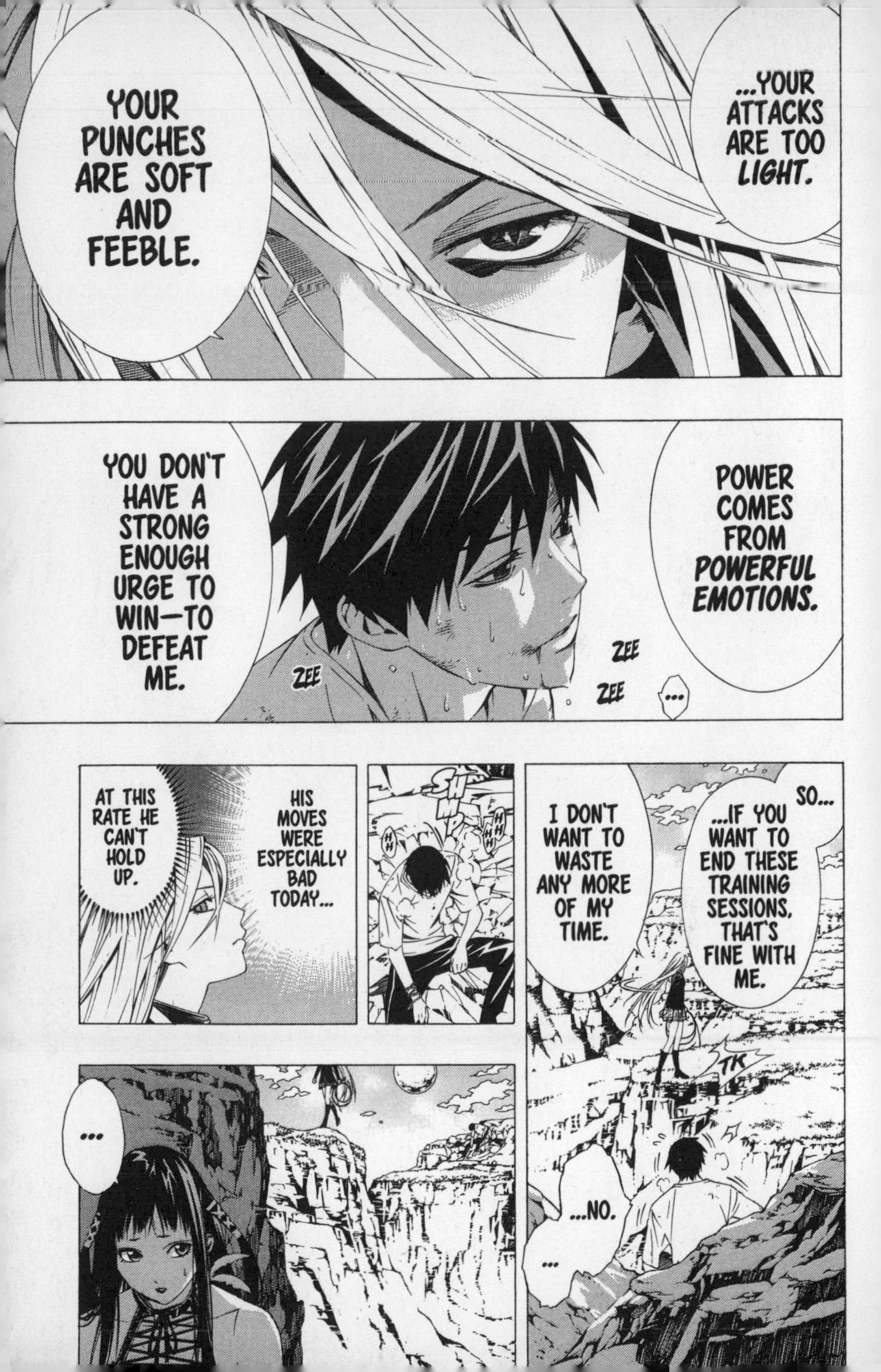
...YOUR ATTACKS ARE TOO LIGHT.
YOUR PUNCHES ARE SOFT AND FEEBLE.
POWER COMES FROM POWERFUL EMOTIONS.
ZEE
ZEE
...
YOU DON'T HAVE A STRONG ENOUGH URGE TO WIN—TO DEFEAT ME.
ZEE
SO...
...IF YOU WANT TO END THESE TRAINING SESSIONS, THAT'S FINE WITH ME.
I DON'T WANT TO WASTE ANY MORE OF MY TIME.
TK
...NO.
...
SHMP
HIS MOVES WERE ESPECIALLY BAD TODAY...
AT THIS RATE HE CAN'T HOLD UP.
...

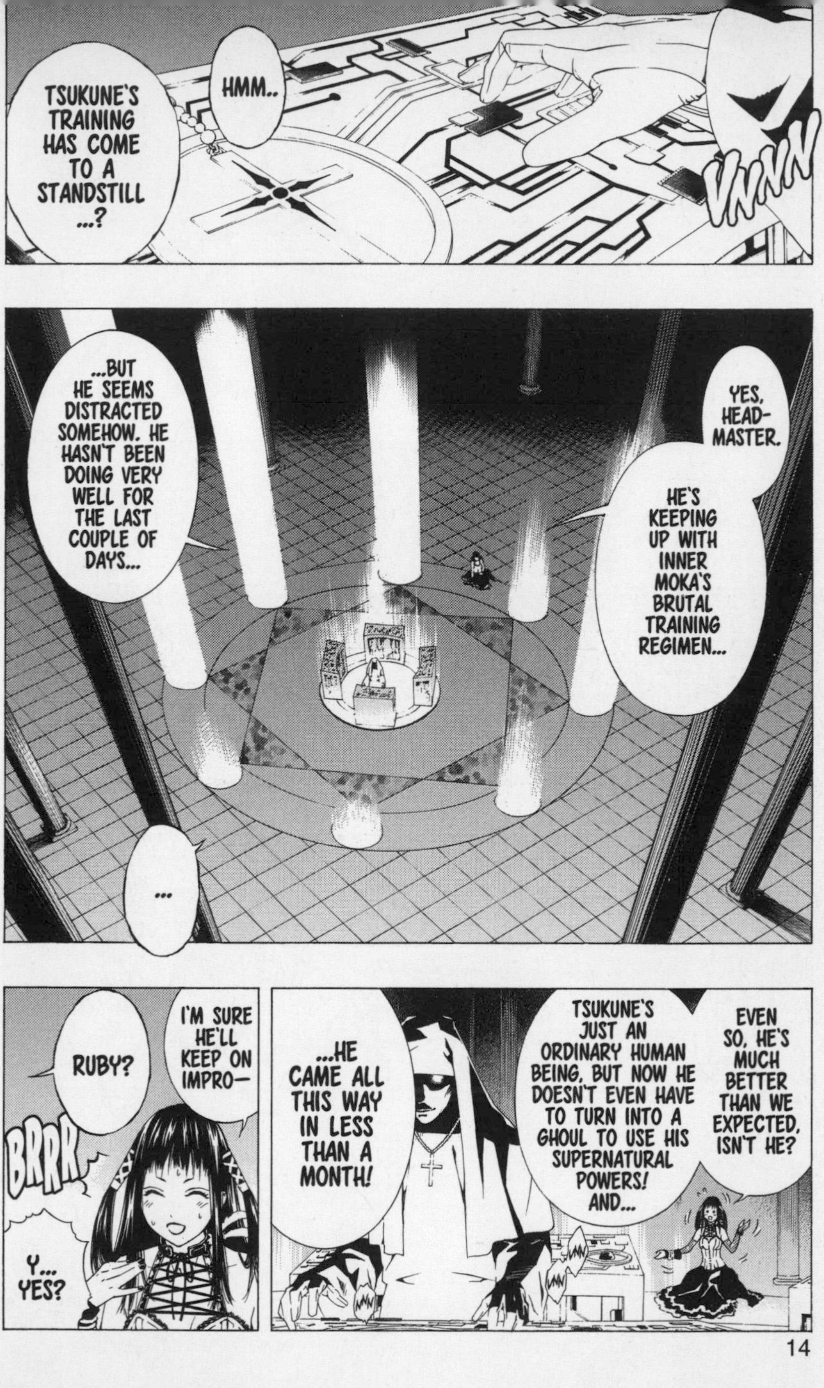
VNNN
HMM..
TSUKUNE'S TRAINING HAS COME TO A STANDSTILL ...?
YES, HEAD-MASTER.
HE'S KEEPING UP WITH INNER MOKA'S BRUTAL TRAINING REGIMEN...
...BUT HE SEEMS DISTRACTED SOMEHOW. HE HASN'T BEEN DOING VERY WELL FOR THE LAST COUPLE OF DAYS...
...
EVEN SO, HE'S MUCH BETTER THAN WE EXPECTED, ISN'T HE?
TSUKUNE'S JUST AN ORDINARY HUMAN BEING, BUT NOW HE DOESN'T EVEN HAVE TO TURN INTO A GHOUL TO USE HIS SUPERNATURAL POWERS! AND...
...HE CAME ALL THIS WAY IN LESS THAN A MONTH!
I'M SURE HE'LL KEEP ON IMPRO—
RUBY?
BRRK
Y... YES?

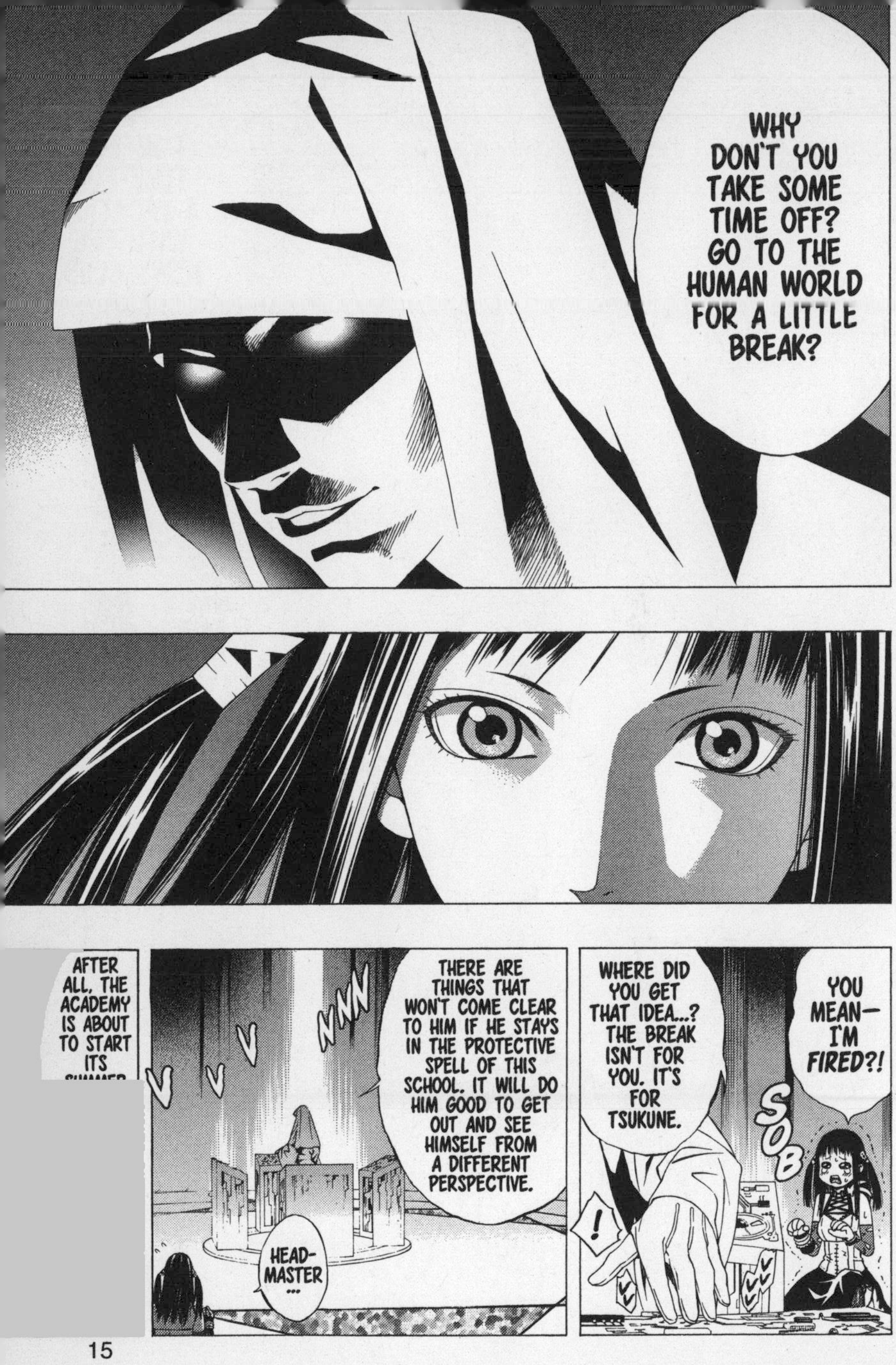
WHY DON'T YOU TAKE SOME TIME OFF? GO TO THE HUMAN WORLD FOR A LITTLE BREAK?
YOU MEAN— I'M *FIRED?!*
SOB
WHERE DID YOU GET THAT IDEA...? THE BREAK ISN'T FOR YOU. IT'S FOR TSUKUNE.
!
THERE ARE THINGS THAT WON'T COME CLEAR TO HIM IF HE STAYS IN THE PROTECTIVE SPELL OF THIS SCHOOL. IT WILL DO HIM GOOD TO GET OUT AND SEE HIMSELF FROM A DIFFERENT PERSPECTIVE.
HEAD-MASTER...
AFTER ALL, THE ACADEMY IS ABOUT TO START ITS

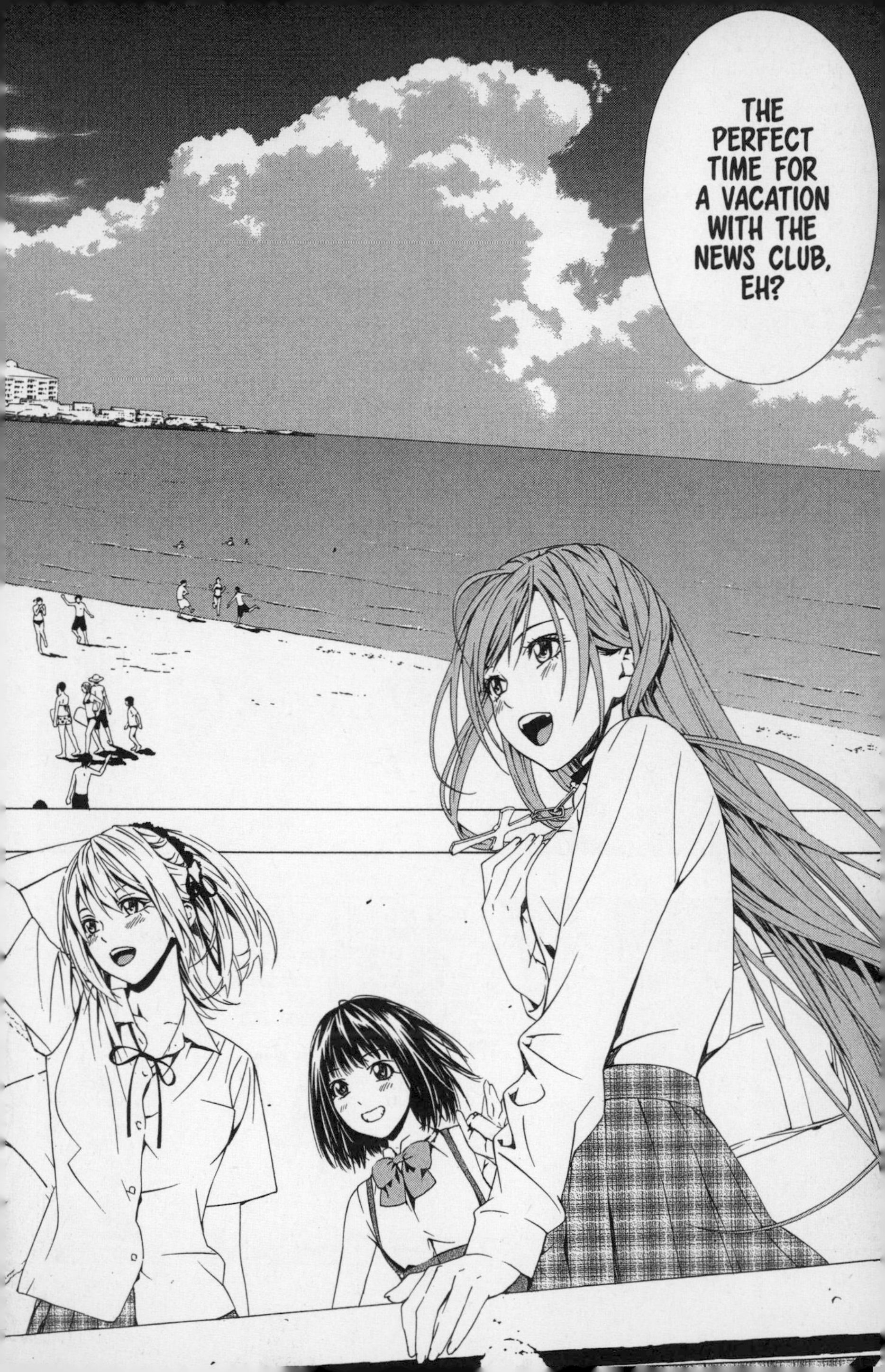
THE PERFECT TIME FOR A VACATION WITH THE NEWS CLUB, EH?

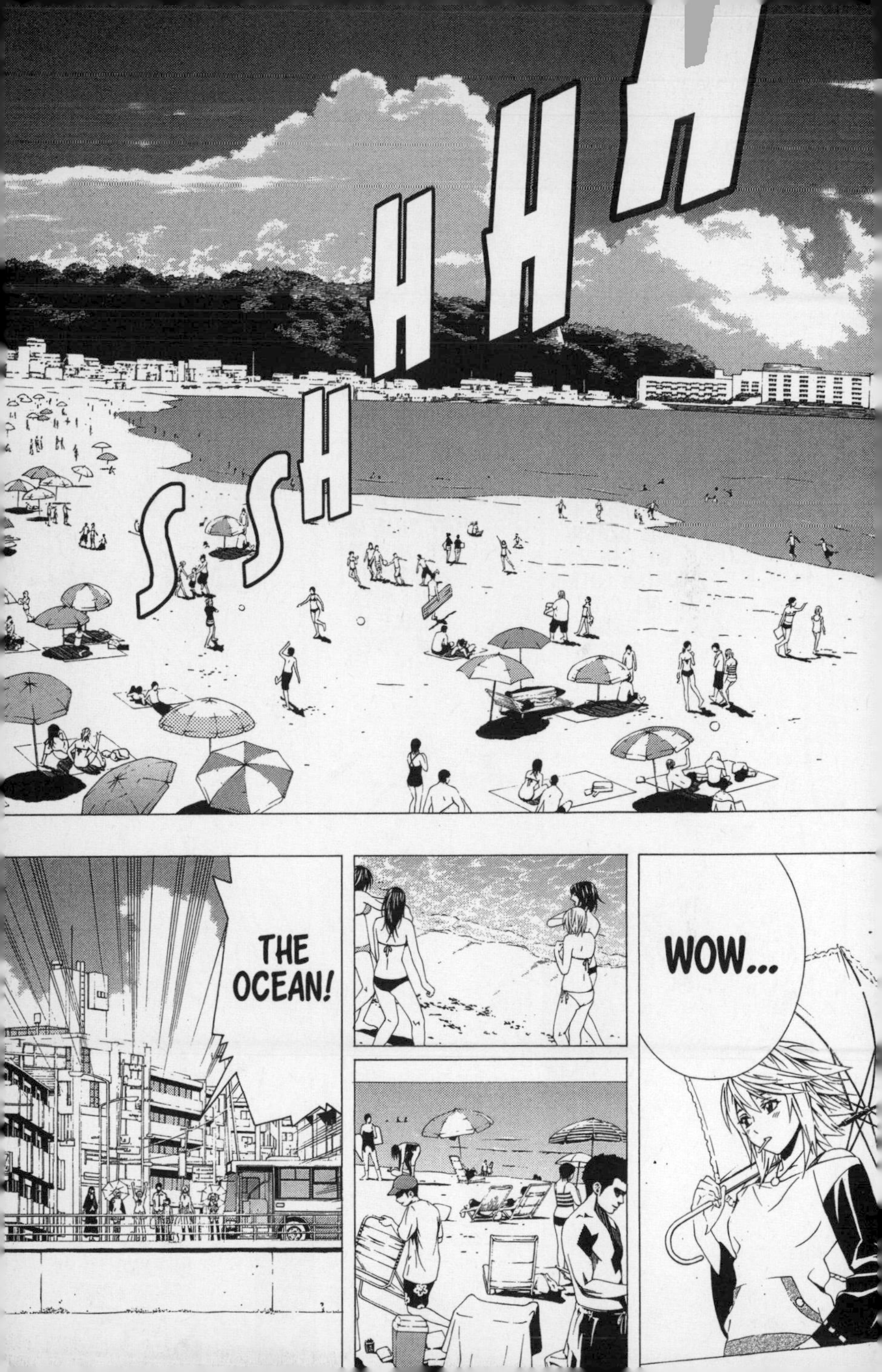
SSHHHH
WOW...
THE OCEAN!

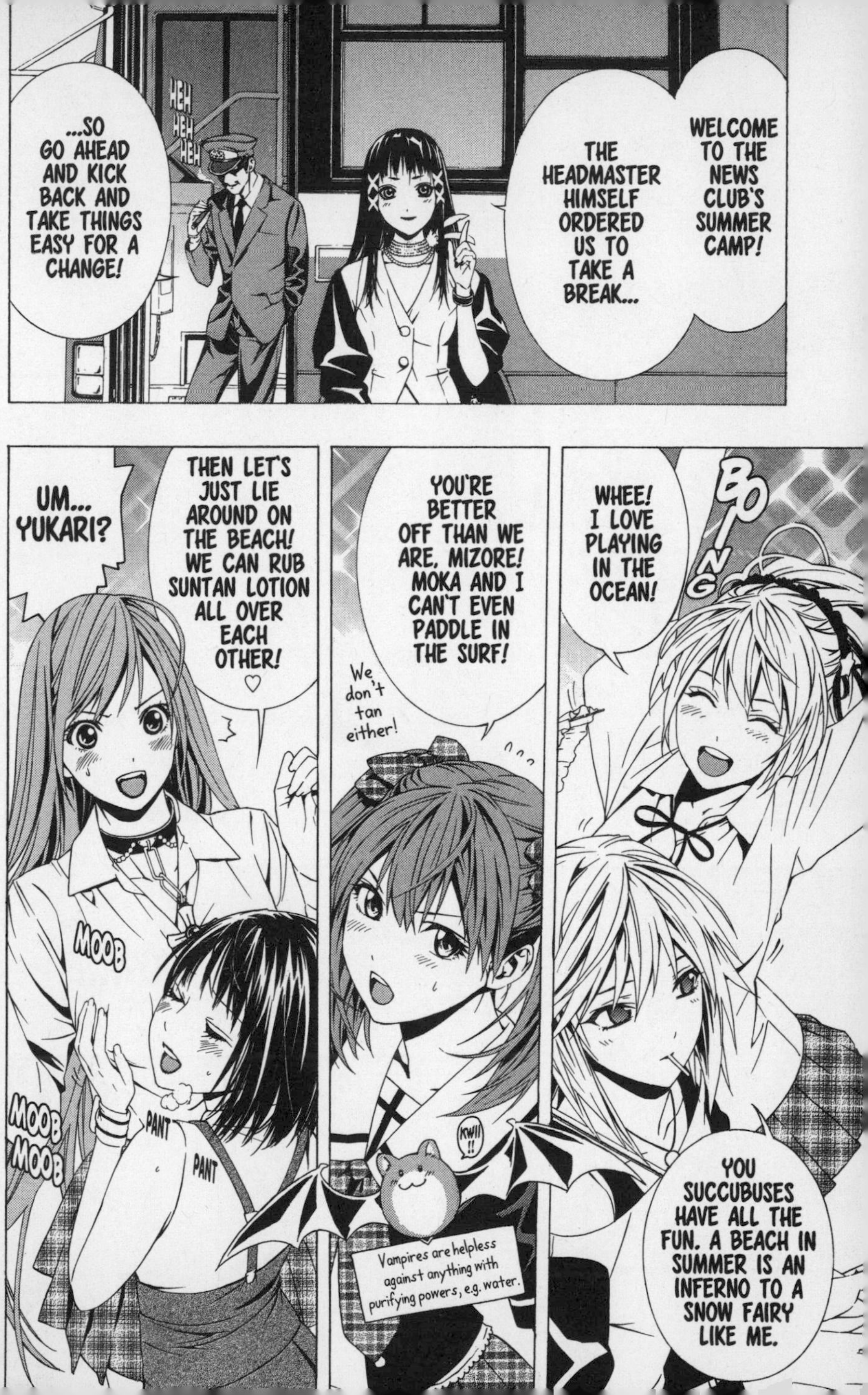
WELCOME TO THE NEWS CLUB'S SUMMER CAMP!
THE HEADMASTER HIMSELF ORDERED US TO TAKE A BREAK...
HEH HEH HEH
...SO GO AHEAD AND KICK BACK AND TAKE THINGS EASY FOR A CHANGE!
BOING
WHEE! I LOVE PLAYING IN THE OCEAN!
YOU SUCCUBUSES HAVE ALL THE FUN. A BEACH IN SUMMER IS AN INFERNO TO A SNOW FAIRY LIKE ME.
YOU'RE BETTER OFF THAN WE ARE, MIZORE! MOKA AND I CAN'T EVEN PADDLE IN THE SURF!
We don't tan either!
KWII!!
Vampires are helpless against anything with purifying powers, e.g. water.
THEN LET'S JUST LIE AROUND ON THE BEACH! WE CAN RUB SUNTAN LOTION ALL OVER EACH OTHER! ♡
UM... YUKARI?
MOOB
PANT PANT
MOOB MOOB

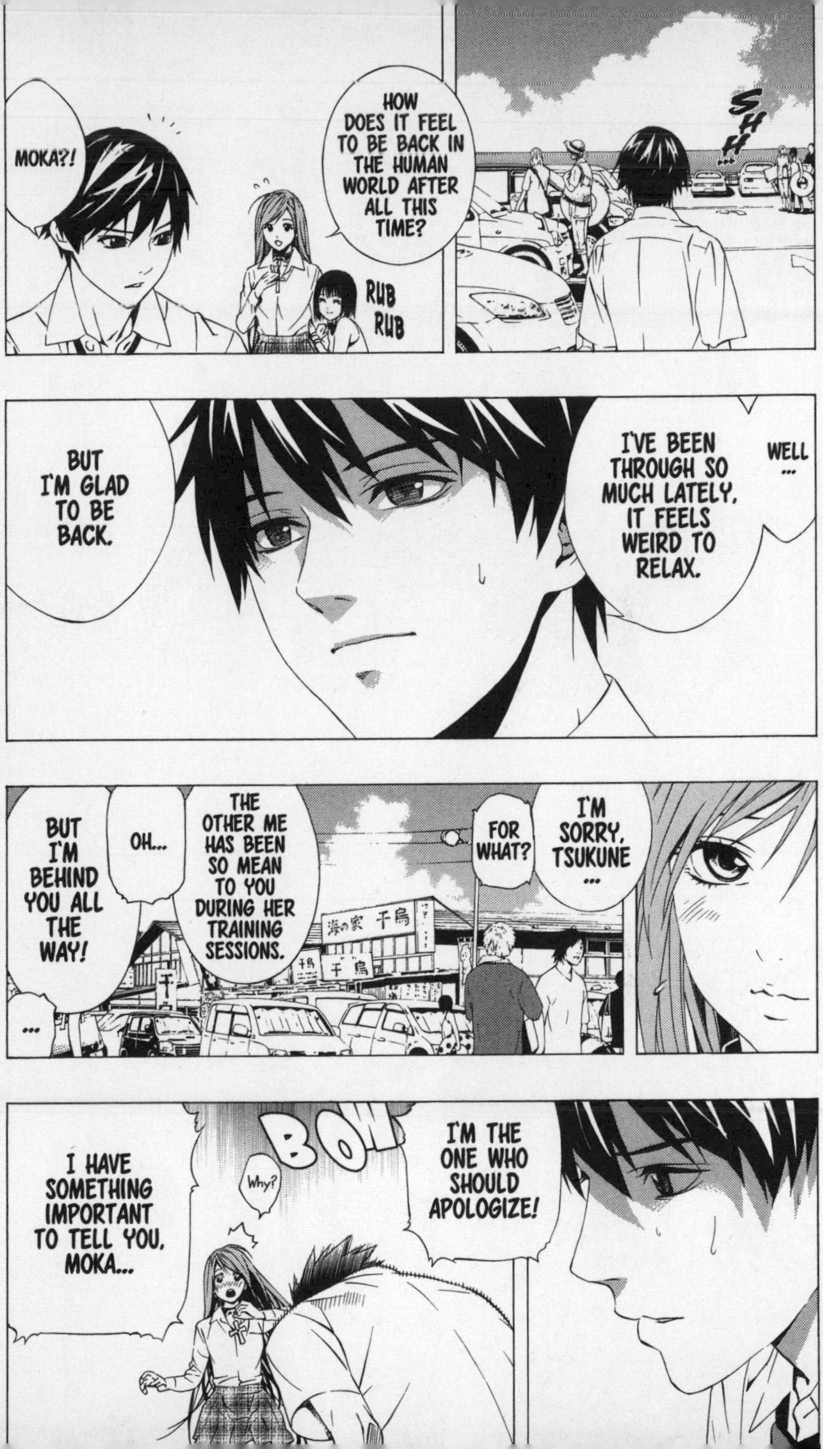
SHH...
HOW DOES IT FEEL TO BE BACK IN THE HUMAN WORLD AFTER ALL THIS TIME?
MOKA?!
RUB RUB
WELL...
I'VE BEEN THROUGH SO MUCH LATELY, IT FEELS WEIRD TO RELAX.
BUT I'M GLAD TO BE BACK.
I'M SORRY, TSUKUNE...
FOR WHAT?
THE OTHER ME HAS BEEN SO MEAN TO YOU DURING HER TRAINING SESSIONS.
OH...
BUT I'M BEHIND YOU ALL THE WAY!
...
I'M THE ONE WHO SHOULD APOLOGIZE!
BOM
Why?
I HAVE SOMETHING IMPORTANT TO TELL YOU, MOKA...

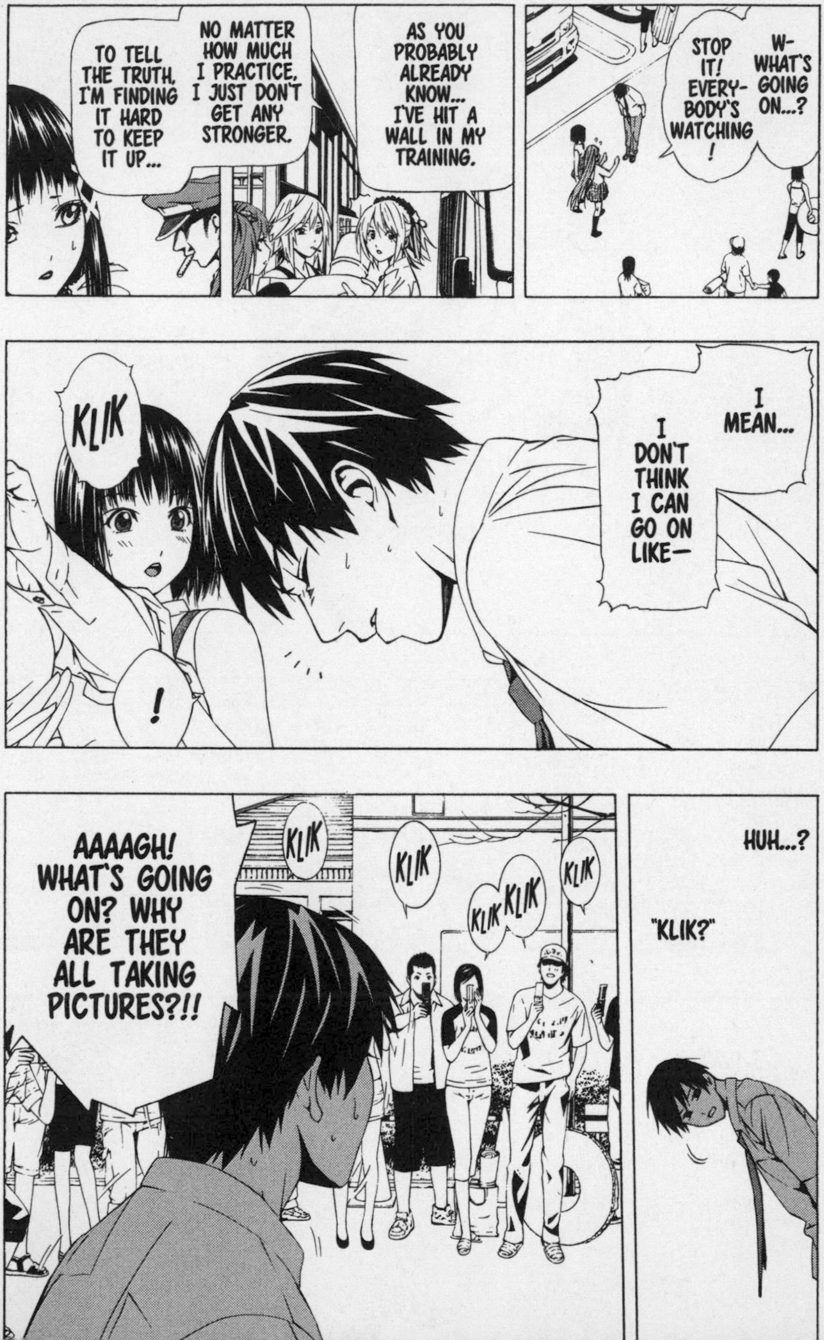
W- WHAT'S GOING ON...?
STOP IT! EVERY-BODY'S WATCHING!
AS YOU PROBABLY ALREADY KNOW... I'VE HIT A WALL IN MY TRAINING.
NO MATTER HOW MUCH I PRACTICE, I JUST DON'T GET ANY STRONGER.
TO TELL THE TRUTH, I'M FINDING IT HARD TO KEEP IT UP...
I MEAN...
I DON'T THINK I CAN GO ON LIKE—
KLIK
!
HUH...?
"KLIK?"
KLIK
KLIK
KLIK
KLIK
KLIK
AAAAGH! WHAT'S GOING ON? WHY ARE THEY ALL TAKING PICTURES?!!

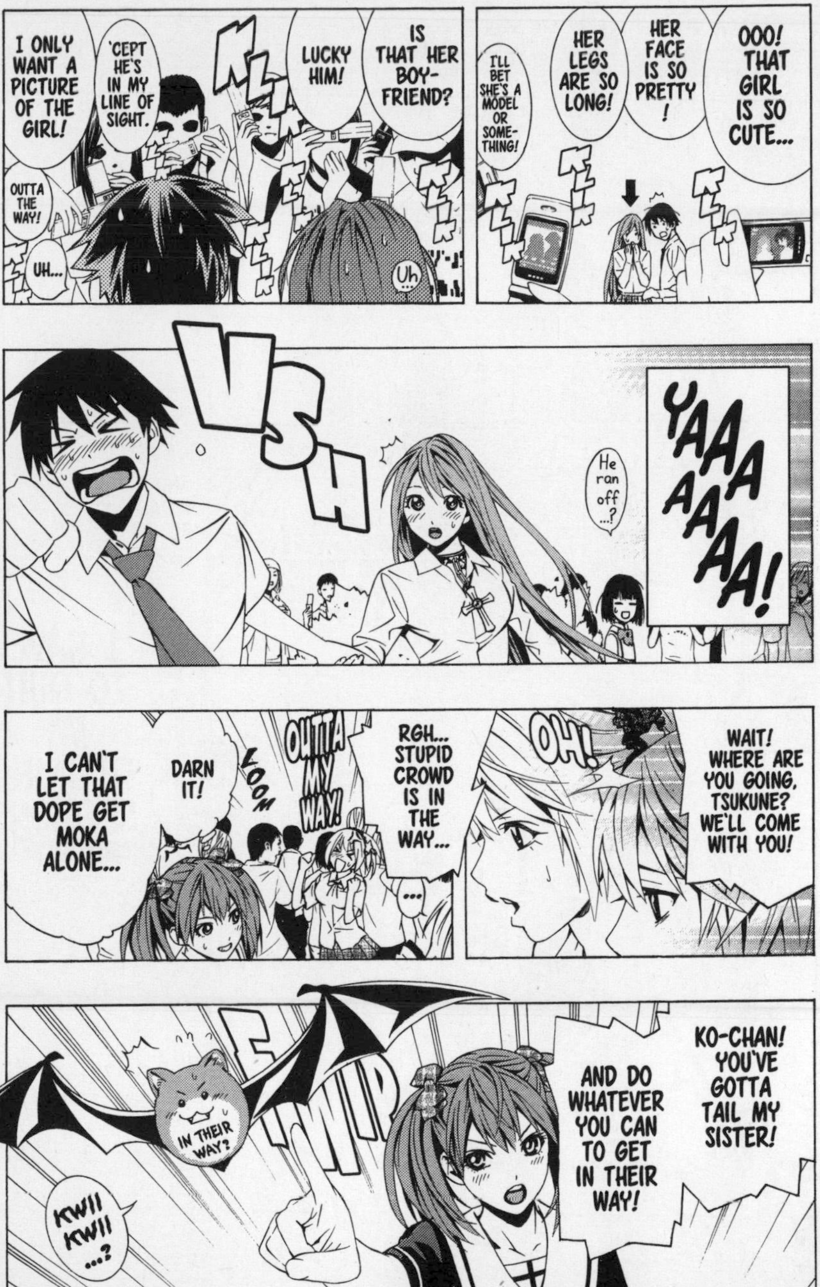
OOO! THAT GIRL IS SO CUTE...
HER FACE IS SO PRETTY!
HER LEGS ARE SO LONG!
I'LL BET SHE'S A MODEL OR SOME-THING!
KLIK
KLIK
KLIK
IS THAT HER BOY-FRIEND?
LUCKY HIM!
'CEPT HE'S IN MY LINE OF SIGHT.
I ONLY WANT A PICTURE OF THE GIRL!
KLIK
OUTTA THE WAY!
Uh...
UH...
YAAAAAAAAA!
He ran off ...?
VSH
WAIT! WHERE ARE YOU GOING, TSUKUNE? WE'LL COME WITH YOU!
OH!
RGH... STUPID CROWD IS IN THE WAY...
OUTTA MY WAY!
VOOM
DARN IT!
I CAN'T LET THAT DOPE GET MOKA ALONE...
...
KO-CHAN! YOU'VE GOTTA TAIL MY SISTER!
AND DO WHATEVER YOU CAN TO GET IN THEIR WAY!
IN THEIR WAY?
KWII KWII ...?

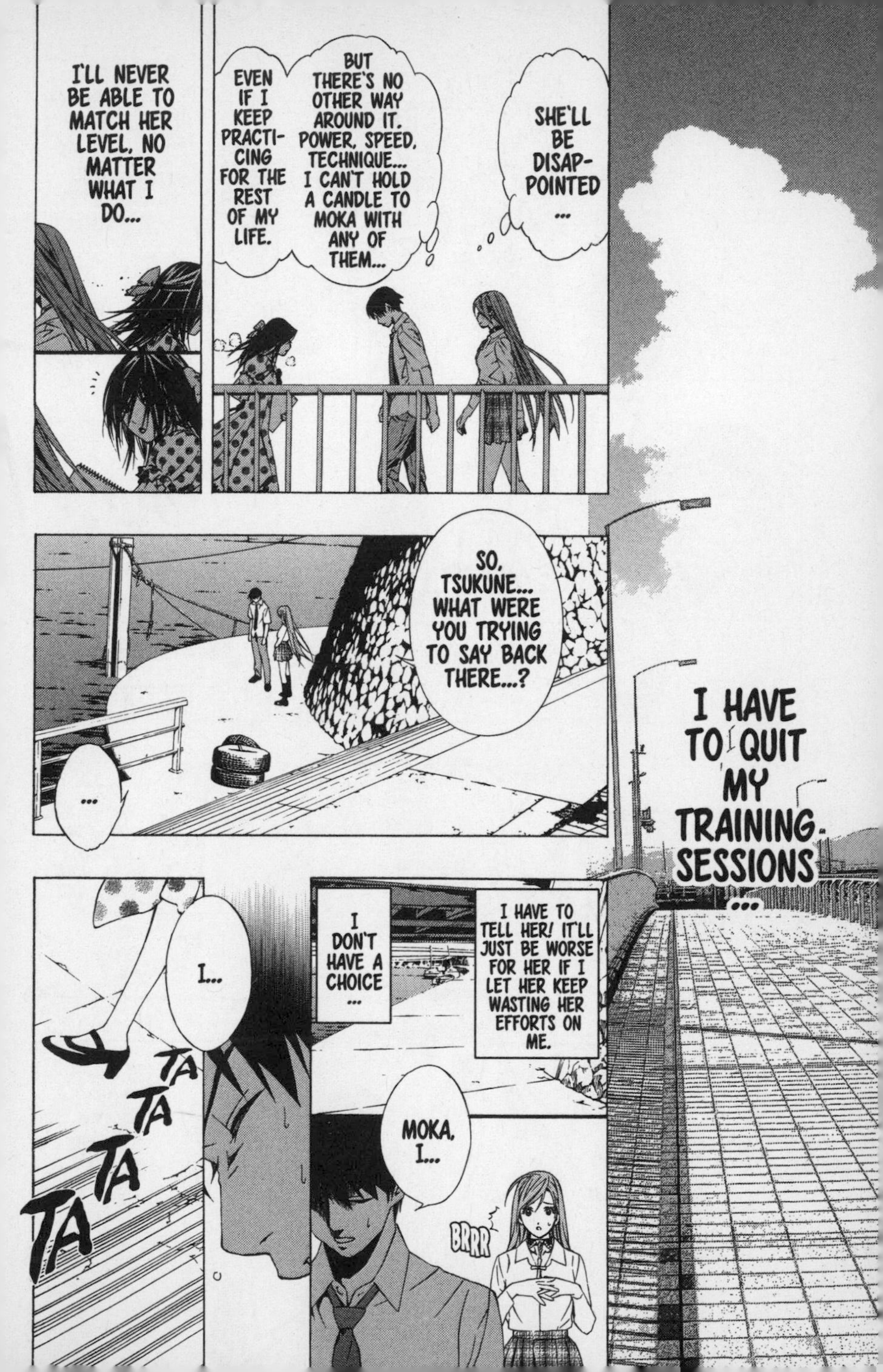
I HAVE TO QUIT MY TRAINING SESSIONS...
SHE'LL BE DISAPPOINTED...
BUT THERE'S NO OTHER WAY AROUND IT. POWER, SPEED, TECHNIQUE... I CAN'T HOLD A CANDLE TO MOKA WITH ANY OF THEM...
EVEN IF I KEEP PRACTICING FOR THE REST OF MY LIFE.
I'LL NEVER BE ABLE TO MATCH HER LEVEL, NO MATTER WHAT I DO...
SO, TSUKUNE... WHAT WERE YOU TRYING TO SAY BACK THERE...?
...
I HAVE TO TELL HER! IT'LL JUST BE WORSE FOR HER IF I LET HER KEEP WASTING HER EFFORTS ON ME.
I DON'T HAVE A CHOICE...
MOKA, I...
BRRR
I...
TA TA TA TA

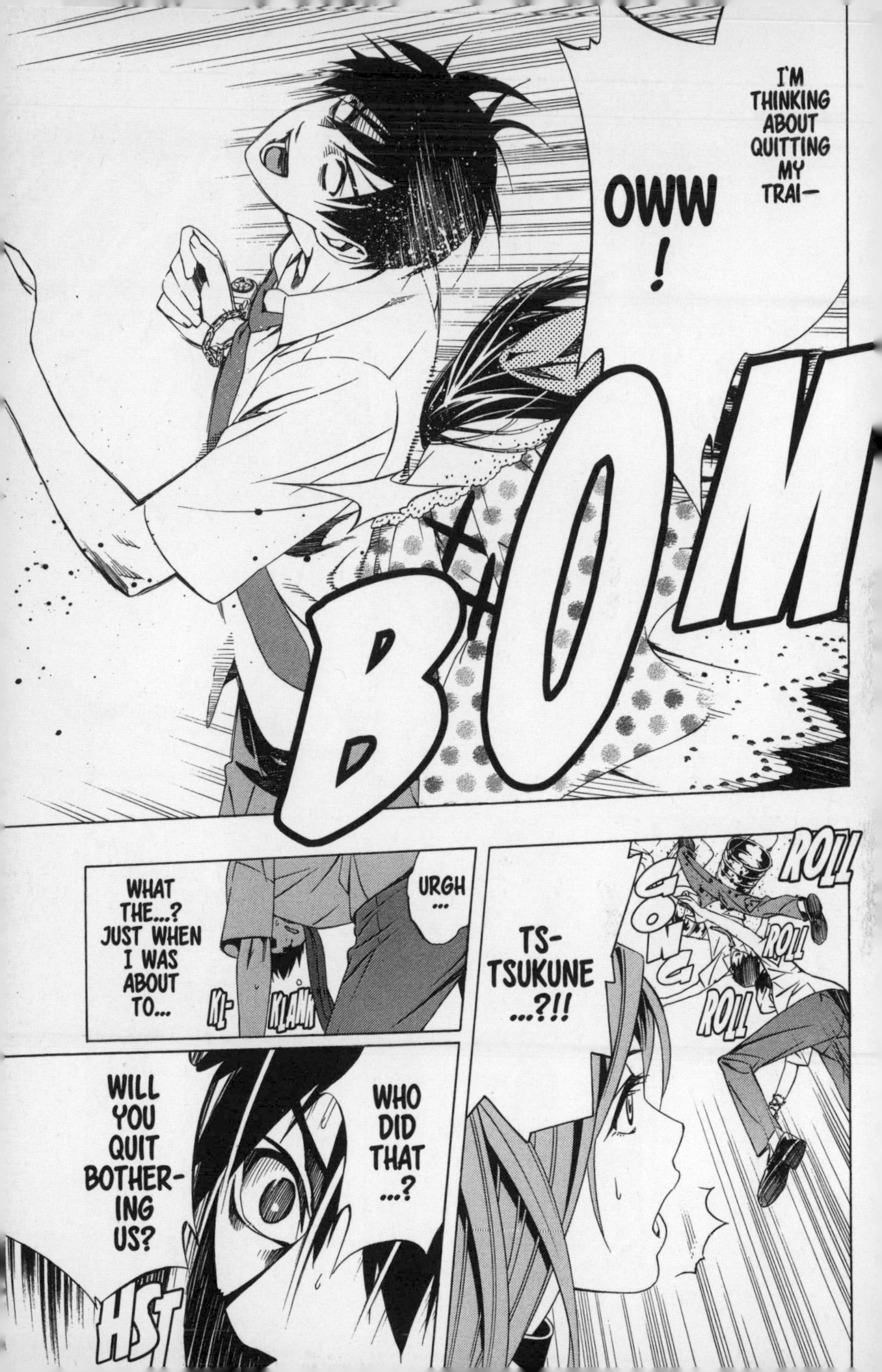
I'M THINKING ABOUT QUITTING MY TRAI—
OWW!
BOOM
ROLL
GONG
ROLL
ROLL
TS-TSUKUNE ...?!!
URGH ...
WHAT THE...? JUST WHEN I WAS ABOUT TO...
KL-
KLANK
WHO DID THAT ...?
WILL YOU QUIT BOTHER-ING US?
HST

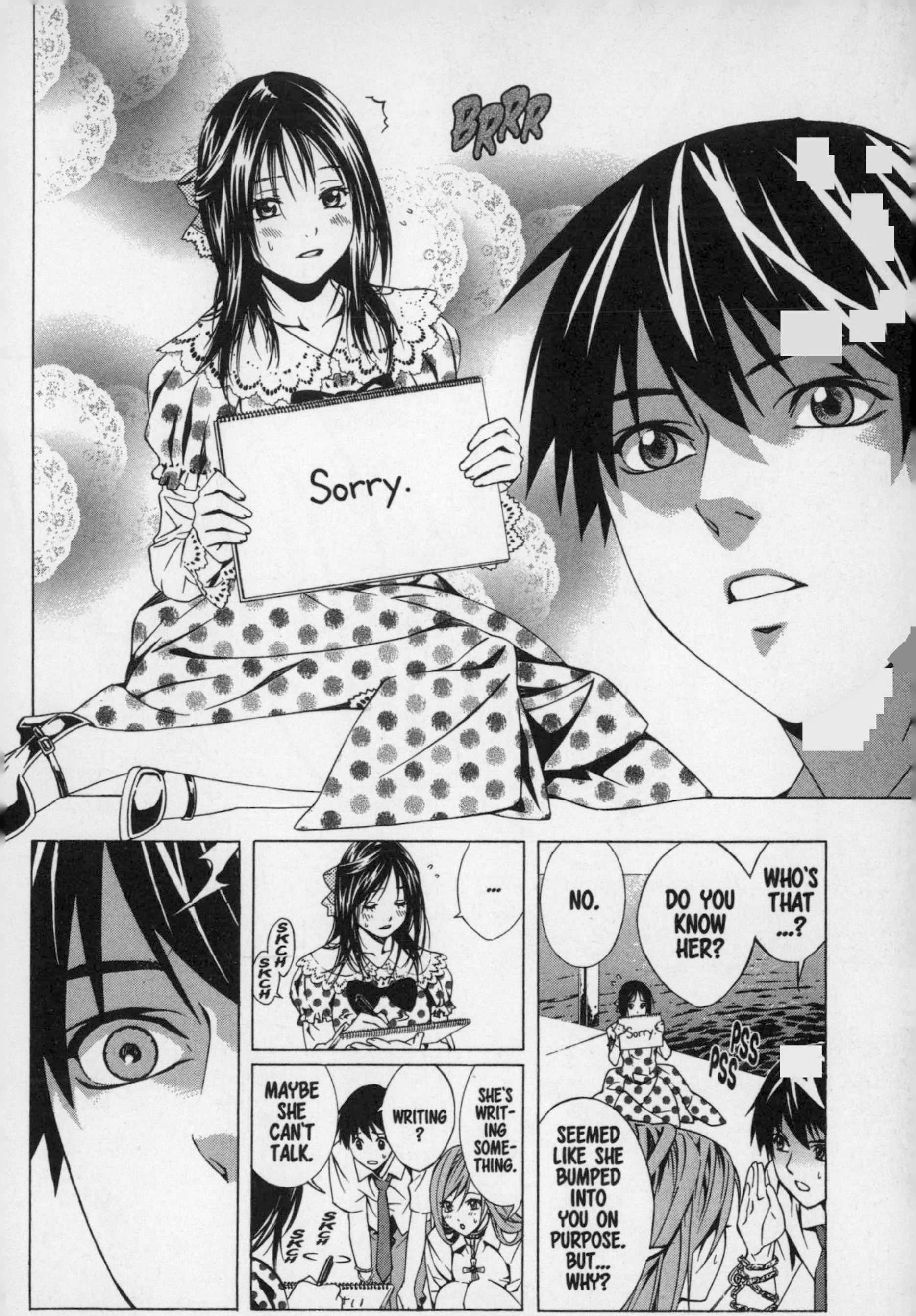
BRRR
Sorry.
WHO'S THAT ...?
DO YOU KNOW HER?
NO.
Sorry.
PSS PSS
SEEMED LIKE SHE BUMPED INTO YOU ON PURPOSE. BUT... WHY?
...
SKCH SKCH
SHE'S WRIT- ING SOME- THING.
WRITING ?
MAYBE SHE CAN'T TALK.
SKCH SKCH

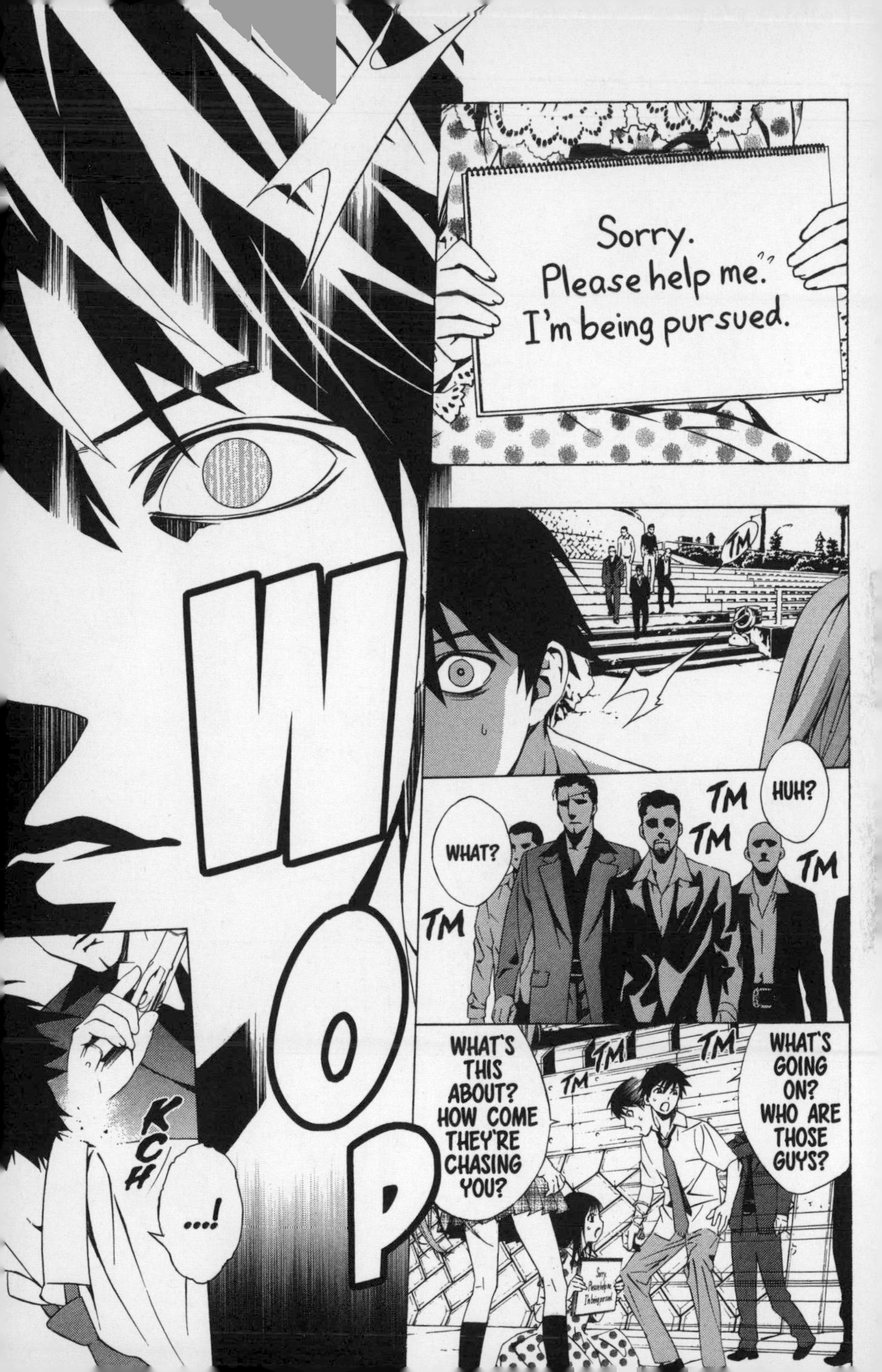
Sorry.
Please help me.
I'm being pursued.
TM
HUH?
TM
TM
TM
WHAT?
TM
WHAT'S GOING ON? WHO ARE THOSE GUYS?
TM
TM
TM
WHAT'S THIS ABOUT? HOW COME THEY'RE CHASING YOU?
WOP
KCH
...!

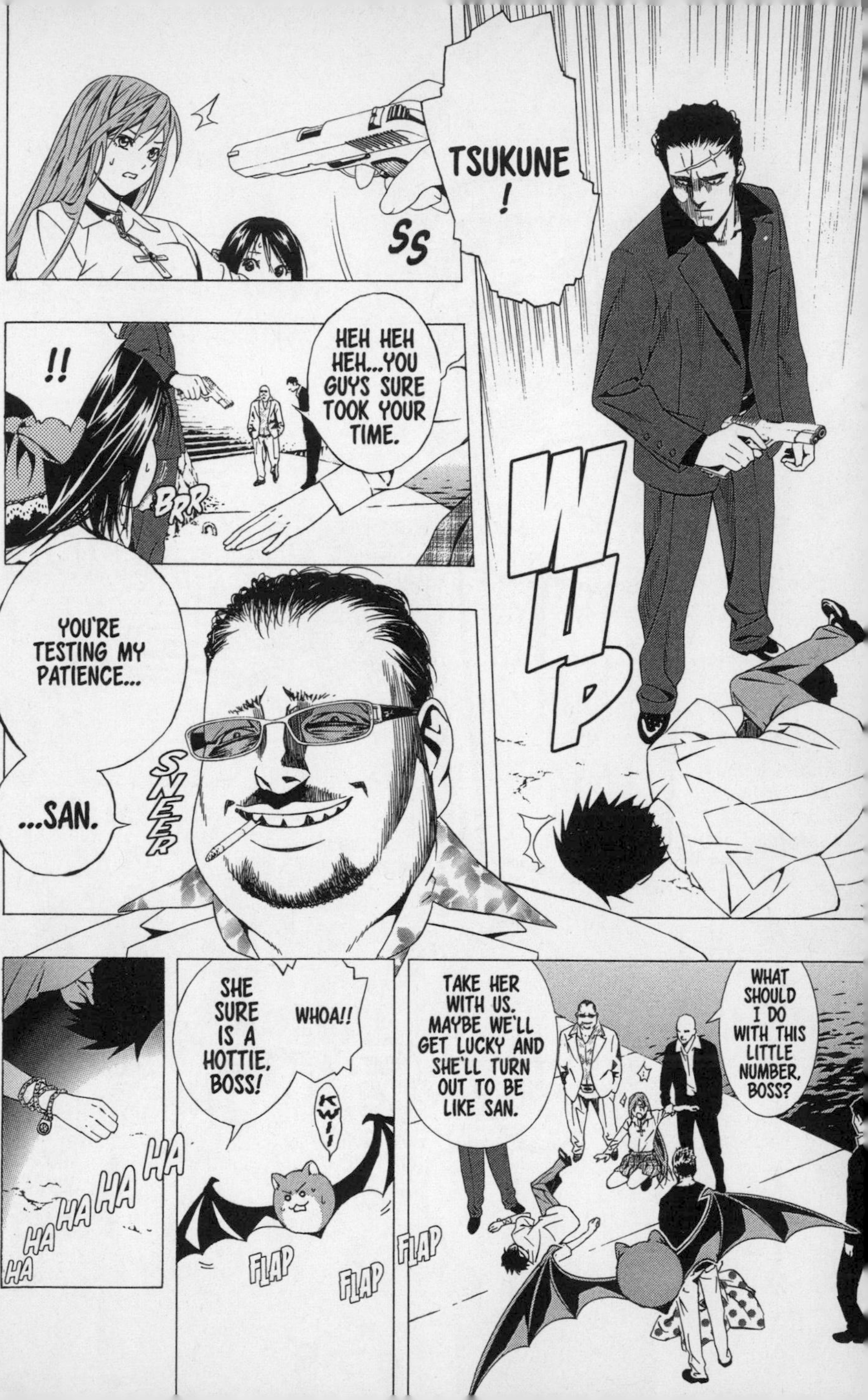
TSUKUNE!
WHUP
SS
!!
HEH HEH HEH...YOU GUYS SURE TOOK YOUR TIME.
BRR
YOU'RE TESTING MY PATIENCE...
...SAN.
SNEER
WHAT SHOULD I DO WITH THIS LITTLE NUMBER, BOSS?
TAKE HER WITH US. MAYBE WE'LL GET LUCKY AND SHE'LL TURN OUT TO BE LIKE SAN.
FLAP
WHOA!!
SHE SURE IS A HOTTIE, BOSS!
KWII
FLAP
FLAP
HA HA HA HA HA HA

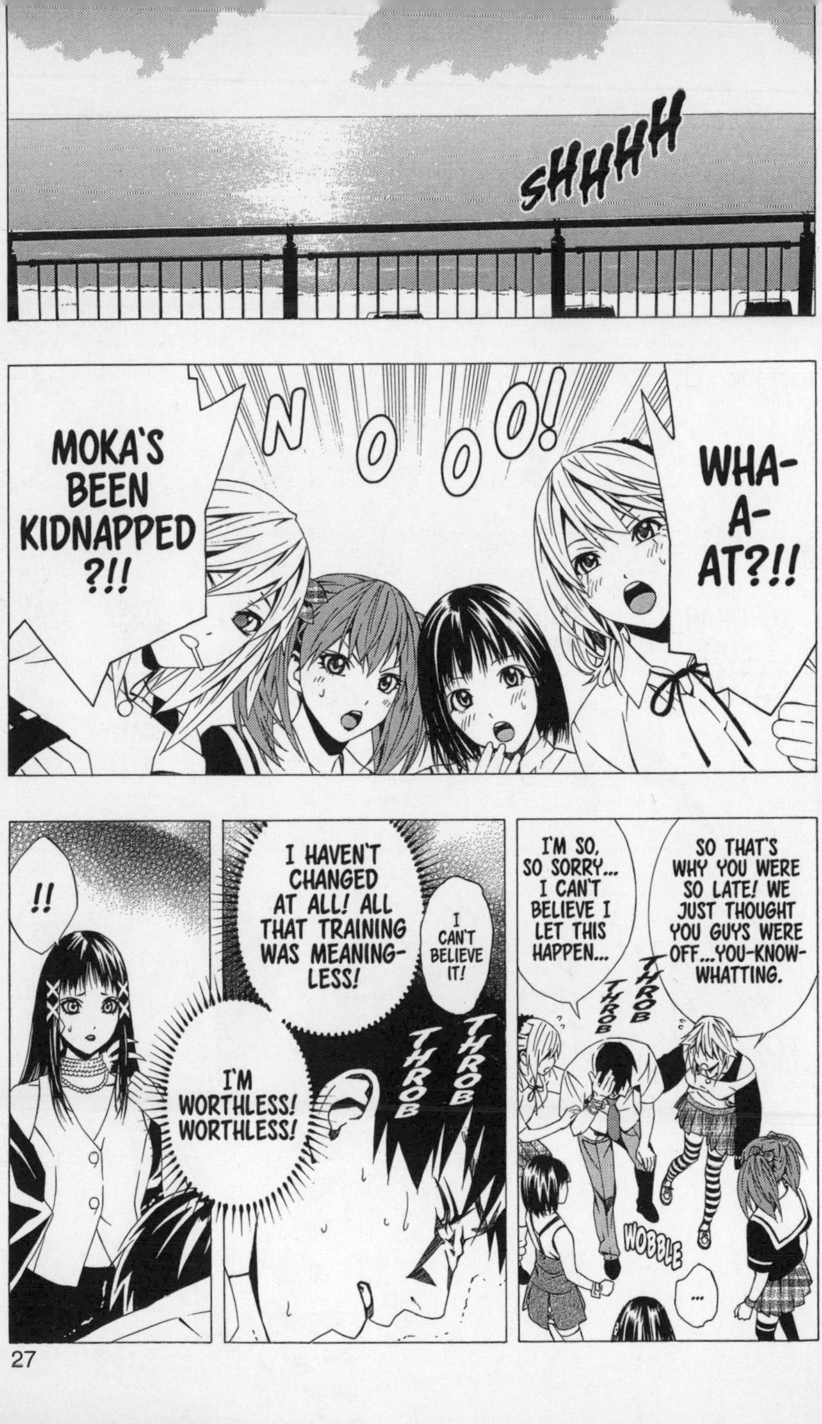
SHHHH
WHA-A-AT?!!
NOOOO!
MOKA'S BEEN KIDNAPPED?!!
SO THAT'S WHY YOU WERE SO LATE! WE JUST THOUGHT YOU GUYS WERE OFF...YOU-KNOW-WHATTING.
I'M SO, SO SORRY... I CAN'T BELIEVE I LET THIS HAPPEN...
THROB THROB
WOBBLE
...
I HAVEN'T CHANGED AT ALL! ALL THAT TRAINING WAS MEANINGLESS!
I CAN'T BELIEVE IT!
THROB THROB
I'M WORTHLESS! WORTHLESS!
!!

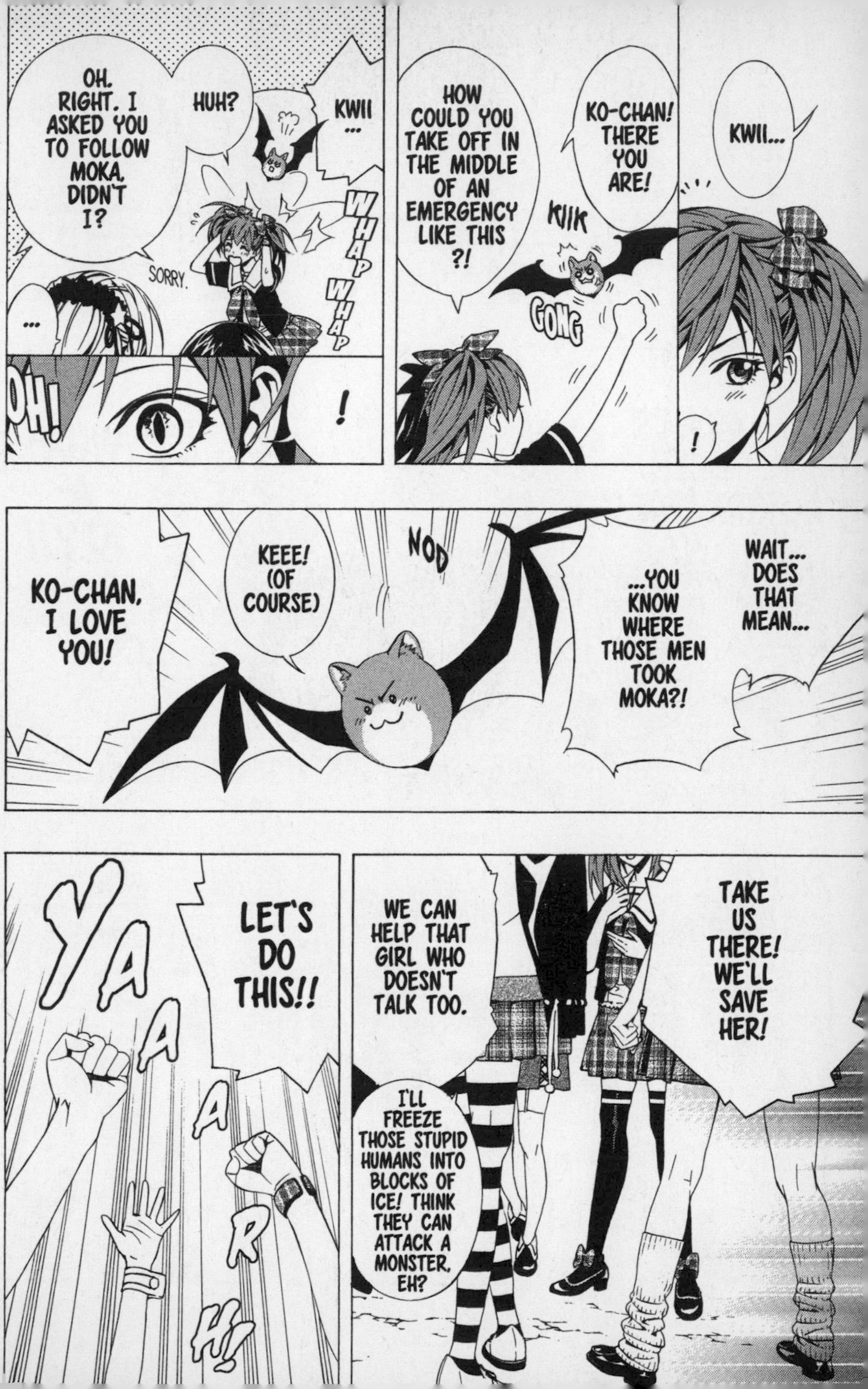
KWII...
!
KO-CHAN! THERE YOU ARE!
KIIK
HOW COULD YOU TAKE OFF IN THE MIDDLE OF AN EMERGENCY LIKE THIS?!
GONG
KWII ...
HUH?
WHAP WHAP WHAP
OH. RIGHT. I ASKED YOU TO FOLLOW MOKA, DIDN'T I?
SORRY.
...
!
OH!
WAIT... DOES THAT MEAN...
...YOU KNOW WHERE THOSE MEN TOOK MOKA?!
NOD
KEEE! (OF COURSE)
KO-CHAN, I LOVE YOU!
TAKE US THERE! WE'LL SAVE HER!
WE CAN HELP THAT GIRL WHO DOESN'T TALK TOO.
I'LL FREEZE THOSE STUPID HUMANS INTO BLOCKS OF ICE! THINK THEY CAN ATTACK A MONSTER, EH?
LET'S DO THIS!!
YAAARH!

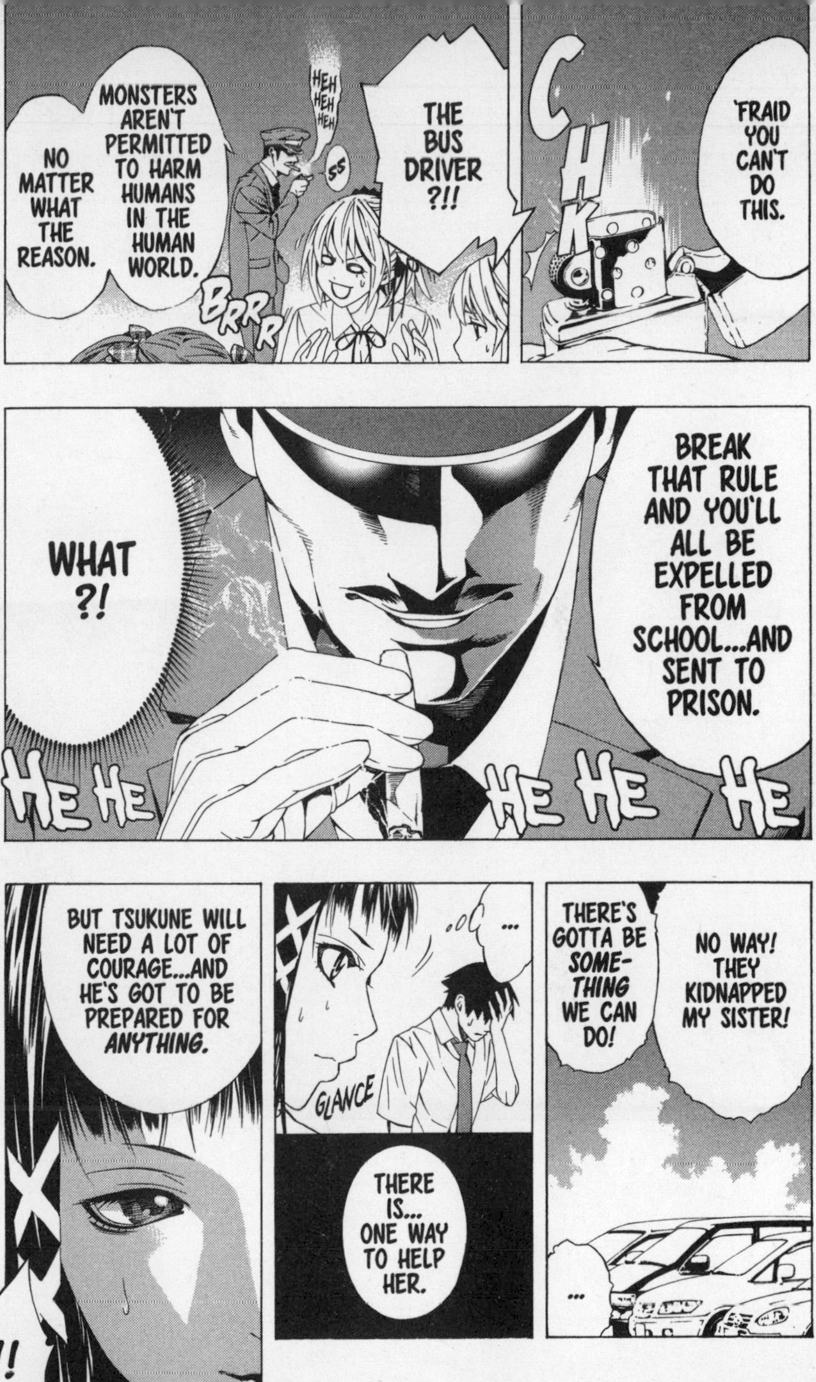
'FRAID YOU CAN'T DO THIS.
CHK
THE BUS DRIVER?!!
MONSTERS AREN'T PERMITTED TO HARM HUMANS IN THE HUMAN WORLD.
NO MATTER WHAT THE REASON.
HEH HEH HEH
SS
BRRR
BREAK THAT RULE AND YOU'LL ALL BE EXPELLED FROM SCHOOL...AND SENT TO PRISON.
WHAT?!
HE HE HE HE HE
NO WAY! THEY KIDNAPPED MY SISTER!
THERE'S GOTTA BE SOMETHING WE CAN DO!
...
...
GLANCE
THERE IS... ONE WAY TO HELP HER.
BUT TSUKUNE WILL NEED A LOT OF COURAGE...AND HE'S GOT TO BE PREPARED FOR ANYTHING.
!!

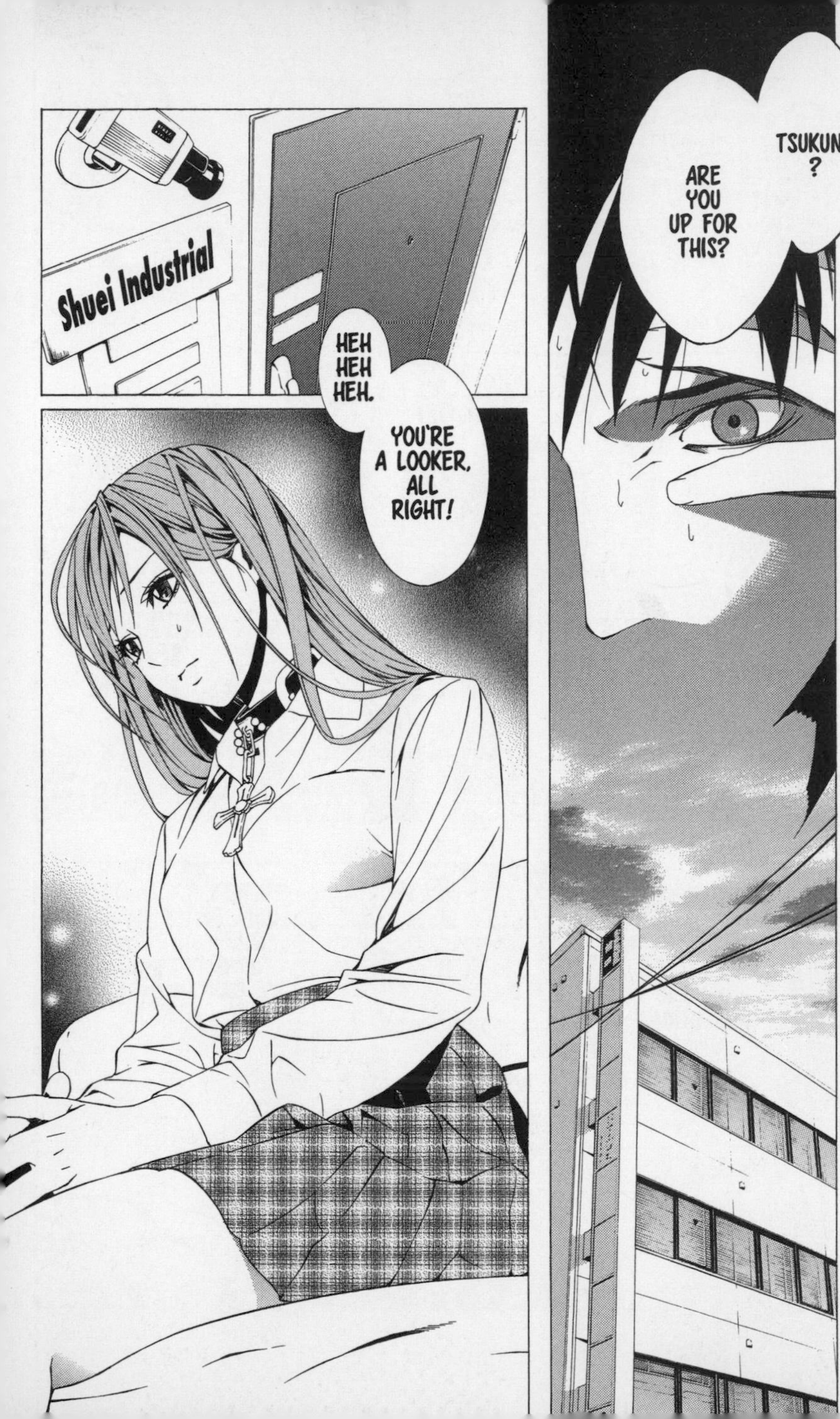
TSUKUNE?
ARE YOU UP FOR THIS?
Shuei Industrial
HEH HEH HEH.
YOU'RE A LOOKER, ALL RIGHT!

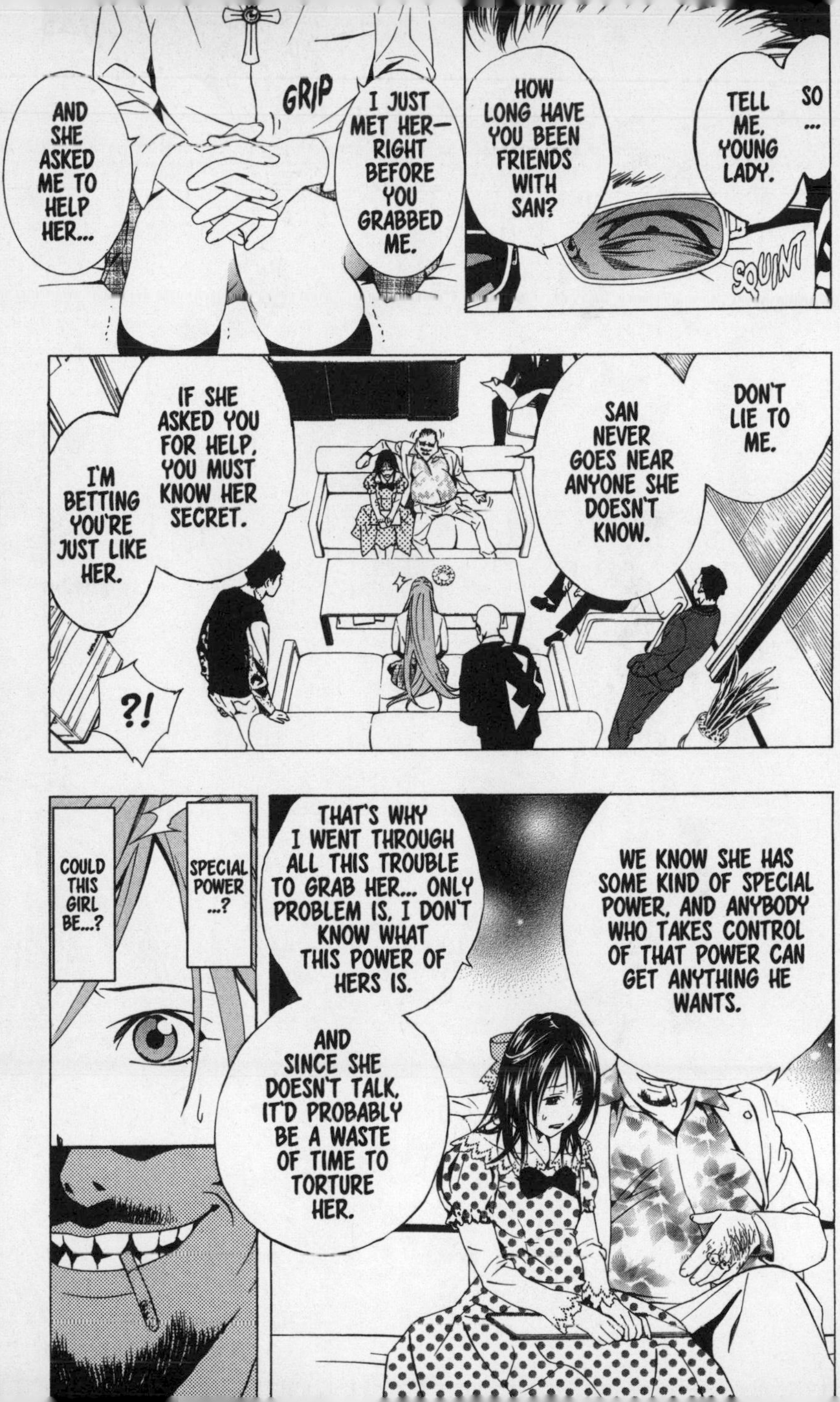
SO ...
TELL ME, YOUNG LADY.
HOW LONG HAVE YOU BEEN FRIENDS WITH SAN?
SQUINT
I JUST MET HER— RIGHT BEFORE YOU GRABBED ME.
GRIP
AND SHE ASKED ME TO HELP HER...
DON'T LIE TO ME.
SAN NEVER GOES NEAR ANYONE SHE DOESN'T KNOW.
IF SHE ASKED YOU FOR HELP, YOU MUST KNOW HER SECRET.
I'M BETTING YOU'RE JUST LIKE HER.
?!
WE KNOW SHE HAS SOME KIND OF SPECIAL POWER, AND ANYBODY WHO TAKES CONTROL OF THAT POWER CAN GET ANYTHING HE WANTS.
THAT'S WHY I WENT THROUGH ALL THIS TROUBLE TO GRAB HER... ONLY PROBLEM IS, I DON'T KNOW WHAT THIS POWER OF HERS IS.
AND SINCE SHE DOESN'T TALK, IT'D PROBABLY BE A WASTE OF TIME TO TORTURE HER.
SPECIAL POWER ...?
COULD THIS GIRL BE...?

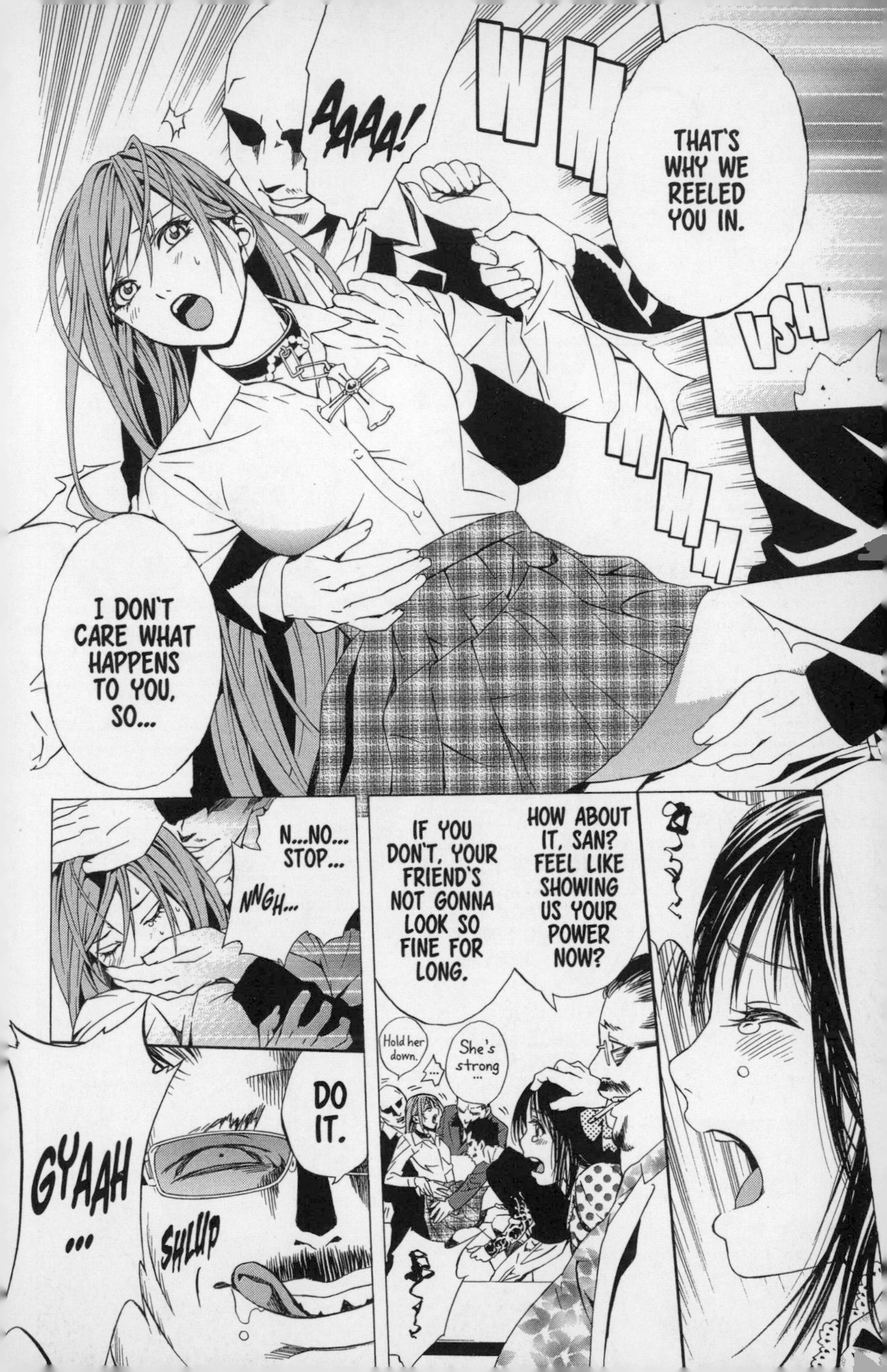
THAT'S WHY WE REELED YOU IN.
AAAAA!
VSH
I DON'T CARE WHAT HAPPENS TO YOU, SO...
HOW ABOUT IT, SAN? FEEL LIKE SHOWING US YOUR POWER NOW?
IF YOU DON'T, YOUR FRIEND'S NOT GONNA LOOK SO FINE FOR LONG.
She's strong ...
...
Hold her down.
N...NO... STOP...
NNGH...
DO IT.
GYAAH ...
SHLUP

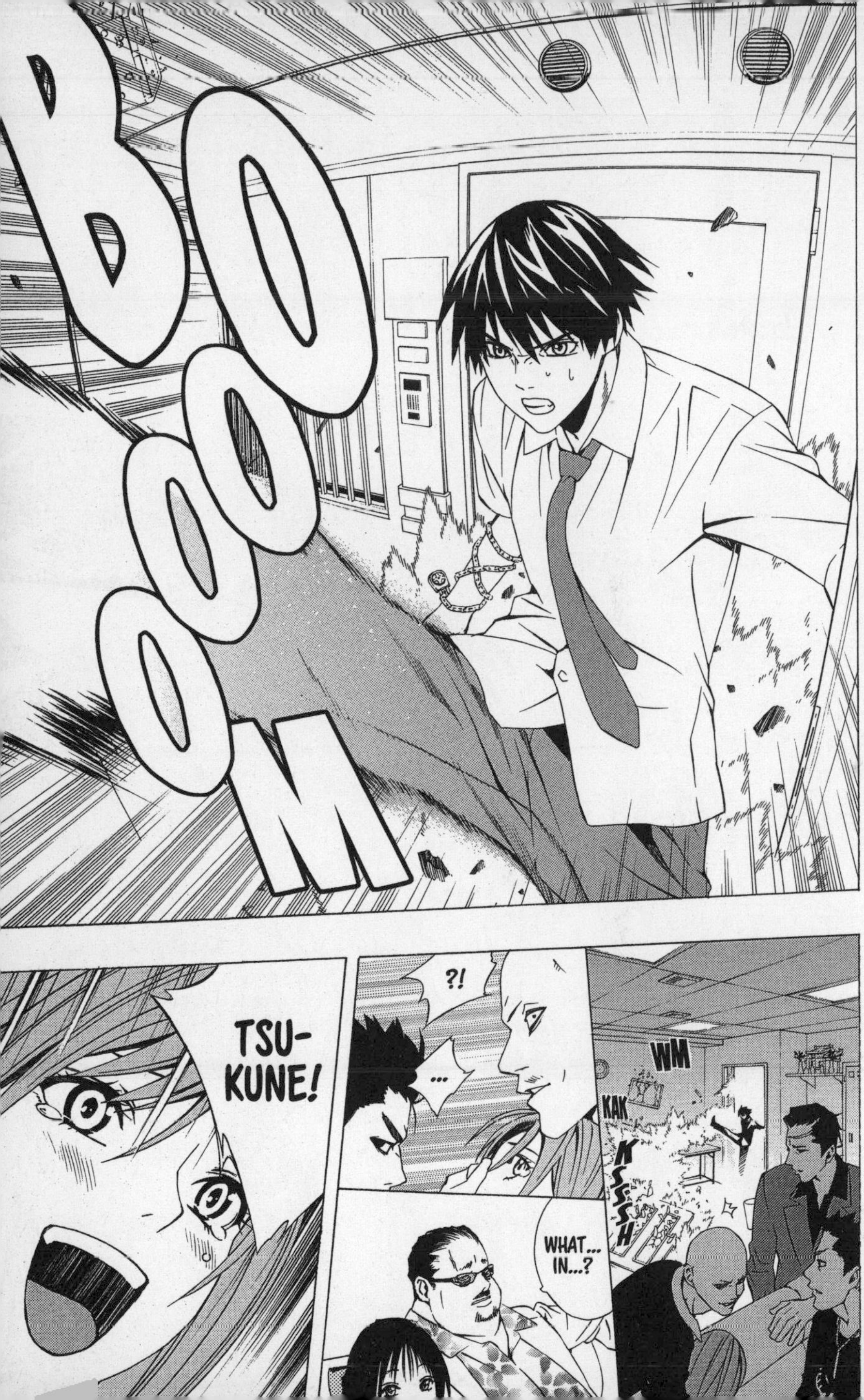
BOOOOOM
WM
KAK
KSSSH
?!
...
WHAT... IN...?
TSU-KUNE!

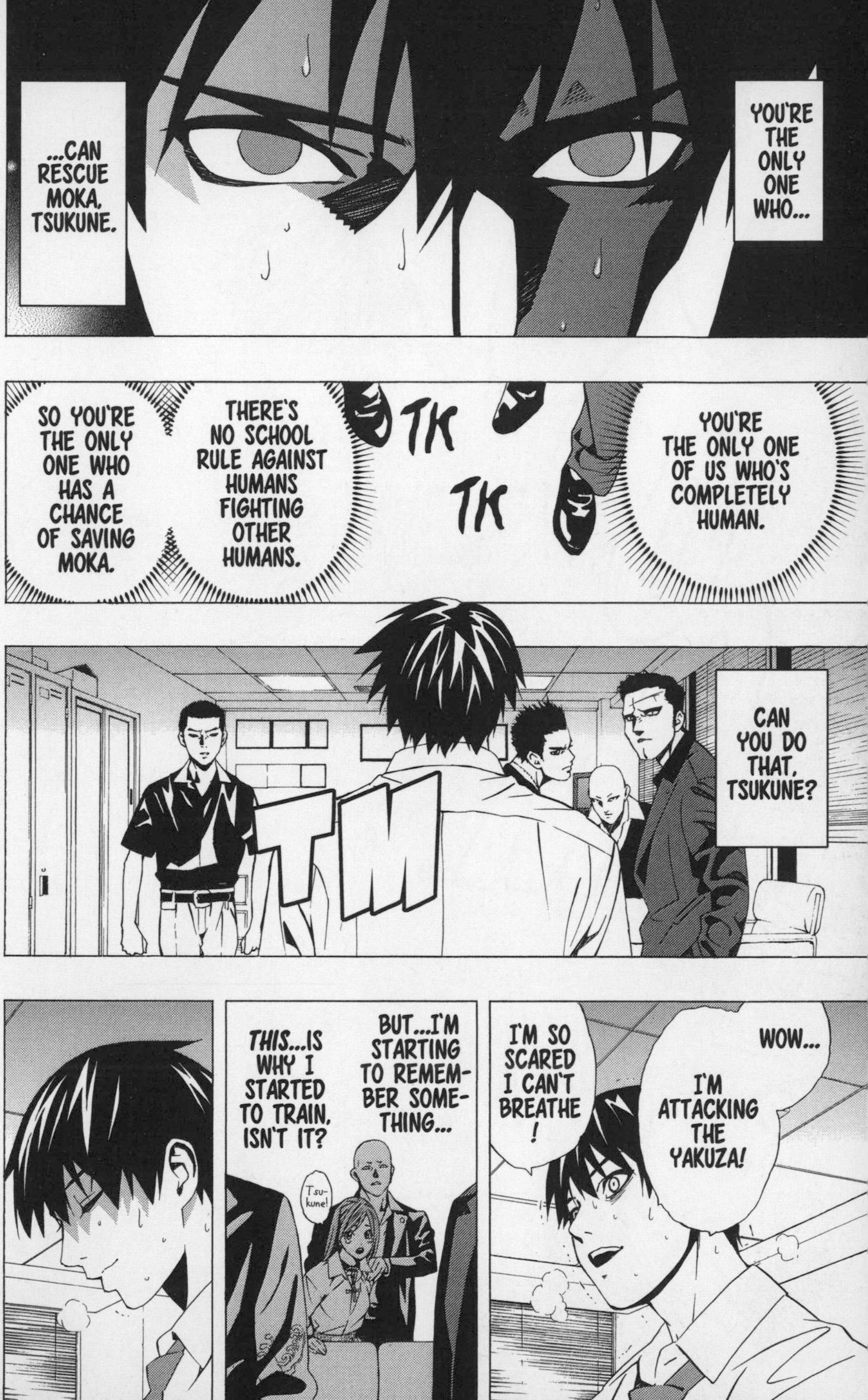
YOU'RE THE ONLY ONE WHO...
...CAN RESCUE MOKA, TSUKUNE.
YOU'RE THE ONLY ONE OF US WHO'S COMPLETELY HUMAN.
TK
TK
THERE'S NO SCHOOL RULE AGAINST HUMANS FIGHTING OTHER HUMANS.
SO YOU'RE THE ONLY ONE WHO HAS A CHANCE OF SAVING MOKA.
CAN YOU DO THAT, TSUKUNE?
TM
WOW...
I'M ATTACKING THE YAKUZA!
I'M SO SCARED I CAN'T BREATHE!
BUT...I'M STARTING TO REMEMBER SOMETHING...
THIS...IS WHY I STARTED TO TRAIN, ISN'T IT?
Tsukune!

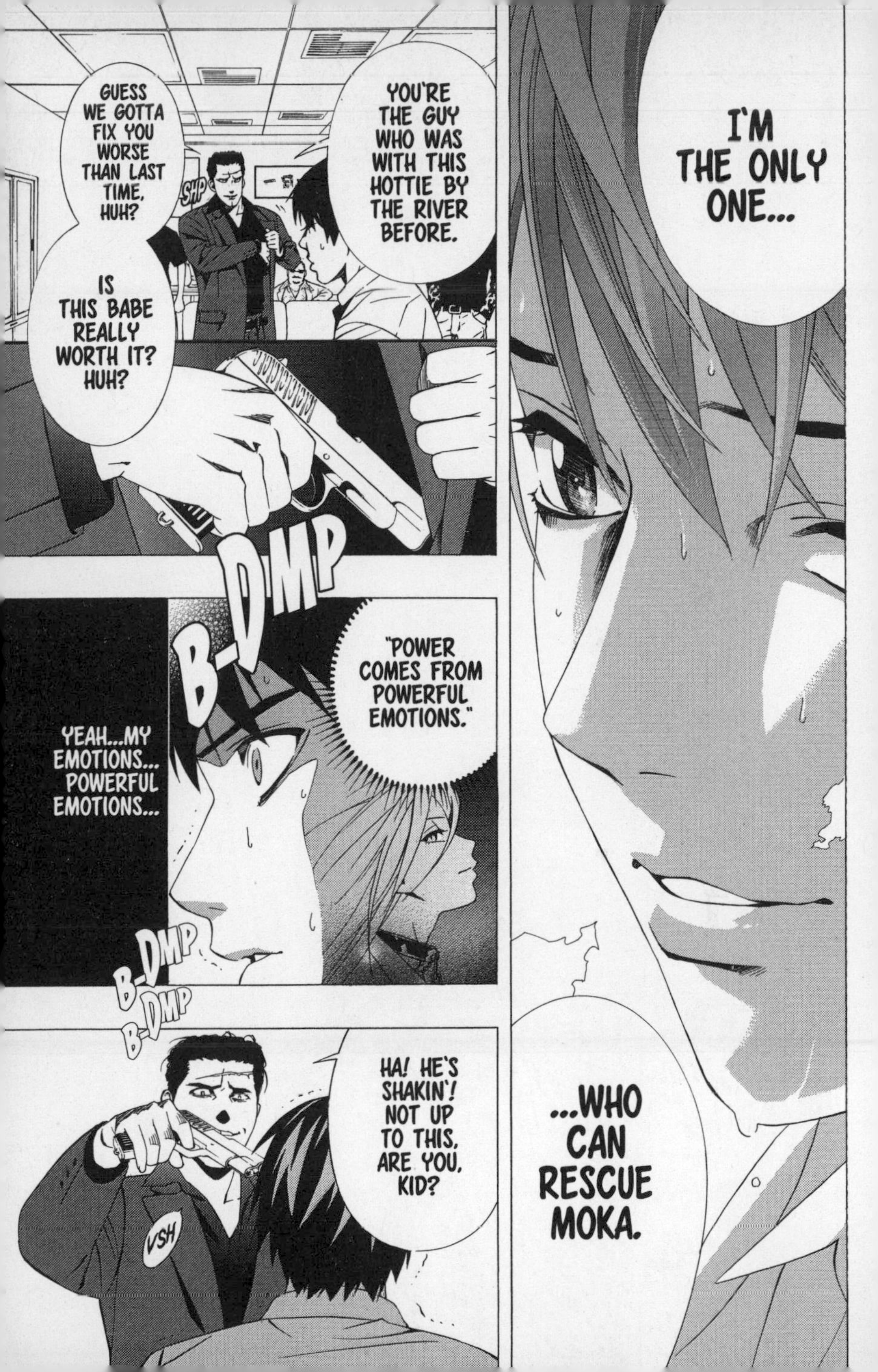
I'M THE ONLY ONE...
...WHO CAN RESCUE MOKA.
YOU'RE THE GUY WHO WAS WITH THIS HOTTIE BY THE RIVER BEFORE.
GUESS WE GOTTA FIX YOU WORSE THAN LAST TIME, HUH?
SHP
IS THIS BABE REALLY WORTH IT? HUH?
B-DMP
"POWER COMES FROM POWERFUL EMOTIONS."
YEAH...MY EMOTIONS... POWERFUL EMOTIONS...
B-DMP
B-DMP
HA! HE'S SHAKIN'! NOT UP TO THIS, ARE YOU, KID?
VSH

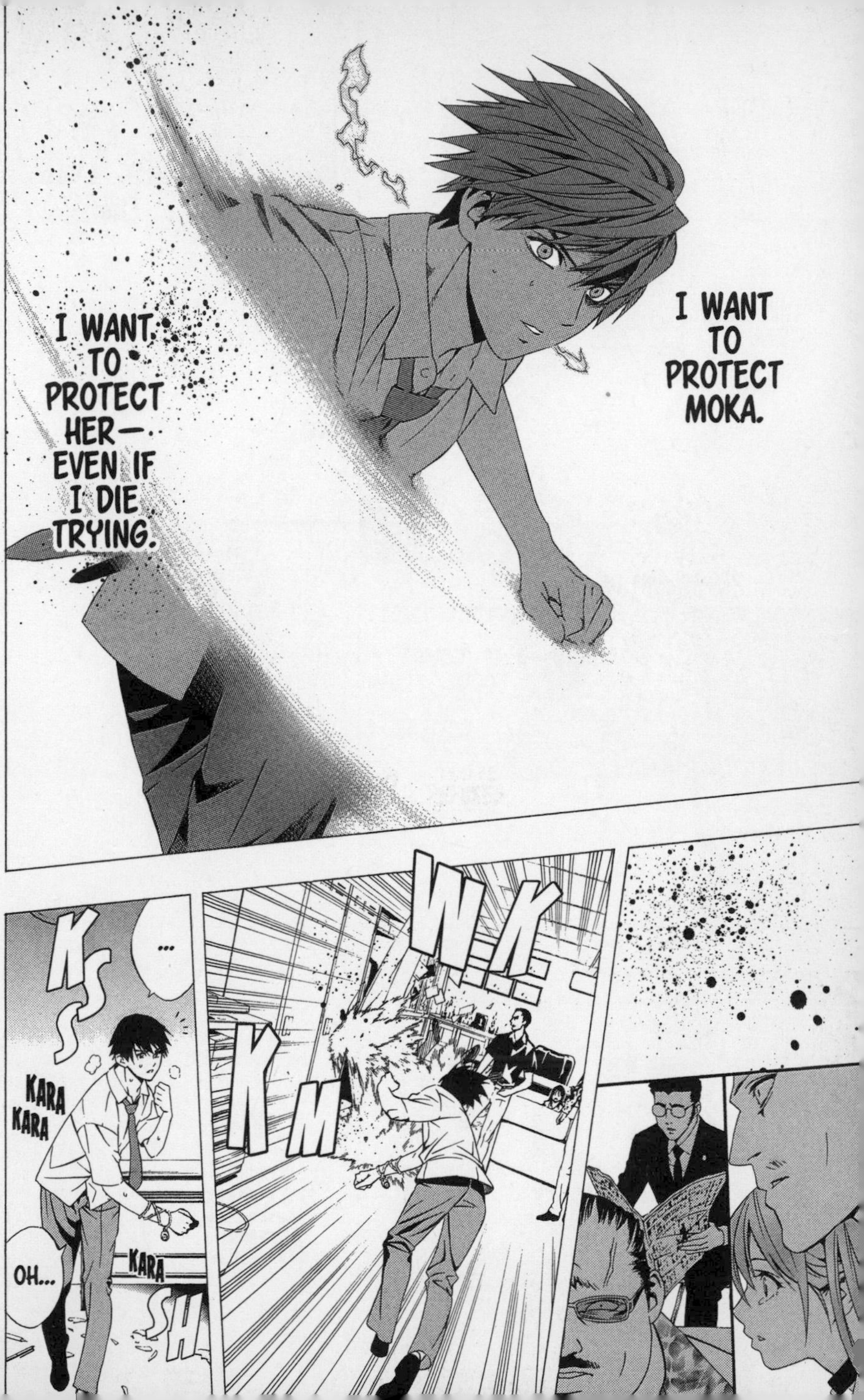
I WANT TO PROTECT MOKA.
I WANT TO PROTECT HER— EVEN IF I DIE TRYING.
W..K...
K M
KS
...
KARA KARA
KARA
OH...
SH

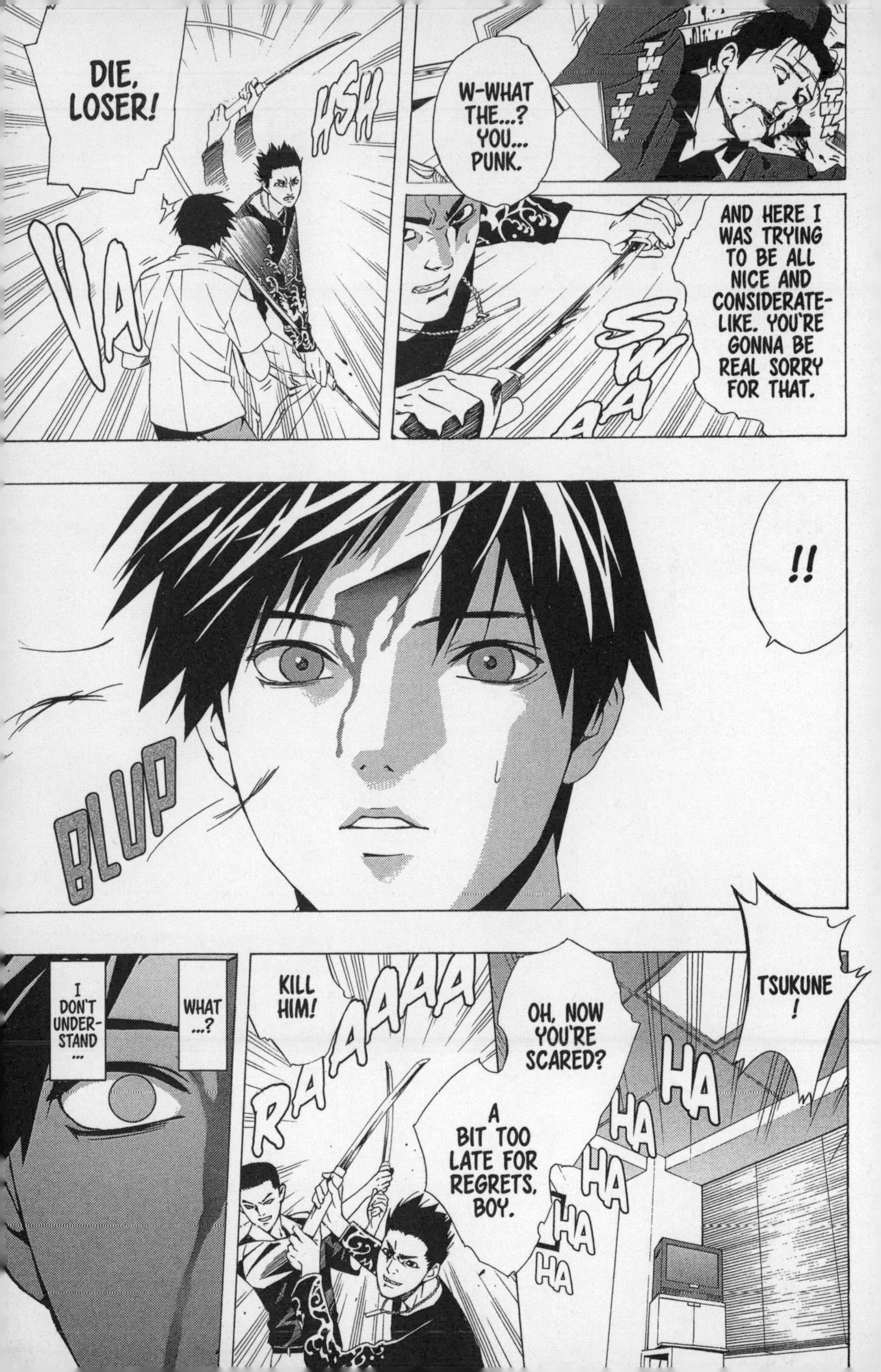
TWK TWK
TWK
W-WHAT THE...? YOU... PUNK.
AND HERE I WAS TRYING TO BE ALL NICE AND CONSIDERATE-LIKE. YOU'RE GONNA BE REAL SORRY FOR THAT.
SWAAA
DIE, LOSER!
HSH
VA
!!
BLUP
TSUKUNE!
HA HA HA HA HA HA
OH, NOW YOU'RE SCARED?
KILL HIM!
RAAAAAA
A BIT TOO LATE FOR REGRETS, BOY.
WHAT...?
I DON'T UNDERSTAND...

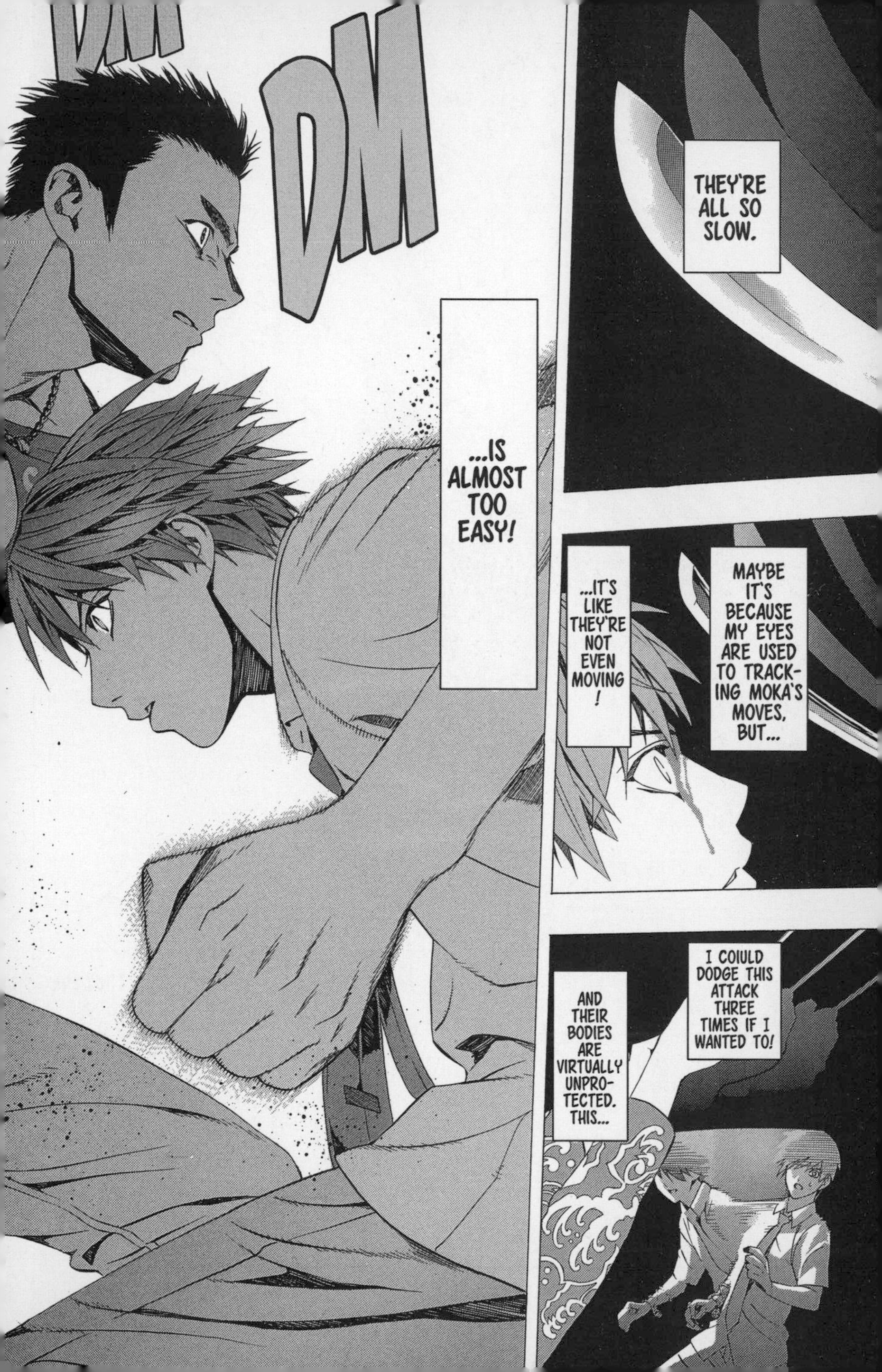
THEY'RE ALL SO SLOW.
MAYBE IT'S BECAUSE MY EYES ARE USED TO TRACKING MOKA'S MOVES, BUT...
...IT'S LIKE THEY'RE NOT EVEN MOVING!
I COIULD DODGE THIS ATTACK THREE TIMES IF I WANTED TO!
AND THEIR BODIES ARE VIRTUALLY UNPROTECTED. THIS...
DM
DM
...IS ALMOST TOO EASY!

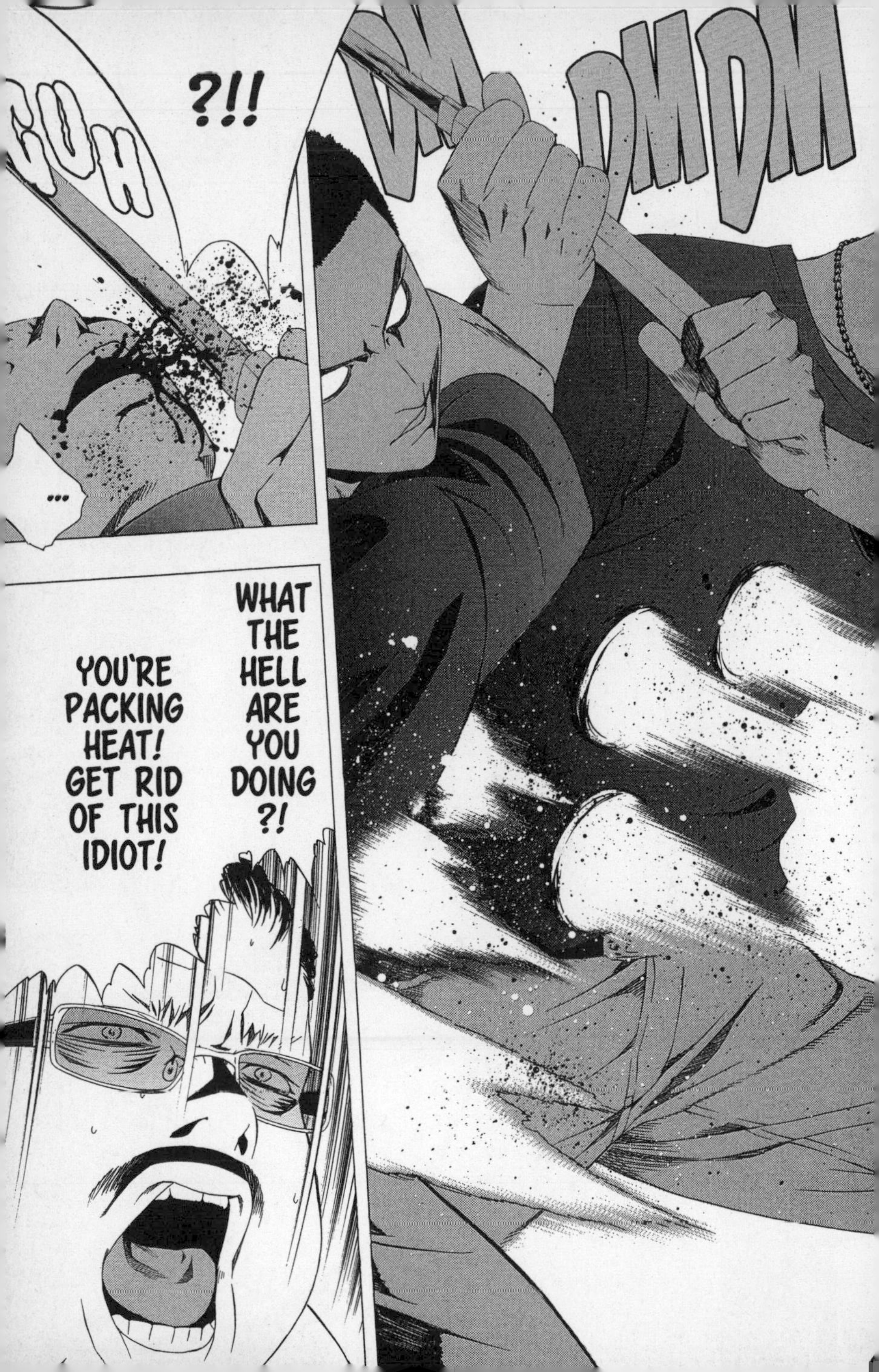
DM
DMDM
GOH
?!!
...
WHAT THE HELL ARE YOU DOING?!
YOU'RE PACKING HEAT! GET RID OF THIS IDIOT!

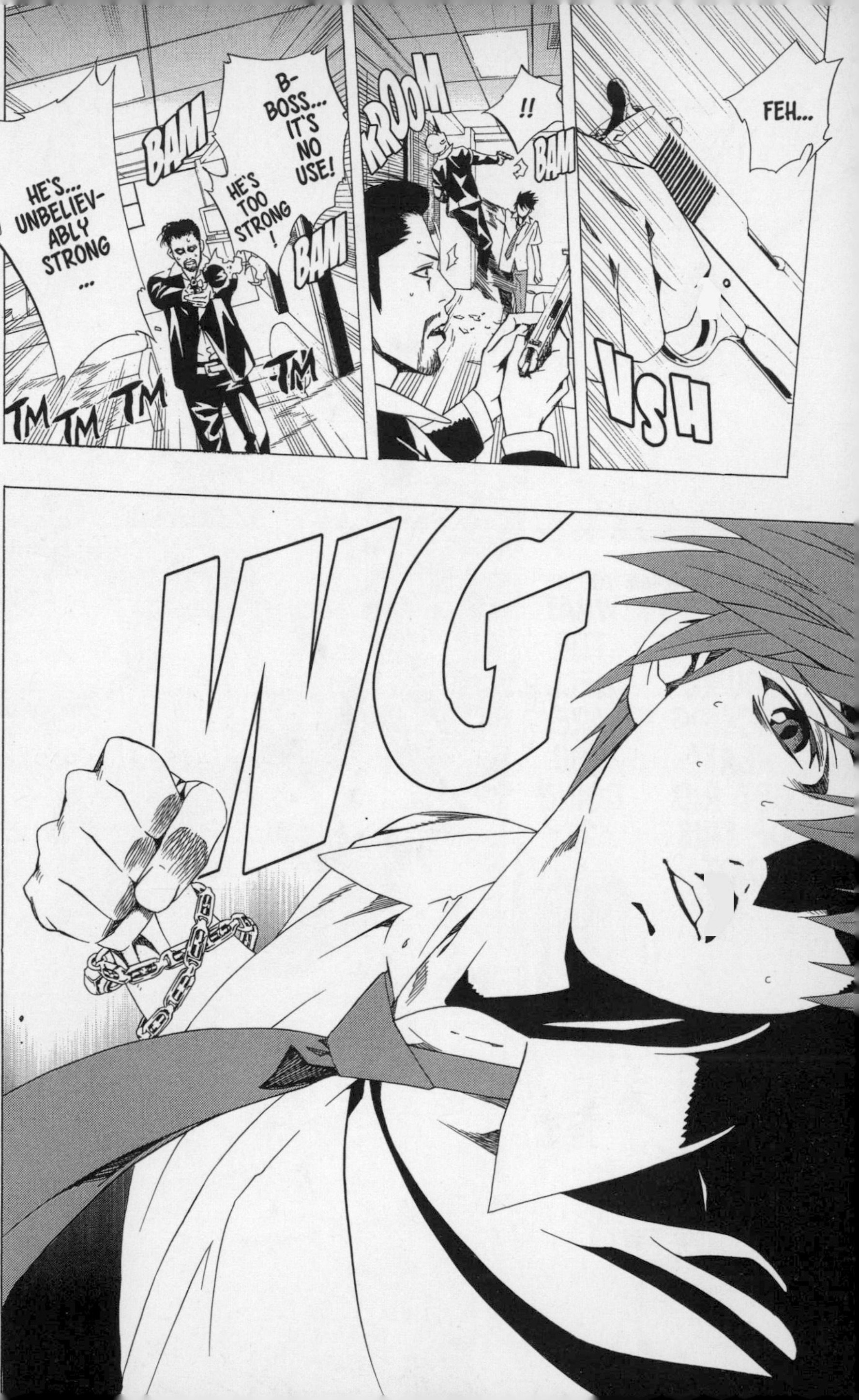
FEH...
VSH
KROOM
!!
BAM
B-BOSS... IT'S NO USE!
HE'S TOO STRONG!
BAM
BAM
HE'S... UNBELIEVABLY STRONG...
TM TM TM TM
WG

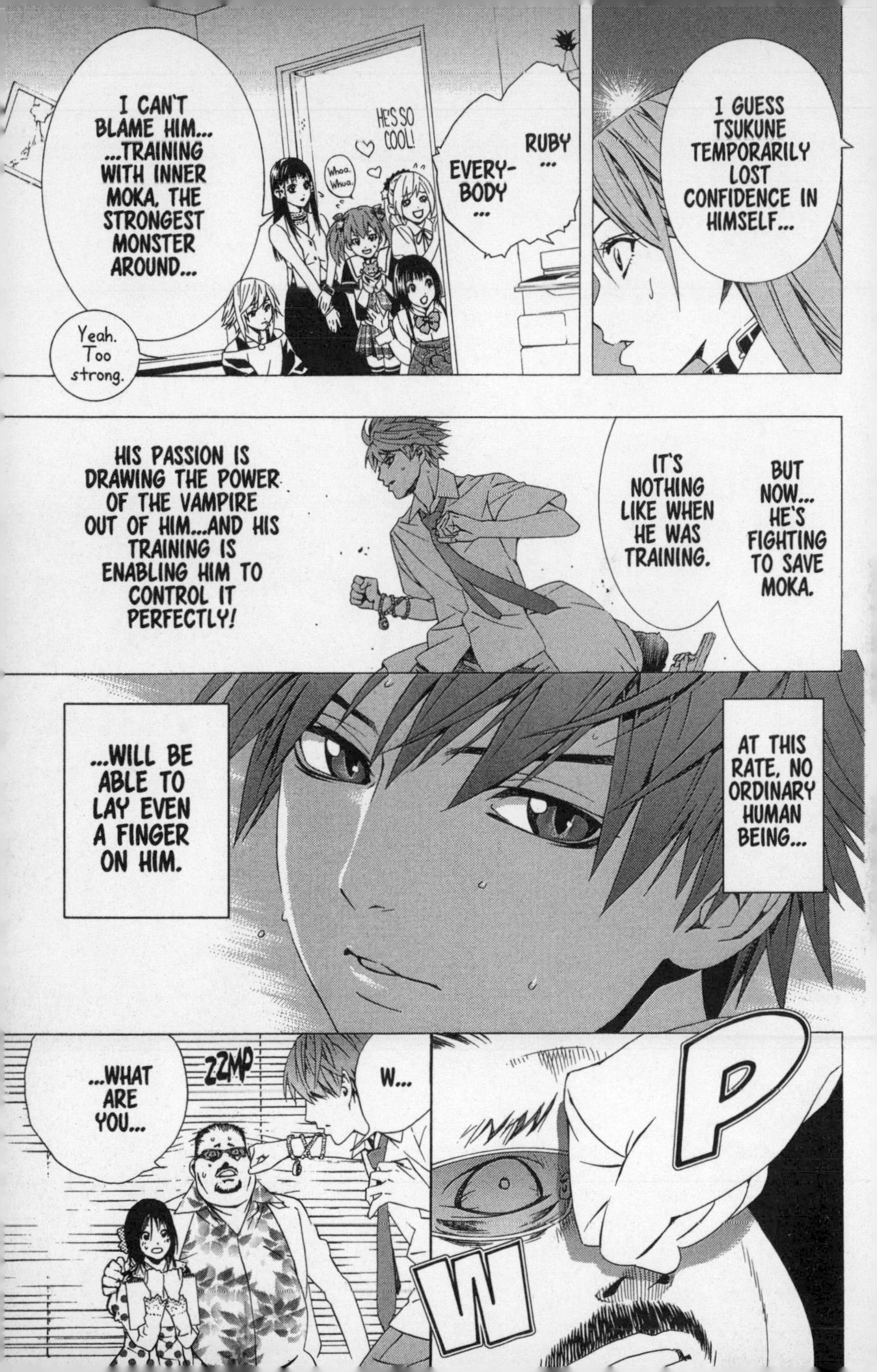
I GUESS TSUKUNE TEMPORARILY LOST CONFIDENCE IN HIMSELF...
RUBY...
EVERY-BODY...
HE'S SO COOL!
Whoa. Whua.
I CAN'T BLAME HIM... ...TRAINING WITH INNER MOKA, THE STRONGEST MONSTER AROUND...
Yeah. Too strong.
BUT NOW... HE'S FIGHTING TO SAVE MOKA.
IT'S NOTHING LIKE WHEN HE WAS TRAINING.
HIS PASSION IS DRAWING THE POWER OF THE VAMPIRE OUT OF HIM...AND HIS TRAINING IS ENABLING HIM TO CONTROL IT PERFECTLY!
AT THIS RATE, NO ORDINARY HUMAN BEING...
...WILL BE ABLE TO LAY EVEN A FINGER ON HIM.
P
W
W...
ZZMP
...WHAT ARE YOU...

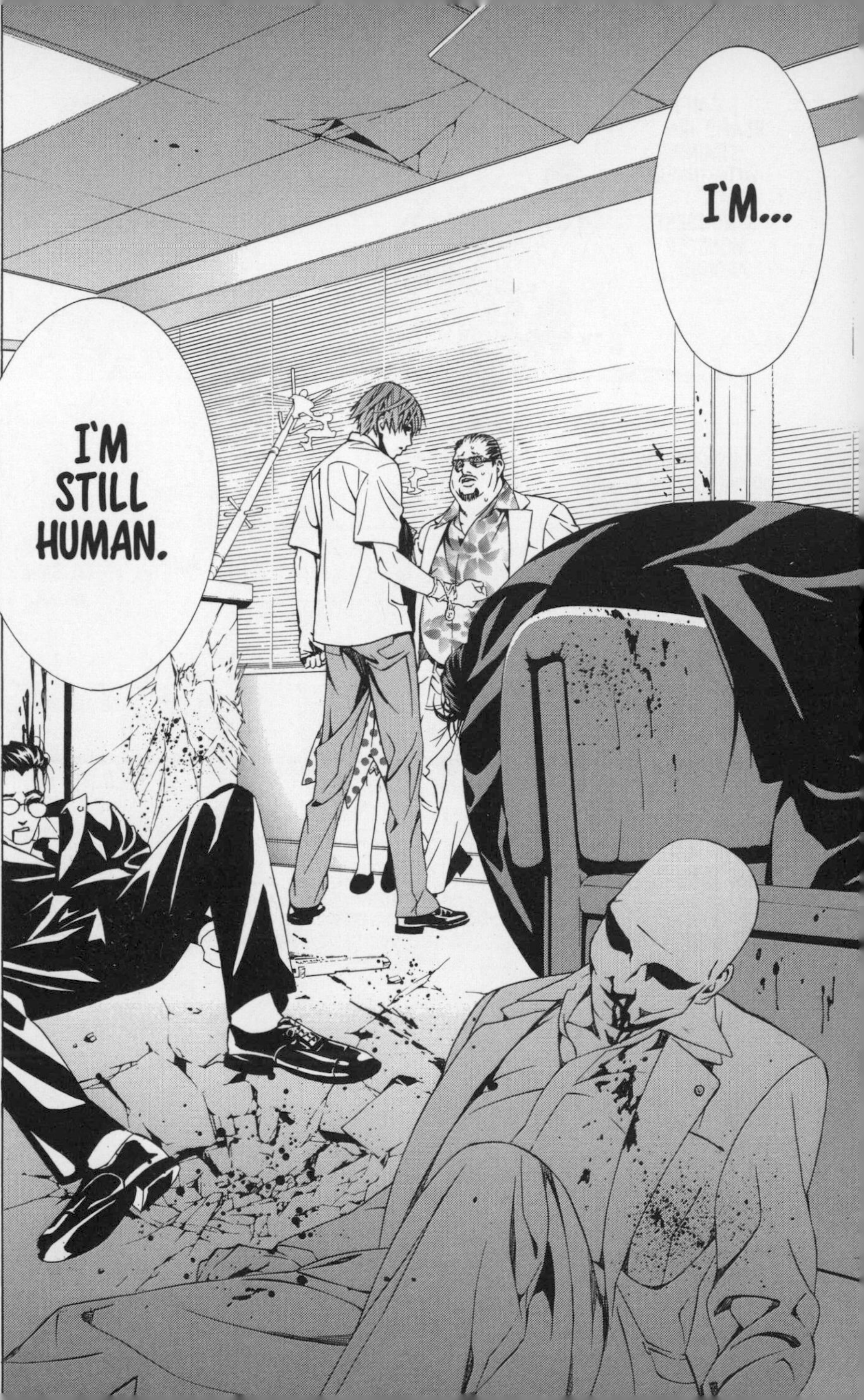
I'M...
I'M STILL HUMAN.

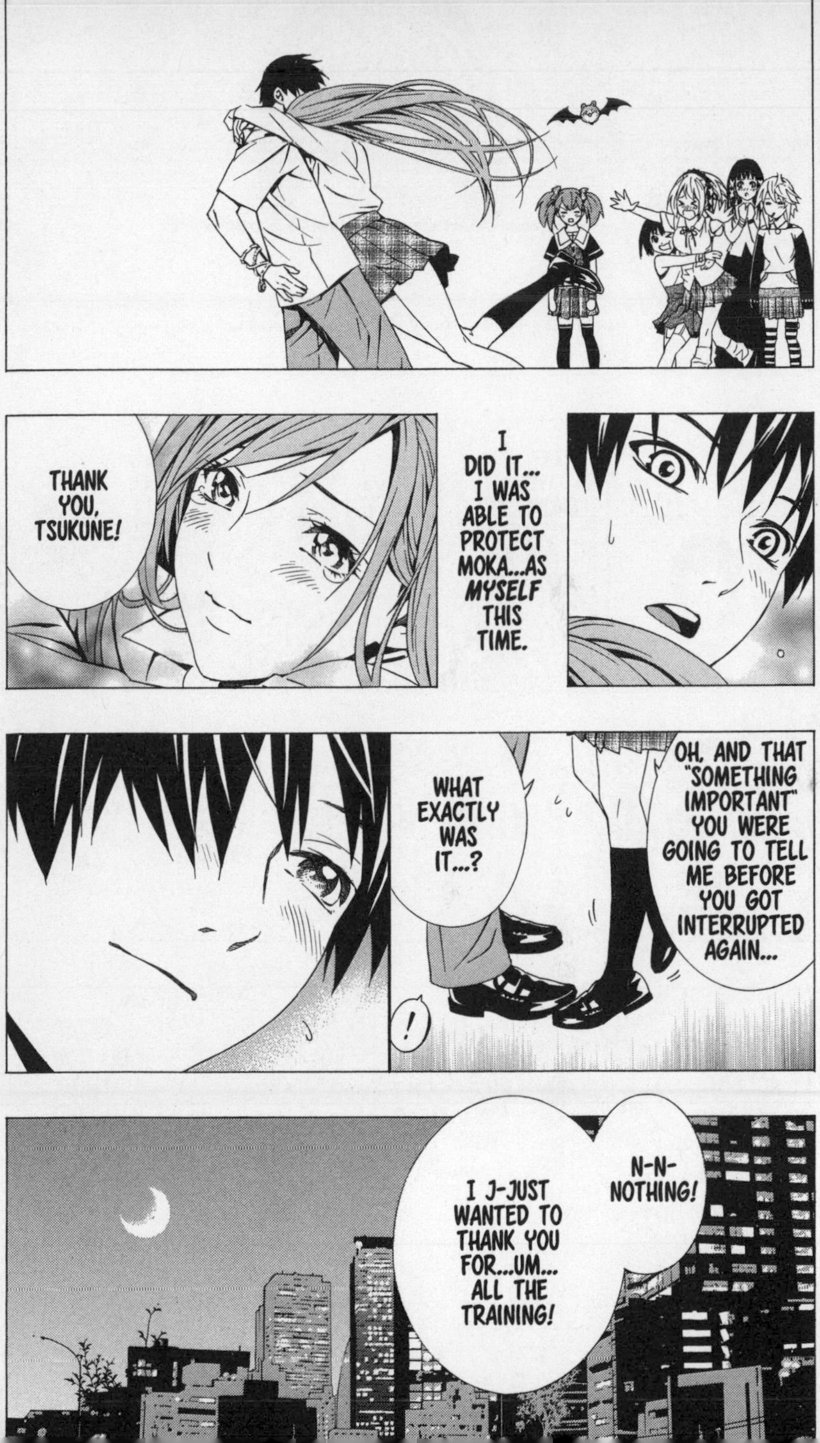
I DID IT... I WAS ABLE TO PROTECT MOKA...AS *MYSELF* THIS TIME.
THANK YOU, TSUKUNE!
OH, AND THAT "SOMETHING IMPORTANT" YOU WERE GOING TO TELL ME BEFORE YOU GOT INTERRUPTED AGAIN...
WHAT EXACTLY WAS IT...?
!
N-N-NOTHING!
I J-JUST WANTED TO THANK YOU FOR...UM... ALL THE TRAINING!

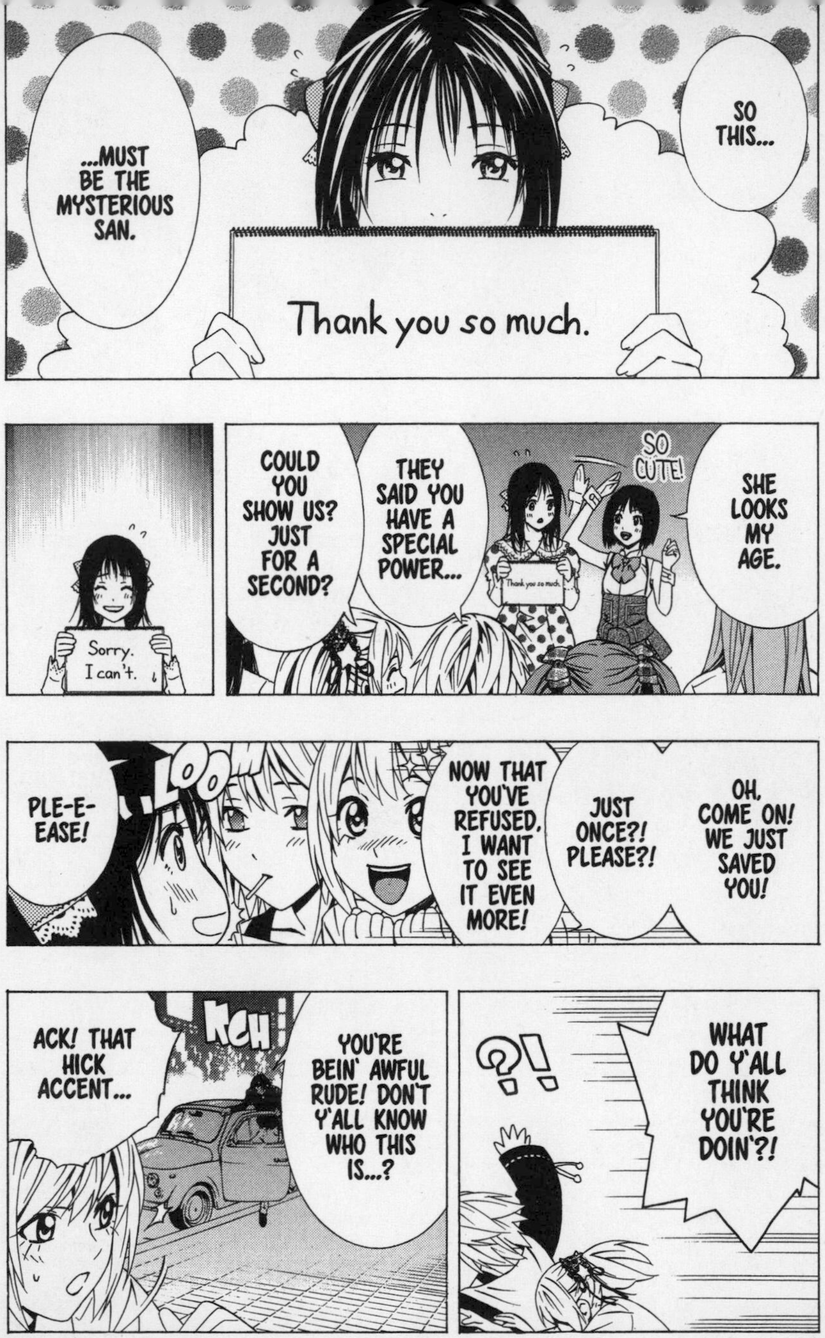
SO THIS...
...MUST BE THE MYSTERIOUS SAN.
Thank you so much.
SO CUTE!
SHE LOOKS MY AGE.
THEY SAID YOU HAVE A SPECIAL POWER...
COULD YOU SHOW US? JUST FOR A SECOND?
Thank you so much.
Sorry. I can't.
OH, COME ON! WE JUST SAVED YOU!
JUST ONCE?! PLEASE?!
NOW THAT YOU'VE REFUSED, I WANT TO SEE IT EVEN MORE!
PLE-E-EASE!
WHAT DO Y'ALL THINK YOU'RE DOIN'?!
?!
KCH
YOU'RE BEIN' AWFUL RUDE! DON'T Y'ALL KNOW WHO THIS IS...?
ACK! THAT HICK ACCENT...

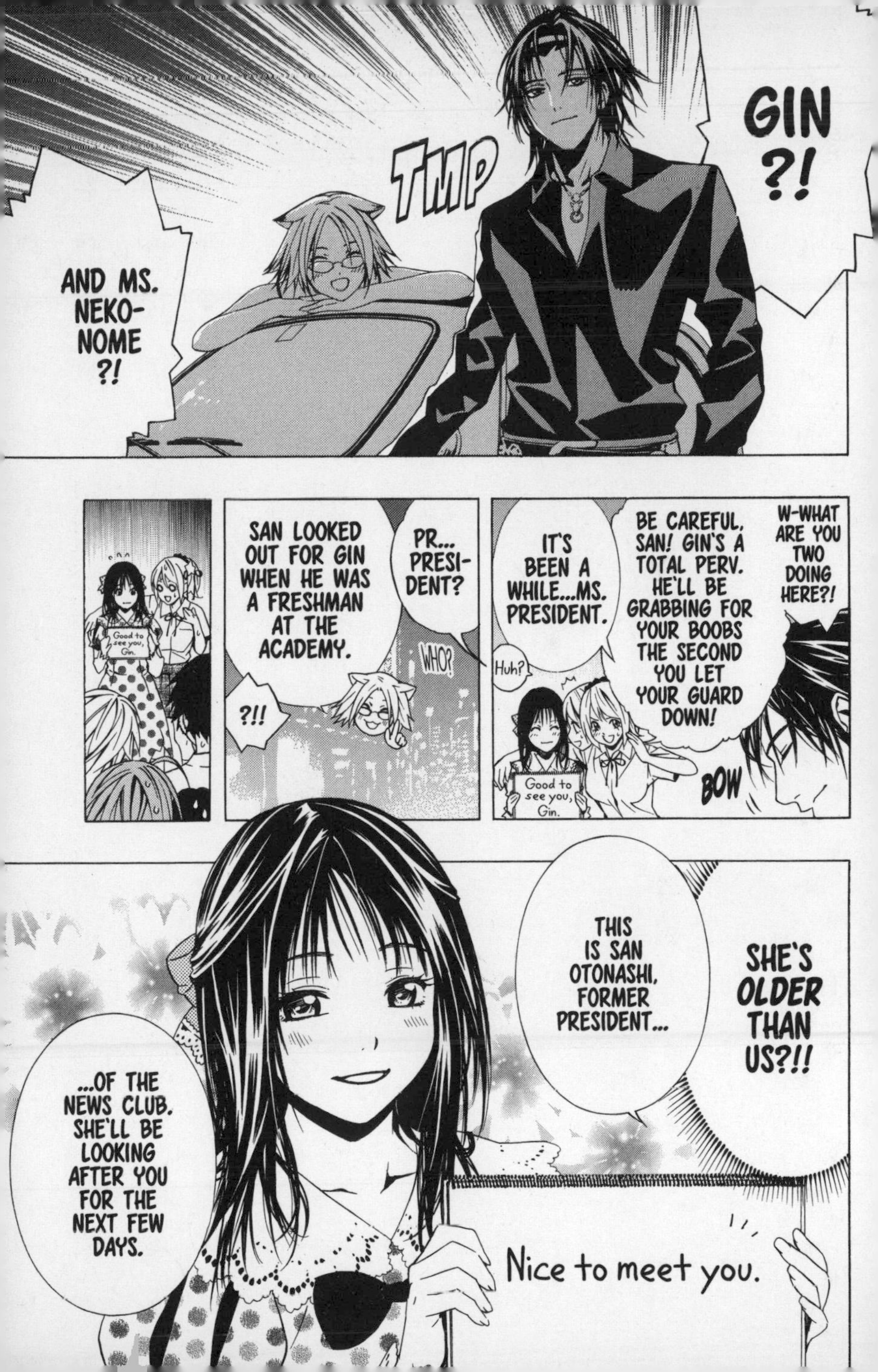
GIN ?!
TMP
AND MS. NEKO-NOME ?!
W-WHAT ARE YOU TWO DOING HERE?!
BE CAREFUL, SAN! GIN'S A TOTAL PERV. HE'LL BE GRABBING FOR YOUR BOOBS THE SECOND YOU LET YOUR GUARD DOWN!
IT'S BEEN A WHILE...MS. PRESIDENT.
Huh?
BOW
Good to see you, Gin.
PR... PRESI-DENT?
SAN LOOKED OUT FOR GIN WHEN HE WAS A FRESHMAN AT THE ACADEMY.
WHO?
?!!
Good to see you, Gin.
SHE'S OLDER THAN US?!!
THIS IS SAN OTONASHI, FORMER PRESIDENT...
...OF THE NEWS CLUB. SHE'LL BE LOOKING AFTER YOU FOR THE NEXT FEW DAYS.
Nice to meet you.

19: How to Grow Up

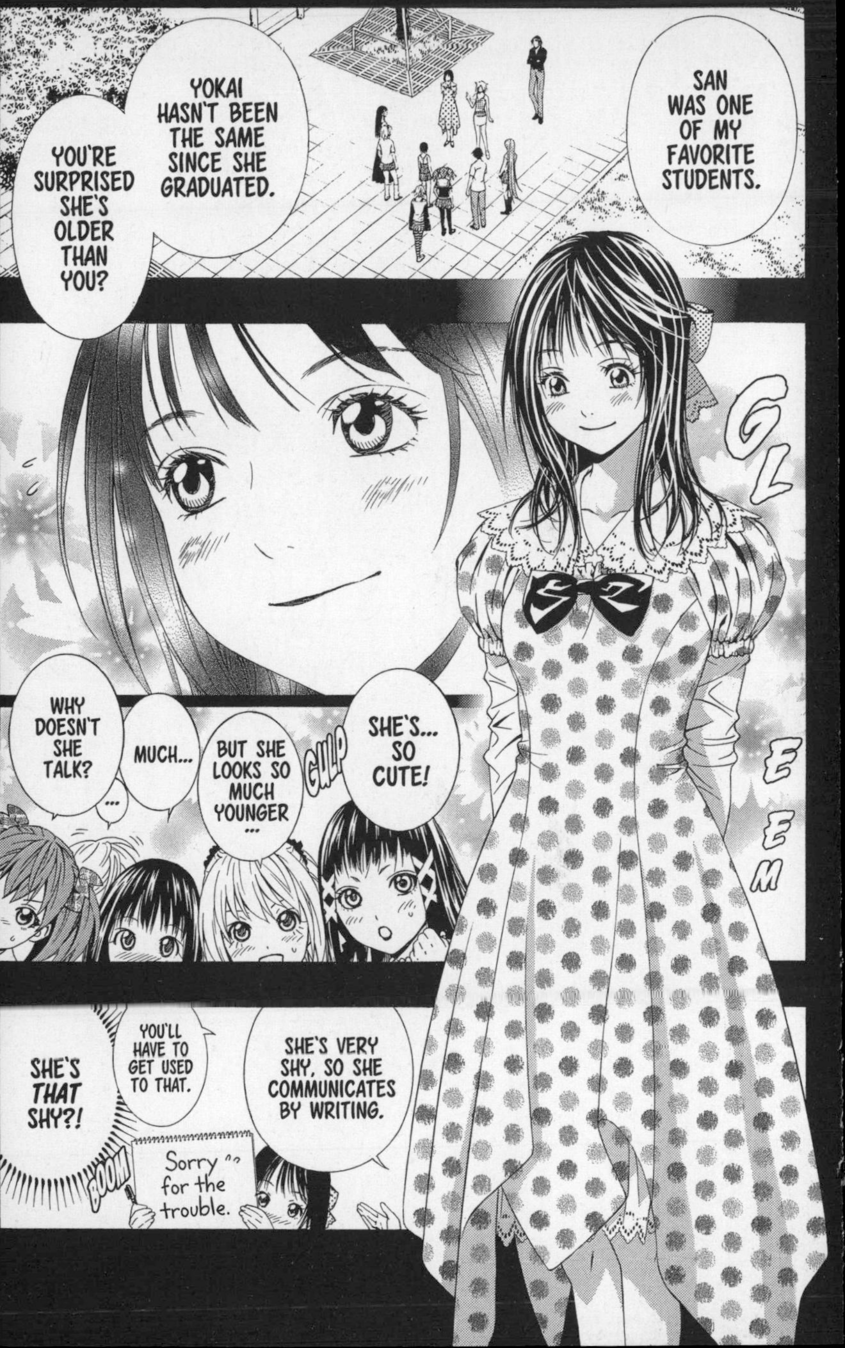
SAN WAS ONE OF MY FAVORITE STUDENTS.
YOKAI HASN'T BEEN THE SAME SINCE SHE GRADUATED.
YOU'RE SURPRISED SHE'S OLDER THAN YOU?
GLEEM
SHE'S... SO CUTE!
GULP
BUT SHE LOOKS SO MUCH YOUNGER ...
MUCH...
WHY DOESN'T SHE TALK?
...
SHE'S VERY SHY, SO SHE COMMUNICATES BY WRITING.
YOU'LL HAVE TO GET USED TO THAT.
Sorry for the trouble.
BOOM
SHE'S *THAT* SHY?!

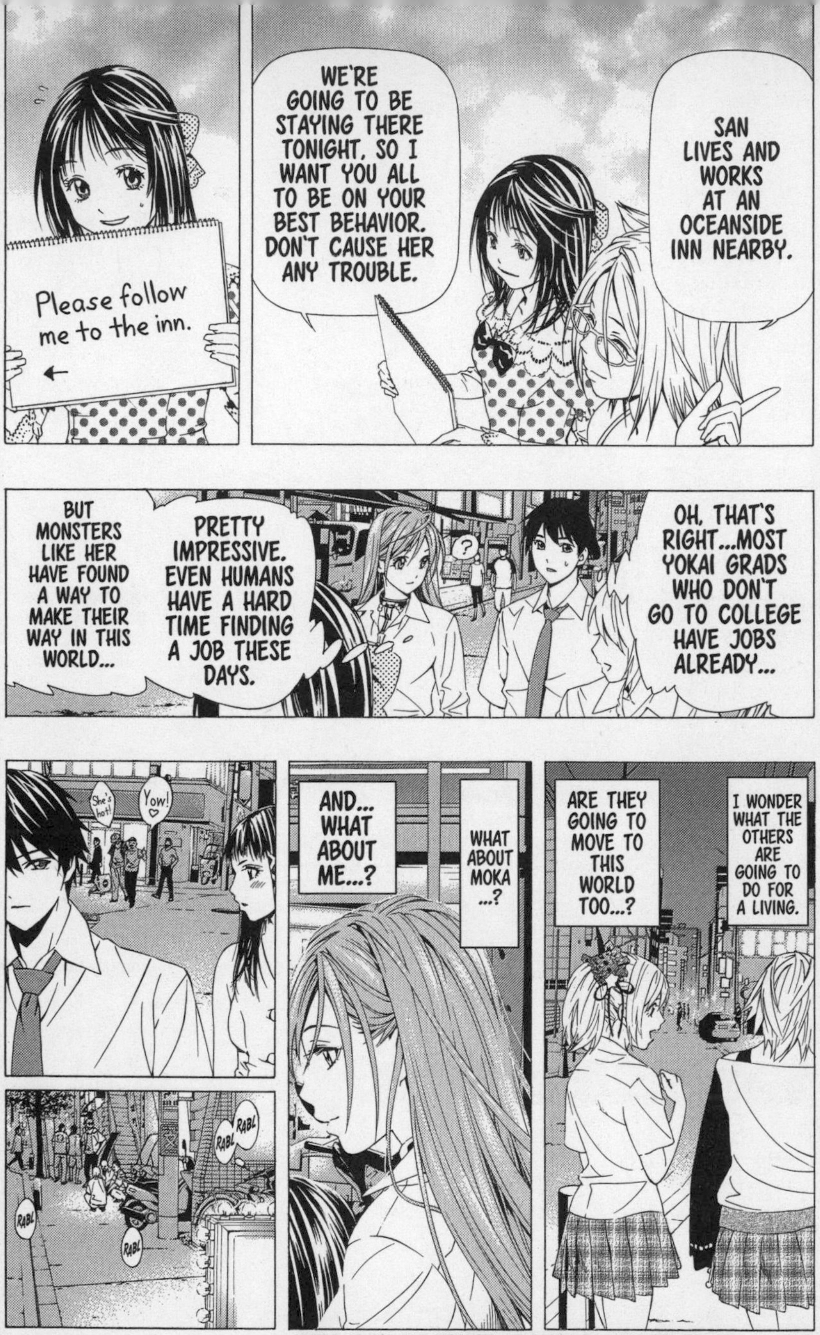
SAN LIVES AND WORKS AT AN OCEANSIDE INN NEARBY.
WE'RE GOING TO BE STAYING THERE TONIGHT, SO I WANT YOU ALL TO BE ON YOUR BEST BEHAVIOR. DON'T CAUSE HER ANY TROUBLE.
Please follow me to the inn. ←
OH, THAT'S RIGHT...MOST YOKAI GRADS WHO DON'T GO TO COLLEGE HAVE JOBS ALREADY...
?
PRETTY IMPRESSIVE. EVEN HUMANS HAVE A HARD TIME FINDING A JOB THESE DAYS.
BUT MONSTERS LIKE HER HAVE FOUND A WAY TO MAKE THEIR WAY IN THIS WORLD...
I WONDER WHAT THE OTHERS ARE GOING TO DO FOR A LIVING.
ARE THEY GOING TO MOVE TO THIS WORLD TOO...?
WHAT ABOUT MOKA ...?
AND... WHAT ABOUT ME...?
Yow! ♡
She's hot!
RABL
RABL
RABL
RABL

*THERE AREN'T ANY MONSTER COLLEGES, SO ANY MONSTER WHO WANTS A HIGHER EDUCATION MUST GO TO THE HUMAN WORLD.

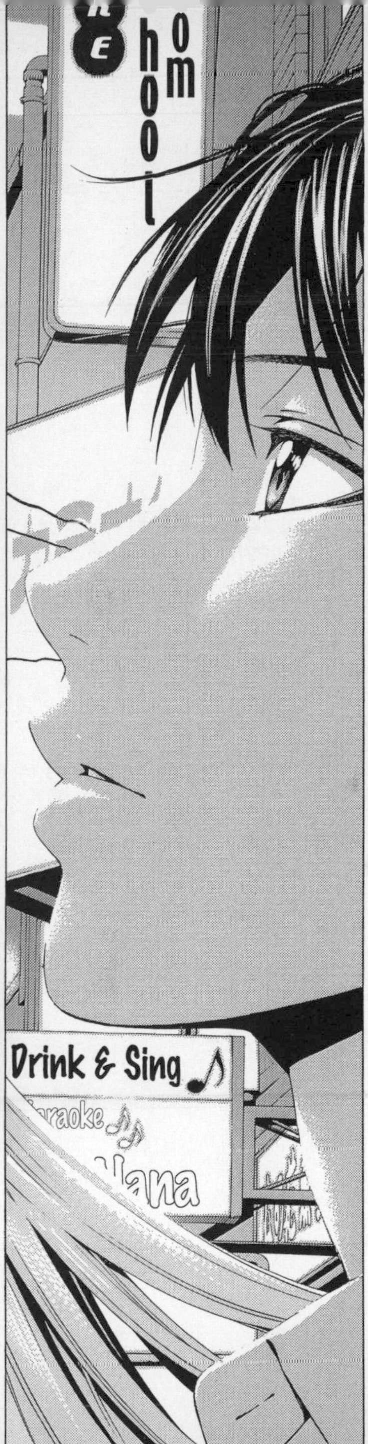
Drink & Sing

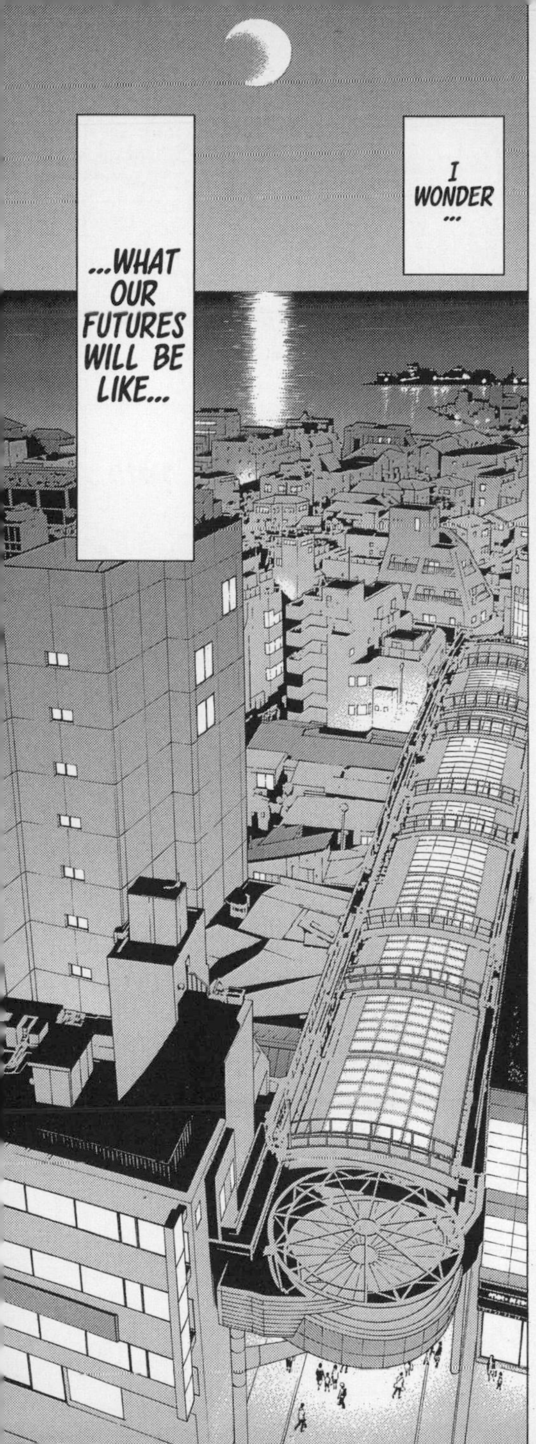
I WONDER ...
...WHAT OUR FUTURES WILL BE LIKE...

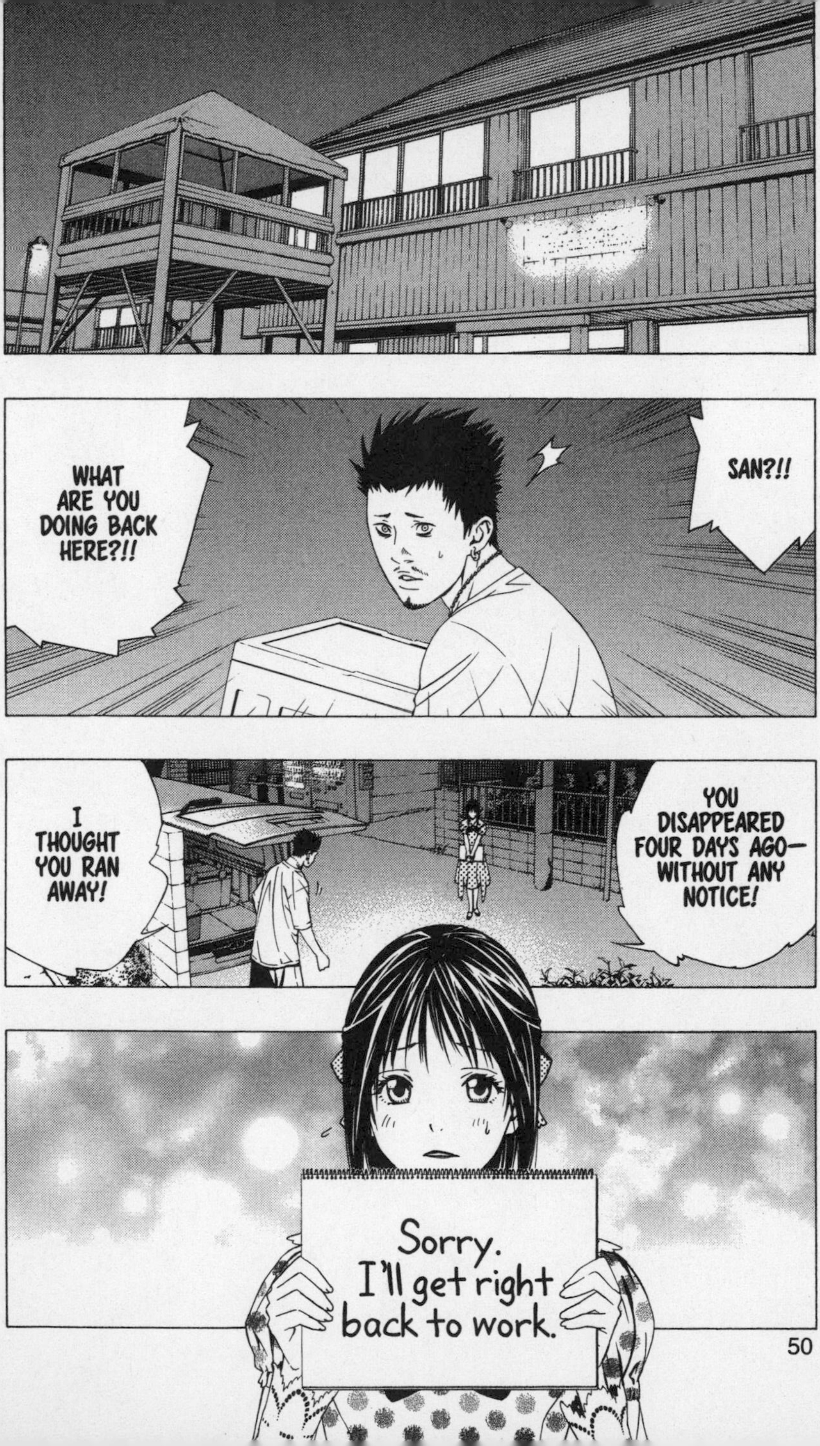
SAN?!!
WHAT ARE YOU DOING BACK HERE?!!
YOU DISAPPEARED FOUR DAYS AGO— WITHOUT ANY NOTICE!
I THOUGHT YOU RAN AWAY!
Sorry. I'll get right back to work.

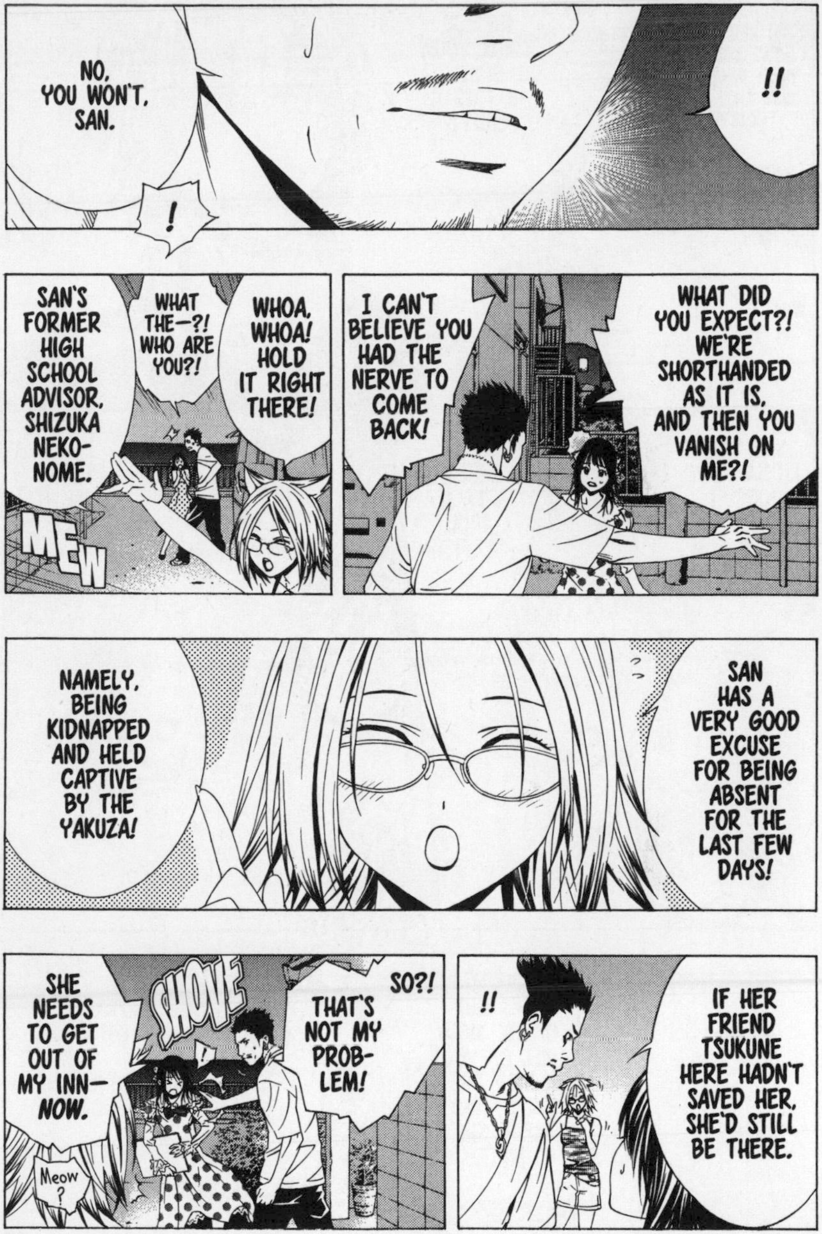
!!
NO, YOU WON'T, SAN.
!
WHAT DID YOU EXPECT?! WE'RE SHORTHANDED AS IT IS, AND THEN YOU VANISH ON ME?!
I CAN'T BELIEVE YOU HAD THE NERVE TO COME BACK!
WHOA, WHOA! HOLD IT RIGHT THERE!
WHAT THE—?! WHO ARE YOU?!
SAN'S FORMER HIGH SCHOOL ADVISOR, SHIZUKA NEKO-NOME.
MEW
SAN HAS A VERY GOOD EXCUSE FOR BEING ABSENT FOR THE LAST FEW DAYS!
NAMELY, BEING KIDNAPPED AND HELD CAPTIVE BY THE YAKUZA!
IF HER FRIEND TSUKUNE HERE HADN'T SAVED HER, SHE'D STILL BE THERE.
!!
SO?! THAT'S NOT MY PROB-LEM!
SHOVE
!
SHE NEEDS TO GET OUT OF MY INN—*NOW.*
Meow ?

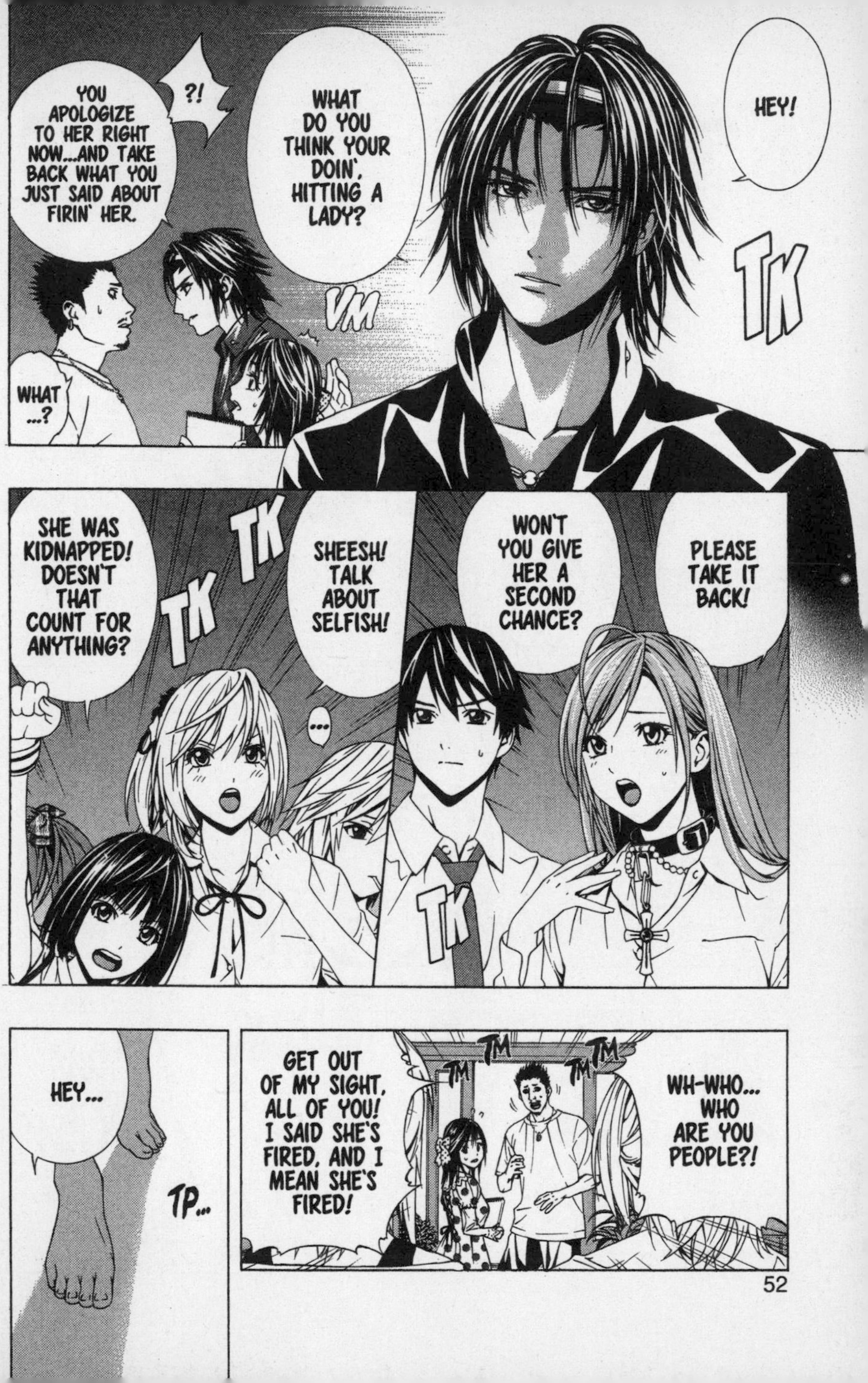
HEY!
TK
WHAT DO YOU THINK YOUR DOIN', HITTING A LADY?
VM
?!
YOU APOLOGIZE TO HER RIGHT NOW...AND TAKE BACK WHAT YOU JUST SAID ABOUT FIRIN' HER.
WHAT ...?
PLEASE TAKE IT BACK!
WON'T YOU GIVE HER A SECOND CHANCE?
TK
SHEESH! TALK ABOUT SELFISH!
TK
TK
SHE WAS KIDNAPPED! DOESN'T THAT COUNT FOR ANYTHING?
...
WH-WHO... WHO ARE YOU PEOPLE?!
TM TM
GET OUT OF MY SIGHT, ALL OF YOU! I SAID SHE'S FIRED, AND I MEAN SHE'S FIRED!
TM TM
HEY...
TP...

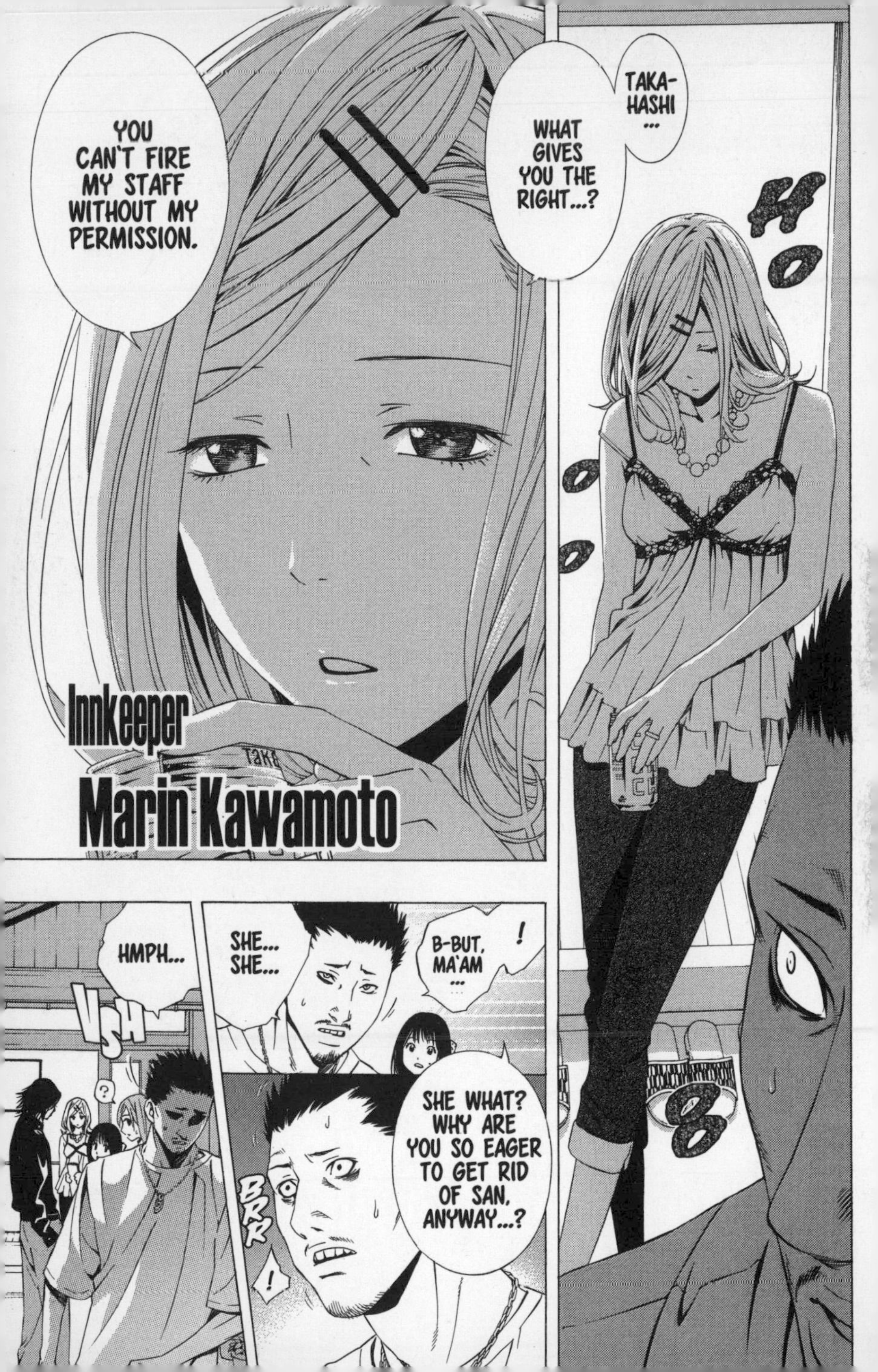

TAKA-HASHI...
WHAT GIVES YOU THE RIGHT...?
HO
OO
YOU CAN'T FIRE MY STAFF WITHOUT MY PERMISSION.
Innkeeper
Marin Kawamoto
!
B-BUT, MA'AM ...
SHE... SHE...
SHE WHAT? WHY ARE YOU SO EAGER TO GET RID OF SAN, ANYWAY...?
BRR
!
HMPH...
VSH
?

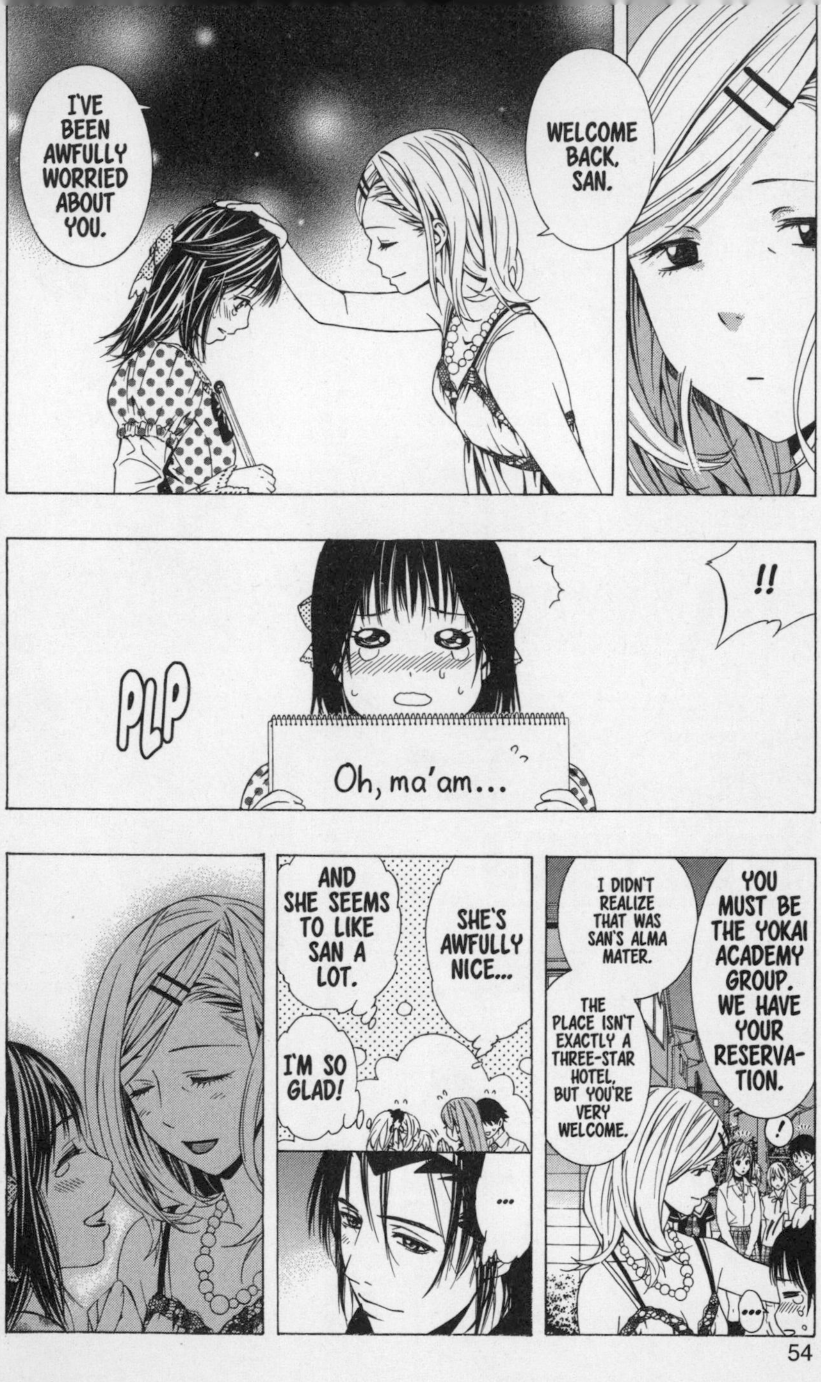
WELCOME BACK, SAN.
I'VE BEEN AWFULLY WORRIED ABOUT YOU.
!!
PLP
Oh, ma'am...
YOU MUST BE THE YOKAI ACADEMY GROUP. WE HAVE YOUR RESERVATION.
I DIDN'T REALIZE THAT WAS SAN'S ALMA MATER.
THE PLACE ISN'T EXACTLY A THREE-STAR HOTEL, BUT YOU'RE VERY WELCOME.
!
...
SHE'S AWFULLY NICE...
AND SHE SEEMS TO LIKE SAN A LOT.
I'M SO GLAD!
...

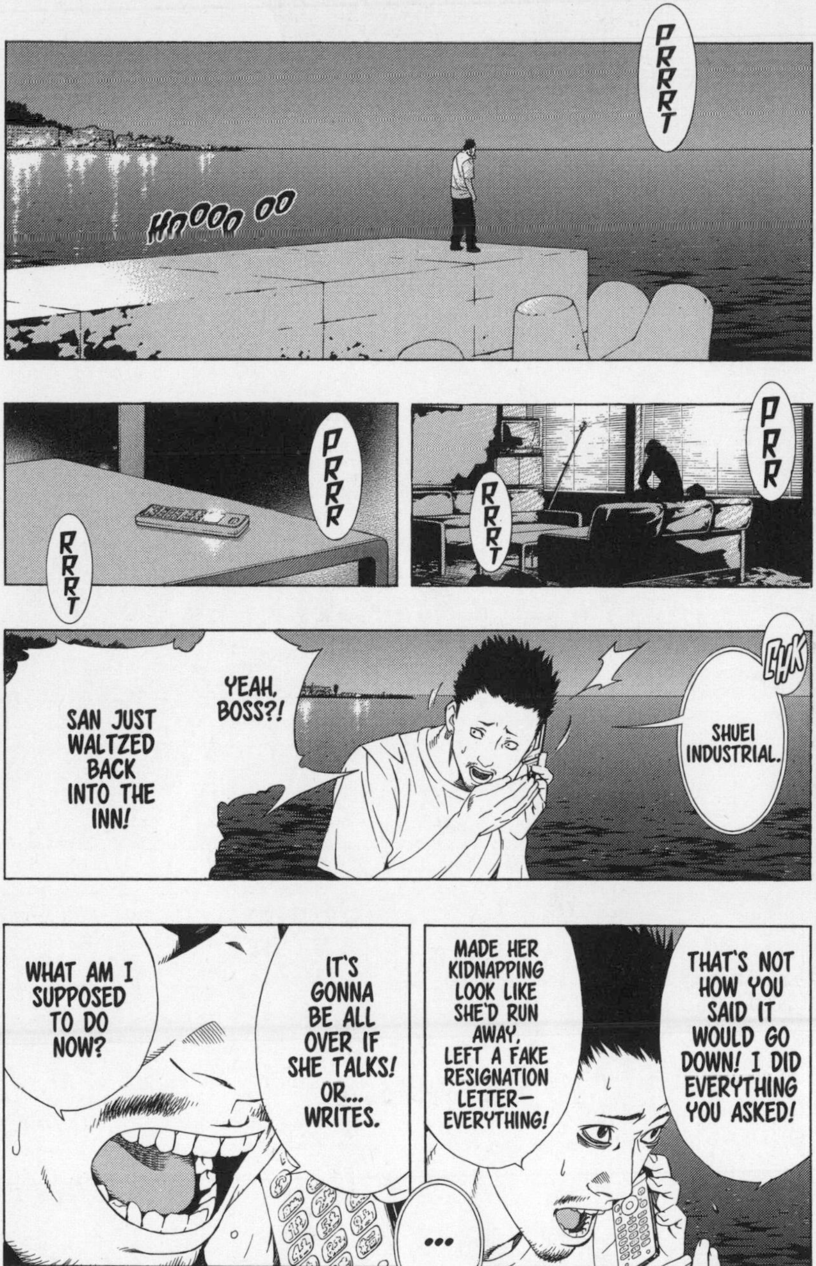
PRRRT
PRR
RRRT
PRRR
RRRT
CHK
SHUEI INDUSTRIAL.
YEAH, BOSS?!
SAN JUST WALTZED BACK INTO THE INN!
THAT'S NOT HOW YOU SAID IT WOULD GO DOWN! I DID EVERYTHING YOU ASKED!
MADE HER KIDNAPPING LOOK LIKE SHE'D RUN AWAY, LEFT A FAKE RESIGNATION LETTER— EVERYTHING!
...
IT'S GONNA BE ALL OVER IF SHE TALKS! OR... WRITES.
WHAT AM I SUPPOSED TO DO NOW?

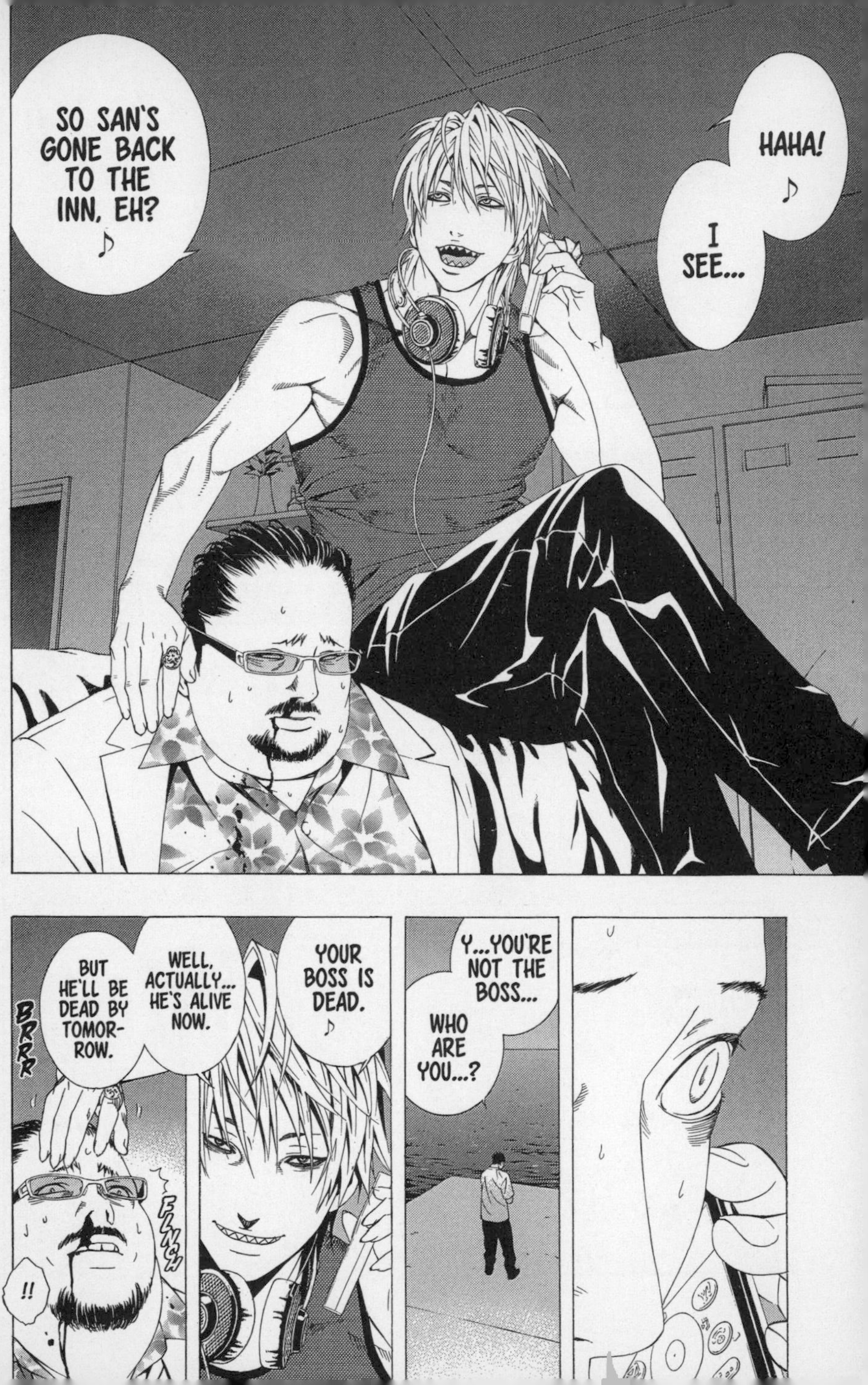
HAHA! ♪
I SEE...
SO SAN'S GONE BACK TO THE INN, EH? ♪
Y...YOU'RE NOT THE BOSS...
WHO ARE YOU...?
YOUR BOSS IS DEAD. ♪
WELL, ACTUALLY... HE'S ALIVE NOW.
BUT HE'LL BE DEAD BY TOMOR-ROW.
BRRR
FLINCH
!!

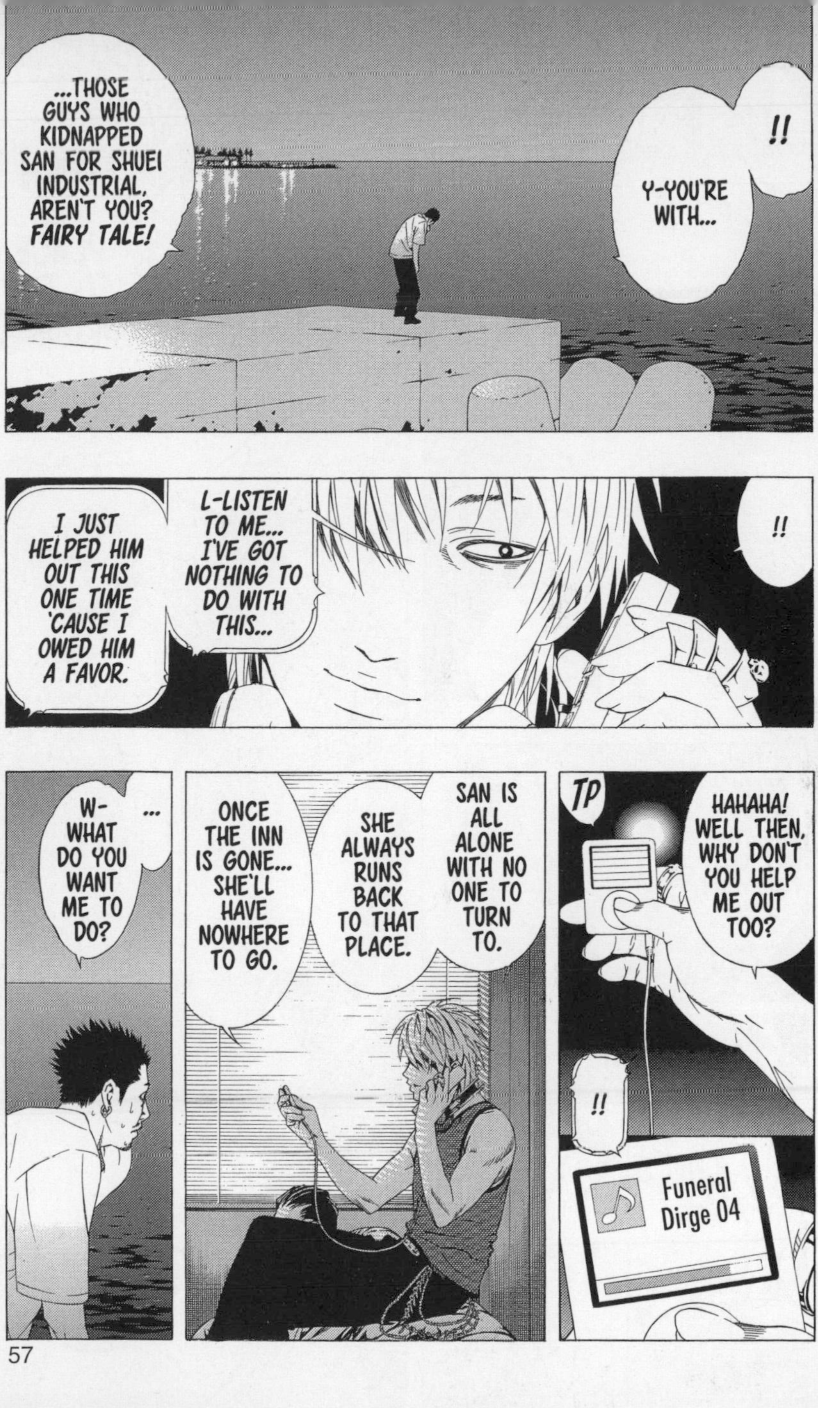
!!
Y-YOU'RE WITH...
...THOSE GUYS WHO KIDNAPPED SAN FOR SHUEI INDUSTRIAL, AREN'T YOU? FAIRY TALE!
!!
L-LISTEN TO ME... I'VE GOT NOTHING TO DO WITH THIS...
I JUST HELPED HIM OUT THIS ONE TIME 'CAUSE I OWED HIM A FAVOR.
TP
HAHAHA! WELL THEN, WHY DON'T YOU HELP ME OUT TOO?
!!
Funeral Dirge 04
SAN IS ALL ALONE WITH NO ONE TO TURN TO.
SHE ALWAYS RUNS BACK TO THAT PLACE.
ONCE THE INN IS GONE... SHE'LL HAVE NOWHERE TO GO.
...
W- WHAT DO YOU WANT ME TO DO?

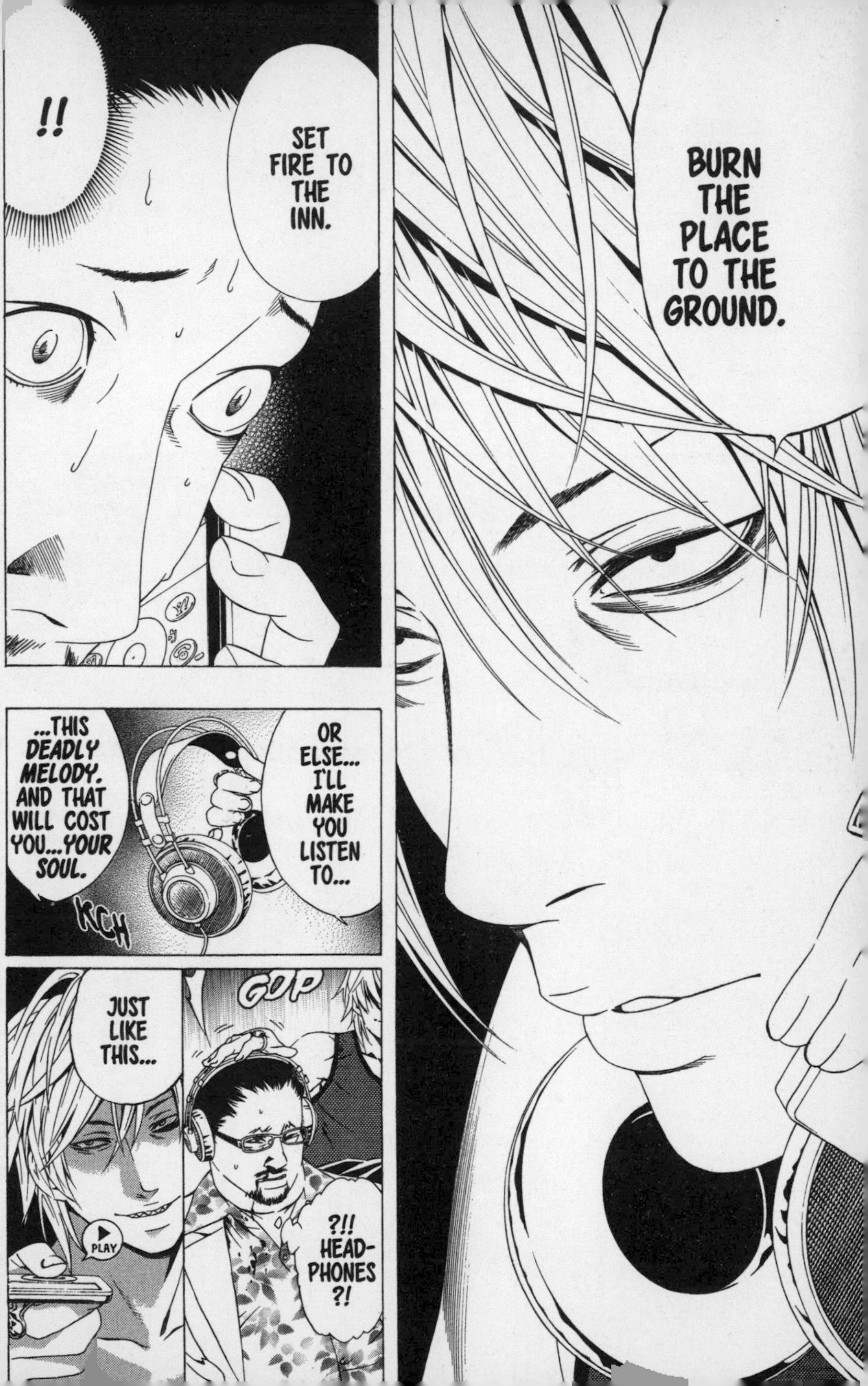
BURN THE PLACE TO THE GROUND.
SET FIRE TO THE INN.
!!
OR ELSE... I'LL MAKE YOU LISTEN TO...
...THIS DEADLY MELODY. AND THAT WILL COST YOU...YOUR SOUL.
KCH
GOP
JUST LIKE THIS...
?!! HEADPHONES?!
PLAY

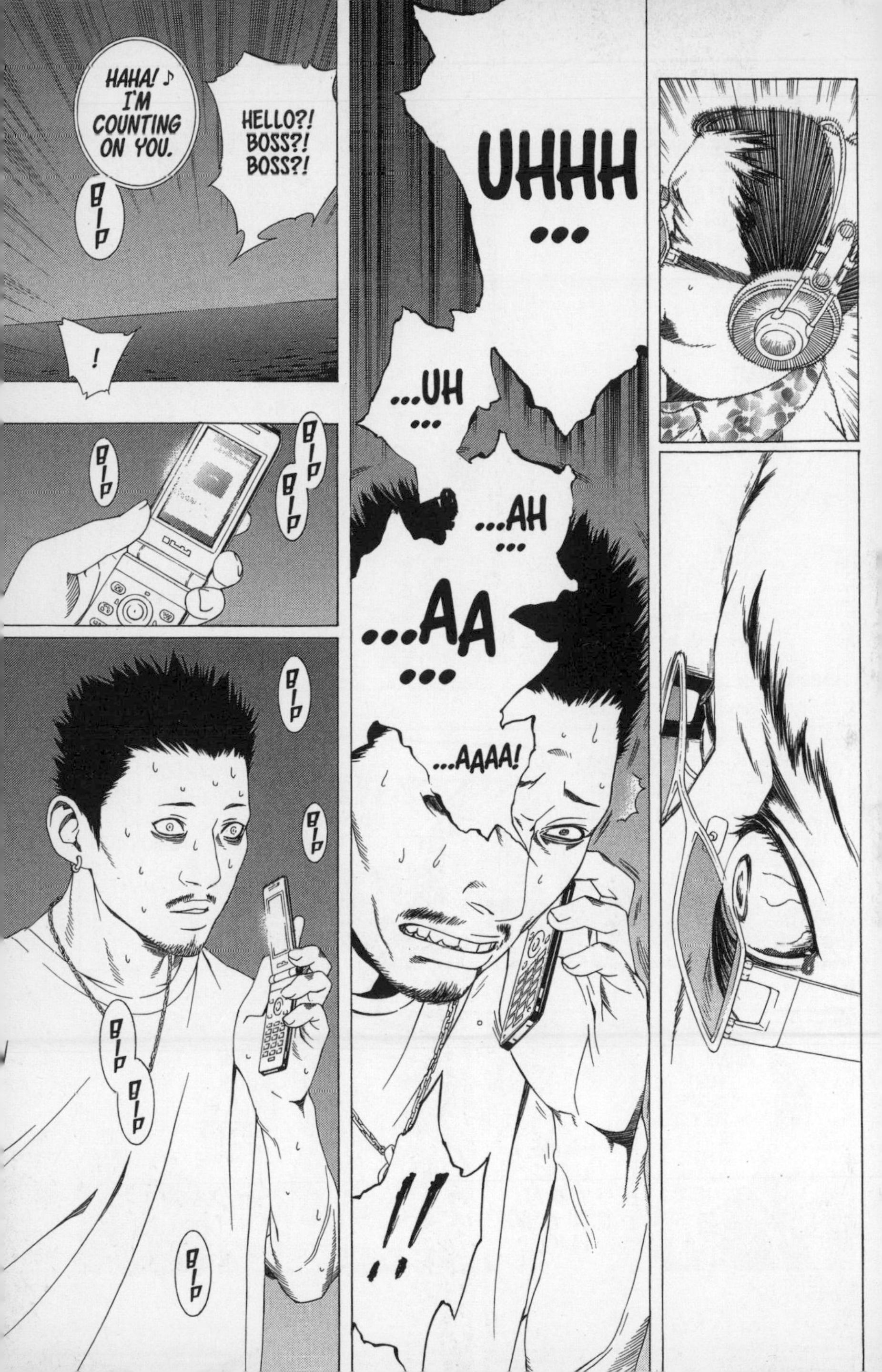
UHHH...
...UH...
...AH...
...AA...
...AAAA!
!!
HAHA! ♪ I'M COUNTING ON YOU.
BLIP
HELLO?! BOSS?! BOSS?!
!
BLIP
BLIP
BLIP
BLIP
BLIP
BLIP
BLIP
BLIP

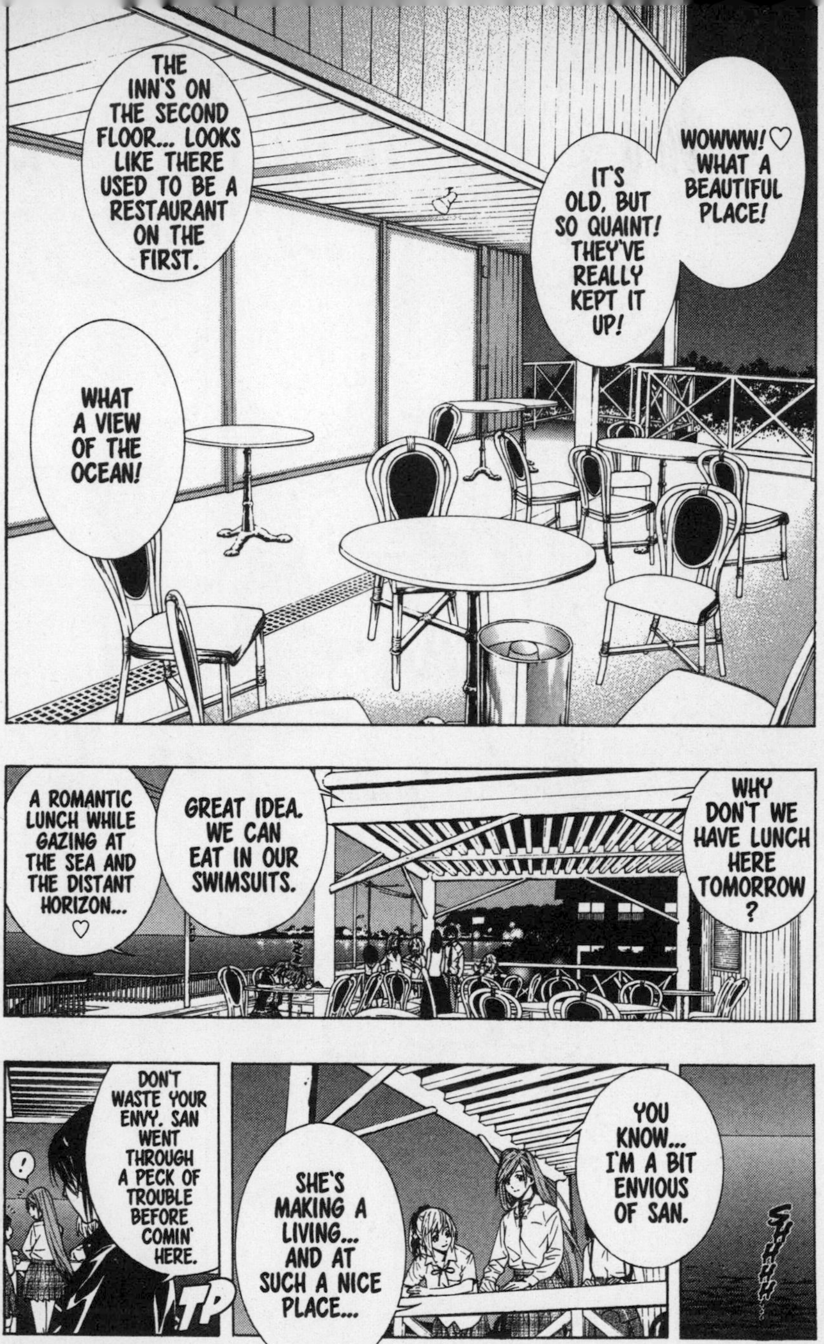
WOWWW! ♡ WHAT A BEAUTIFUL PLACE!
IT'S OLD, BUT SO QUAINT! THEY'VE REALLY KEPT IT UP!
THE INN'S ON THE SECOND FLOOR... LOOKS LIKE THERE USED TO BE A RESTAURANT ON THE FIRST.
WHAT A VIEW OF THE OCEAN!
WHY DON'T WE HAVE LUNCH HERE TOMORROW?
GREAT IDEA. WE CAN EAT IN OUR SWIMSUITS.
A ROMANTIC LUNCH WHILE GAZING AT THE SEA AND THE DISTANT HORIZON... ♡
SHHHHH...
YOU KNOW... I'M A BIT ENVIOUS OF SAN.
SHE'S MAKING A LIVING... AND AT SUCH A NICE PLACE...
!
DON'T WASTE YOUR ENVY. SAN WENT THROUGH A PECK OF TROUBLE BEFORE COMIN' HERE.
TP

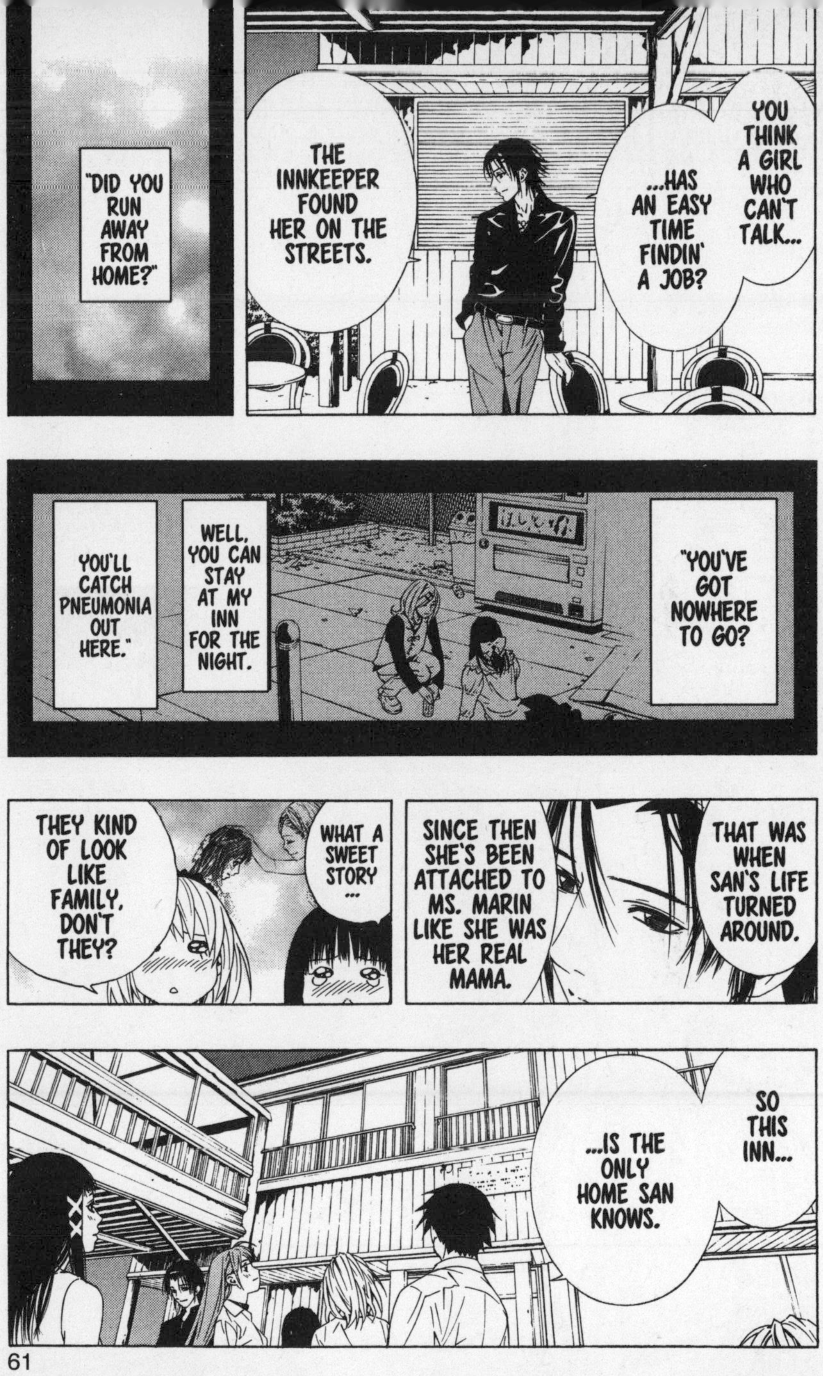
YOU THINK A GIRL WHO CAN'T TALK...
...HAS AN EASY TIME FINDIN' A JOB?
THE INNKEEPER FOUND HER ON THE STREETS.
"DID YOU RUN AWAY FROM HOME?"
"YOU'VE GOT NOWHERE TO GO?
WELL, YOU CAN STAY AT MY INN FOR THE NIGHT.
YOU'LL CATCH PNEUMONIA OUT HERE."
THAT WAS WHEN SAN'S LIFE TURNED AROUND.
SINCE THEN SHE'S BEEN ATTACHED TO MS. MARIN LIKE SHE WAS HER REAL MAMA.
WHAT A SWEET STORY...
THEY KIND OF LOOK LIKE FAMILY, DON'T THEY?
SO THIS INN...
...IS THE ONLY HOME SAN KNOWS.

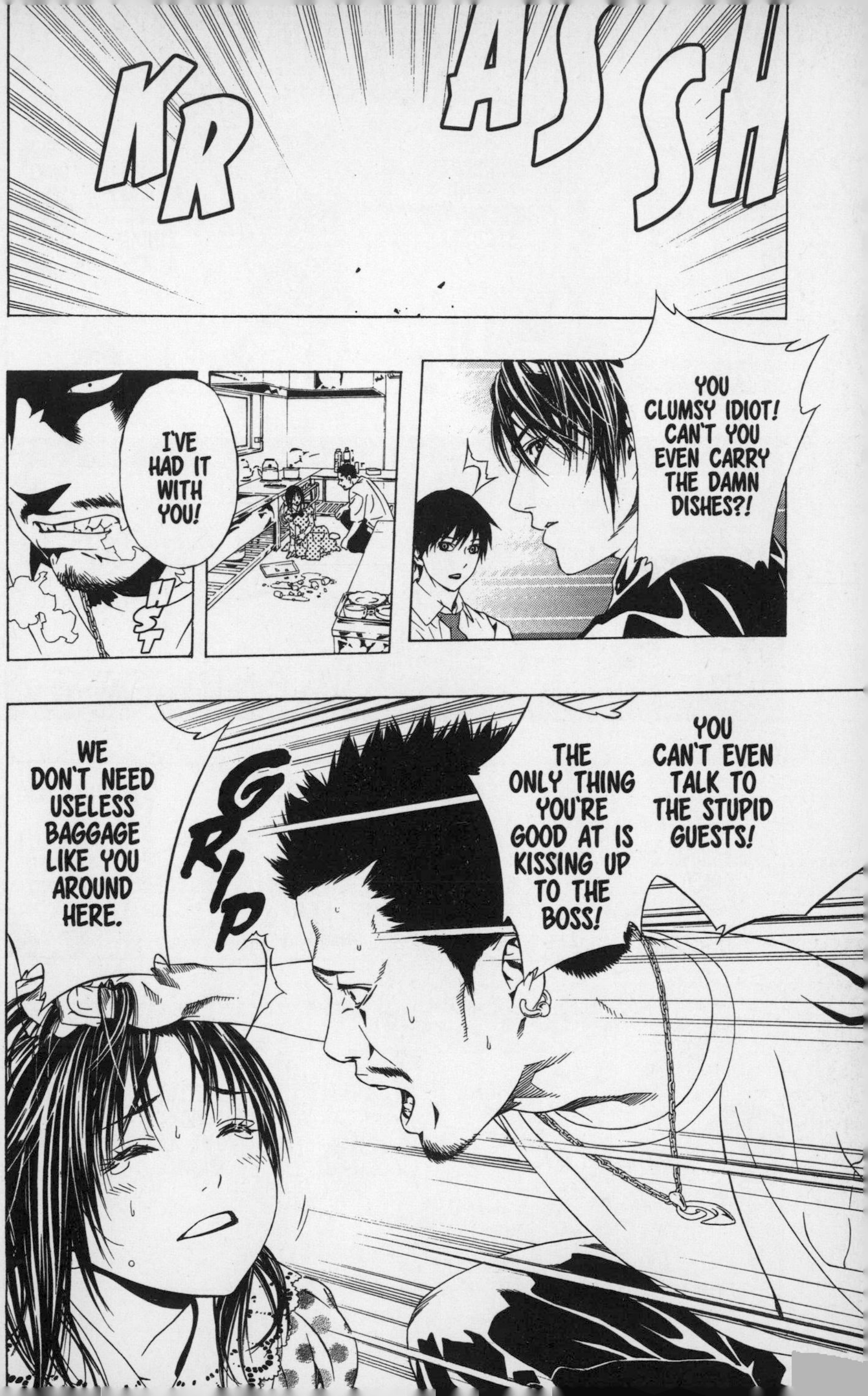
KRASSH
YOU CLUMSY IDIOT! CAN'T YOU EVEN CARRY THE DAMN DISHES?!
I'VE HAD IT WITH YOU!
HST
YOU CAN'T EVEN TALK TO THE STUPID GUESTS!
THE ONLY THING YOU'RE GOOD AT IS KISSING UP TO THE BOSS!
GRIP
WE DON'T NEED USELESS BAGGAGE LIKE YOU AROUND HERE.

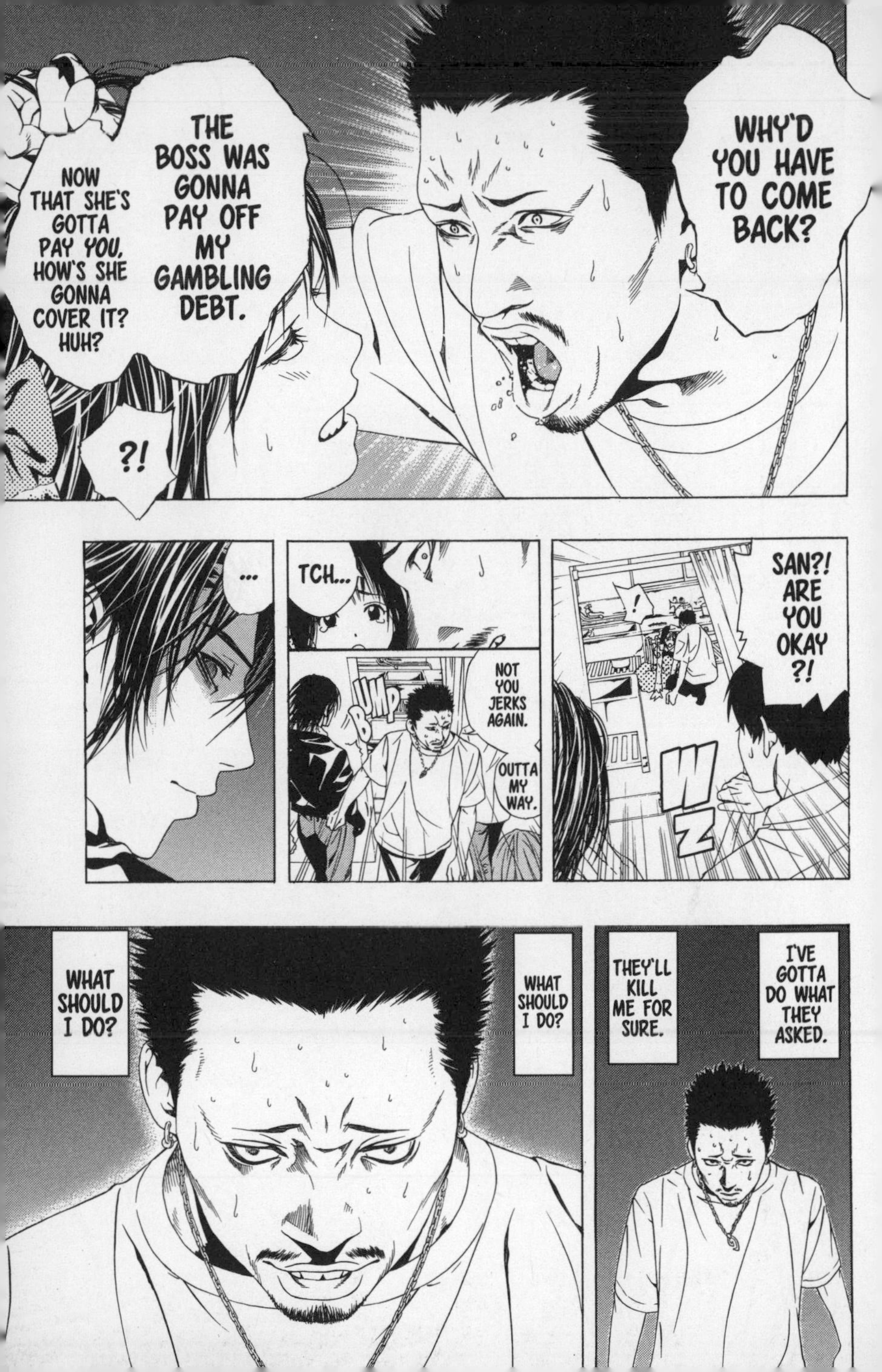
WHY'D YOU HAVE TO COME BACK?
THE BOSS WAS GONNA PAY OFF MY GAMBLING DEBT.
NOW THAT SHE'S GOTTA PAY YOU, HOW'S SHE GONNA COVER IT? HUH?
?!
SAN?! ARE YOU OKAY?!
!
WZ
TCH...
NOT YOU JERKS AGAIN.
BUMP
OUTTA MY WAY.
...
I'VE GOTTA DO WHAT THEY ASKED.
THEY'LL KILL ME FOR SURE.
WHAT SHOULD I DO?
WHAT SHOULD I DO?

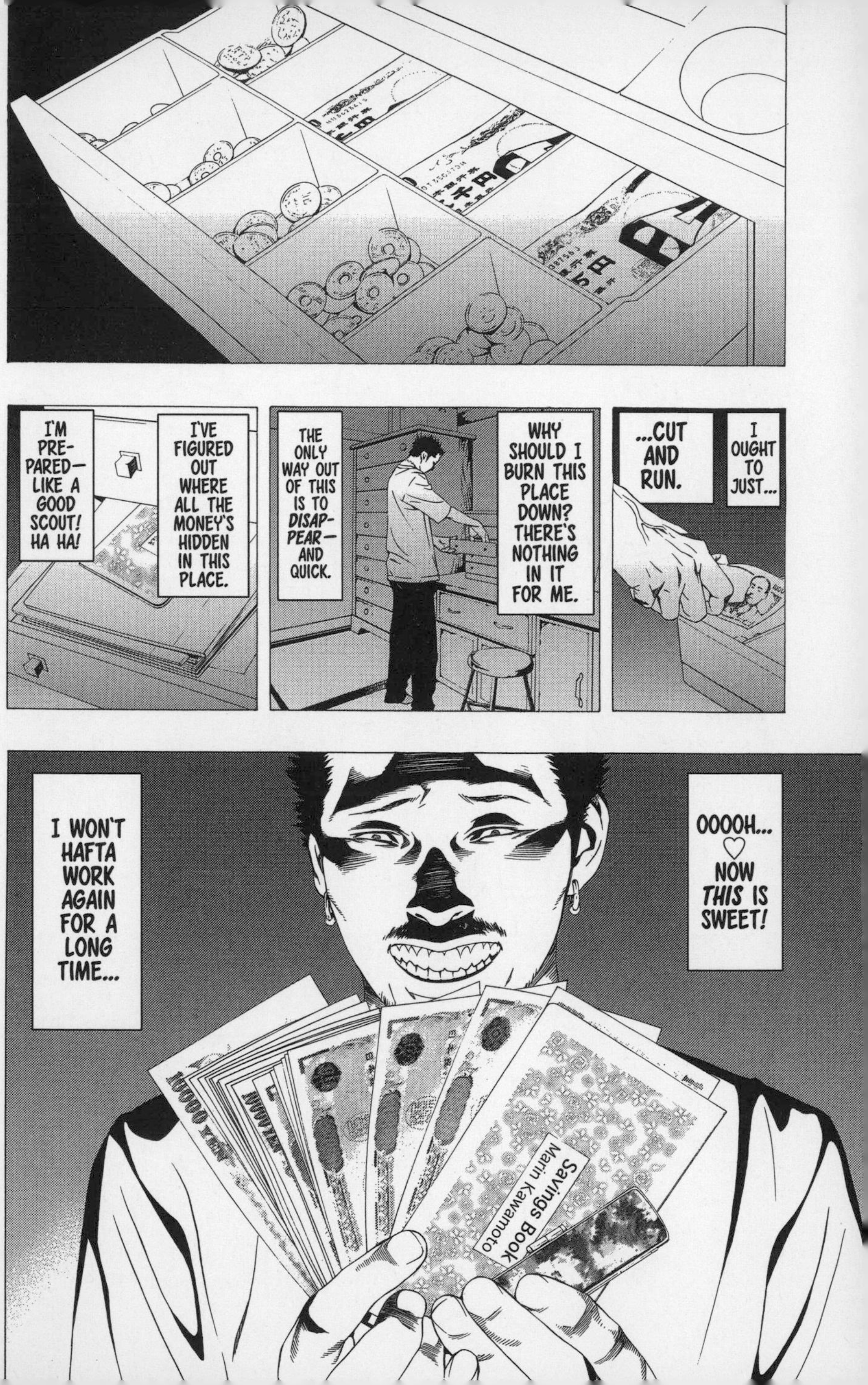
I OUGHT TO JUST...
...CUT AND RUN.
WHY SHOULD I BURN THIS PLACE DOWN? THERE'S NOTHING IN IT FOR ME.
THE ONLY WAY OUT OF THIS IS TO *DISAPPEAR*—AND QUICK.
I'VE FIGURED OUT WHERE ALL THE MONEY'S HIDDEN IN THIS PLACE.
I'M PREPARED—LIKE A GOOD SCOUT! HA HA!
OOOOH... ♡ NOW *THIS* IS SWEET!
I WON'T HAFTA WORK AGAIN FOR A LONG TIME...
Savings Book
Marin Kawamoto

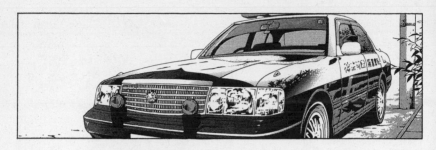

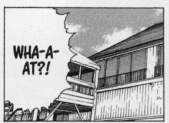

HUH ?
?
WHAT'S ALL THAT NOISE ABOUT?
DM DM
DM DM
WHA-A-AT?!
ALL THE INN'S MONEY WAS STOLEN?!
...
Please cooperate with the investigation.
YOU THINK IT WAS THAT TAKAHASHI GUY?!
DAMN YOU, TAKA-HASHI!
WE'LL GET HIM! WE'LL TEAR HIM INTO LITTLE PIECES!
Ohh...
CALM DOWN.
HOW DO YOU INTEND TO FIND HIM WITHOUT A SINGLE CLUE TO HIS WHERE-ABOUTS?

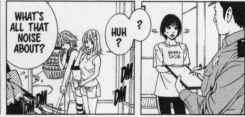

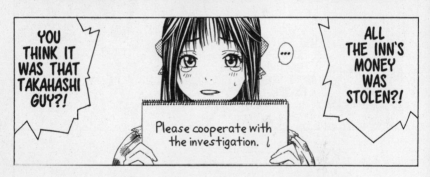

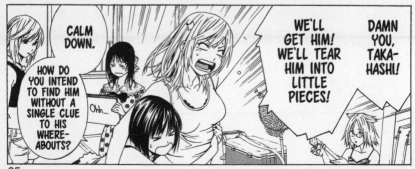

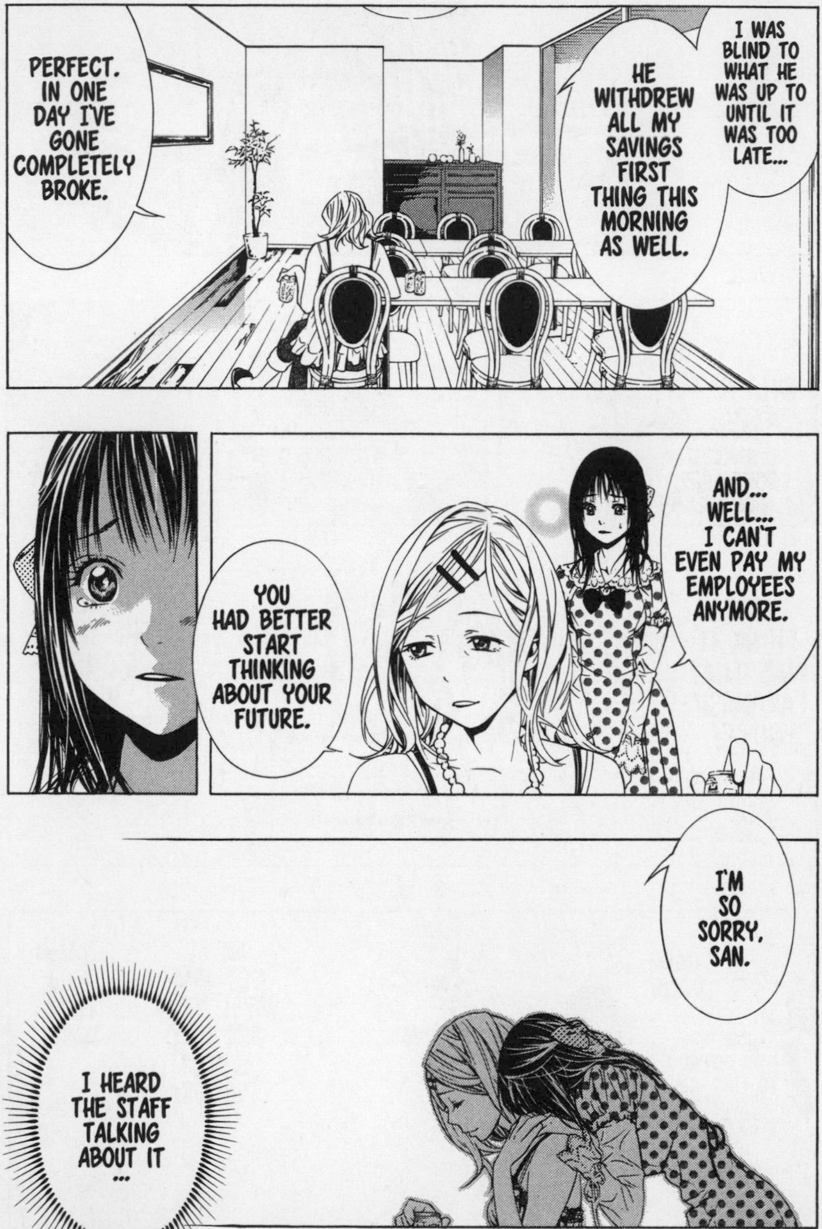
I WAS BLIND TO WHAT HE WAS UP TO UNTIL IT WAS TOO LATE...
HE WITHDREW ALL MY SAVINGS FIRST THING THIS MORNING AS WELL.
PERFECT. IN ONE DAY I'VE GONE COMPLETELY BROKE.
AND... WELL... I CAN'T EVEN PAY MY EMPLOYEES ANYMORE.
YOU HAD BETTER START THINKING ABOUT YOUR FUTURE.
I'M SO SORRY, SAN.
I HEARD THE STAFF TALKING ABOUT IT ...

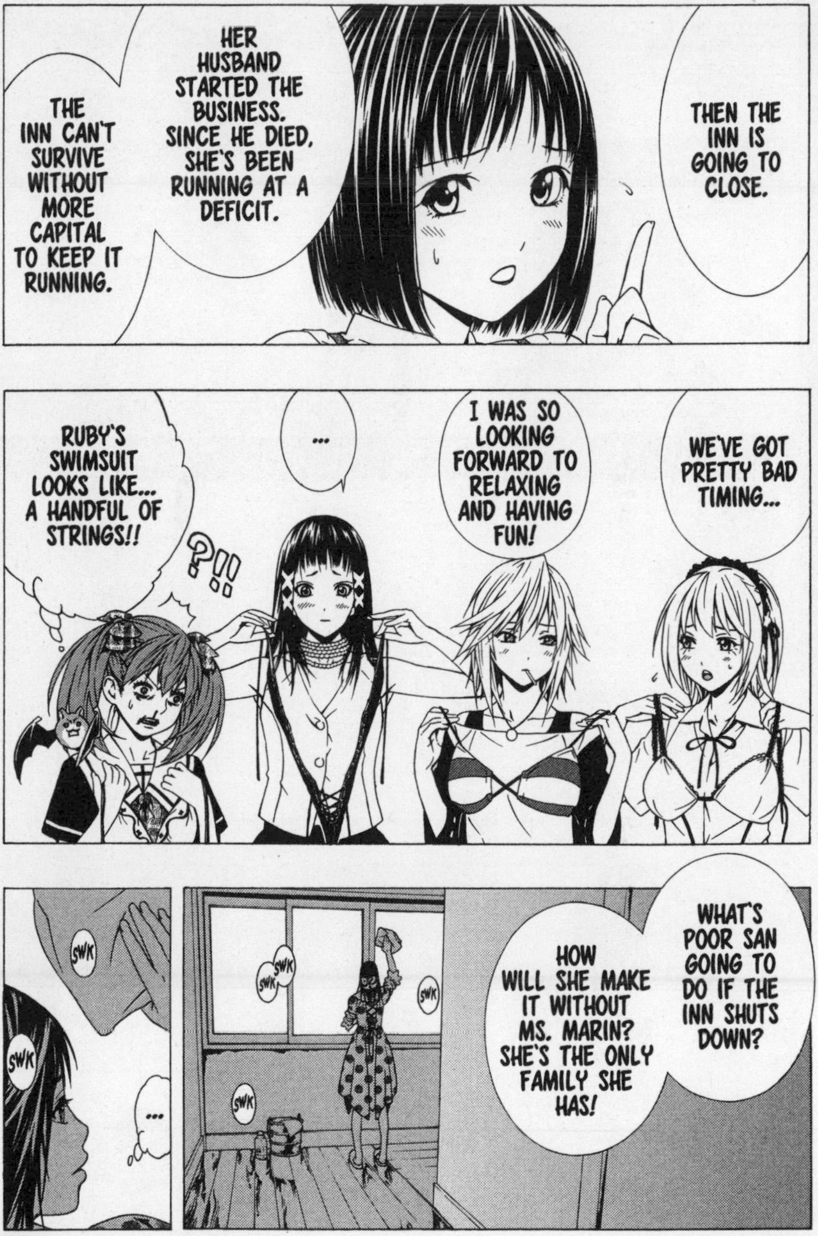
THEN THE INN IS GOING TO CLOSE.
HER HUSBAND STARTED THE BUSINESS. SINCE HE DIED, SHE'S BEEN RUNNING AT A DEFICIT.
THE INN CAN'T SURVIVE WITHOUT MORE CAPITAL TO KEEP IT RUNNING.
WE'VE GOT PRETTY BAD TIMING...
I WAS SO LOOKING FORWARD TO RELAXING AND HAVING FUN!
...
?!!
RUBY'S SWIMSUIT LOOKS LIKE... A HANDFUL OF STRINGS!!
WHAT'S POOR SAN GOING TO DO IF THE INN SHUTS DOWN?
HOW WILL SHE MAKE IT WITHOUT MS. MARIN? SHE'S THE ONLY FAMILY SHE HAS!
SWK
SWK
SWK
SWK
SWK
SWK
SWK
...

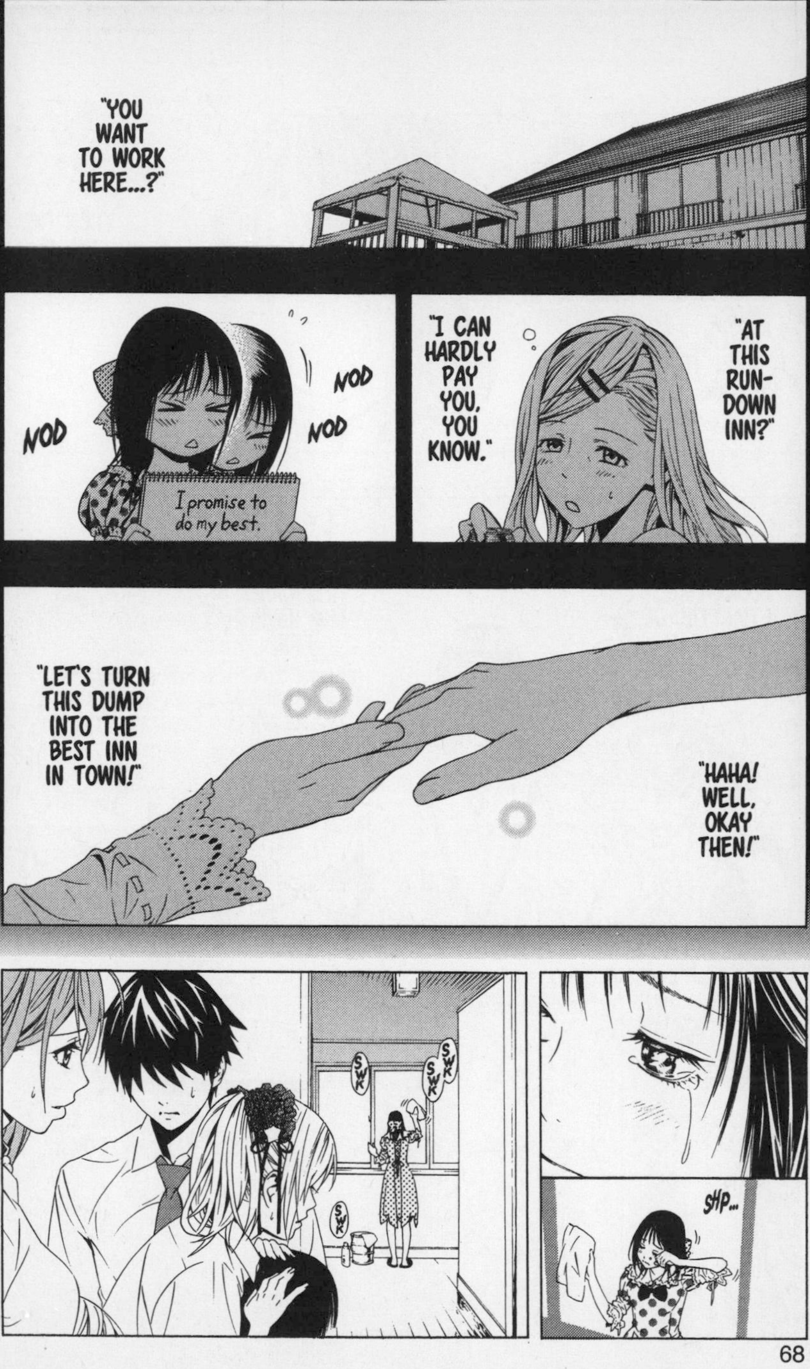
"YOU WANT TO WORK HERE...?"
"AT THIS RUN-DOWN INN?"
"I CAN HARDLY PAY YOU, YOU KNOW."
NOD
NOD
NOD
I promise to do my best.
"HAHA! WELL, OKAY THEN!"
"LET'S TURN THIS DUMP INTO THE BEST INN IN TOWN!"
SHP...
SWK
SWK
SWK
SWK

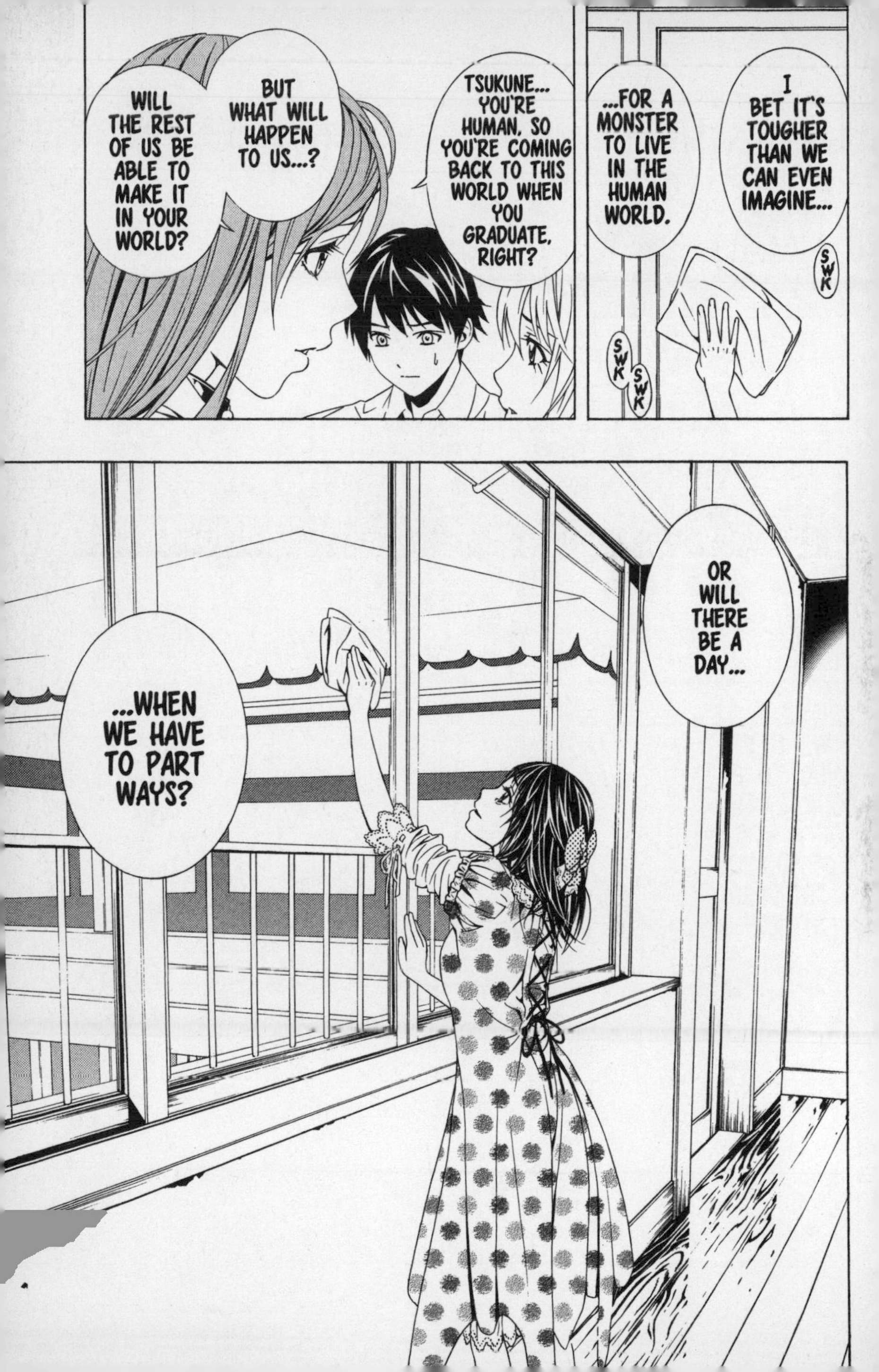
I BET IT'S TOUGHER THAN WE CAN EVEN IMAGINE...
SWK
...FOR A MONSTER TO LIVE IN THE HUMAN WORLD.
SWK
SWK
SWK
TSUKUNE... YOU'RE HUMAN, SO YOU'RE COMING BACK TO THIS WORLD WHEN YOU GRADUATE, RIGHT?
BUT WHAT WILL HAPPEN TO US...?
WILL THE REST OF US BE ABLE TO MAKE IT IN YOUR WORLD?
OR WILL THERE BE A DAY...
...WHEN WE HAVE TO PART WAYS?

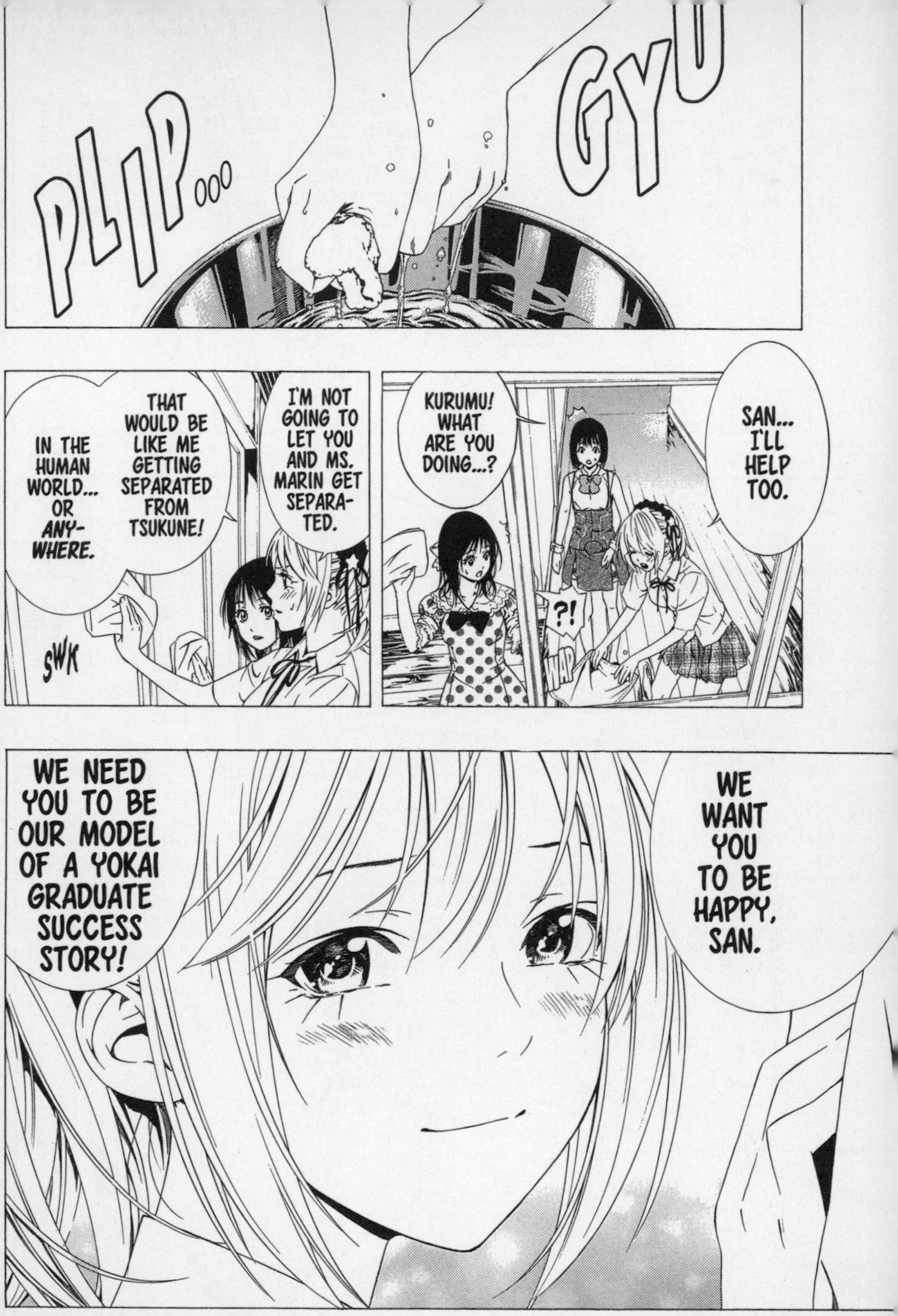
GYU
PLIP...
SAN... I'LL HELP TOO.
KURUMU! WHAT ARE YOU DOING...?
?!
WAP
I'M NOT GOING TO LET YOU AND MS. MARIN GET SEPARATED.
THAT WOULD BE LIKE ME GETTING SEPARATED FROM TSUKUNE!
IN THE HUMAN WORLD... OR ANY-WHERE.
SWK
WE WANT YOU TO BE HAPPY, SAN.
WE NEED YOU TO BE OUR MODEL OF A YOKAI GRADUATE SUCCESS STORY!

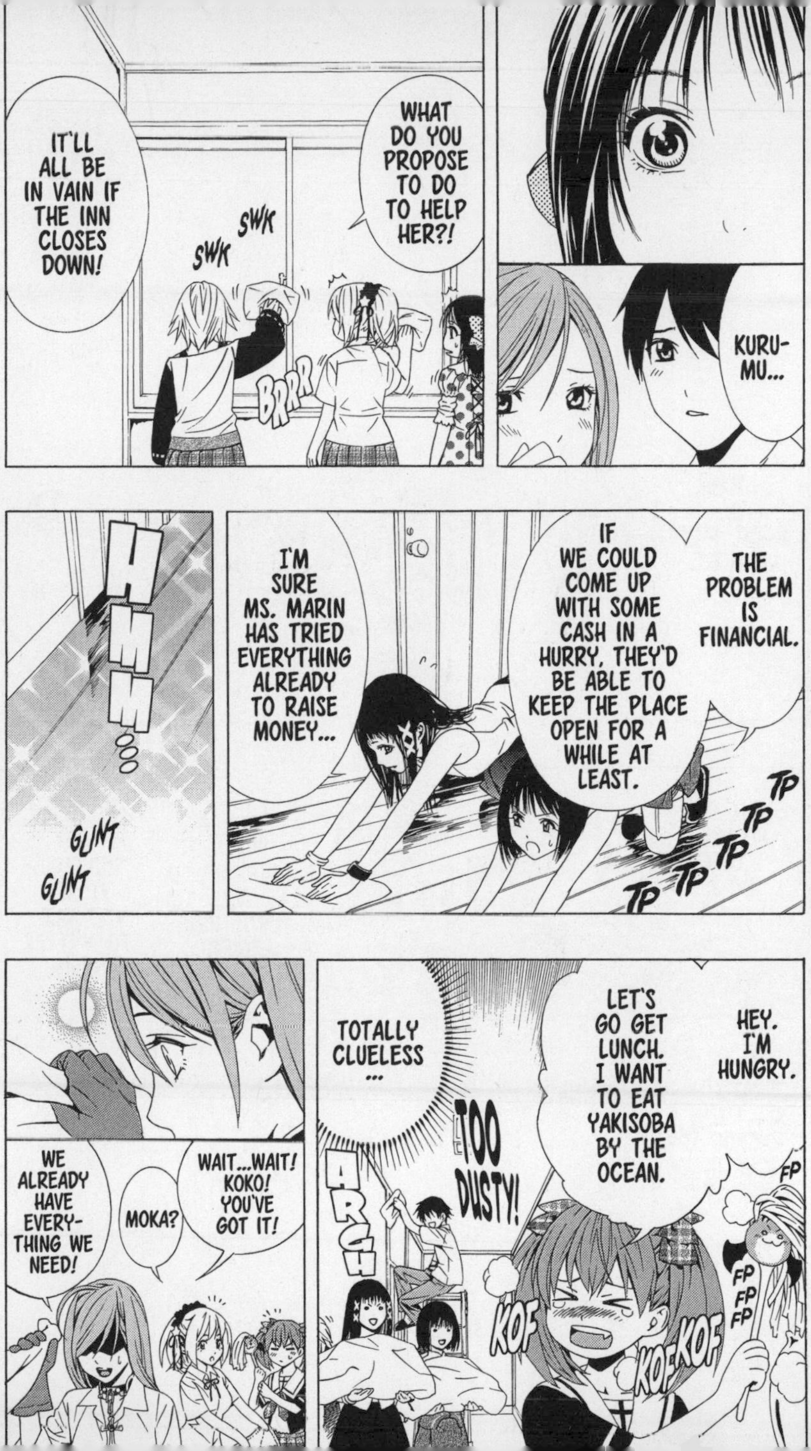
KURU-MU...
WHAT DO YOU PROPOSE TO DO TO HELP HER?!
SWK
SWK
IT'LL ALL BE IN VAIN IF THE INN CLOSES DOWN!
BRRR
THE PROBLEM IS FINANCIAL.
IF WE COULD COME UP WITH SOME CASH IN A HURRY, THEY'D BE ABLE TO KEEP THE PLACE OPEN FOR A WHILE AT LEAST.
I'M SURE MS. MARIN HAS TRIED EVERYTHING ALREADY TO RAISE MONEY...
TP TP TP TP TP TP
HMMM
GLINT
GLINT
HEY. I'M HUNGRY.
LET'S GO GET LUNCH. I WANT TO EAT YAKISOBA BY THE OCEAN.
TOTALLY CLUELESS ...
TOO DUSTY!
ARGH
FP FP FP FP
KOF
KOF KOF
WAIT...WAIT! KOKO! YOU'VE GOT IT!
MOKA?
WE ALREADY HAVE EVERY-THING WE NEED!

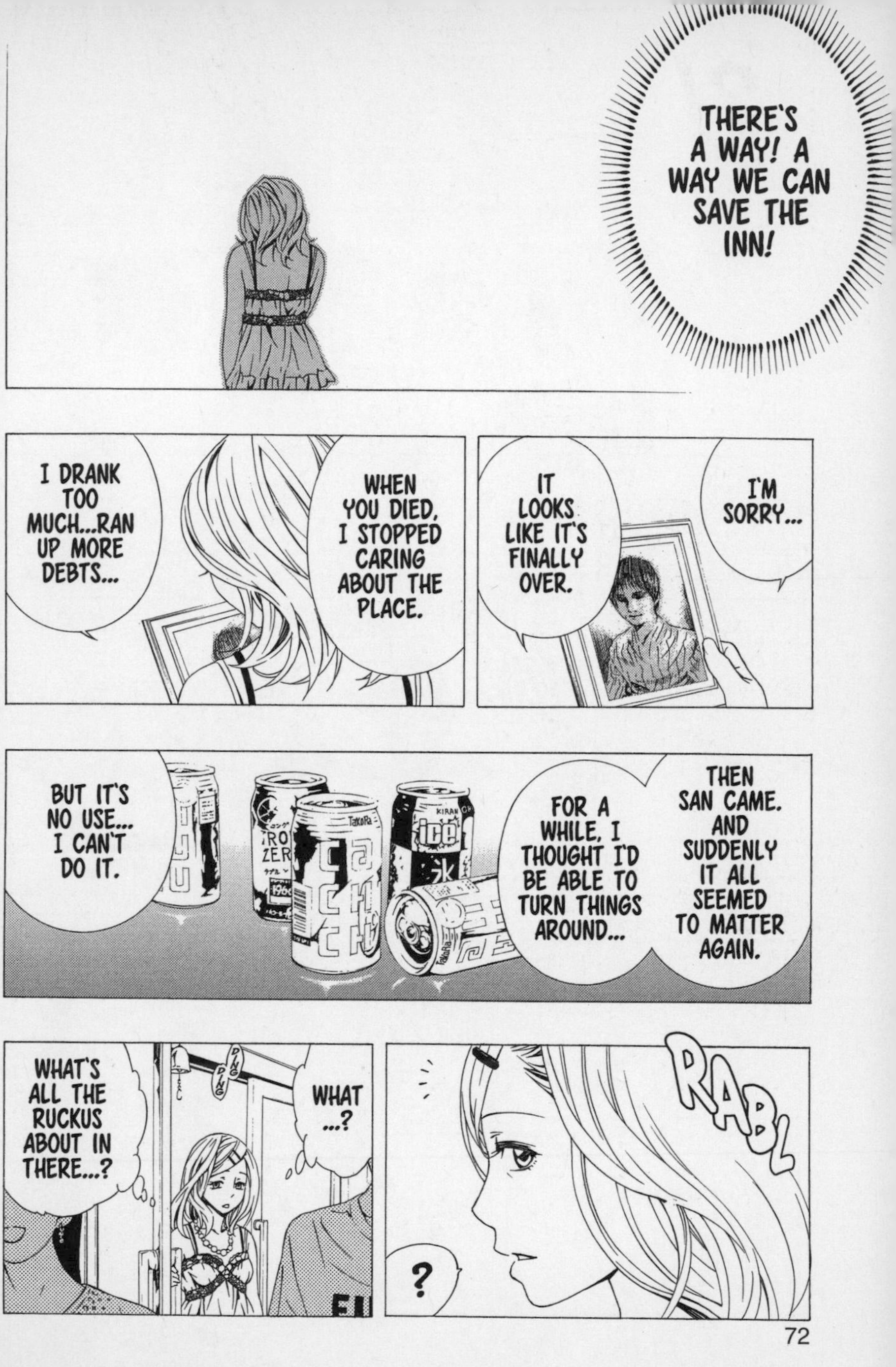
THERE'S A WAY! A WAY WE CAN SAVE THE INN!
I'M SORRY...
IT LOOKS LIKE IT'S FINALLY OVER.
WHEN YOU DIED, I STOPPED CARING ABOUT THE PLACE.
I DRANK TOO MUCH...RAN UP MORE DEBTS...
THEN SAN CAME. AND SUDDENLY IT ALL SEEMED TO MATTER AGAIN.
FOR A WHILE, I THOUGHT I'D BE ABLE TO TURN THINGS AROUND...
BUT IT'S NO USE... I CAN'T DO IT.
RABL
?
WHAT ...?
DING DING
WHAT'S ALL THE RUCKUS ABOUT IN THERE...?

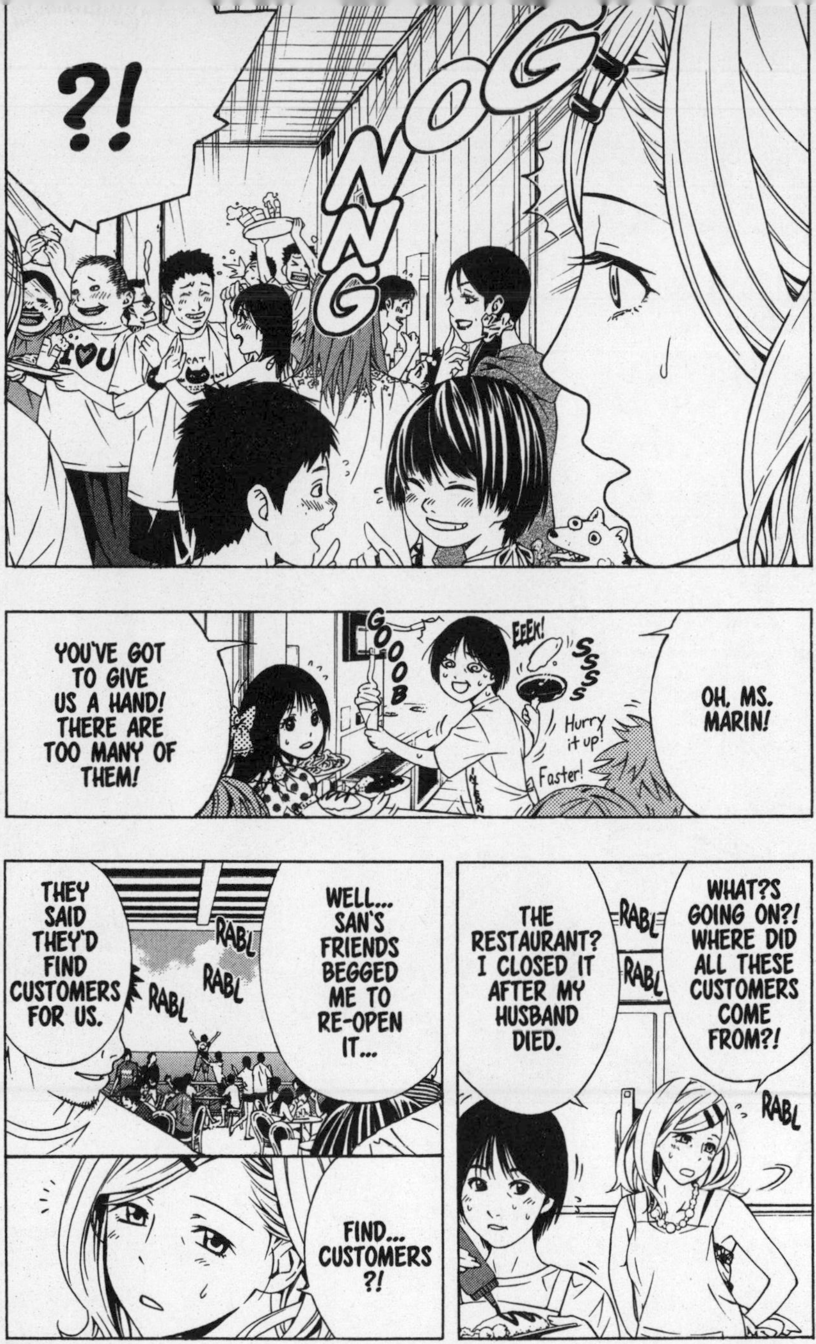
?!
NOG
NANG
OH, MS. MARIN!
EEEK!
SSSS
Hurry it up!
Faster!
GOOOB
INTERN
YOU'VE GOT TO GIVE US A HAND! THERE ARE TOO MANY OF THEM!
WHAT?S GOING ON?! WHERE DID ALL THESE CUSTOMERS COME FROM?!
RABL
RABL
RABL
THE RESTAURANT? I CLOSED IT AFTER MY HUSBAND DIED.
RABL
WELL... SAN'S FRIENDS BEGGED ME TO RE-OPEN IT...
RABL
RABL
RABL
THEY SAID THEY'D FIND CUSTOMERS FOR US.
FIND... CUSTOMERS ?!

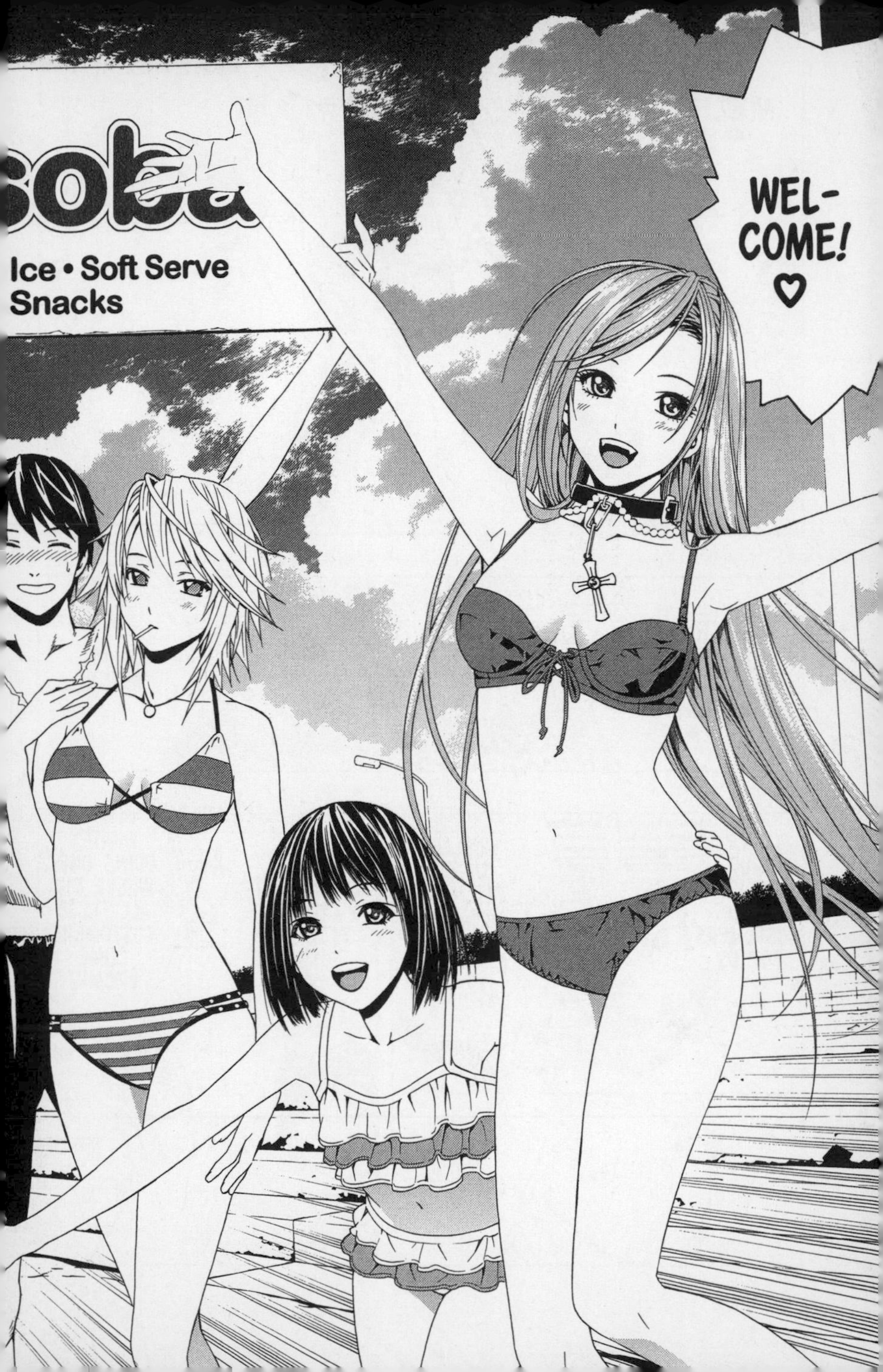
WEL-
COME!
♡
Soba
Ice • Soft Serve
Snacks

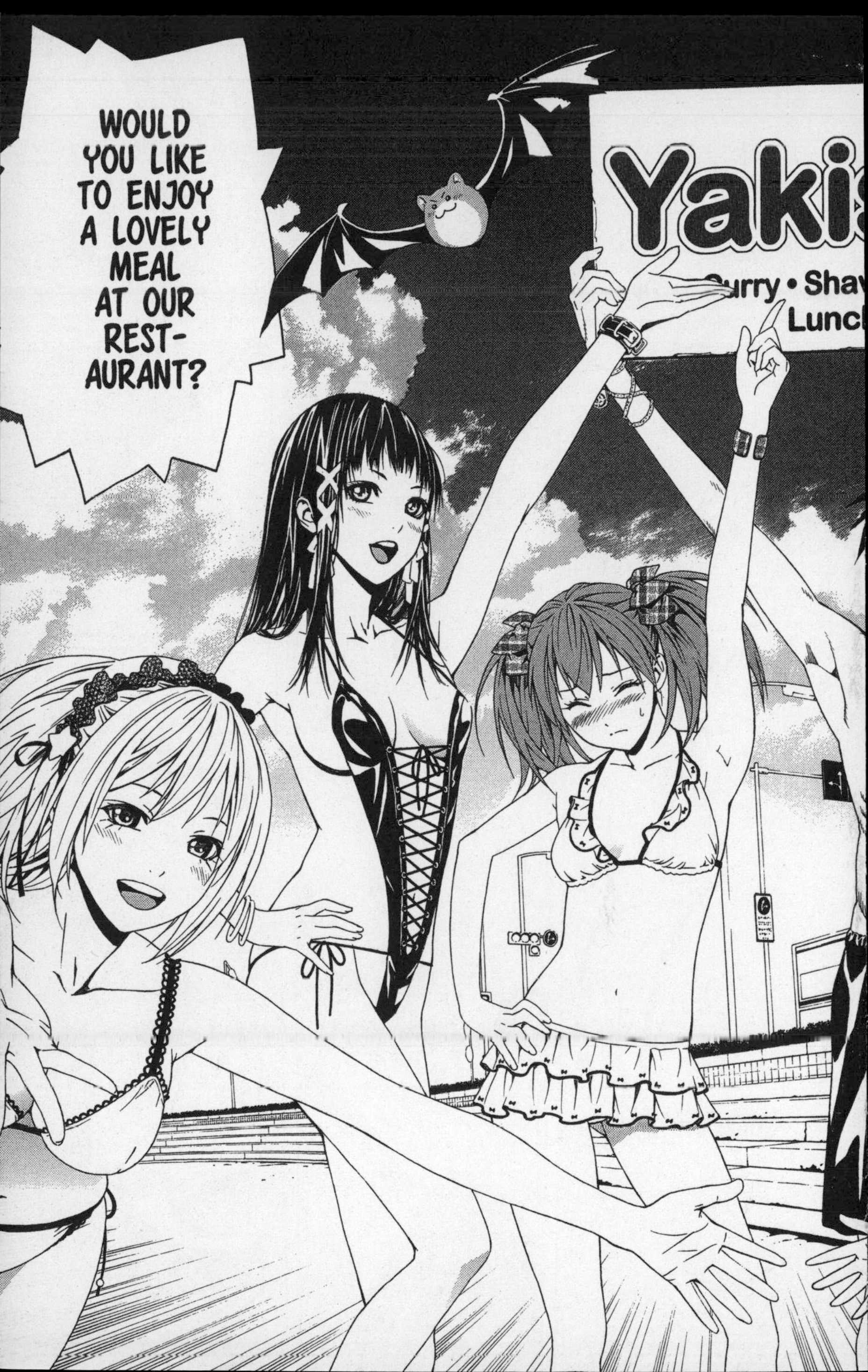
WOULD YOU LIKE TO ENJOY A LOVELY MEAL AT OUR REST- AURANT?
Yaki
urry • Sha
Lunc

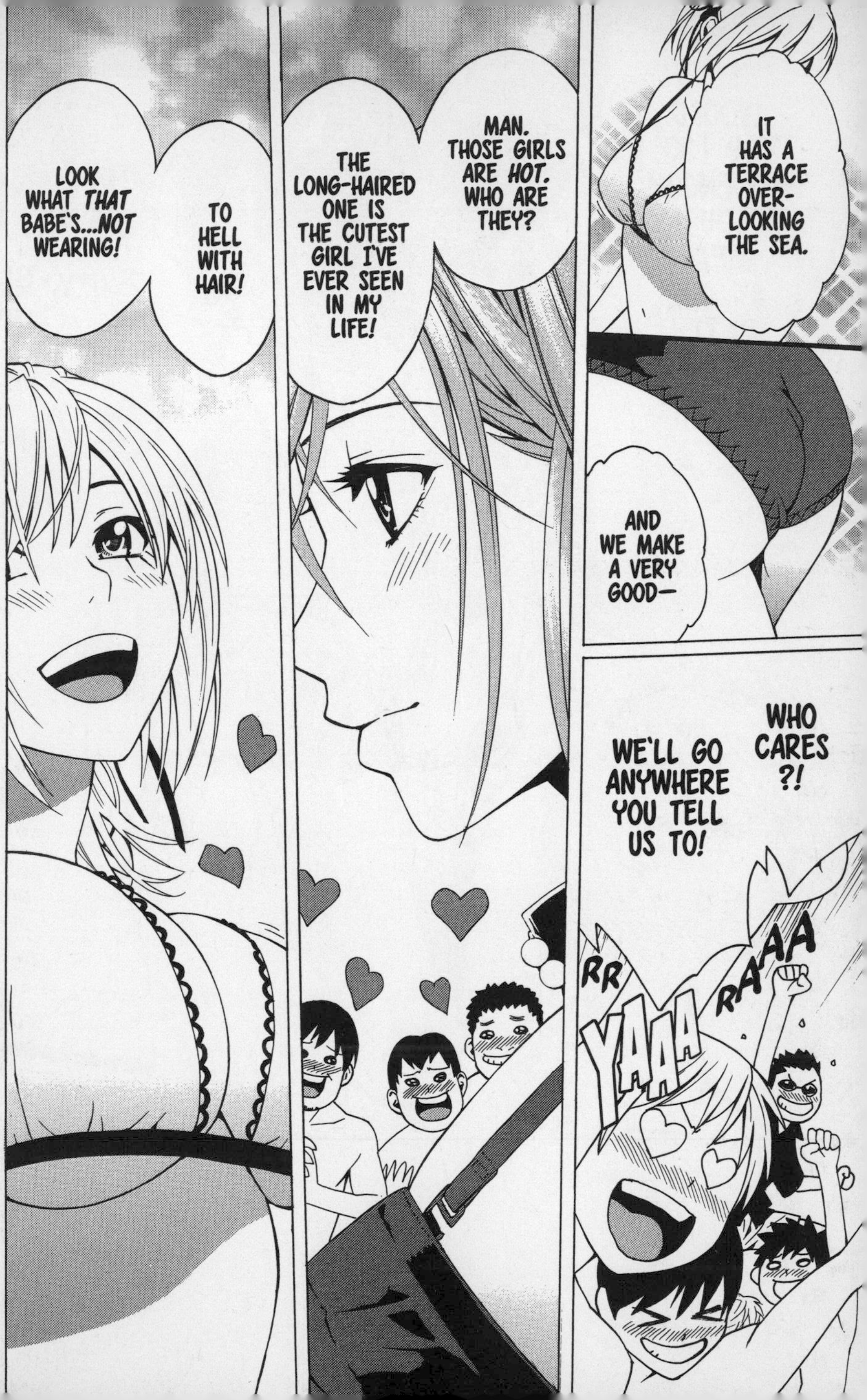
IT HAS A TERRACE OVER-LOOKING THE SEA.
AND WE MAKE A VERY GOOD—
WHO CARES?!
WE'LL GO ANYWHERE YOU TELL US TO!
RR
RAAAA
YAAA
MAN. THOSE GIRLS ARE *HOT*. WHO ARE THEY?
THE LONG-HAIRED ONE IS THE CUTEST GIRL I'VE EVER SEEN IN MY LIFE!
TO HELL WITH HAIR!
LOOK WHAT *THAT* BABE'S...*NOT* WEARING!

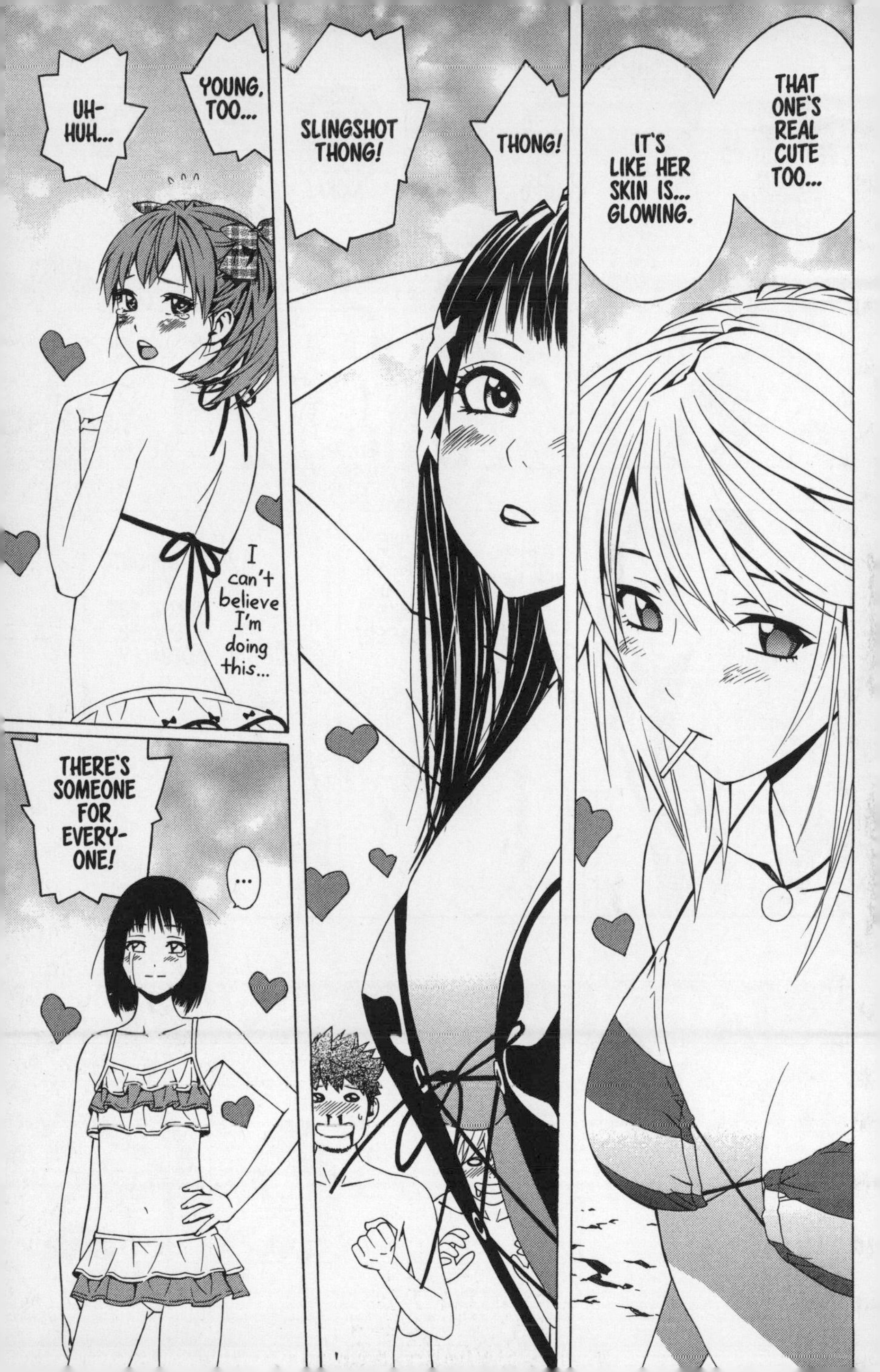
THAT ONE'S REAL CUTE TOO...
IT'S LIKE HER SKIN IS... GLOWING.
THONG!
SLINGSHOT THONG!
YOUNG, TOO...
UH-HUH...
I can't believe I'm doing this...
THERE'S SOMEONE FOR EVERY-ONE!
...

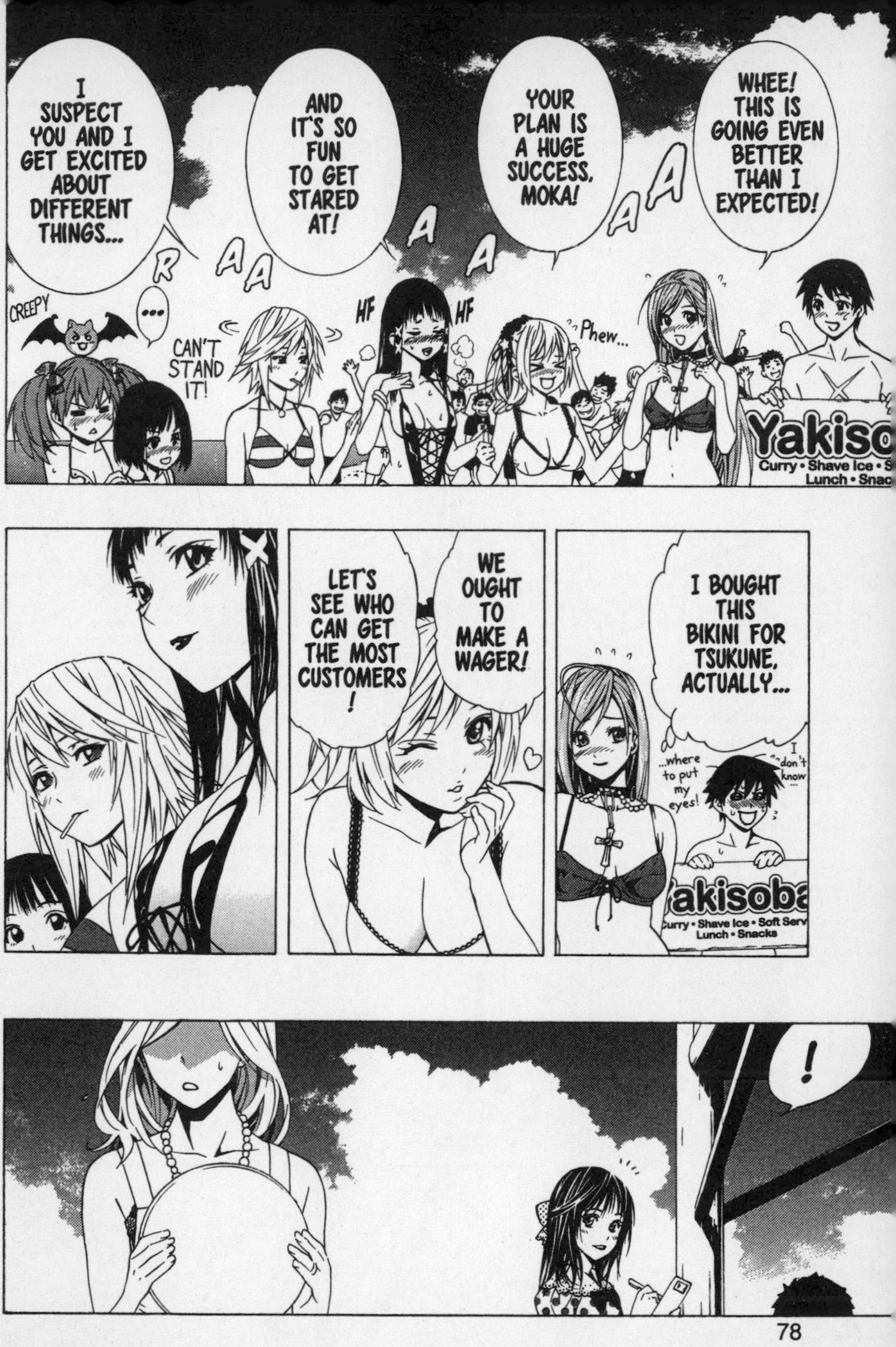
WHEE! THIS IS GOING EVEN BETTER THAN I EXPECTED!
YOUR PLAN IS A HUGE SUCCESS, MOKA!
AND IT'S SO FUN TO GET STARED AT!
I SUSPECT YOU AND I GET EXCITED ABOUT DIFFERENT THINGS...
RAAAAAAA
Yakiso
Curry • Shave Ice • S
Lunch • Snac
Phew...
HF
HF
CAN'T STAND IT!
...
CREEPY
I BOUGHT THIS BIKINI FOR TSUKUNE, ACTUALLY...
I don't know...
...where to put my eyes!
akisoba
urry • Shave Ice • Soft Serv
Lunch • Snacks
WE OUGHT TO MAKE A WAGER!
LET'S SEE WHO CAN GET THE MOST CUSTOMERS!
!

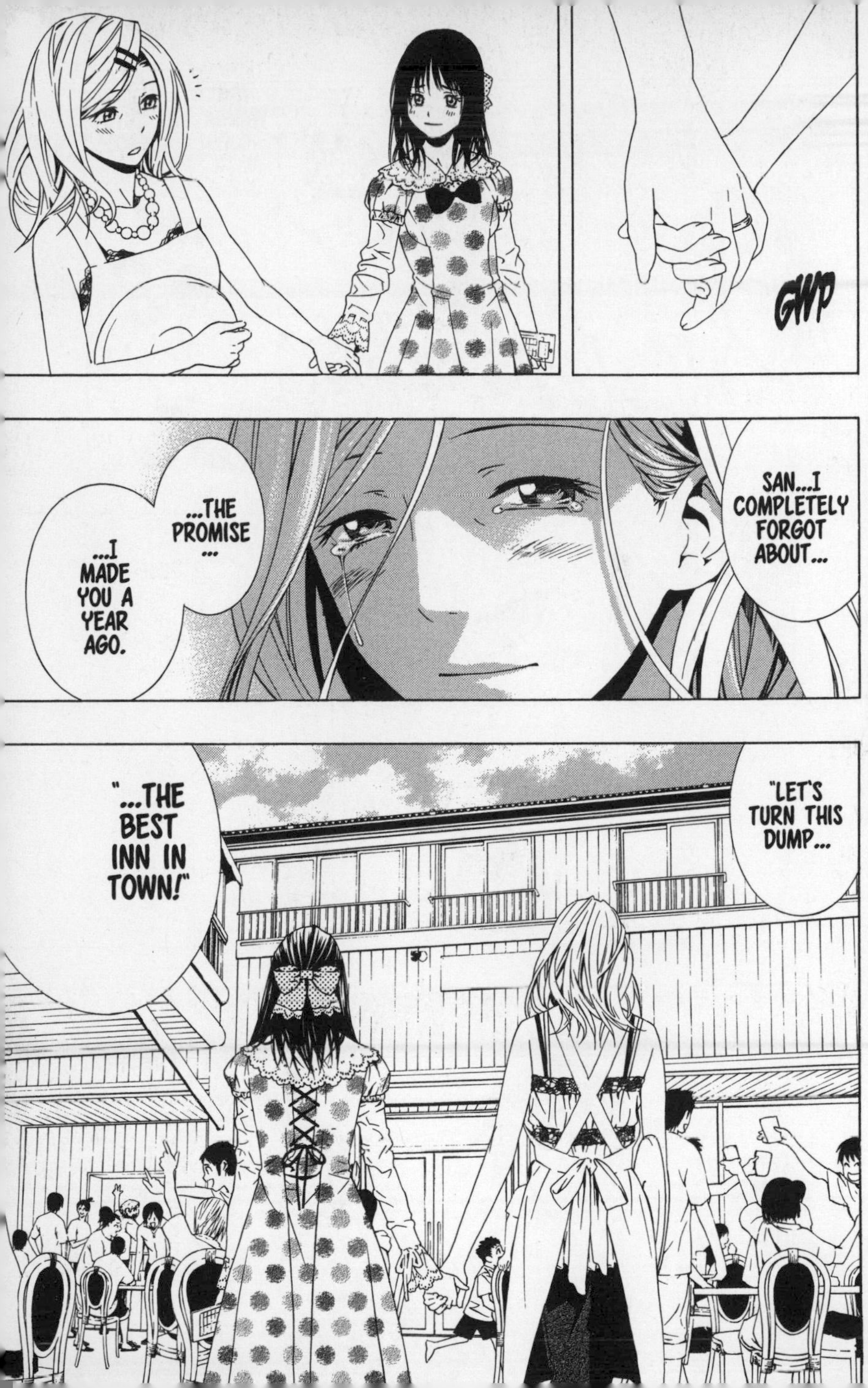
GWP
SAN...I COMPLETELY FORGOT ABOUT...
...THE PROMISE ...
...I MADE YOU A YEAR AGO.
"LET'S TURN THIS DUMP...
"...THE BEST INN IN TOWN!"

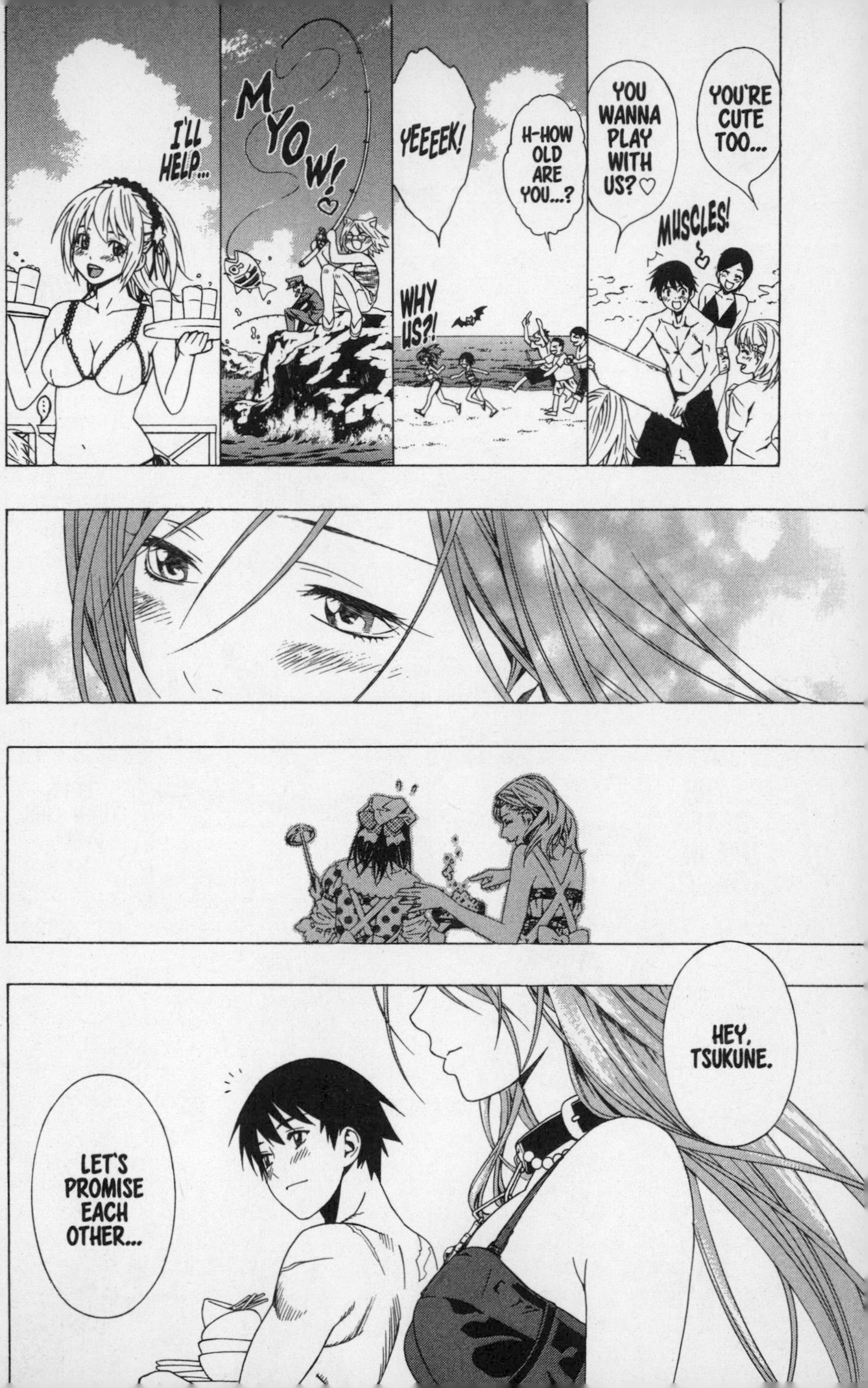
YOU'RE CUTE TOO...
YOU WANNA PLAY WITH US? ♡
MUSCLES!
H-HOW OLD ARE YOU...?
YEEEEK!
WHY US?!
MYOW! ♡
I'LL HELP...
HEY, TSUKUNE.
LET'S PROMISE EACH OTHER...

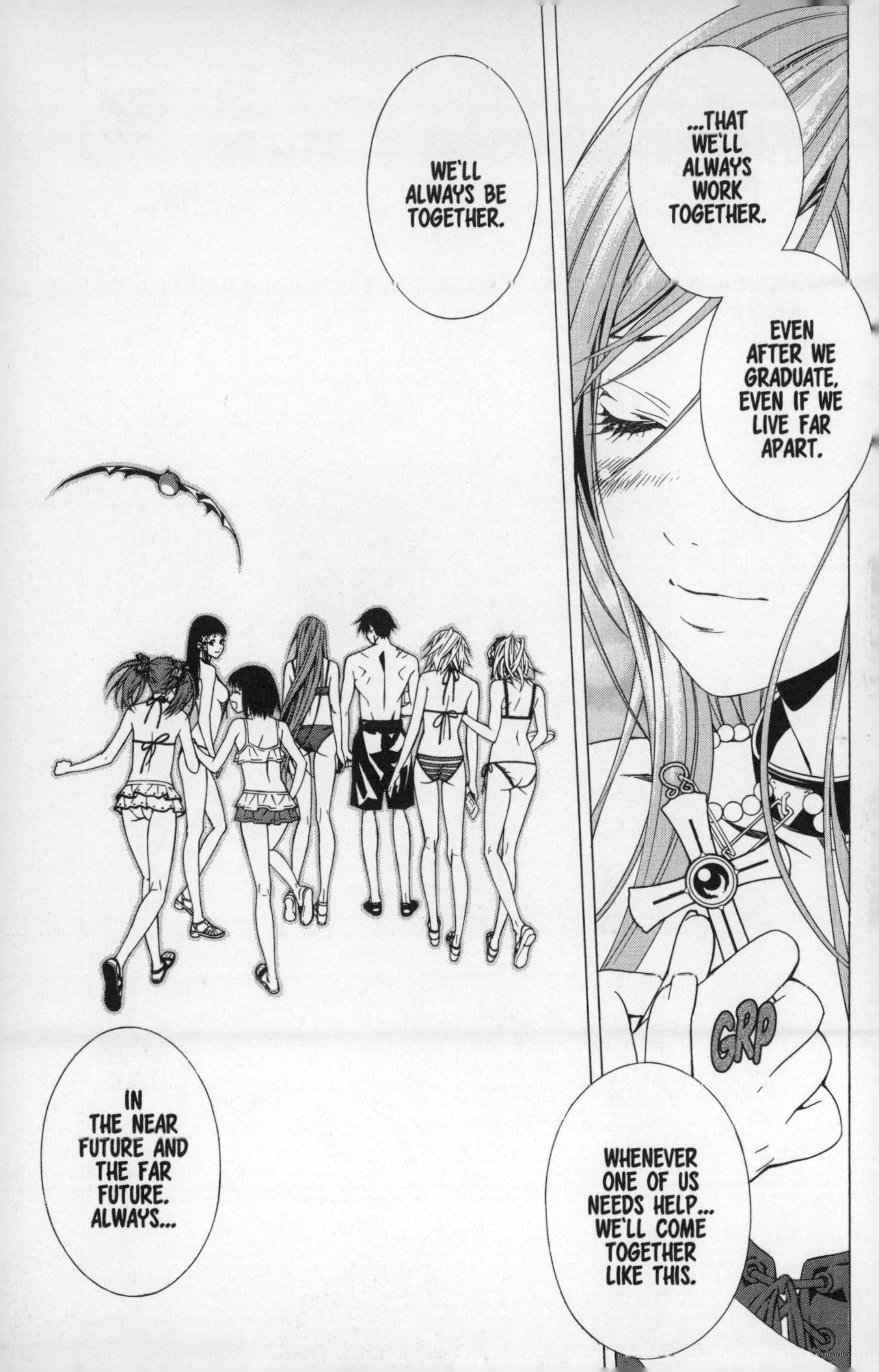
...THAT WE'LL ALWAYS WORK TOGETHER.
EVEN AFTER WE GRADUATE, EVEN IF WE LIVE FAR APART.
GRP
WHENEVER ONE OF US NEEDS HELP... WE'LL COME TOGETHER LIKE THIS.
WE'LL ALWAYS BE TOGETHER.
IN THE NEAR FUTURE AND THE FAR FUTURE. ALWAYS...

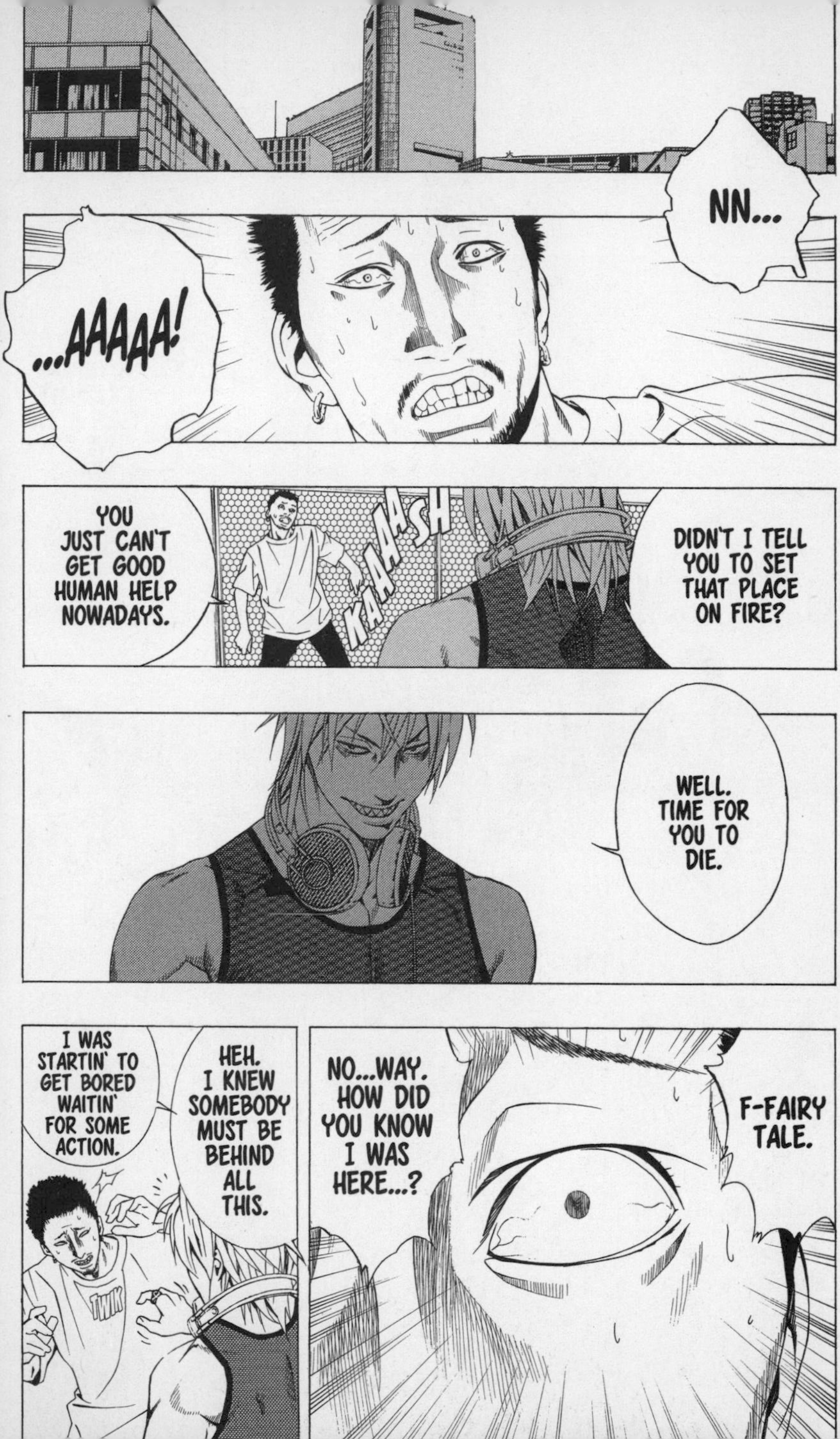
NN...
...AAAAA!
DIDN'T I TELL YOU TO SET THAT PLACE ON FIRE?
KAAAASH
YOU JUST CAN'T GET GOOD HUMAN HELP NOWADAYS.
WELL. TIME FOR YOU TO DIE.
F-FAIRY TALE.
NO...WAY. HOW DID YOU KNOW I WAS HERE...?
HEH. I KNEW SOMEBODY MUST BE BEHIND ALL THIS.
I WAS STARTIN' TO GET BORED WAITIN' FOR SOME ACTION.
TWIK

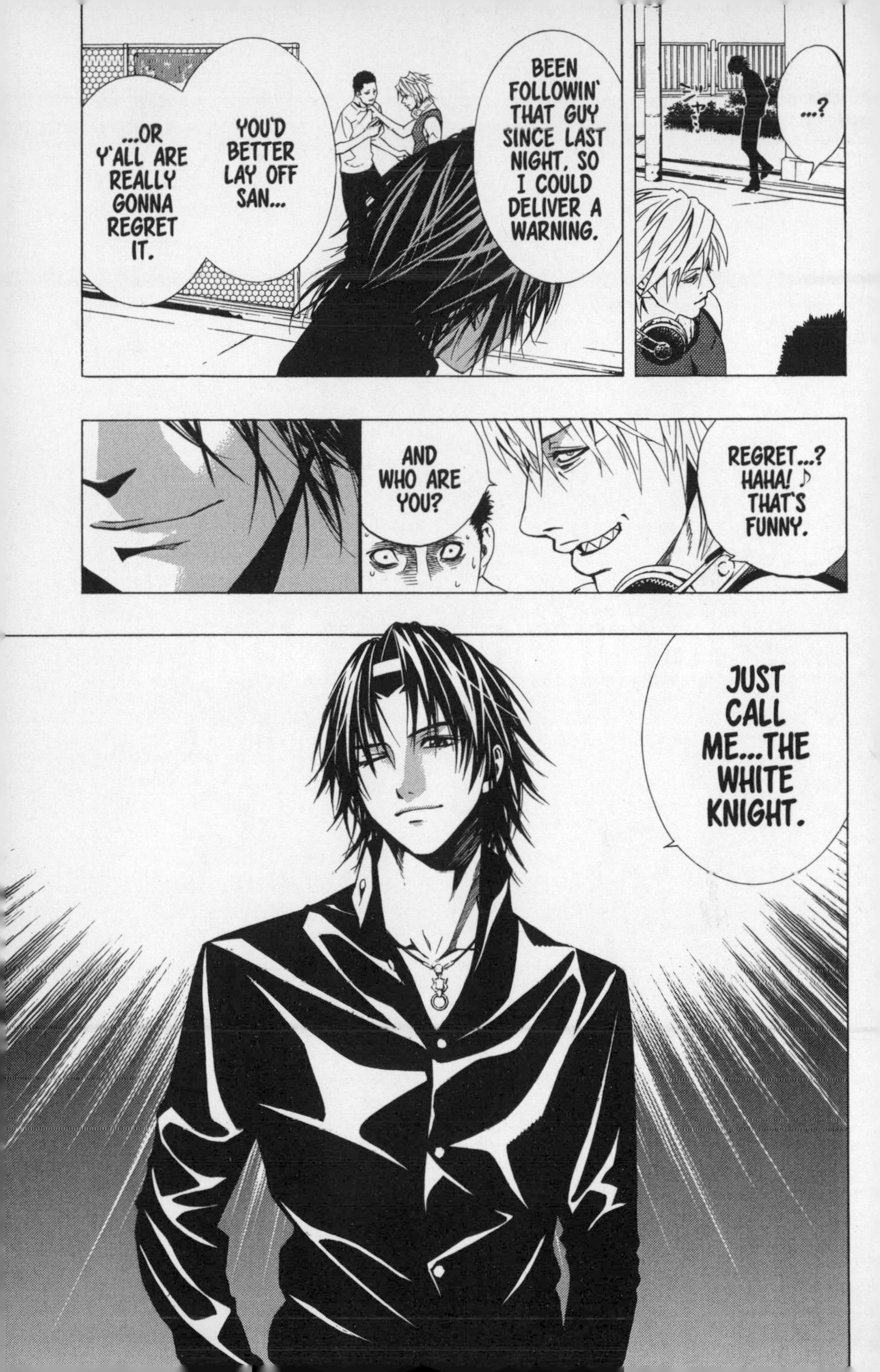
...?
BEEN FOLLOWIN' THAT GUY SINCE LAST NIGHT, SO I COULD DELIVER A WARNING.
YOU'D BETTER LAY OFF SAN...
...OR Y'ALL ARE REALLY GONNA REGRET IT.
REGRET...? HAHA! ♪ THAT'S FUNNY.
AND WHO ARE YOU?
JUST CALL ME...THE WHITE KNIGHT.

20: The Angel's Song...

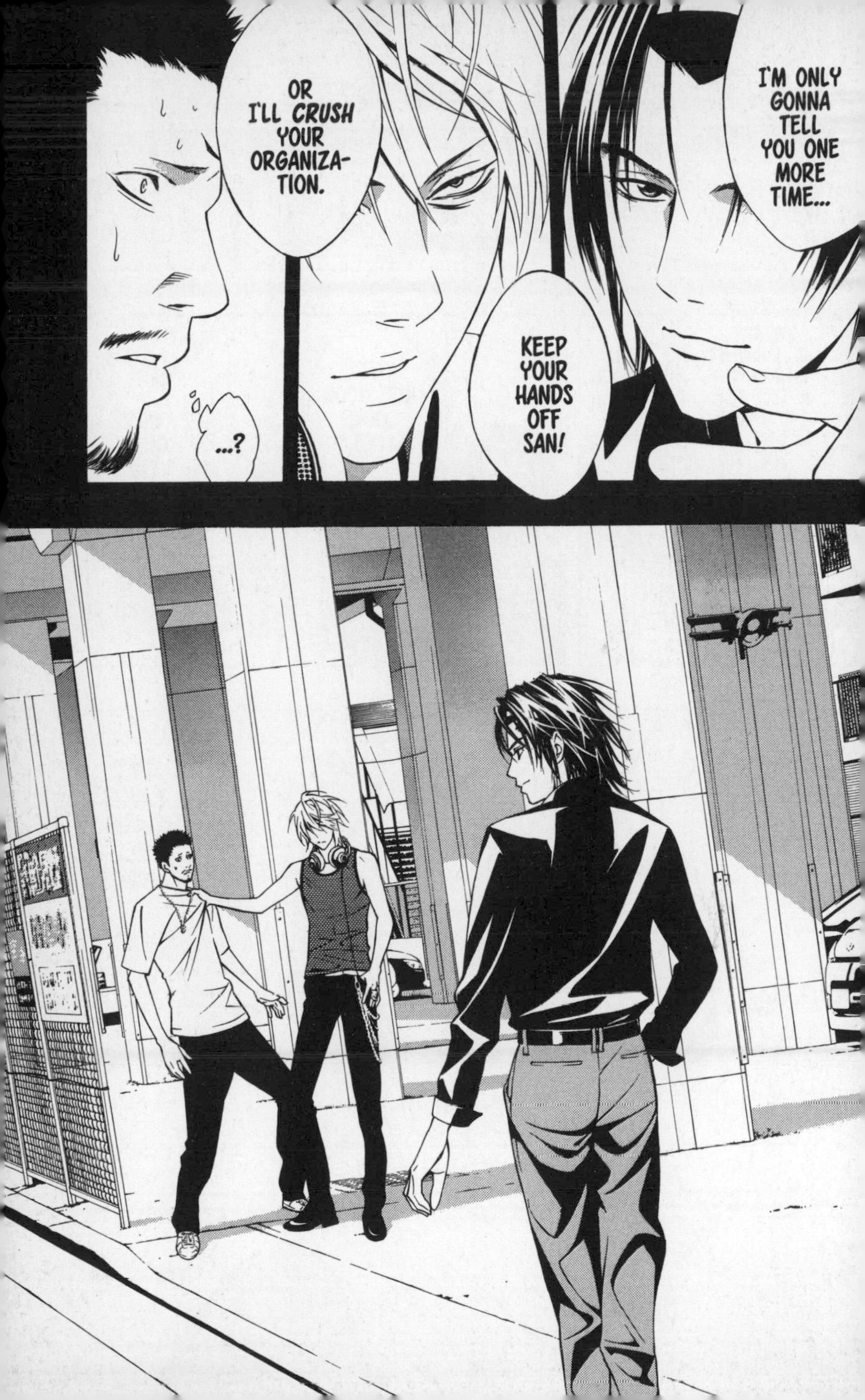
I'M ONLY GONNA TELL YOU ONE MORE TIME...
KEEP YOUR HANDS OFF SAN!
OR I'LL *CRUSH* YOUR ORGANIZA-TION.
...?

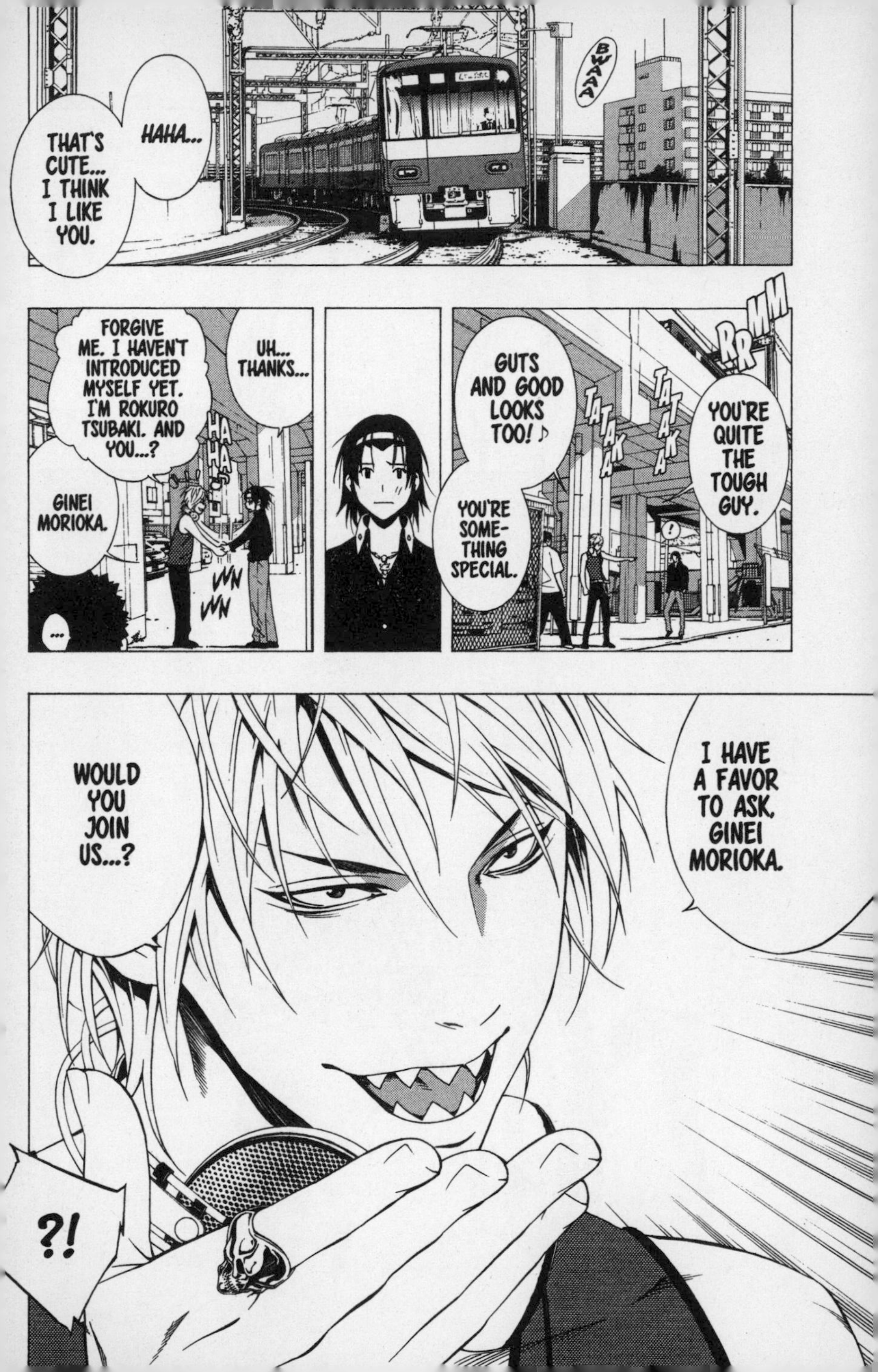
BWAAA
HAHA...
THAT'S CUTE... I THINK I LIKE YOU.
RRMM
YOU'RE QUITE THE TOUGH GUY.
TATAKA
TATAKA
!
GUTS AND GOOD LOOKS TOO! ♪
YOU'RE SOMETHING SPECIAL.
UH... THANKS...
FORGIVE ME. I HAVEN'T INTRODUCED MYSELF YET. I'M ROKURO TSUBAKI. AND YOU...?
HA HA ♪
VVN VVN
GINEI MORIOKA.
...
I HAVE A FAVOR TO ASK. GINEI MORIOKA.
WOULD YOU JOIN US...?
?!

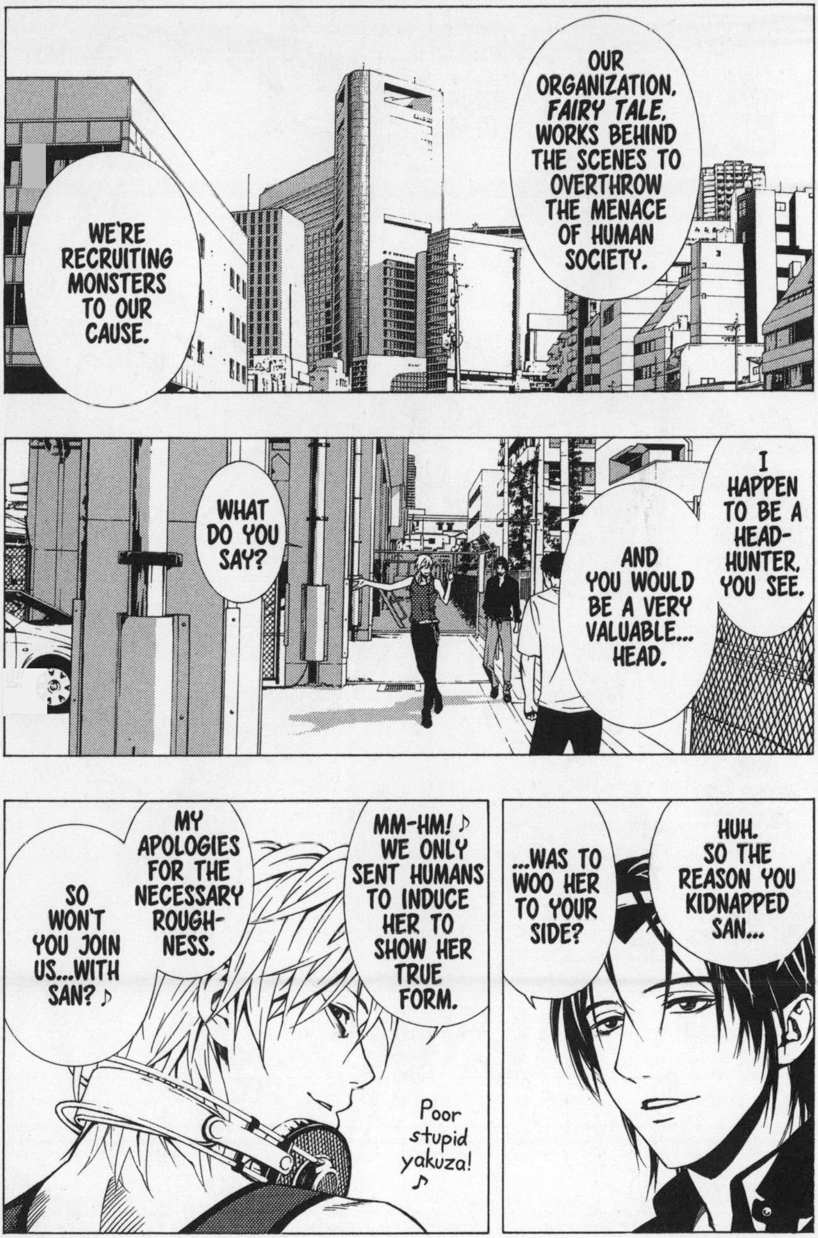
OUR ORGANIZATION, *FAIRY TALE*, WORKS BEHIND THE SCENES TO OVERTHROW THE MENACE OF HUMAN SOCIETY.
WE'RE RECRUITING MONSTERS TO OUR CAUSE.
I HAPPEN TO BE A HEAD-HUNTER, YOU SEE.
AND YOU WOULD BE A VERY VALUABLE... HEAD.
WHAT DO YOU SAY?
HUH. SO THE REASON YOU KIDNAPPED SAN...
...WAS TO WOO HER TO YOUR SIDE?
MM-HM! ♪ WE ONLY SENT HUMANS TO INDUCE HER TO SHOW HER TRUE FORM.
MY APOLOGIES FOR THE NECESSARY ROUGH-NESS.
SO WON'T YOU JOIN US...WITH SAN? ♪
Poor stupid yakuza! ♪

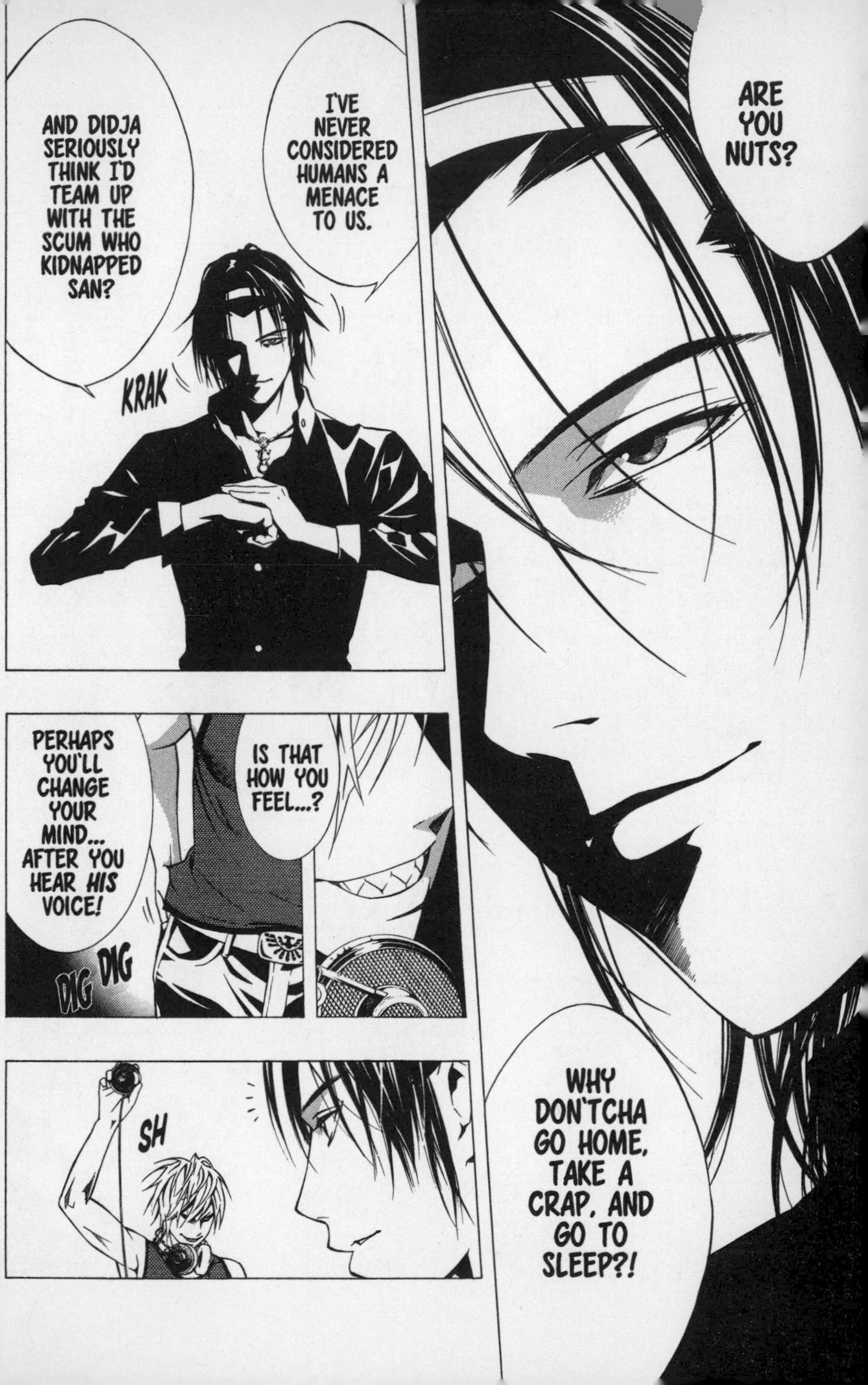
ARE YOU NUTS?
WHY DON'TCHA GO HOME, TAKE A CRAP, AND GO TO SLEEP?!
I'VE NEVER CONSIDERED HUMANS A MENACE TO US.
AND DIDJA SERIOUSLY THINK I'D TEAM UP WITH THE SCUM WHO KIDNAPPED SAN?
KRAK
IS THAT HOW YOU FEEL...?
PERHAPS YOU'LL CHANGE YOUR MIND... AFTER YOU HEAR HIS VOICE!
DIG DIG
SH

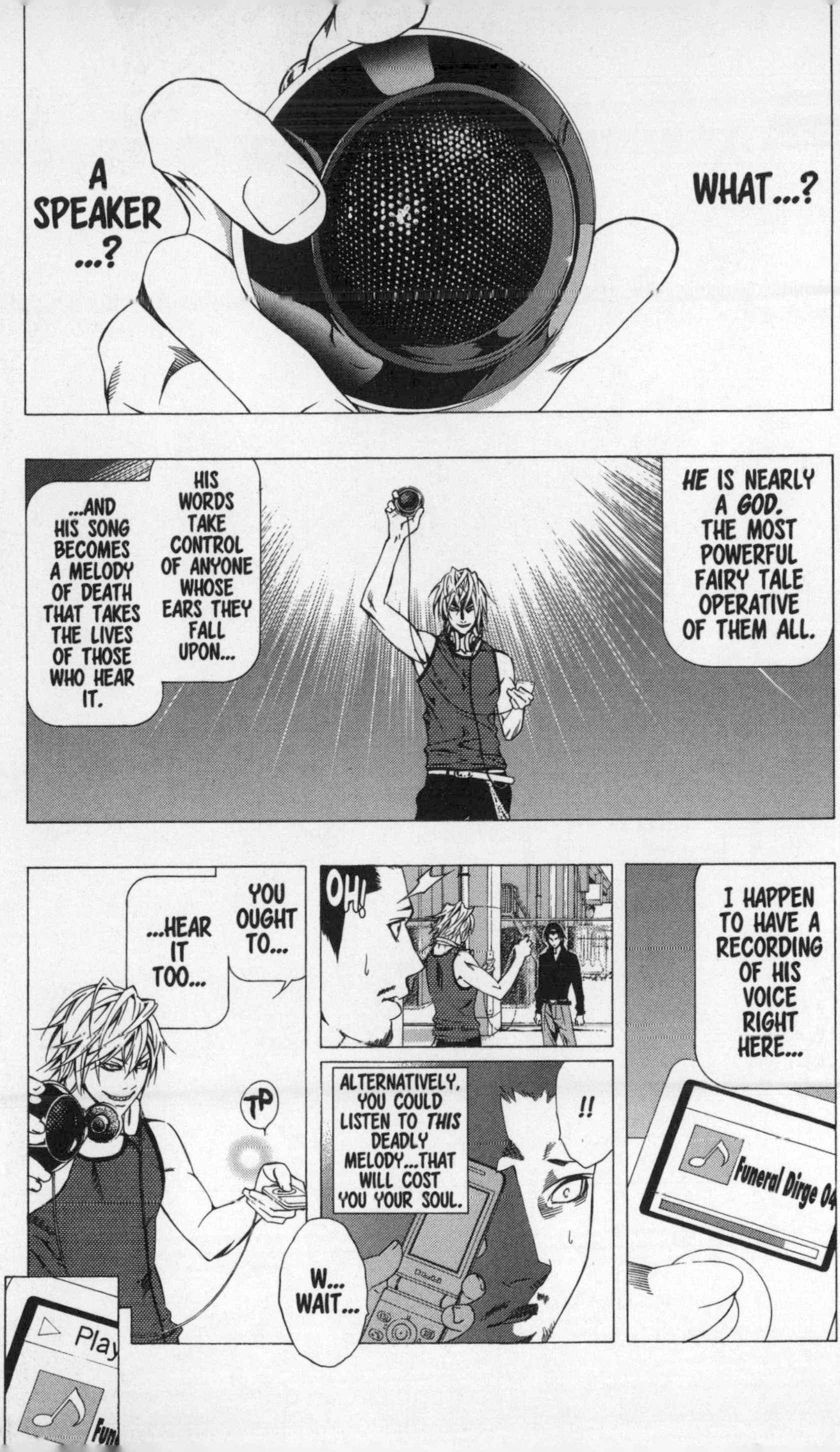
WHAT...?
A SPEAKER ...?
HE IS NEARLY A GOD. THE MOST POWERFUL FAIRY TALE OPERATIVE OF THEM ALL.
HIS WORDS TAKE CONTROL OF ANYONE WHOSE EARS THEY FALL UPON...
...AND HIS SONG BECOMES A MELODY OF DEATH THAT TAKES THE LIVES OF THOSE WHO HEAR IT.
I HAPPEN TO HAVE A RECORDING OF HIS VOICE RIGHT HERE...
Funeral Dirge 04
OH!
!!
ALTERNATIVELY, YOU COULD LISTEN TO THIS DEADLY MELODY...THAT WILL COST YOU YOUR SOUL.
W... WAIT...
YOU OUGHT TO...
...HEAR IT TOO...
TP
Play

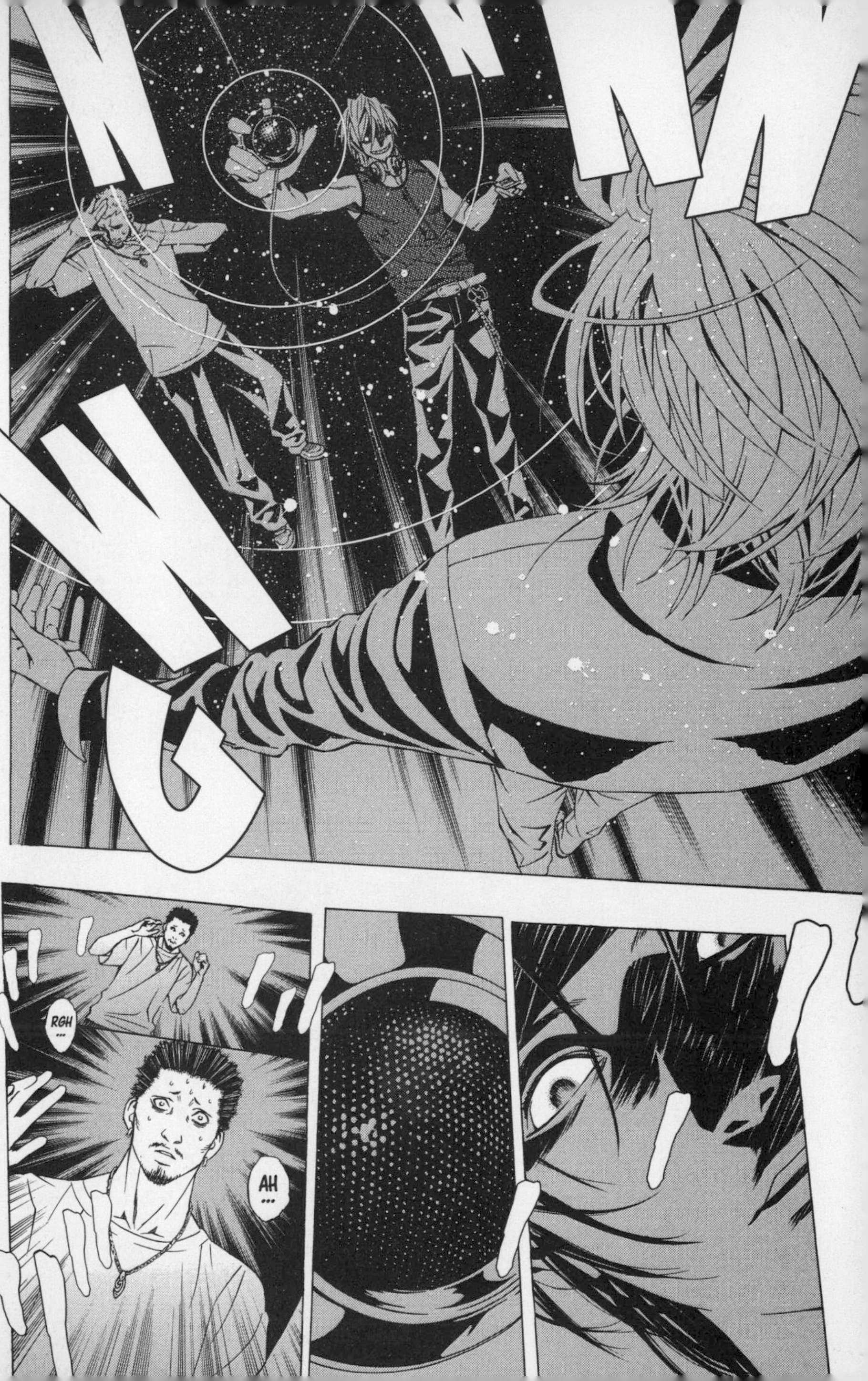

RGH...
AH...

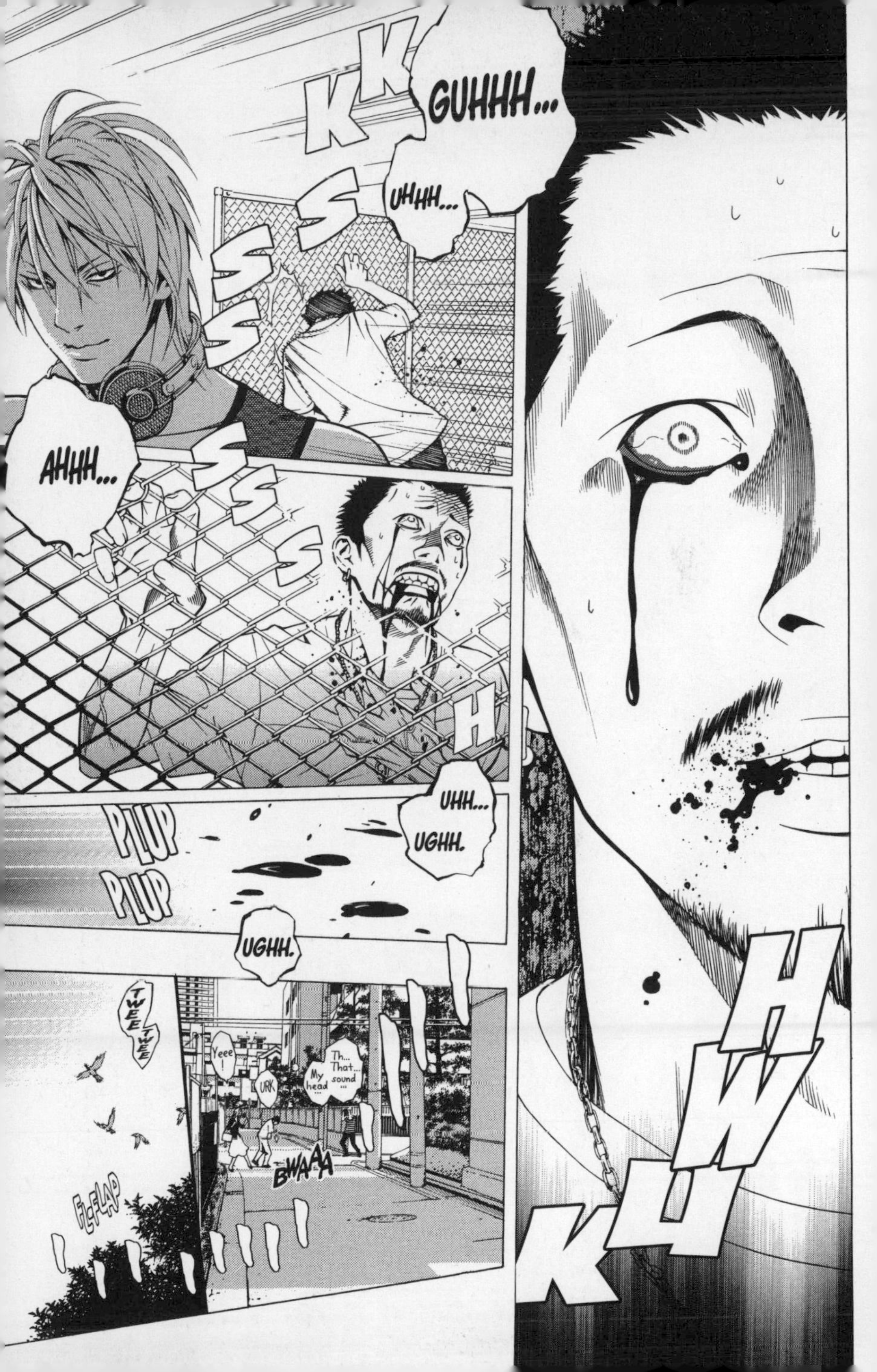
HWUK
KK
GUHHH...
UHHH...
SSS
SS
AHHH...
SSS
H
UHH... UGHH.
PLUP
PLUP
UGHH.
TWEE TWEE
Th... That... sound...
My head...
URK
Yeee!
BWAAA
FL-FLAP

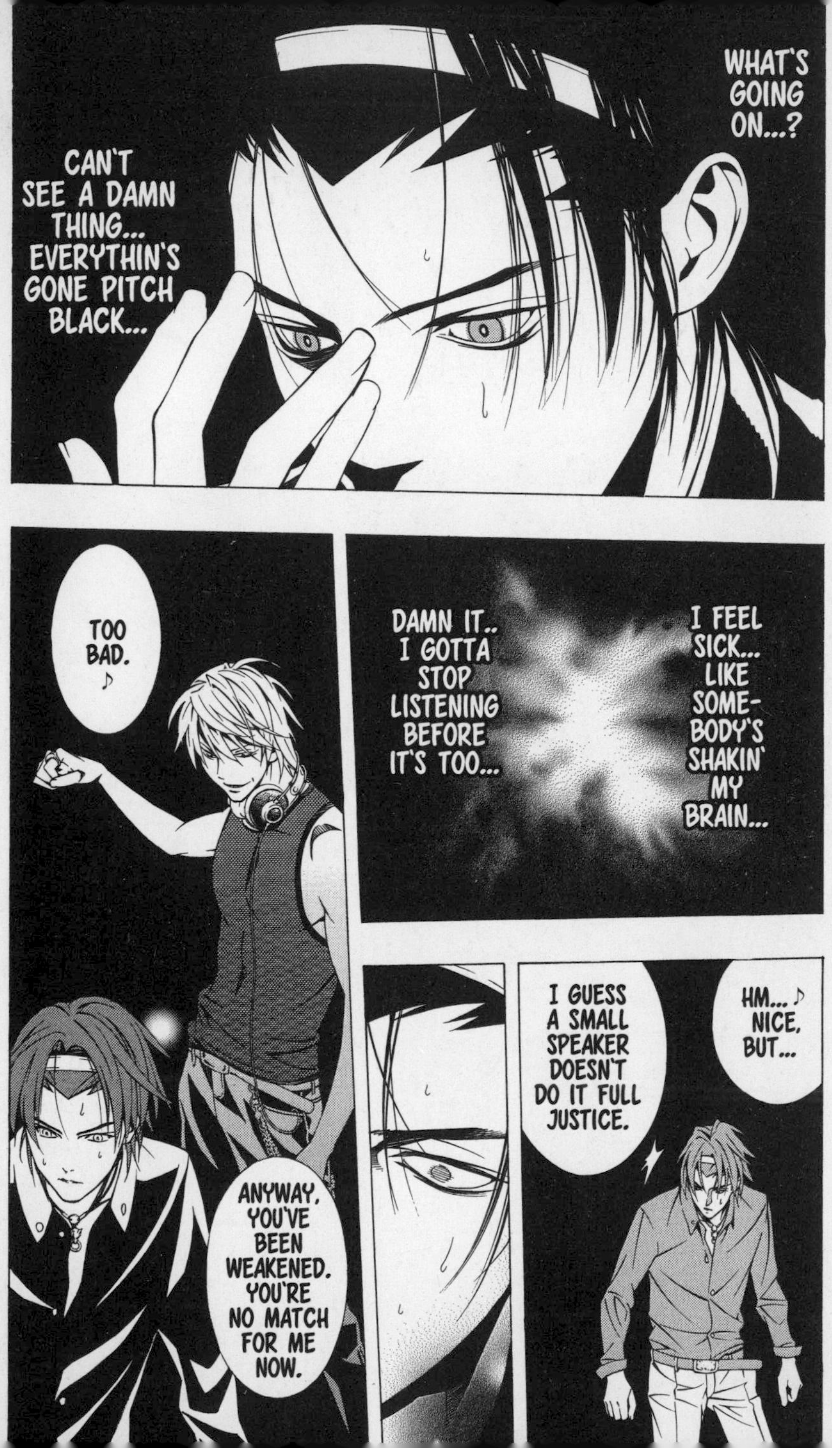
WHAT'S GOING ON...?
CAN'T SEE A DAMN THING... EVERYTHIN'S GONE PITCH BLACK...
I FEEL SICK... LIKE SOMEBODY'S SHAKIN' MY BRAIN...
DAMN IT.. I GOTTA STOP LISTENING BEFORE IT'S TOO...
HM...♪ NICE, BUT...
I GUESS A SMALL SPEAKER DOESN'T DO IT FULL JUSTICE.
TOO BAD. ♪
ANYWAY, YOU'VE BEEN WEAKENED. YOU'RE NO MATCH FOR ME NOW.

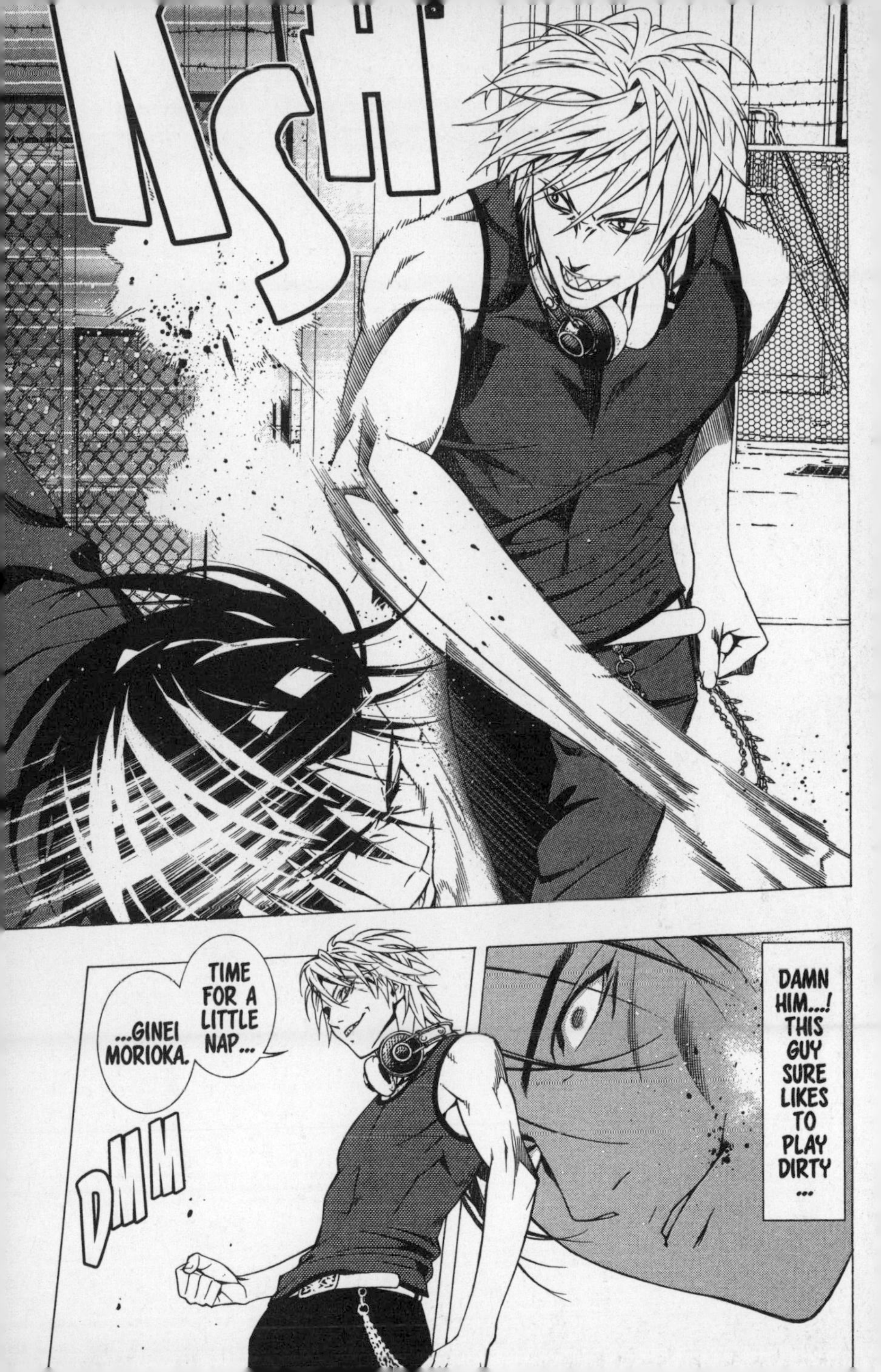
NSH
DAMN HIM...! THIS GUY SURE LIKES TO PLAY DIRTY...
TIME FOR A LITTLE NAP...
...GINEI MORIOKA.
DMM

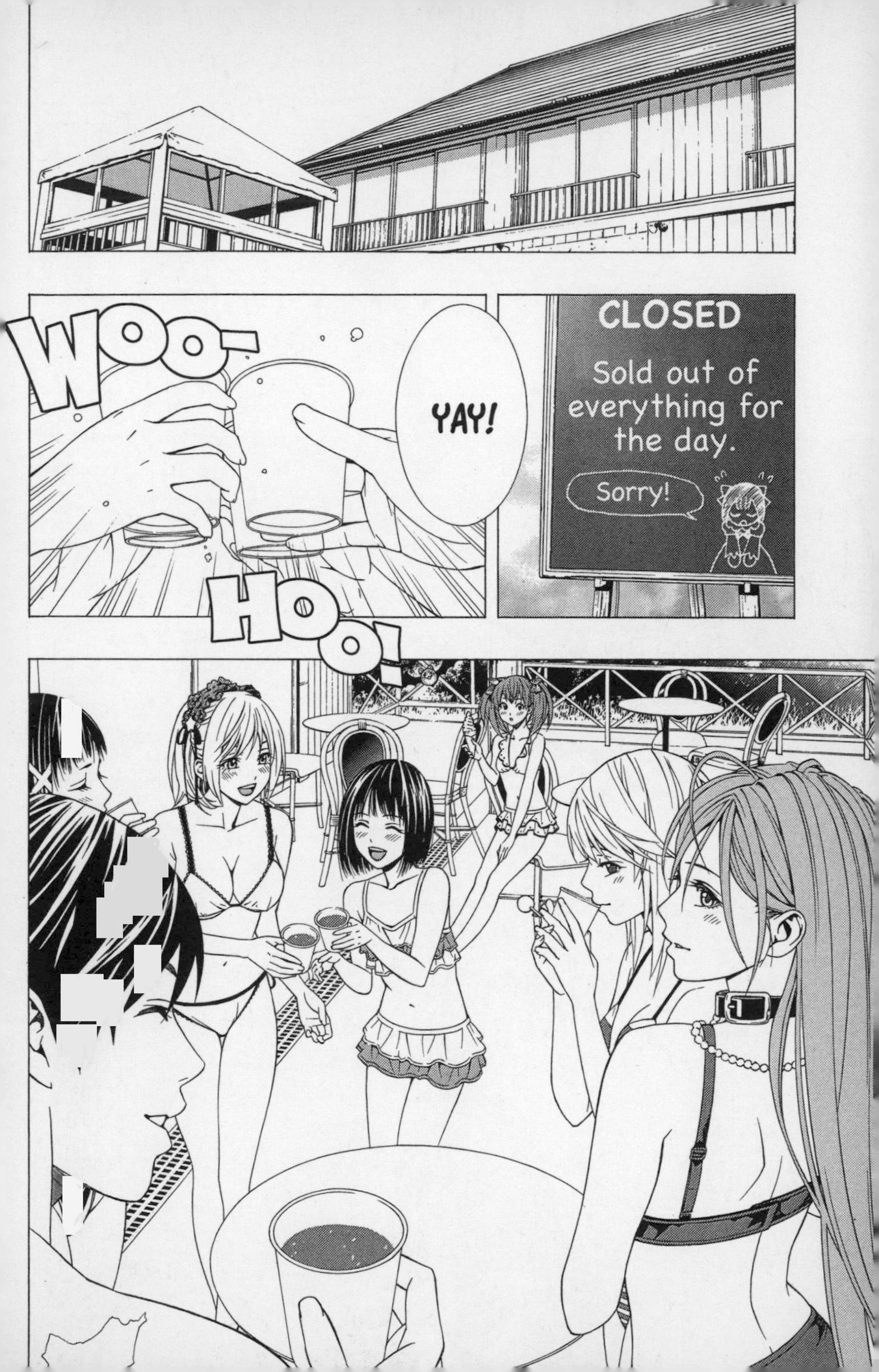
CLOSED
Sold out of everything for the day.
Sorry!
WOO-
YAY!
HOO!

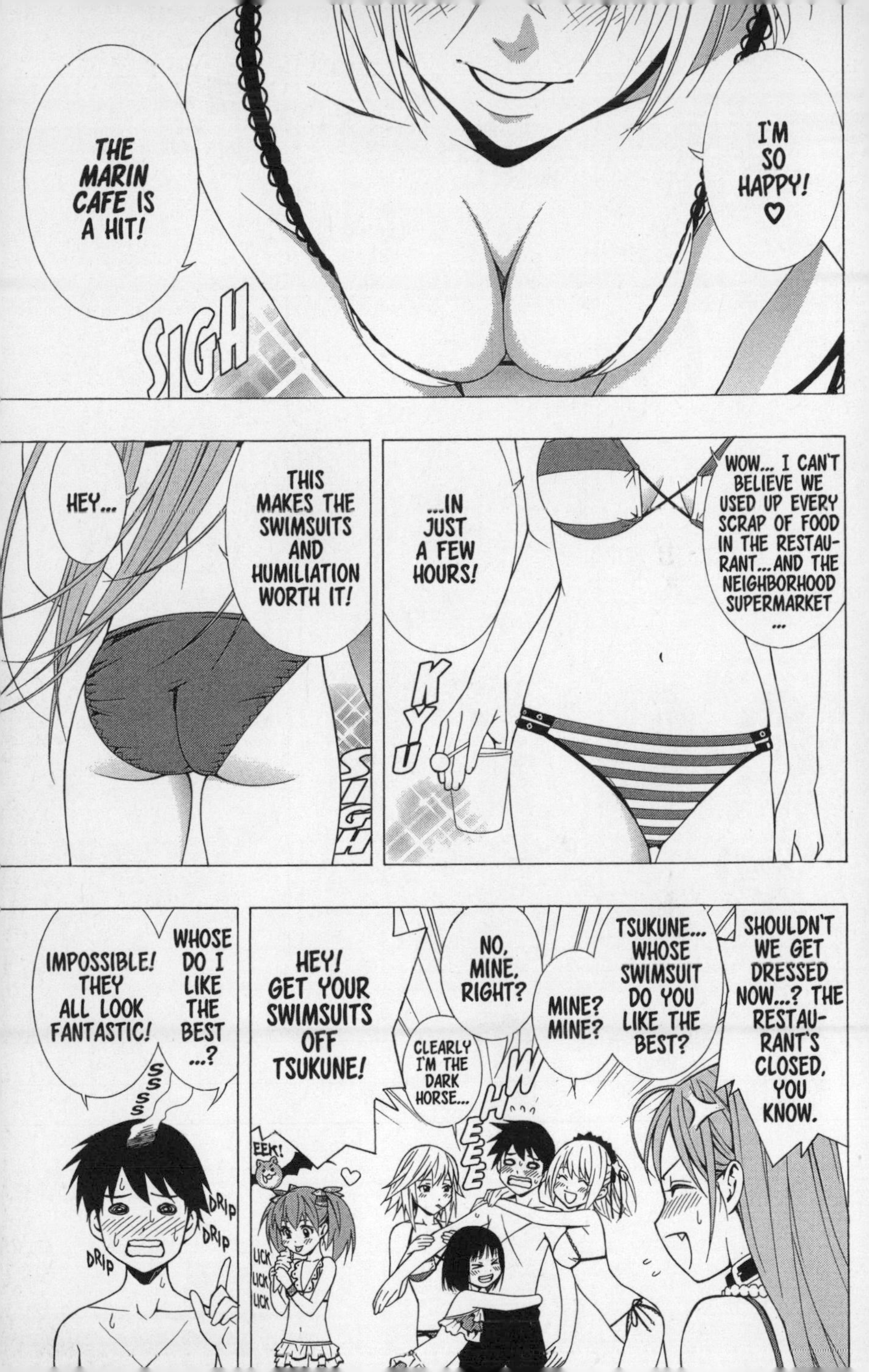
I'M SO HAPPY! ♡
THE MARIN CAFE IS A HIT!
SIGH
WOW... I CAN'T BELIEVE WE USED UP EVERY SCRAP OF FOOD IN THE RESTAURANT...AND THE NEIGHBORHOOD SUPERMARKET ...
...IN JUST A FEW HOURS!
KYU
THIS MAKES THE SWIMSUITS AND HUMILIATION WORTH IT!
HEY...
SIGH
SHOULDN'T WE GET DRESSED NOW...? THE RESTAURANT'S CLOSED, YOU KNOW.
TSUKUNE... WHOSE SWIMSUIT DO YOU LIKE THE BEST?
MINE? MINE?
NO, MINE, RIGHT?
CLEARLY I'M THE DARK HORSE...
WHEEE
HEY! GET YOUR SWIMSUITS OFF TSUKUNE!
EEK!
LICK LICK LICK
WHOSE DO I LIKE THE BEST ...?
IMPOSSIBLE! THEY ALL LOOK FANTASTIC!
SSSS
DRIP DRIP DRIP

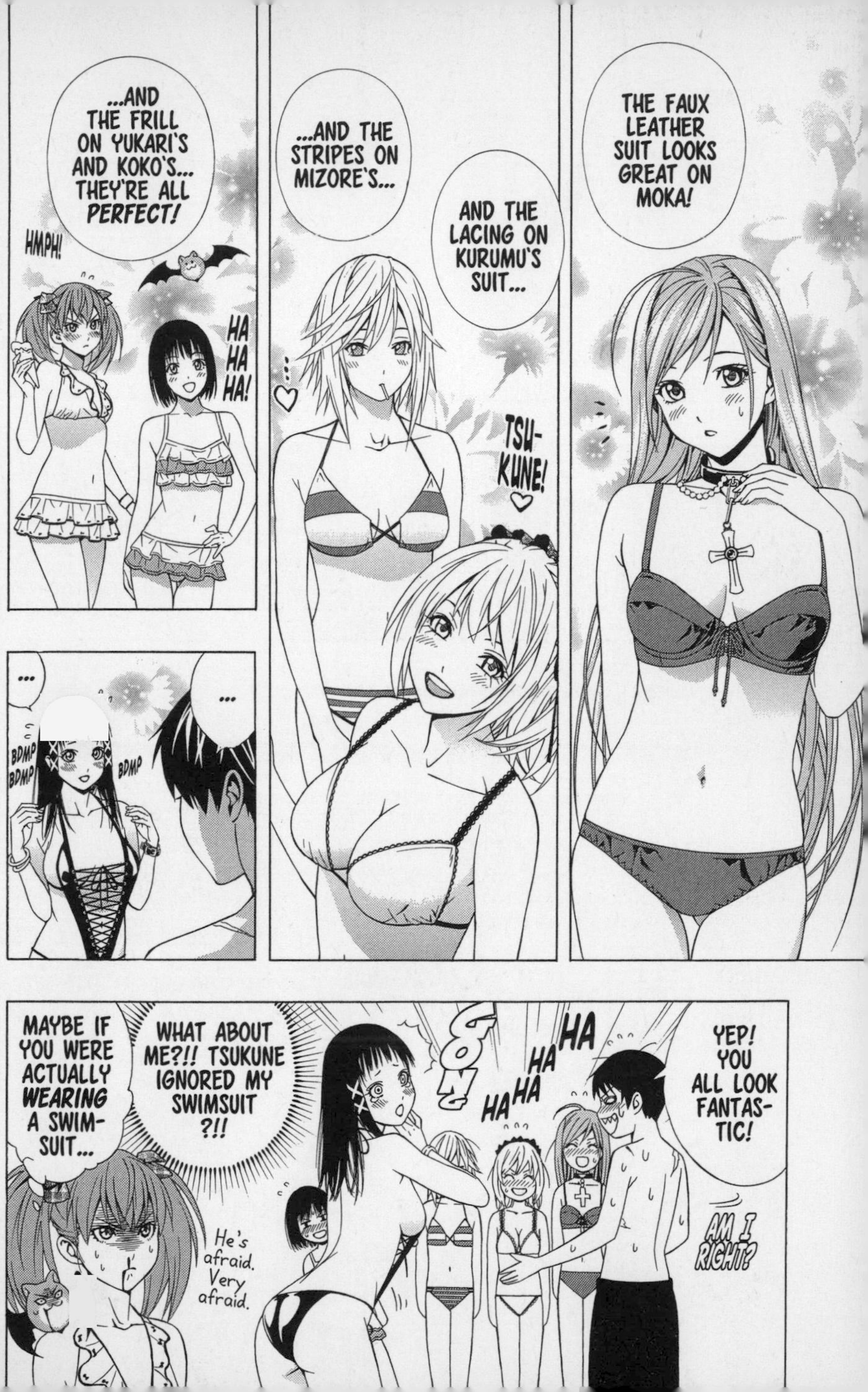
THE FAUX LEATHER SUIT LOOKS GREAT ON MOKA!
...AND THE STRIPES ON MIZORE'S...
AND THE LACING ON KURUMU'S SUIT...
TSU-KUNE!
...AND THE FRILL ON YUKARI'S AND KOKO'S... THEY'RE ALL PERFECT!
HMPH!
HA HA HA!
...
...
BDMP BDMP
BDMP
YEP! YOU ALL LOOK FANTAS-TIC!
AM I RIGHT?
HA HA HA HA
WHAT ABOUT ME?!! TSUKUNE IGNORED MY SWIMSUIT?!!
MAYBE IF YOU WERE ACTUALLY WEARING A SWIM-SUIT...
He's afraid. Very afraid.

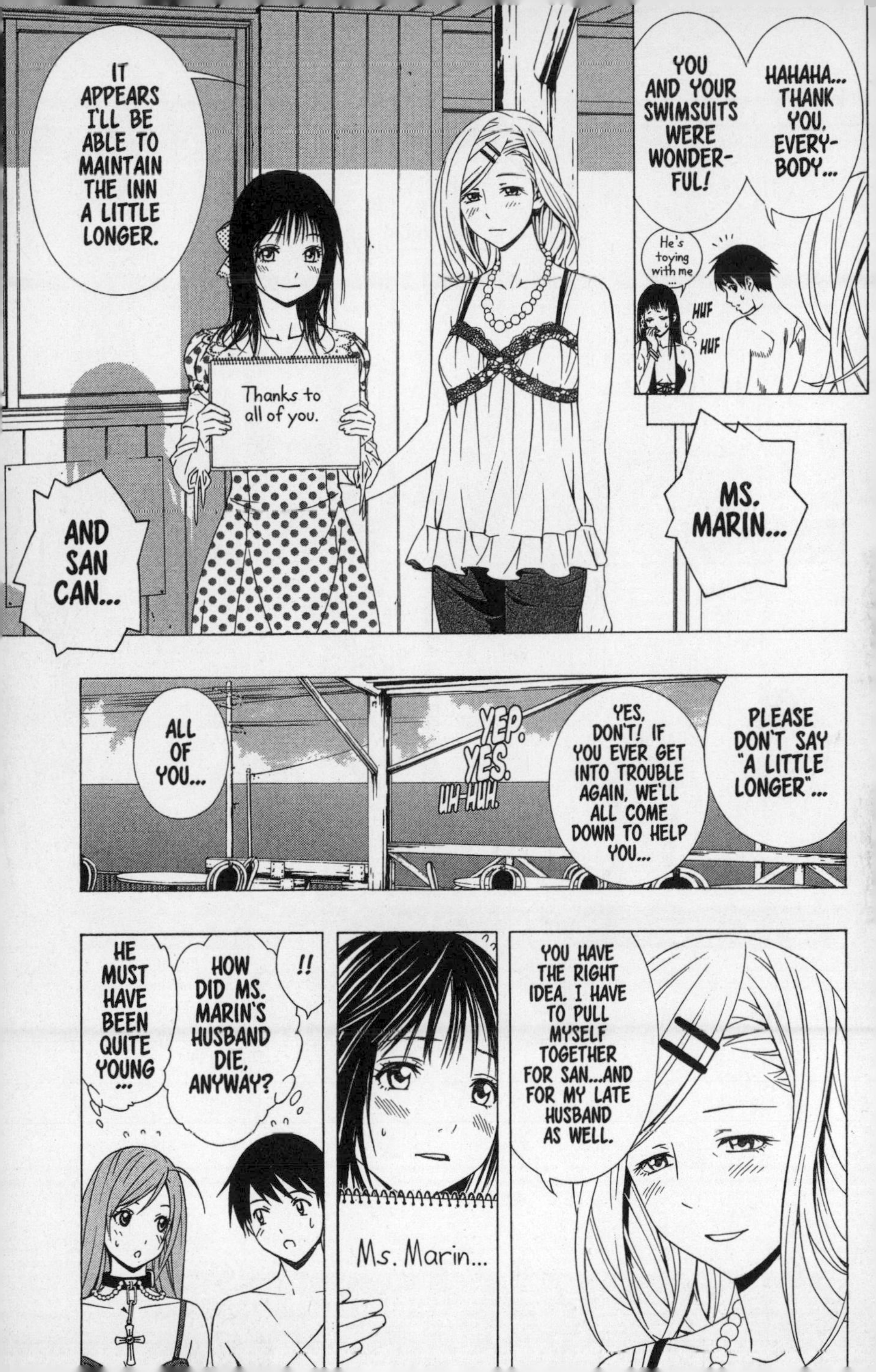
HAHAHA... THANK YOU, EVERYBODY...
YOU AND YOUR SWIMSUITS WERE WONDERFUL!
He's toying with me...
HUF
HUF
MS. MARIN...
IT APPEARS I'LL BE ABLE TO MAINTAIN THE INN A LITTLE LONGER.
Thanks to all of you.
AND SAN CAN...
PLEASE DON'T SAY "A LITTLE LONGER"...
YES, DON'T! IF YOU EVER GET INTO TROUBLE AGAIN, WE'LL ALL COME DOWN TO HELP YOU...
YEP.
YES.
UH-HUH.
ALL OF YOU...
YOU HAVE THE RIGHT IDEA. I HAVE TO PULL MYSELF TOGETHER FOR SAN...AND FOR MY LATE HUSBAND AS WELL.
Ms. Marin...
!!
HOW DID MS. MARIN'S HUSBAND DIE, ANYWAY?
HE MUST HAVE BEEN QUITE YOUNG...

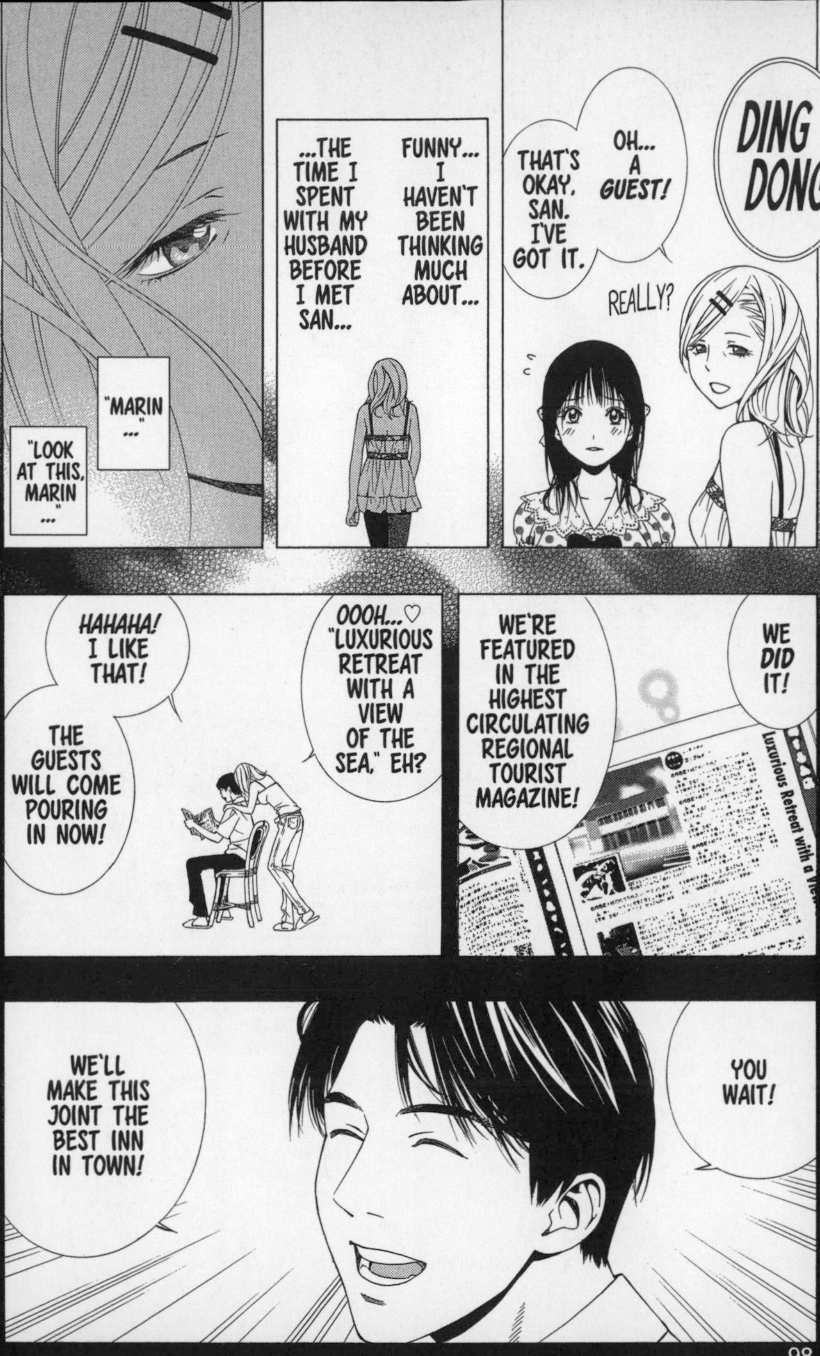
DING DONG
OH... A GUEST!
THAT'S OKAY, SAN. I'VE GOT IT.
REALLY?
FUNNY... I HAVEN'T BEEN THINKING MUCH ABOUT...
...THE TIME I SPENT WITH MY HUSBAND BEFORE I MET SAN...
"MARIN"...
"LOOK AT THIS, MARIN"...
WE DID IT!
WE'RE FEATURED IN THE HIGHEST CIRCULATING REGIONAL TOURIST MAGAZINE!
Luxurious Retreat with a
OOOH...♡ "LUXURIOUS RETREAT WITH A VIEW OF THE SEA," EH?
HAHAHA! I LIKE THAT!
THE GUESTS WILL COME POURING IN NOW!
YOU WAIT!
WE'LL MAKE THIS JOINT THE BEST INN IN TOWN!

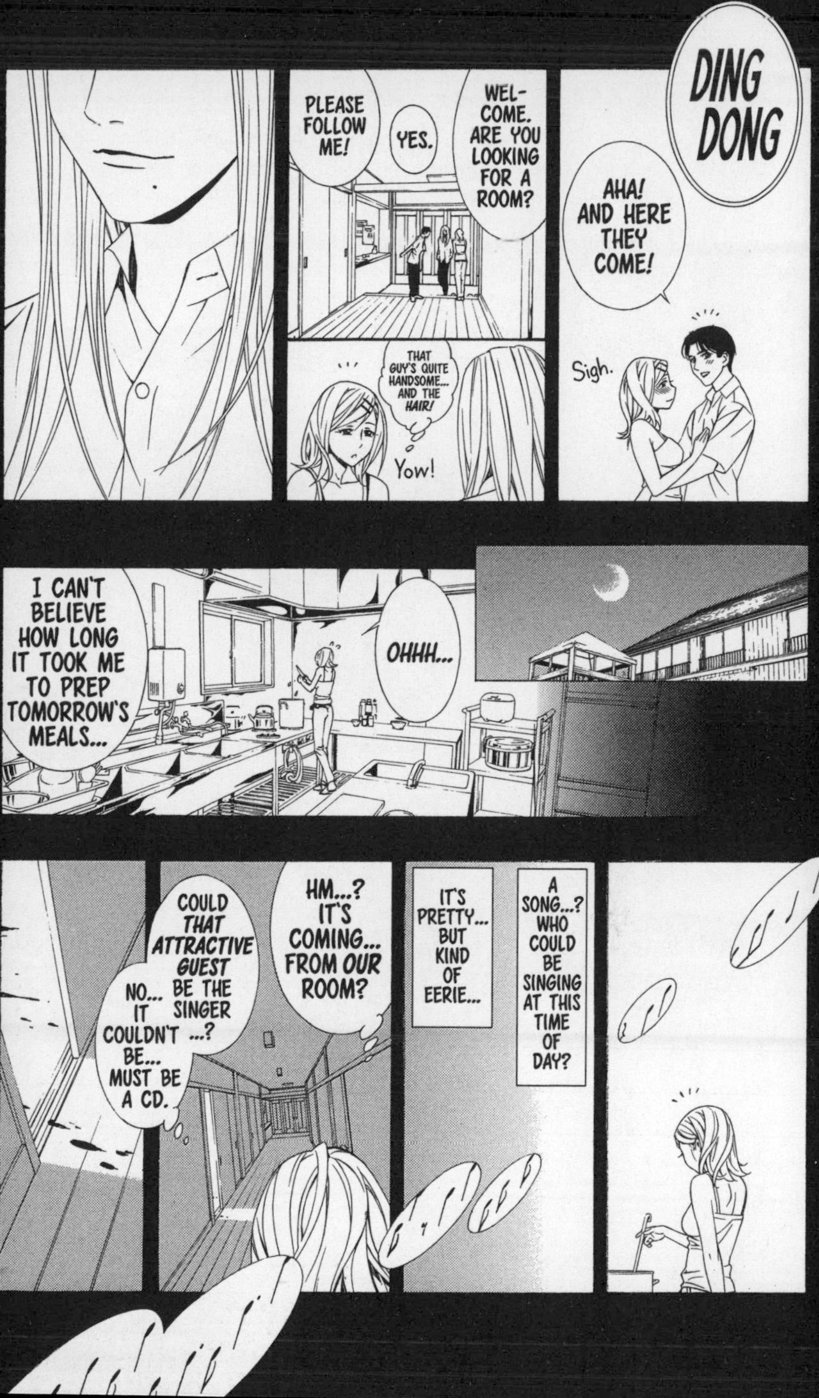
DING DONG
AHA! AND HERE THEY COME!
Sigh.
WEL-COME. ARE YOU LOOKING FOR A ROOM?
YES.
PLEASE FOLLOW ME!
THAT GUY'S QUITE HANDSOME... AND THE HAIR!
Yow!
OHHH...
I CAN'T BELIEVE HOW LONG IT TOOK ME TO PREP TOMORROW'S MEALS...
A SONG...? WHO COULD BE SINGING AT THIS TIME OF DAY?
IT'S PRETTY... BUT KIND OF EERIE...
HM...? IT'S COMING... FROM OUR ROOM?
COULD THAT ATTRACTIVE GUEST BE THE SINGER ...?
NO... IT COULDN'T BE... MUST BE A CD.

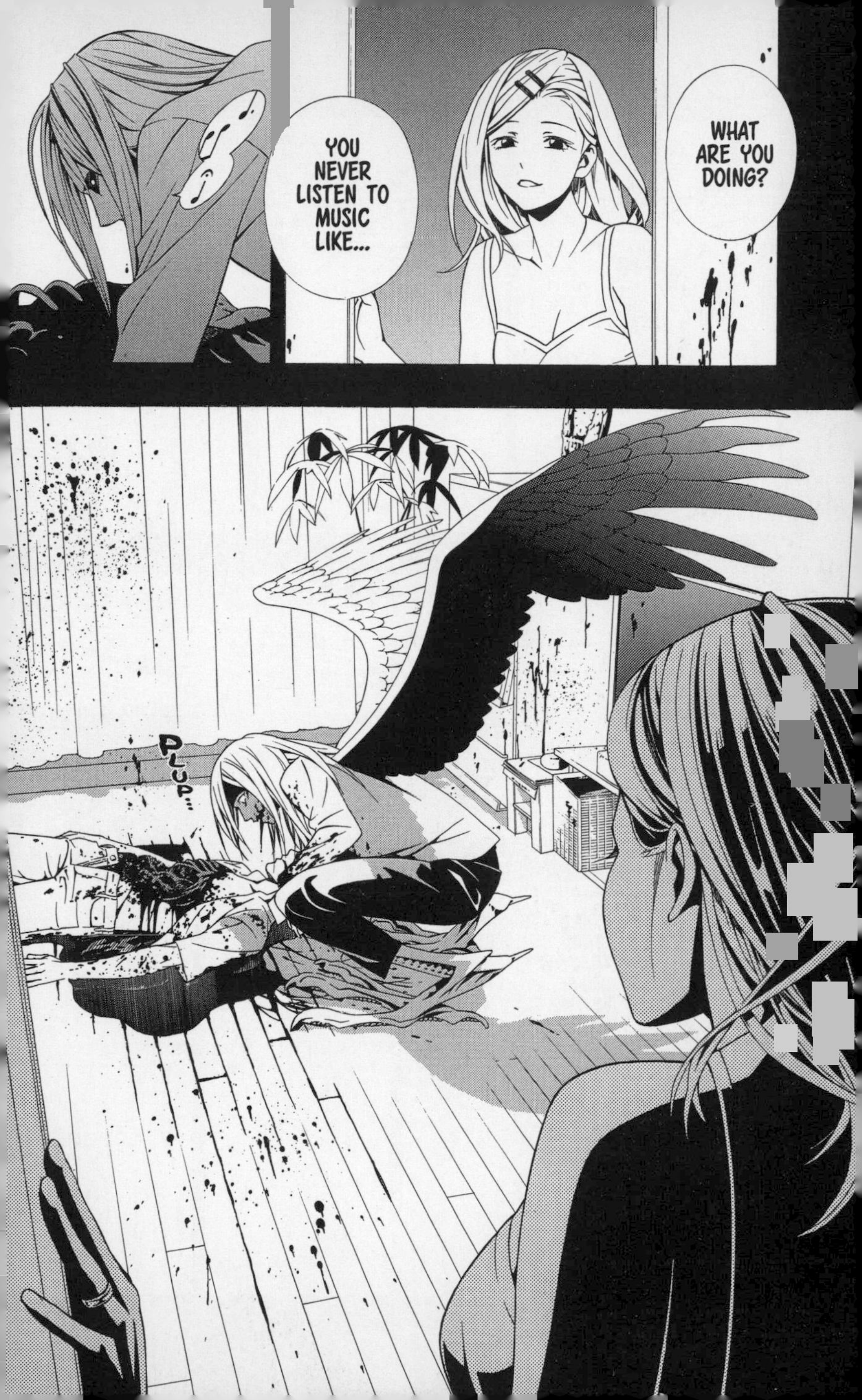
WHAT ARE YOU DOING?
YOU NEVER LISTEN TO MUSIC LIKE...
PLUP...

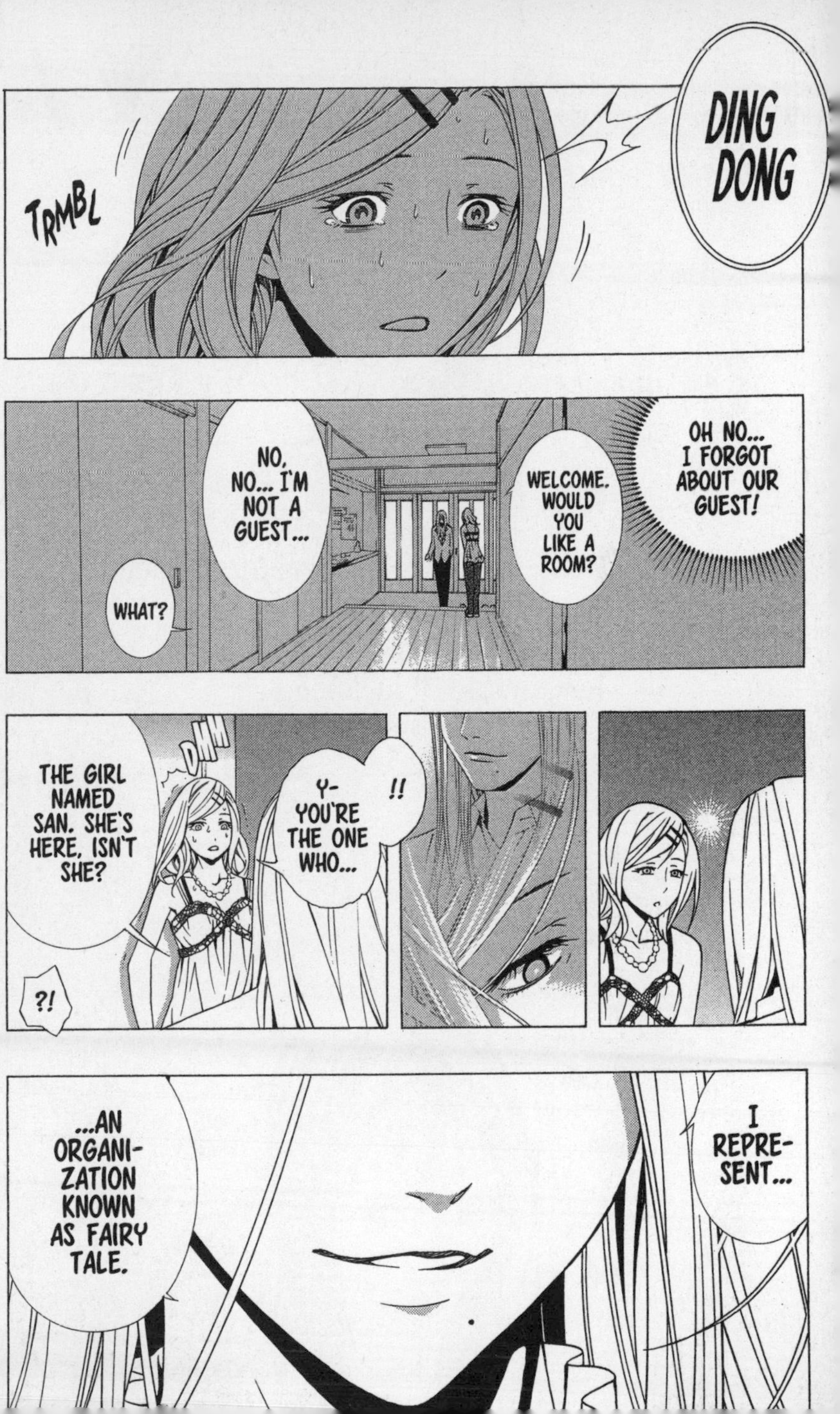
DING DONG
TRMBL
OH NO... I FORGOT ABOUT OUR GUEST!
WELCOME. WOULD YOU LIKE A ROOM?
NO, NO... I'M NOT A GUEST...
WHAT?
Y- YOU'RE THE ONE WHO...
!!
DMM
THE GIRL NAMED SAN. SHE'S HERE, ISN'T SHE?
?!
I REPRESENT...
...AN ORGANIZATION KNOWN AS FAIRY TALE.

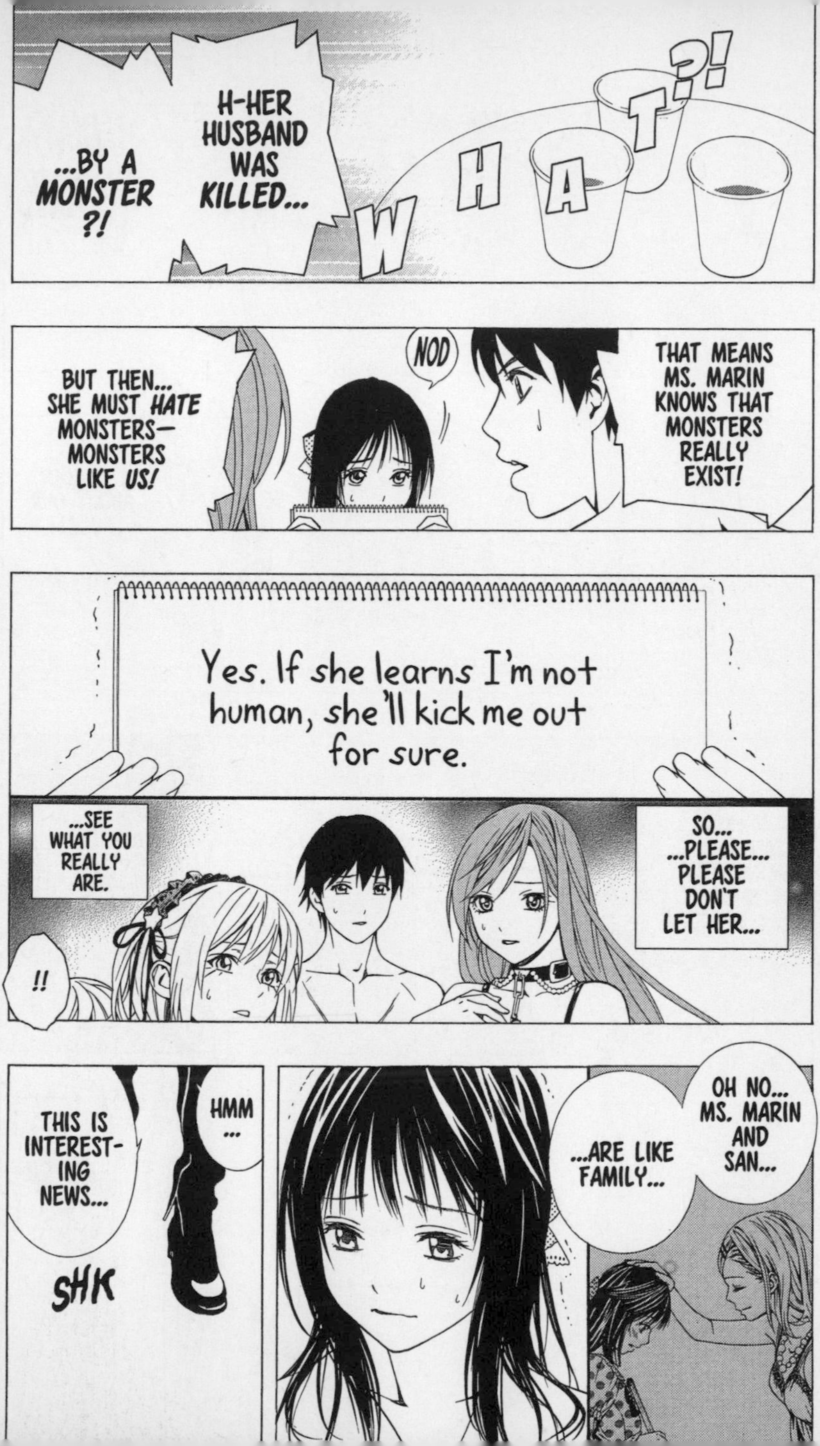
WHAT?!
H-HER HUSBAND WAS KILLED...
...BY A MONSTER ?!
THAT MEANS MS. MARIN KNOWS THAT MONSTERS REALLY EXIST!
NOD
BUT THEN... SHE MUST HATE MONSTERS—MONSTERS LIKE US!
Yes. If she learns I'm not human, she'll kick me out for sure.
SO... ...PLEASE... PLEASE DON'T LET HER...
...SEE WHAT YOU REALLY ARE.
!!
OH NO... MS. MARIN AND SAN...
...ARE LIKE FAMILY...
HMM ...
THIS IS INTEREST-ING NEWS...
SHK

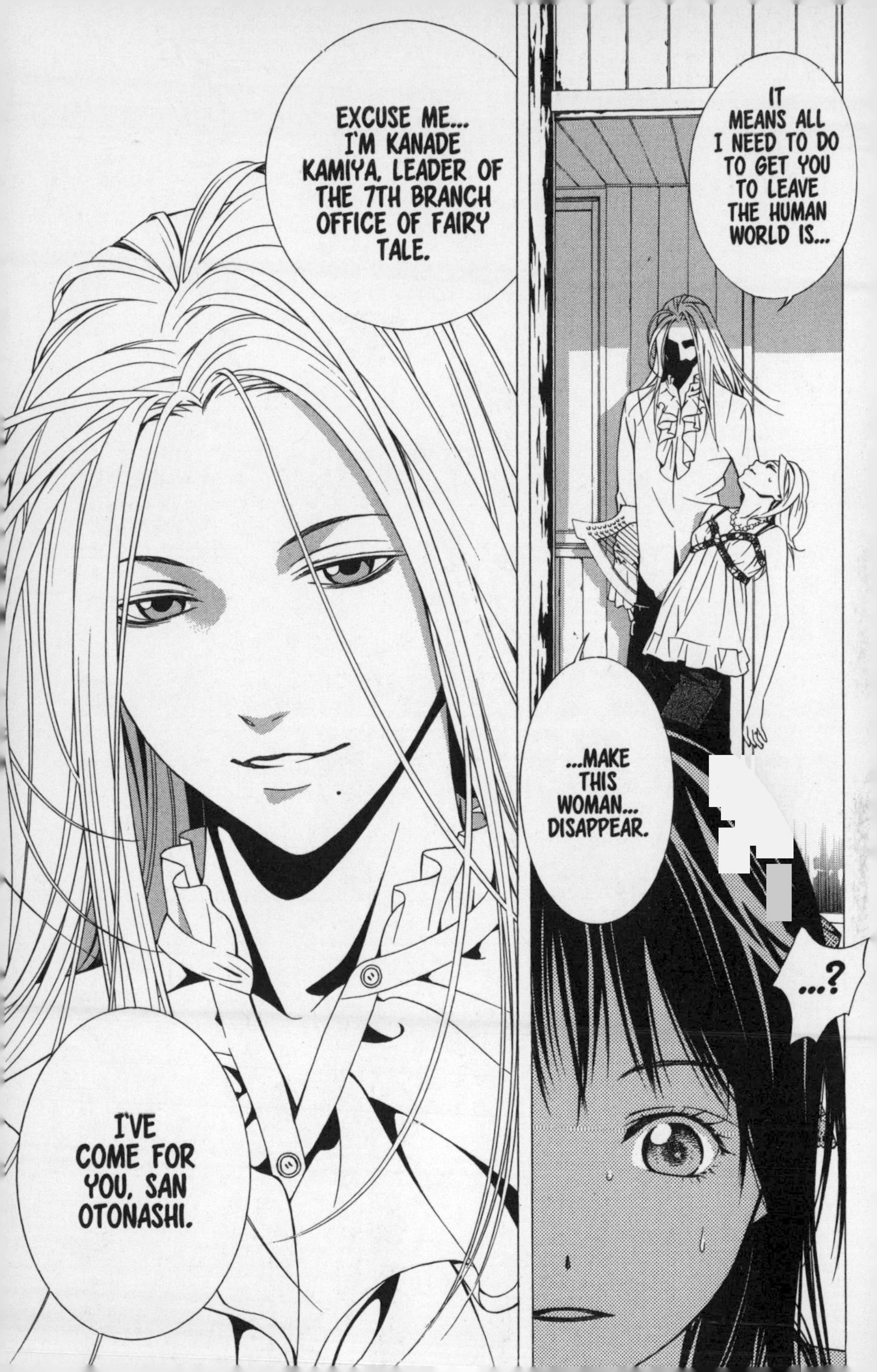
IT MEANS ALL I NEED TO DO TO GET YOU TO LEAVE THE HUMAN WORLD IS...
...MAKE THIS WOMAN... DISAPPEAR.
...?
EXCUSE ME... I'M KANADE KAMIYA, LEADER OF THE 7TH BRANCH OFFICE OF FAIRY TALE.
I'VE COME FOR YOU, SAN OTONASHI.

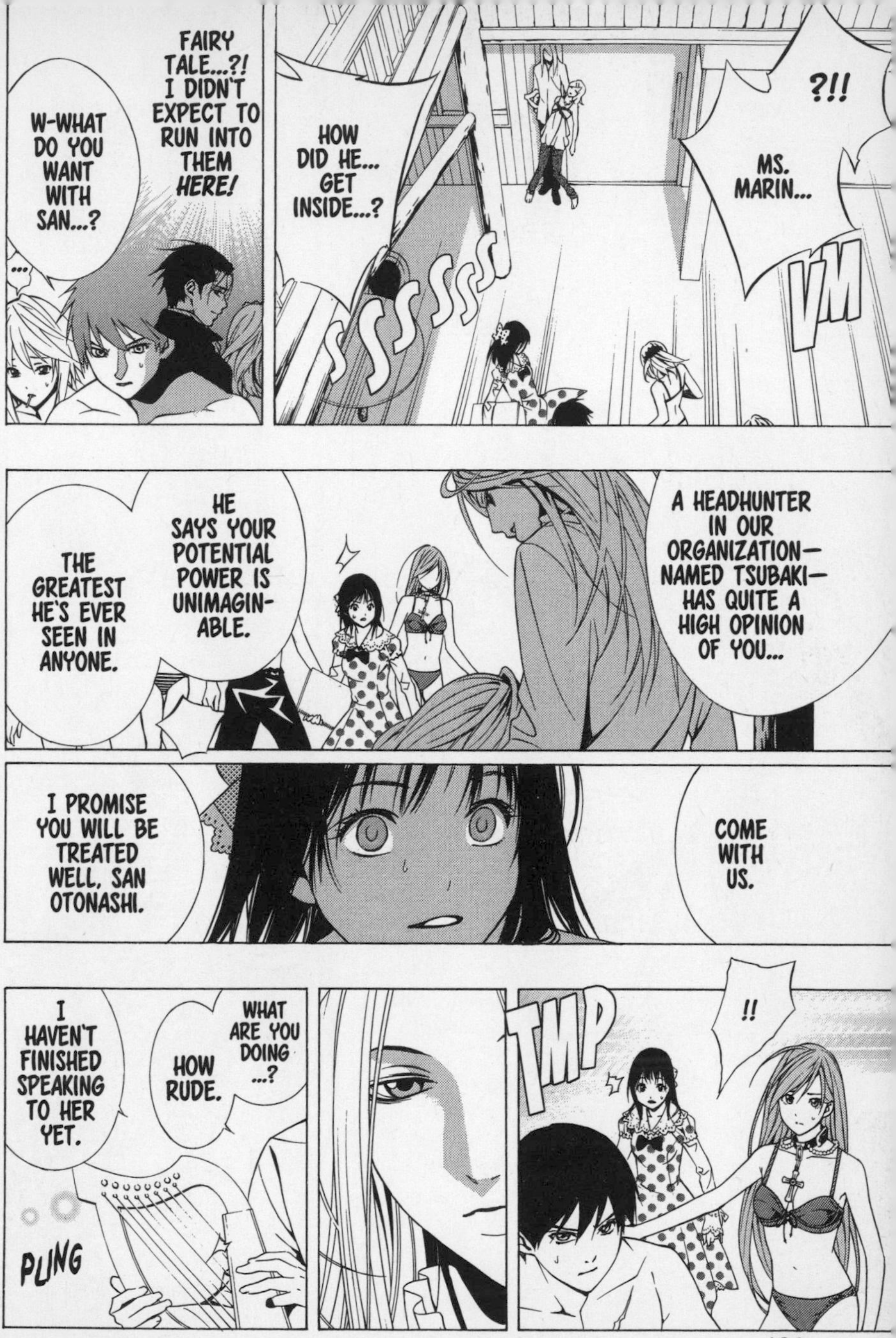
?!!
MS. MARIN...
VM
HOW DID HE... GET INSIDE...?
SSSSSS
FAIRY TALE...?! I DIDN'T EXPECT TO RUN INTO THEM HERE!
W-WHAT DO YOU WANT WITH SAN...?
...
A HEADHUNTER IN OUR ORGANIZATION—NAMED TSUBAKI—HAS QUITE A HIGH OPINION OF YOU...
HE SAYS YOUR POTENTIAL POWER IS UNIMAGIN-ABLE.
THE GREATEST HE'S EVER SEEN IN ANYONE.
COME WITH US.
I PROMISE YOU WILL BE TREATED WELL, SAN OTONASHI.
!!
TMP
WHAT ARE YOU DOING ...?
HOW RUDE.
I HAVEN'T FINISHED SPEAKING TO HER YET.
PLING

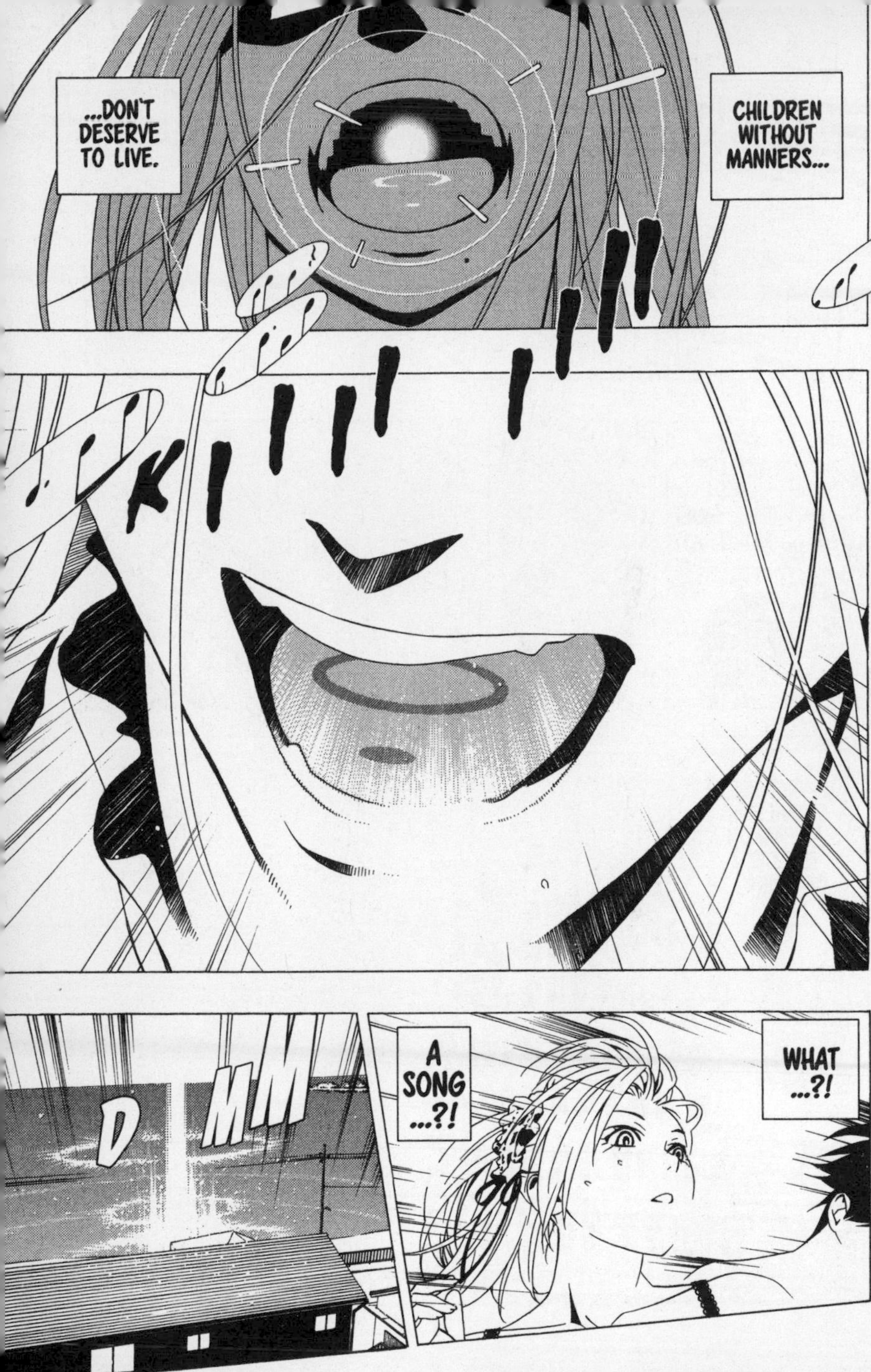
CHILDREN WITHOUT MANNERS...
...DON'T DESERVE TO LIVE.
WHAT ...?!
A SONG ...?!
DMM

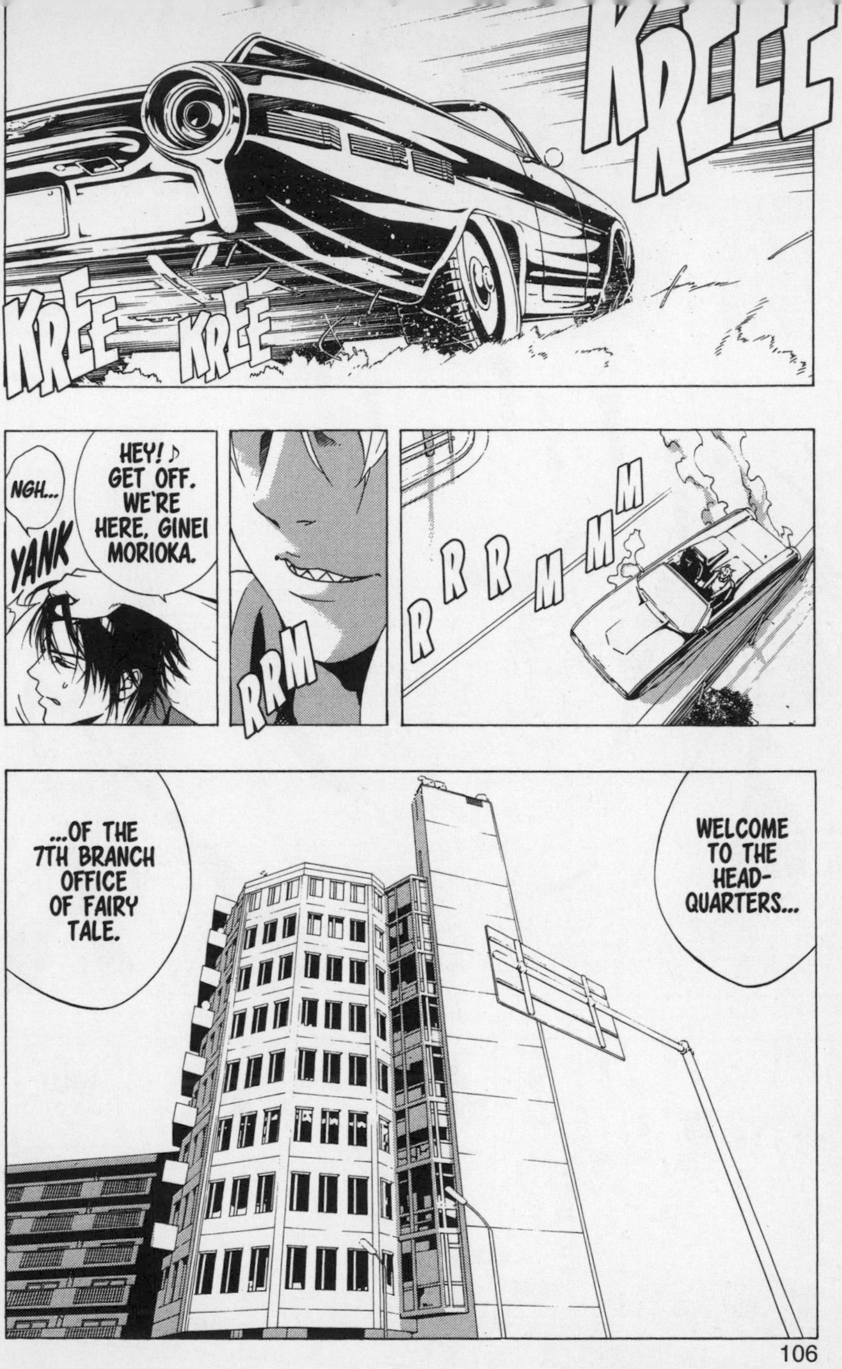
KREEE
KREE KREE
RRRRMMMM
RRM
HEY! ♪ GET OFF. WE'RE HERE, GINEI MORIOKA.
NGH...
YANK
WELCOME TO THE HEAD-QUARTERS...
...OF THE 7TH BRANCH OFFICE OF FAIRY TALE.

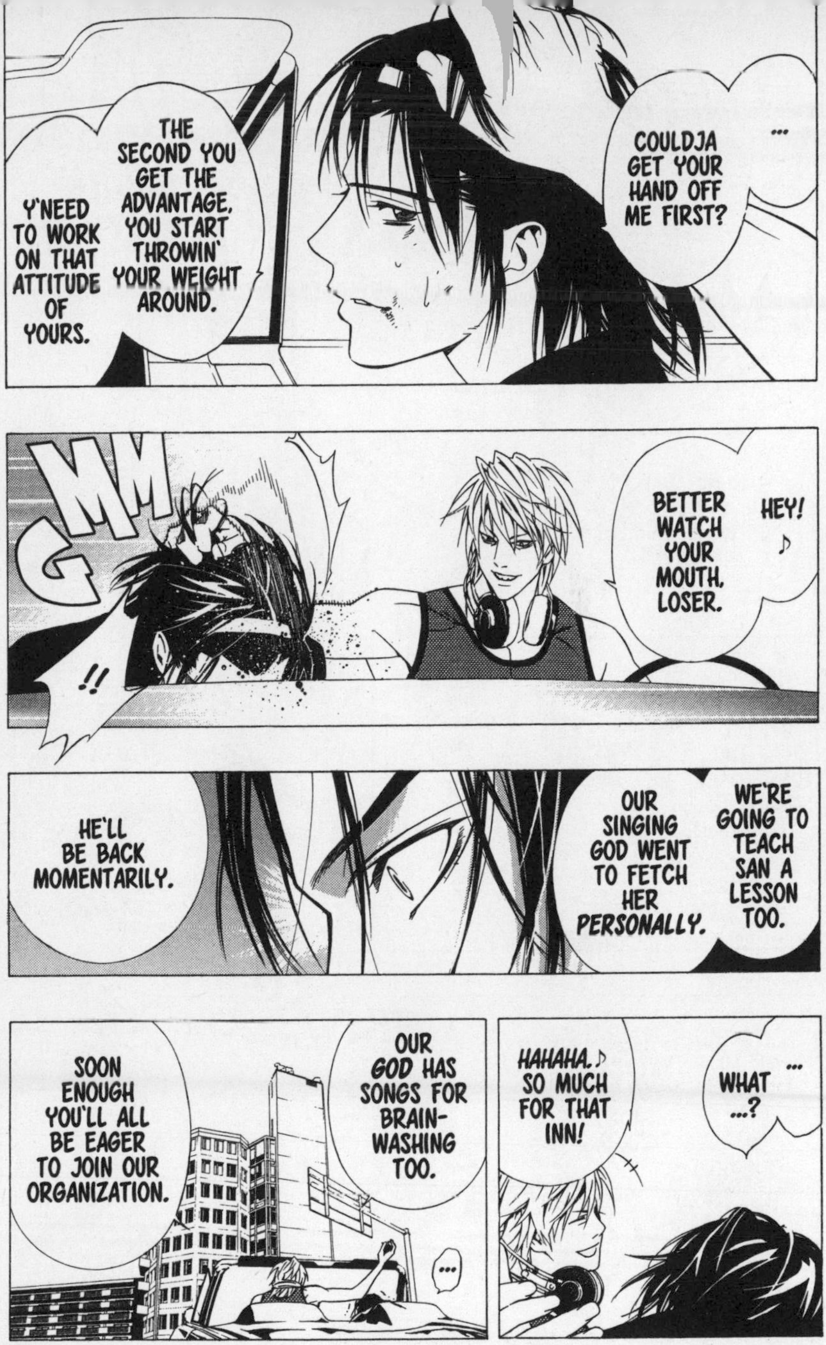
...
COULDJA GET YOUR HAND OFF ME FIRST?
THE SECOND YOU GET THE ADVANTAGE, YOU START THROWIN' YOUR WEIGHT AROUND.
Y'NEED TO WORK ON THAT ATTITUDE OF YOURS.
HEY! ♪
BETTER WATCH YOUR MOUTH, LOSER.
GMM
!!
WE'RE GOING TO TEACH SAN A LESSON TOO.
OUR SINGING GOD WENT TO FETCH HER *PERSONALLY*.
HE'LL BE BACK MOMENTARILY.
... WHAT ...?
HAHAHA.♪ SO MUCH FOR THAT INN!
OUR *GOD* HAS SONGS FOR BRAIN-WASHING TOO.
SOON ENOUGH YOU'LL ALL BE EAGER TO JOIN OUR ORGANIZATION.
...

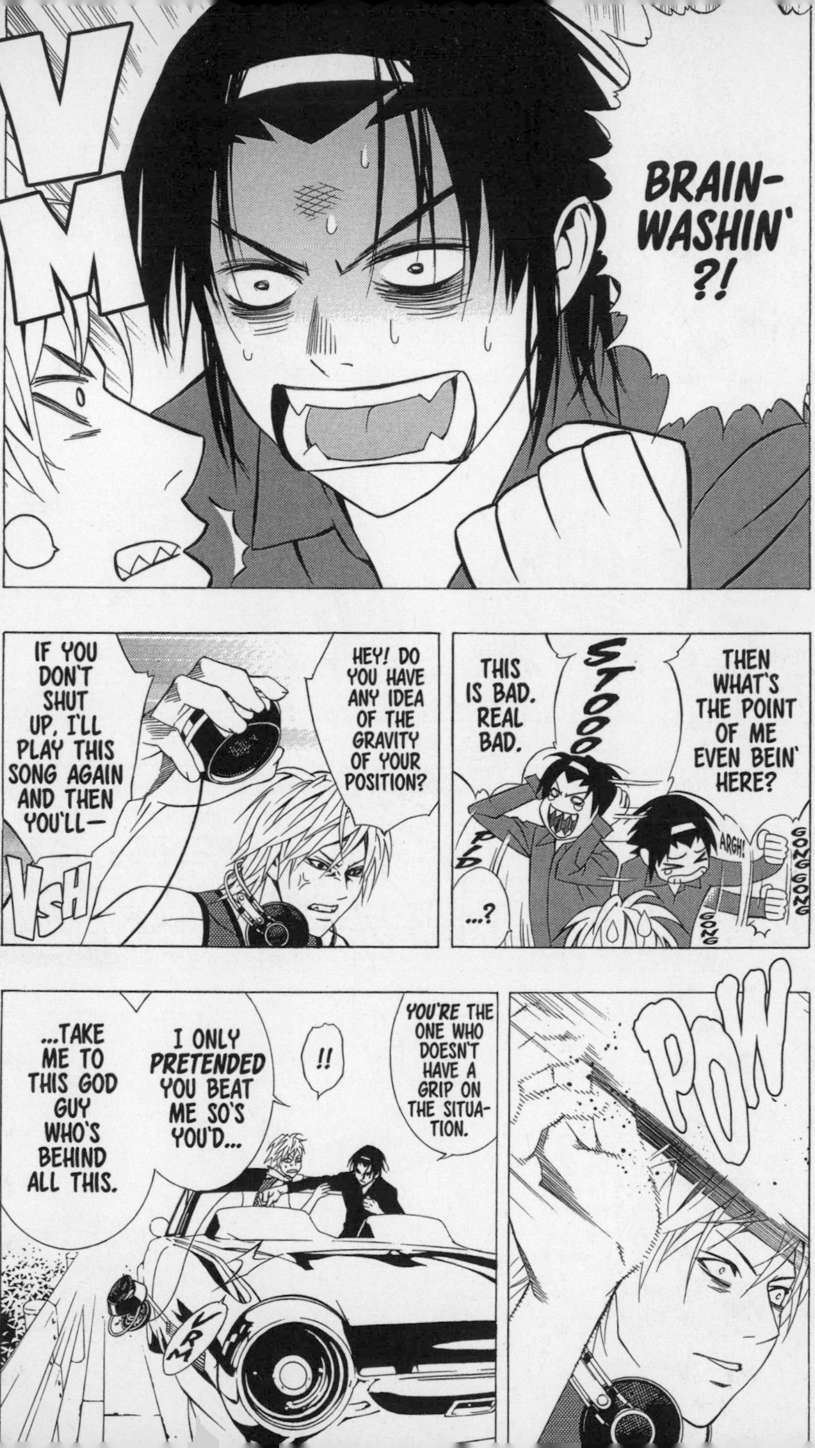
BRAIN-WASHIN'?!
VM
THEN WHAT'S THE POINT OF ME EVEN BEIN' HERE?
THIS IS BAD. REAL BAD.
ARGH!
GONG GONG GONG
...?
HEY! DO YOU HAVE ANY IDEA OF THE GRAVITY OF YOUR POSITION?
IF YOU DON'T SHUT UP, I'LL PLAY THIS SONG AGAIN AND THEN YOU'LL—
VSH
POW
YOU'RE THE ONE WHO DOESN'T HAVE A GRIP ON THE SITUATION.
!!
I ONLY PRETENDED YOU BEAT ME SO'S YOU'D...
...TAKE ME TO THIS GOD GUY WHO'S BEHIND ALL THIS.
VRM

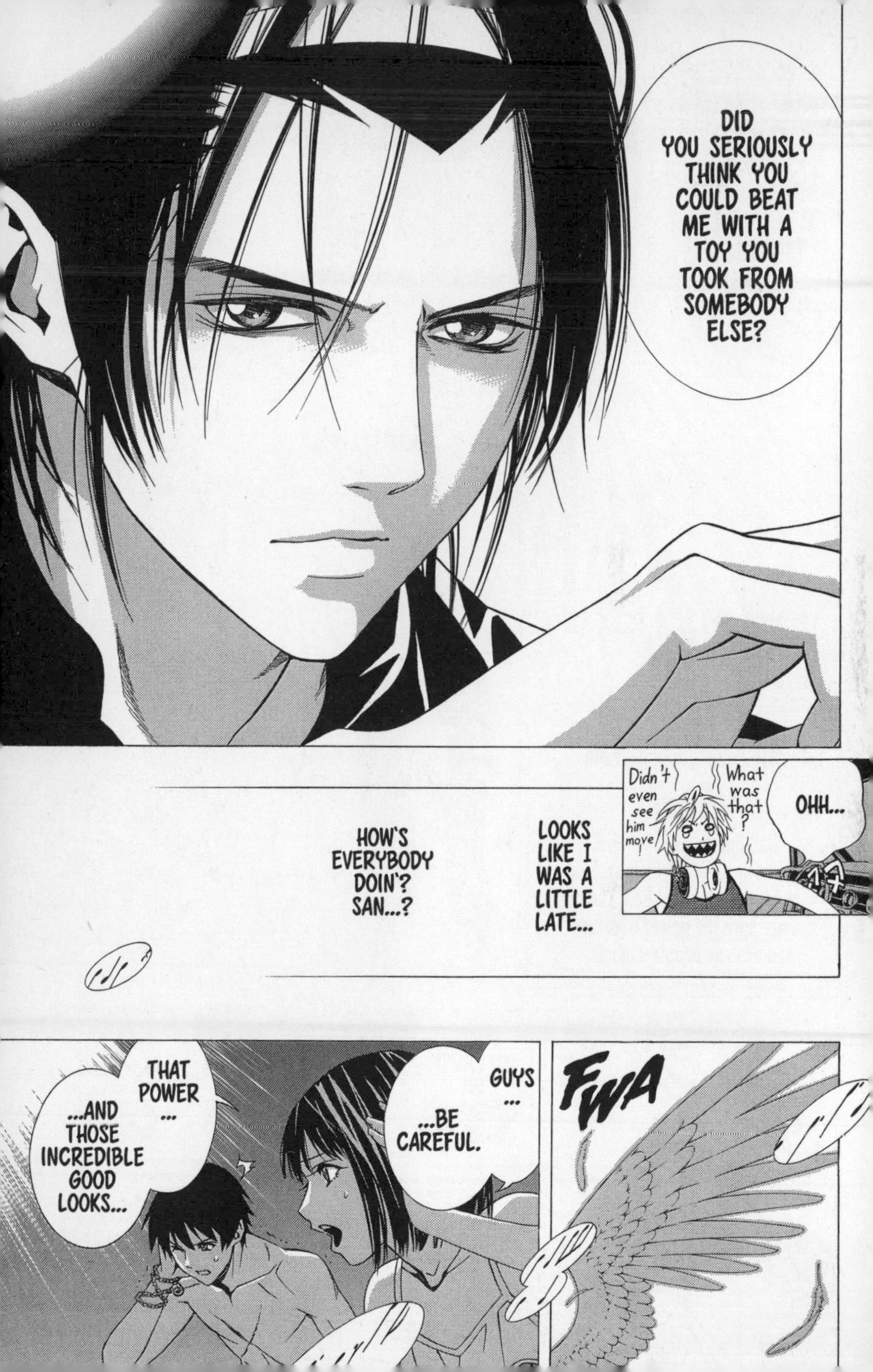
DID YOU SERIOUSLY THINK YOU COULD BEAT ME WITH A TOY YOU TOOK FROM SOMEBODY ELSE?
OHH...
What was that?
Didn't even see him move!
LOOKS LIKE I WAS A LITTLE LATE...
HOW'S EVERYBODY DOIN'? SAN...?
FWA
GUYS... ...BE CAREFUL.
THAT POWER... ...AND THOSE INCREDIBLE GOOD LOOKS...

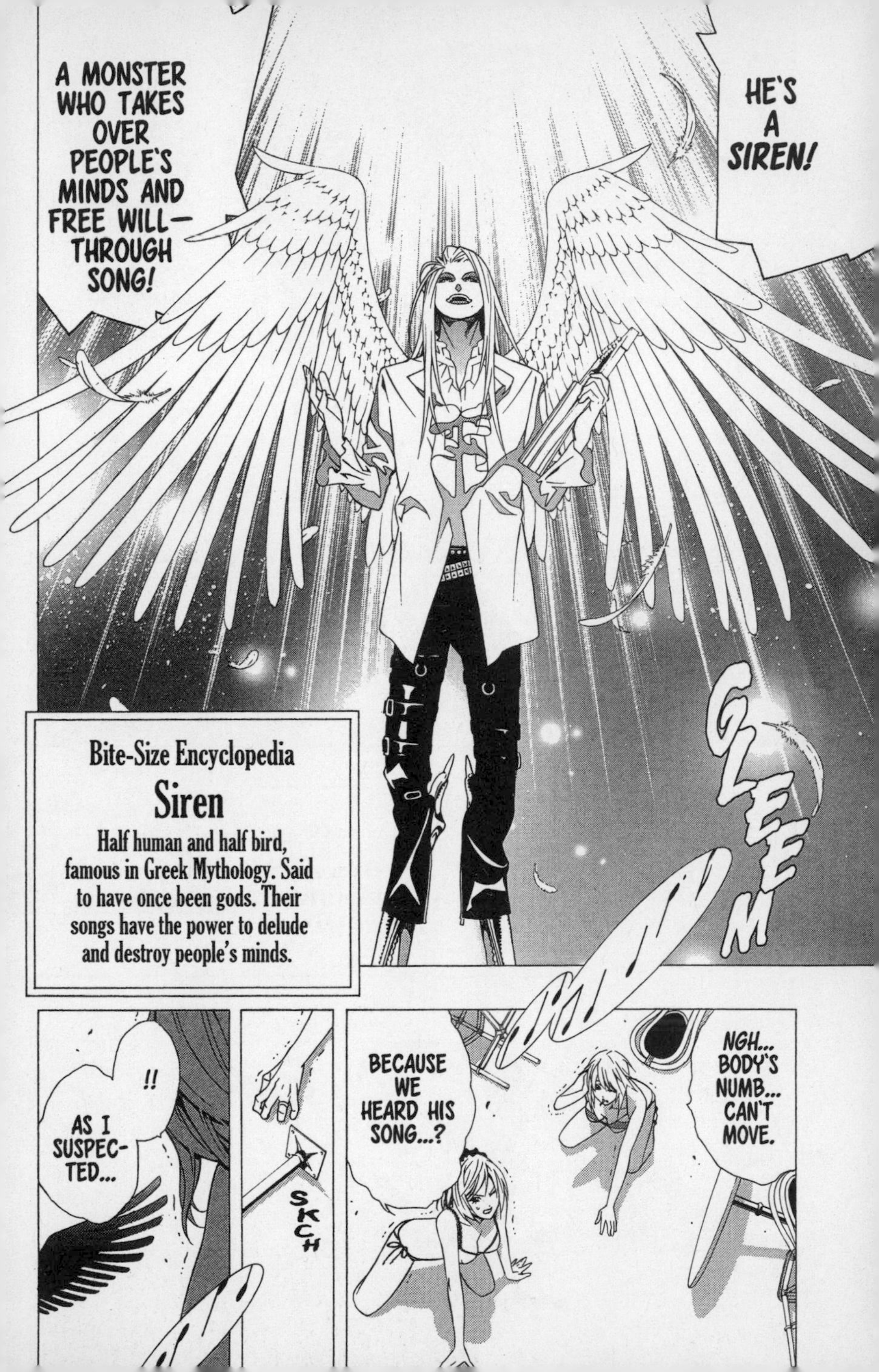
HE'S A SIREN!
A MONSTER WHO TAKES OVER PEOPLE'S MINDS AND FREE WILL— THROUGH SONG!
GLEEM
Bite-Size Encyclopedia
Siren
Half human and half bird, famous in Greek Mythology. Said to have once been gods. Their songs have the power to delude and destroy people's minds.
NGH... BODY'S NUMB... CAN'T MOVE.
BECAUSE WE HEARD HIS SONG...?
SKCH
!!
AS I SUSPEC-TED...

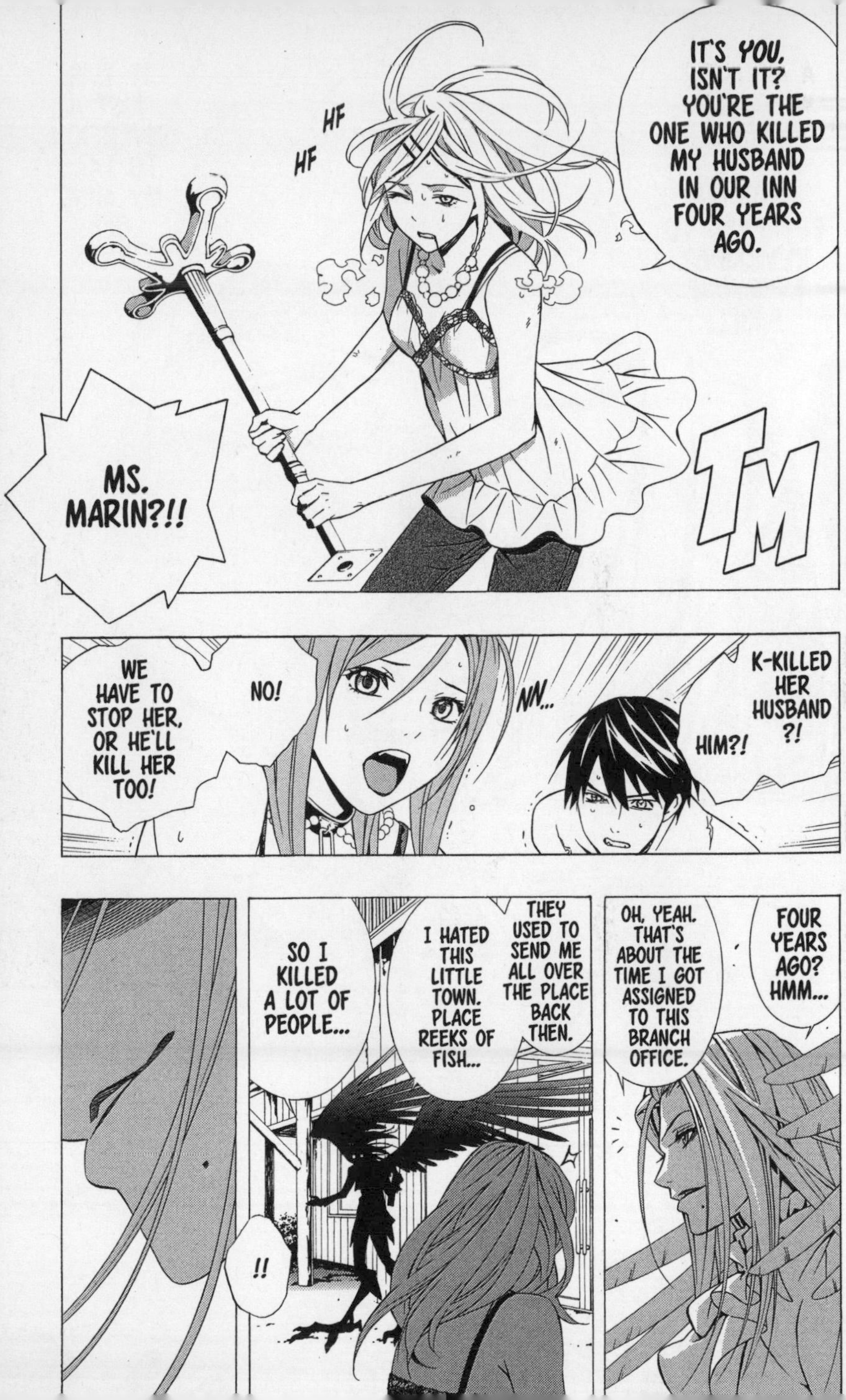
IT'S YOU, ISN'T IT? YOU'RE THE ONE WHO KILLED MY HUSBAND IN OUR INN FOUR YEARS AGO.
HF HF
TM
MS. MARIN?!!
K-KILLED HER HUSBAND ?!
HIM?!
NN...
NO!
WE HAVE TO STOP HER, OR HE'LL KILL HER TOO!
FOUR YEARS AGO? HMM...
OH, YEAH. THAT'S ABOUT THE TIME I GOT ASSIGNED TO THIS BRANCH OFFICE.
THEY USED TO SEND ME ALL OVER THE PLACE BACK THEN.
I HATED THIS LITTLE TOWN. PLACE REEKS OF FISH...
SO I KILLED A LOT OF PEOPLE...
!!

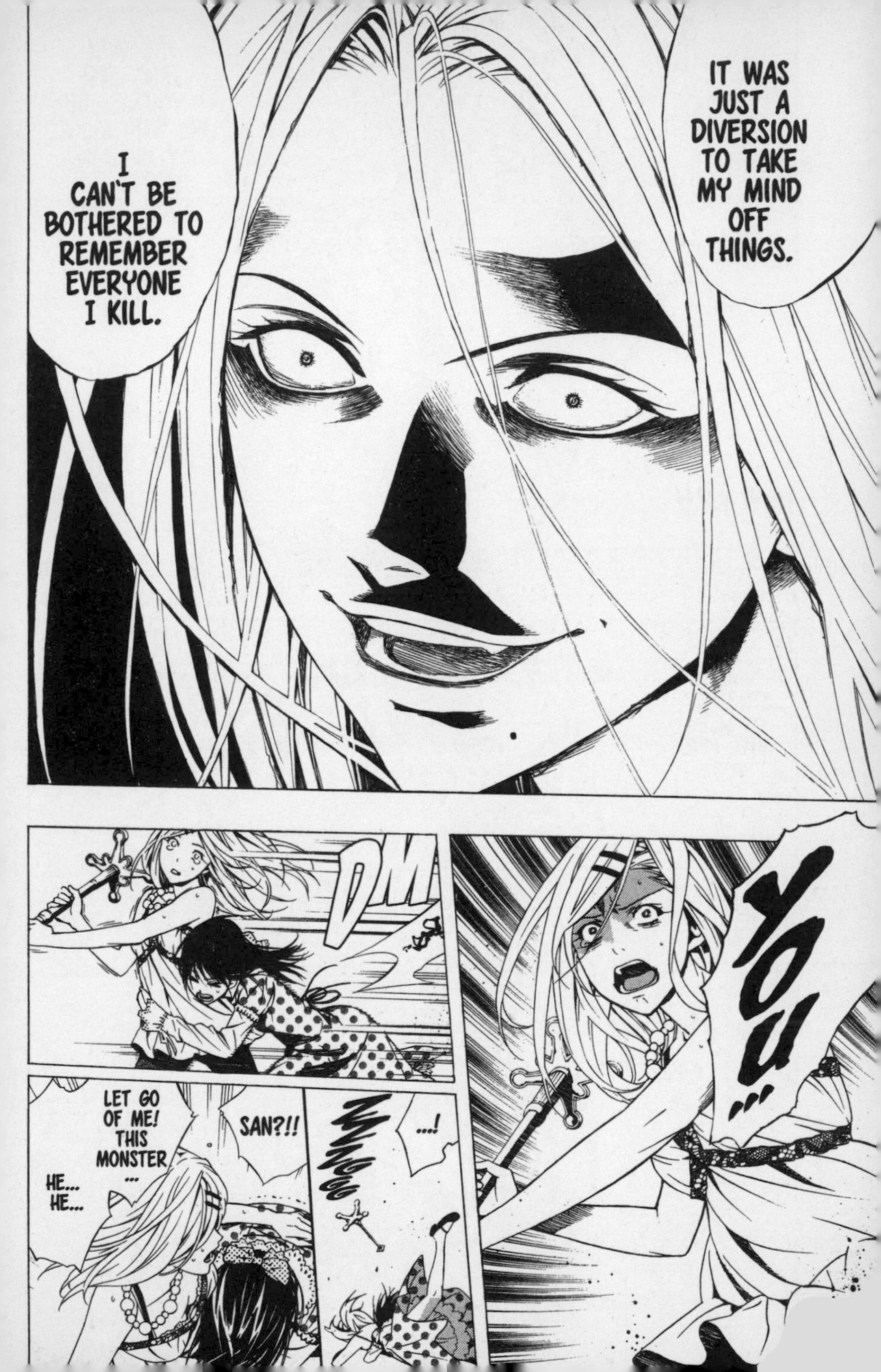
IT WAS JUST A DIVERSION TO TAKE MY MIND OFF THINGS.
I CAN'T BE BOTHERED TO REMEMBER EVERYONE I KILL.
YOU...!!
DM
...!
SAN?!!
LET GO OF ME! THIS MONSTER ...
HE... HE...

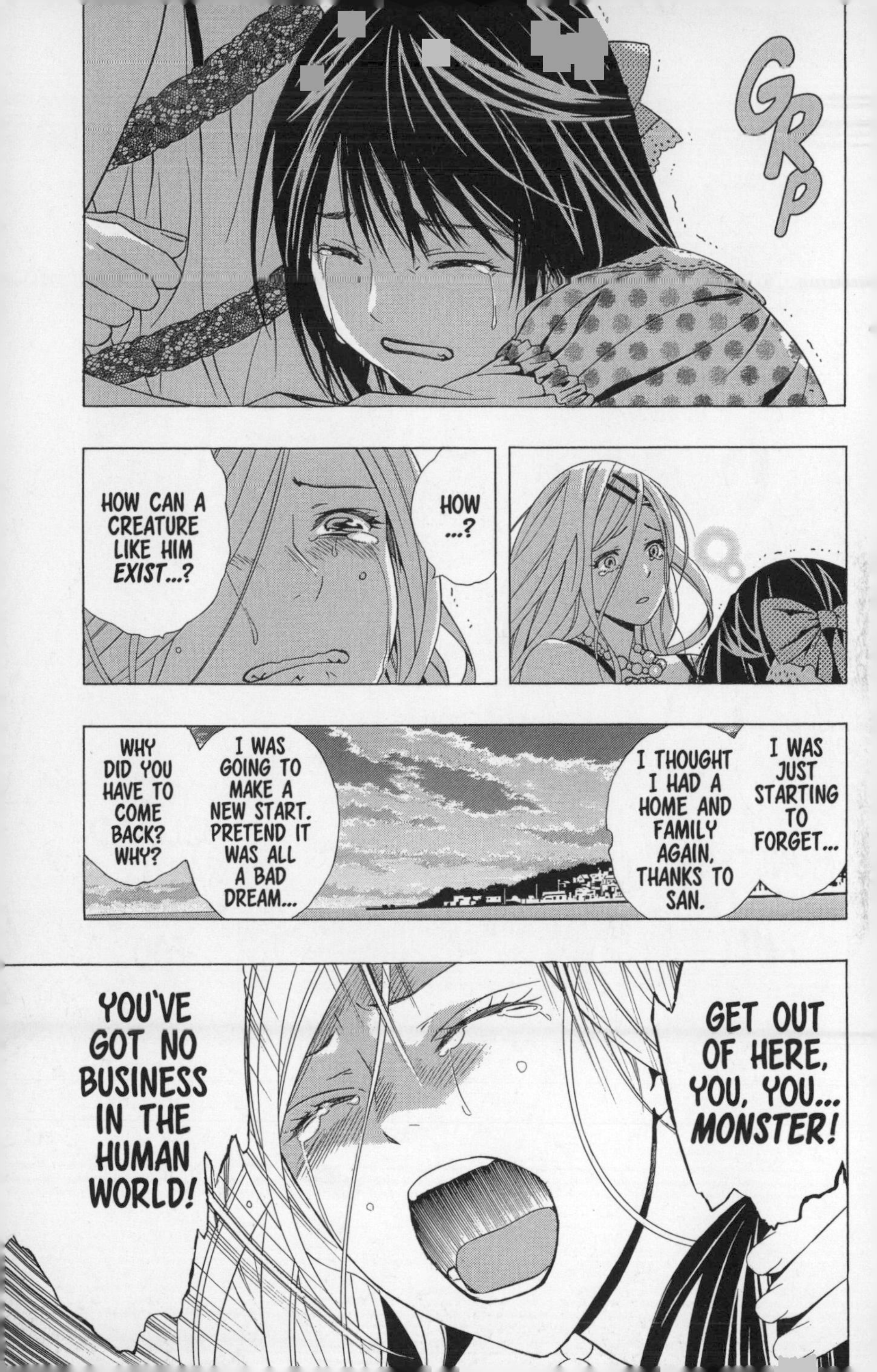
GRP
HOW ...?
HOW CAN A CREATURE LIKE HIM EXIST...?
I WAS JUST STARTING TO FORGET...
I THOUGHT I HAD A HOME AND FAMILY AGAIN, THANKS TO SAN.
I WAS GOING TO MAKE A NEW START. PRETEND IT WAS ALL A BAD DREAM...
WHY DID YOU HAVE TO COME BACK? WHY?
GET OUT OF HERE, YOU, YOU... MONSTER!
YOU'VE GOT NO BUSINESS IN THE HUMAN WORLD!

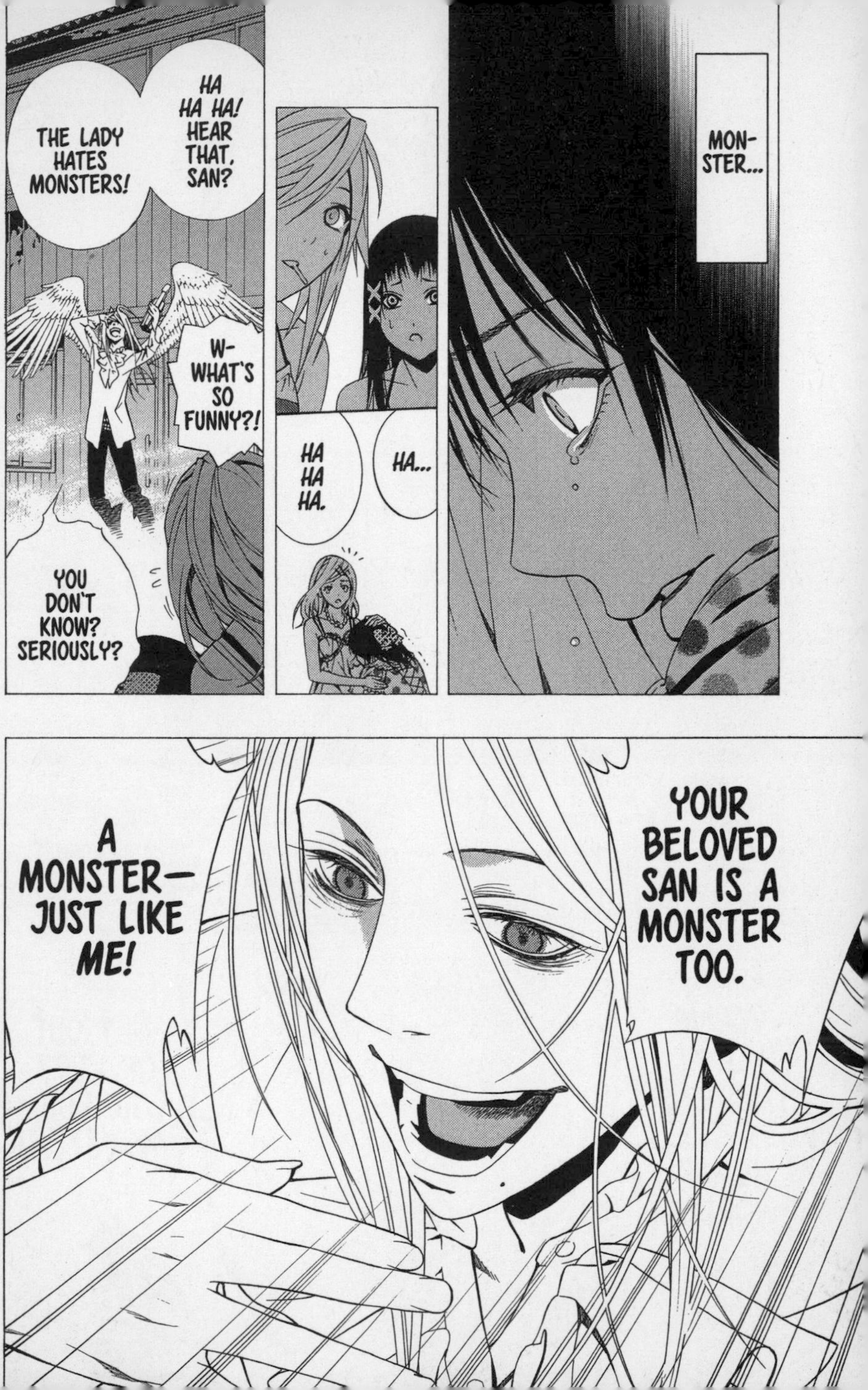
MON-STER...
HA...
HA HA HA.
HA HA HA! HEAR THAT, SAN?
THE LADY HATES MONSTERS!
W-WHAT'S SO FUNNY?!
YOU DON'T KNOW? SERIOUSLY?
YOUR BELOVED SAN IS A MONSTER TOO.
A MONSTER—JUST LIKE ME!

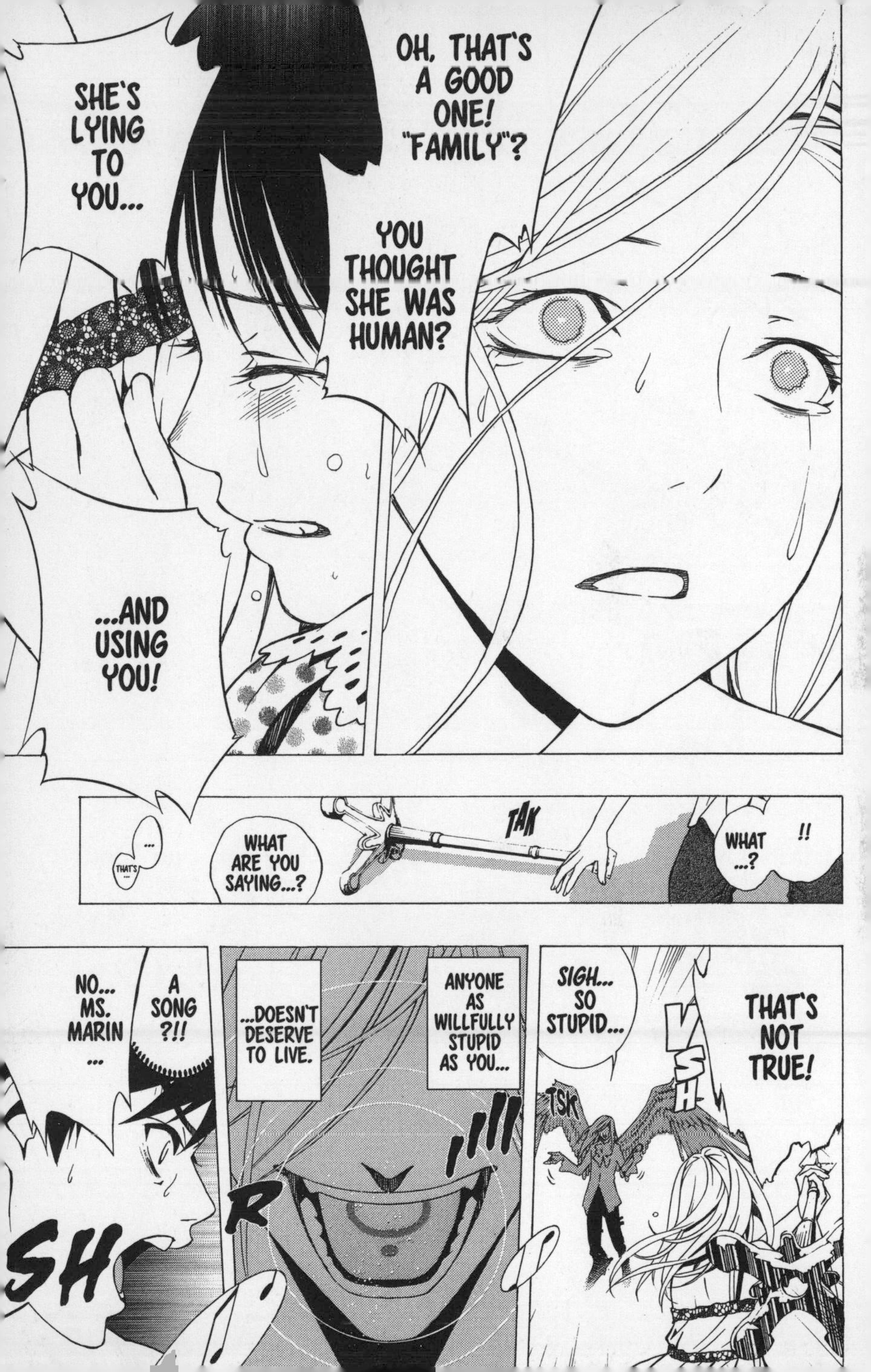
OH, THAT'S A GOOD ONE! "FAMILY"?
YOU THOUGHT SHE WAS HUMAN?
SHE'S LYING TO YOU...
...AND USING YOU!
!!
WHAT ...?
TAK
WHAT ARE YOU SAYING...?
...
THAT'S ...
THAT'S NOT TRUE!
VSSH
SIGH... SO STUPID...
TSK
ANYONE AS WILLFULLY STUPID AS YOU...
...DOESN'T DESERVE TO LIVE.
R
A SONG ?!!
NO... MS. MARIN ...
SH

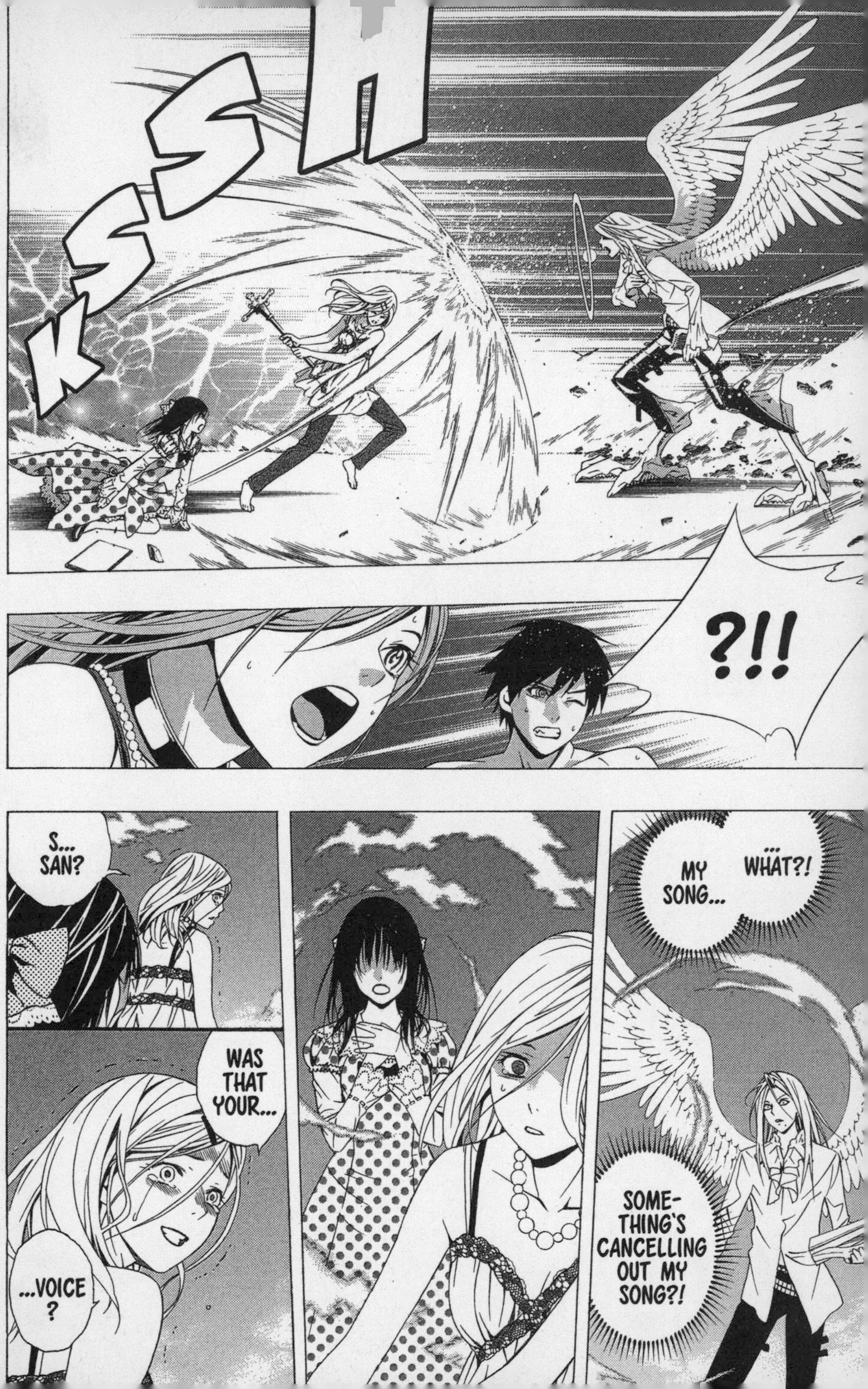
KSSH
?!!
...WHAT?!
MY SONG...
SOME-THING'S CANCELLING OUT MY SONG?!
S... SAN?
WAS THAT YOUR...
...VOICE?

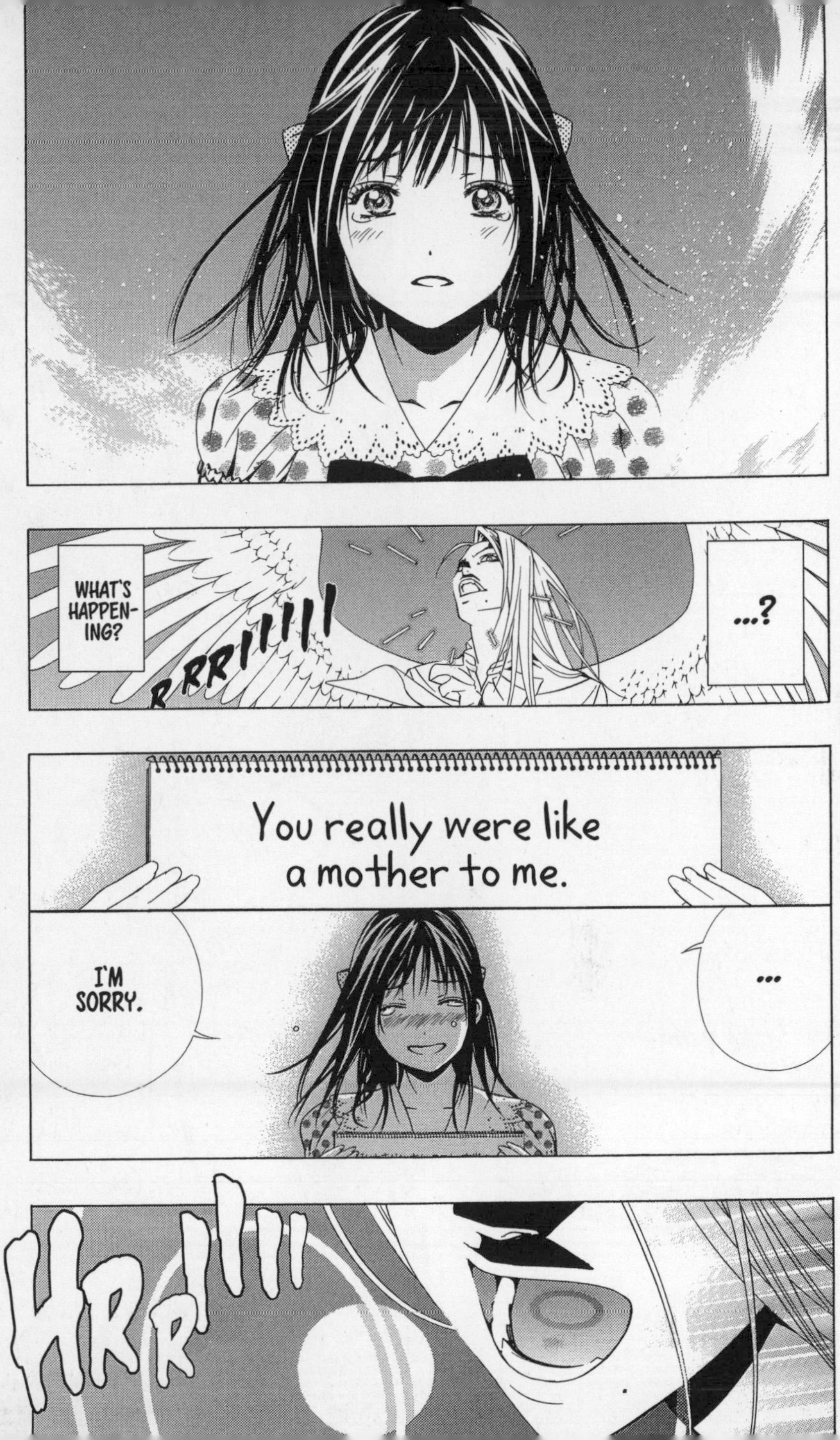
...?
WHAT'S HAPPENING?
RRRIIIII
You really were like a mother to me.
...
I'M SORRY.
HRRIIII

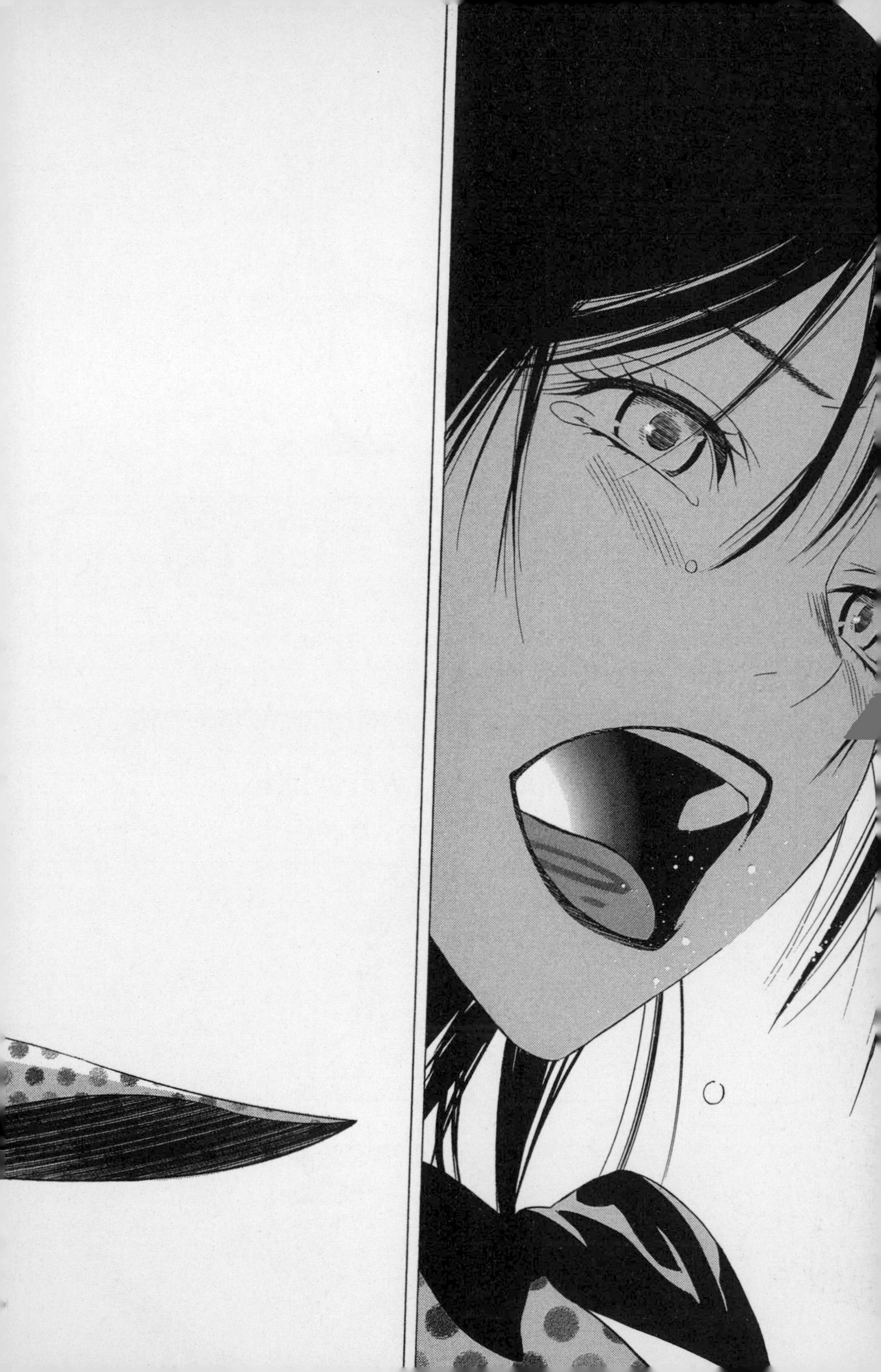

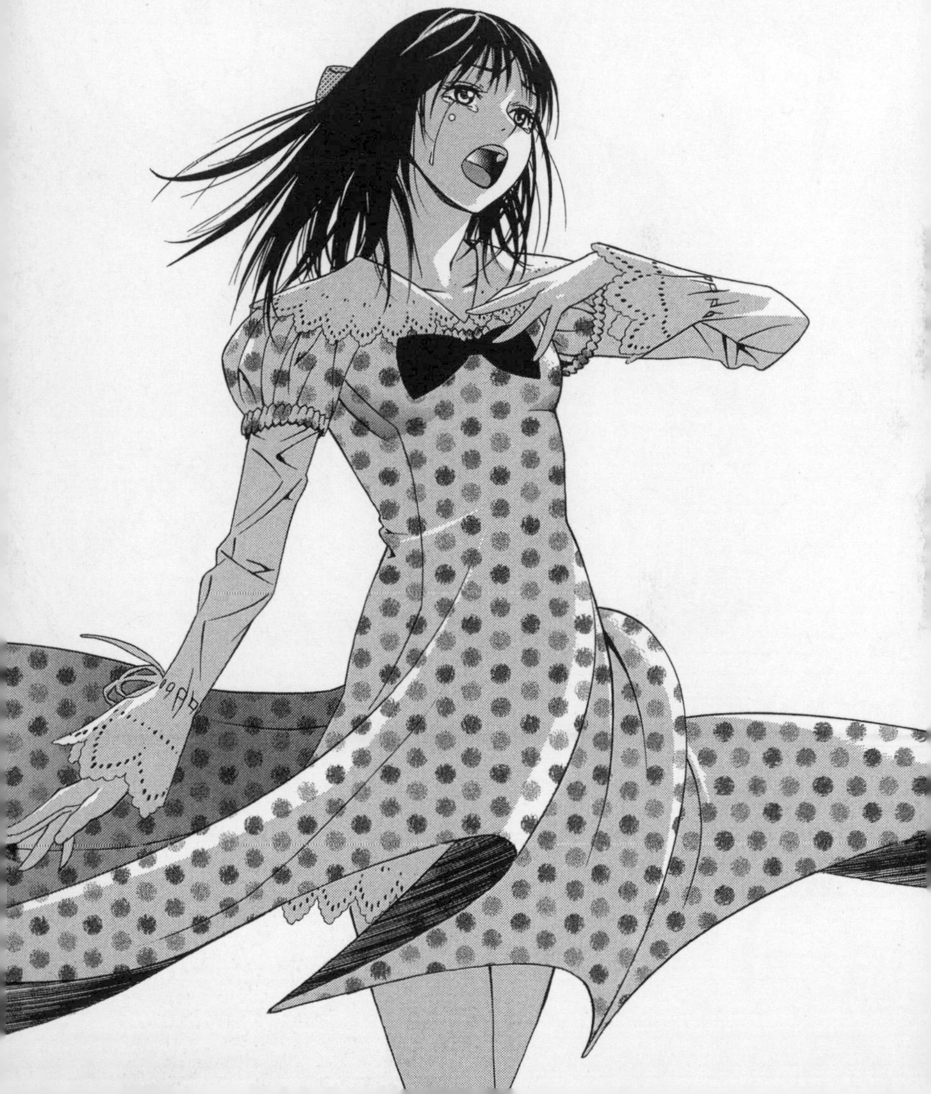

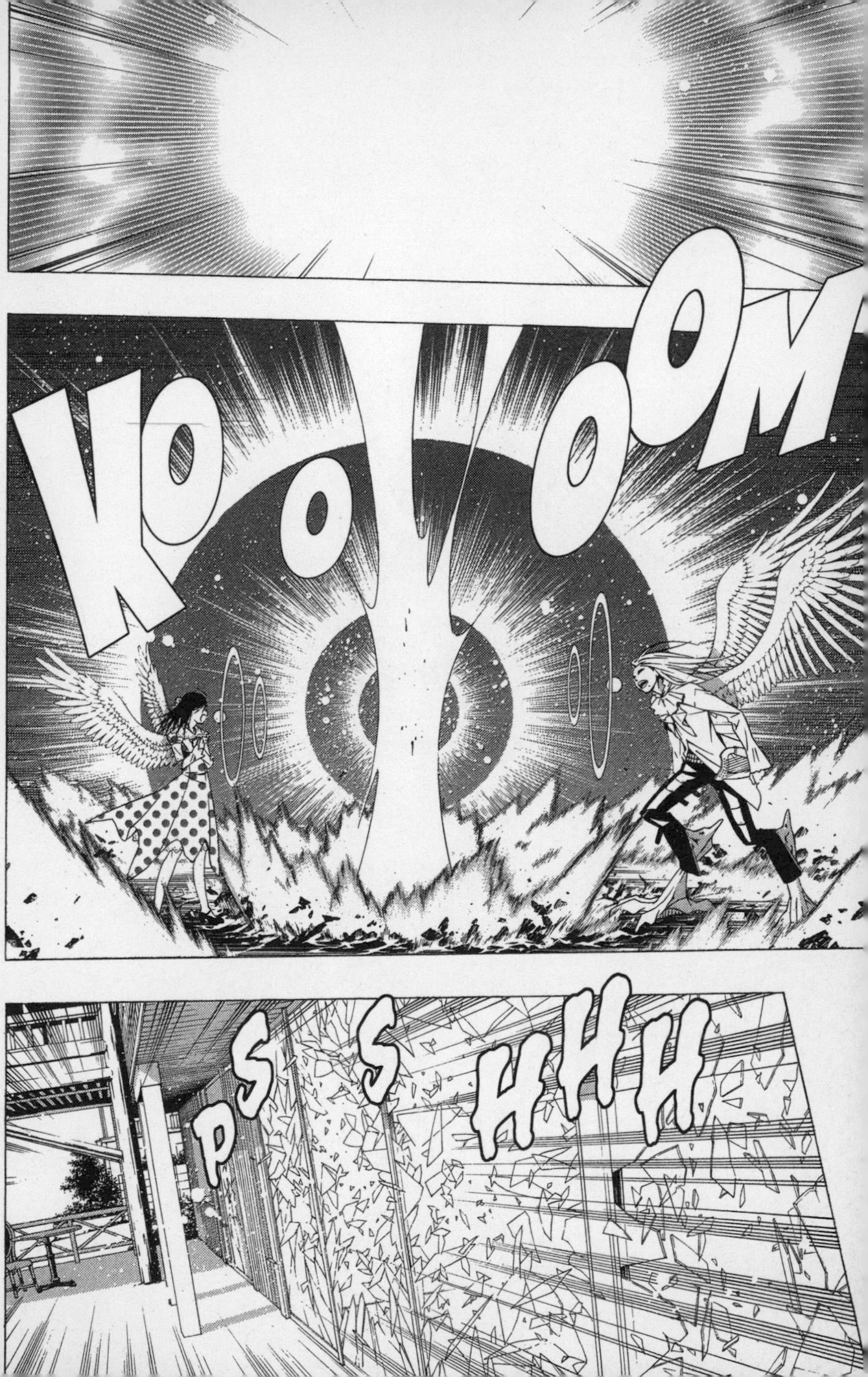
KOOOOM
PSSHHH

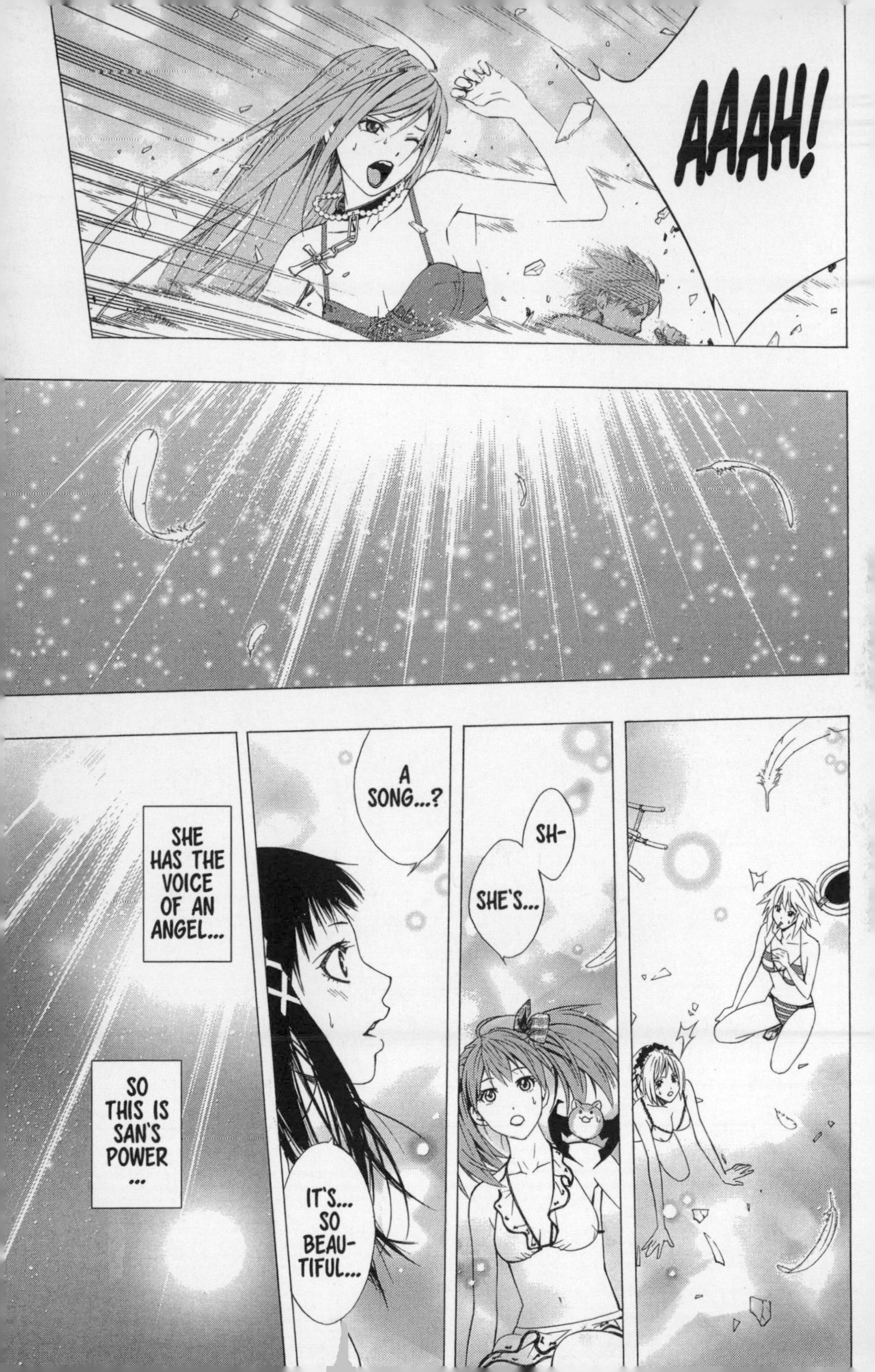
AAAH!
SH-
SHE'S...
A SONG...?
IT'S... SO BEAUTIFUL...
SHE HAS THE VOICE OF AN ANGEL...
SO THIS IS SAN'S POWER...

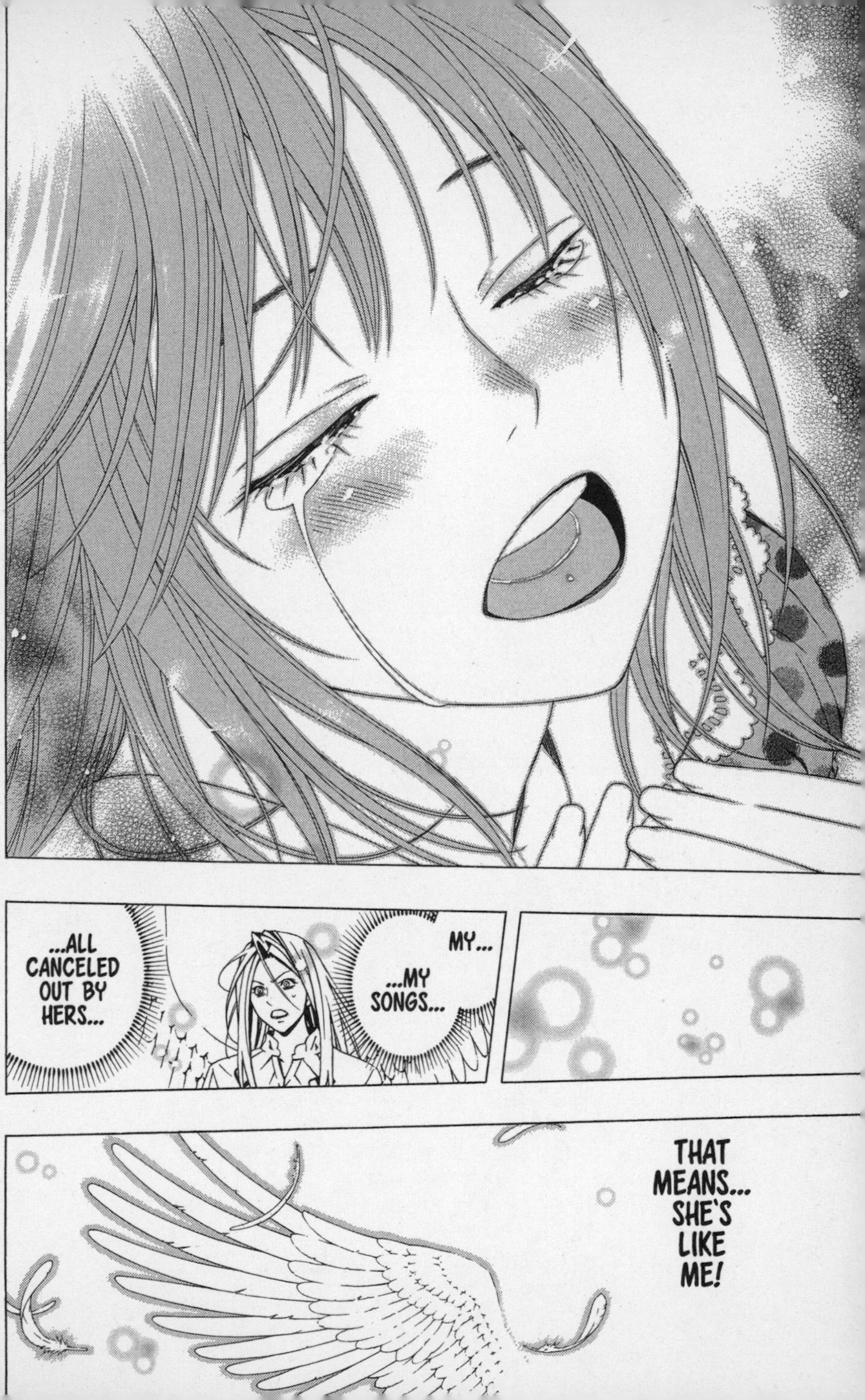
MY...
...MY SONGS...
...ALL CANCELED OUT BY HERS...
THAT MEANS... SHE'S LIKE ME!

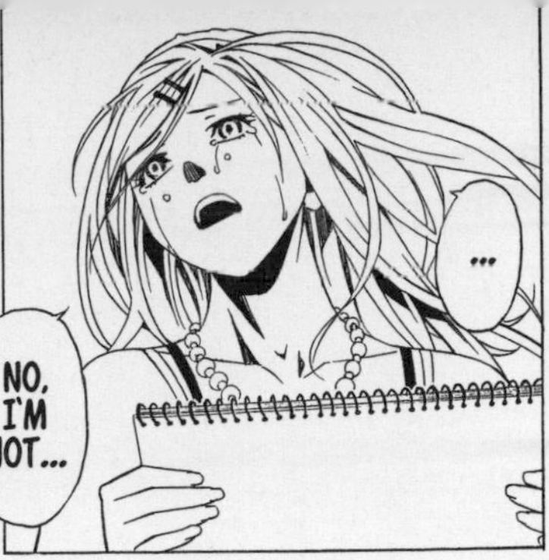
...
NO, I'M NOT...
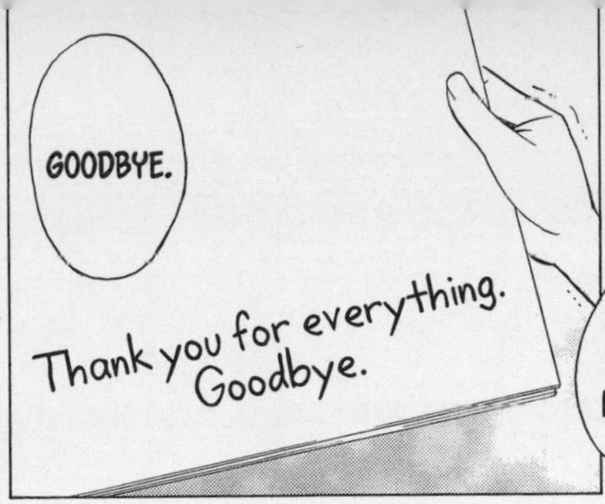
GOODBYE.
Thank you for everything. Goodbye.
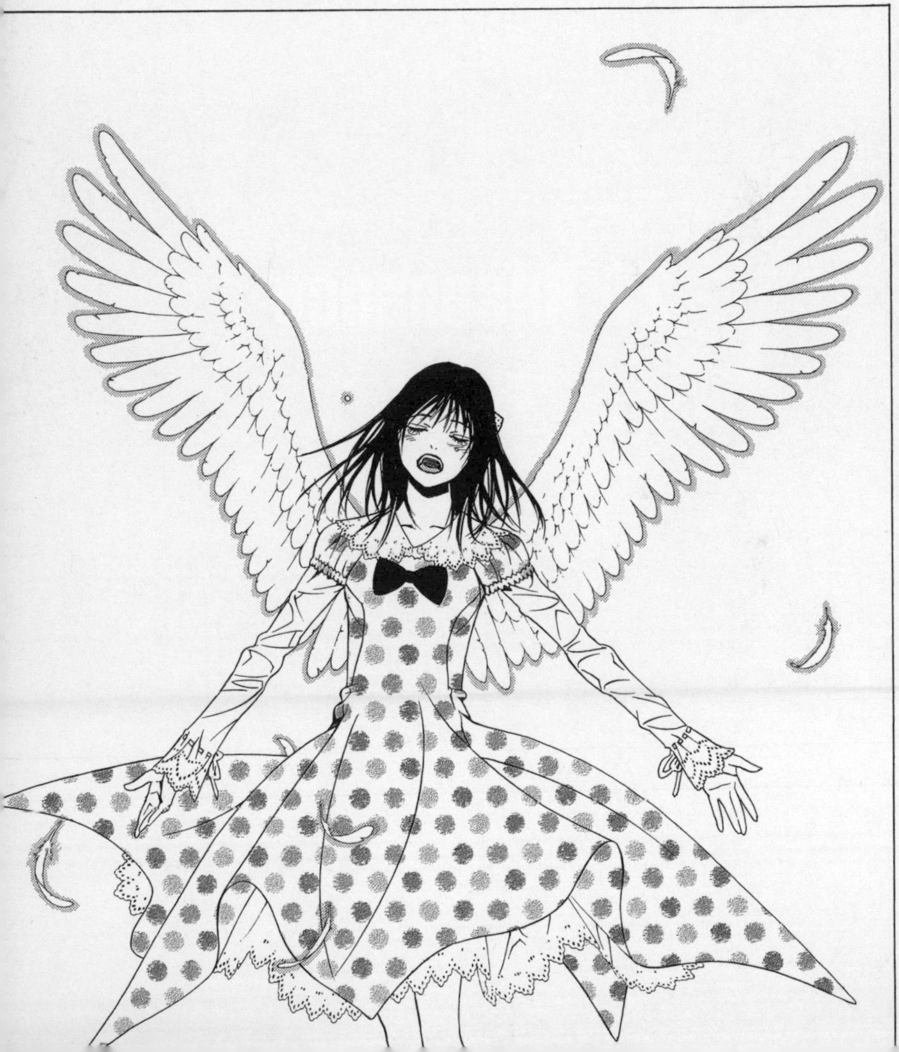

21: Resonance

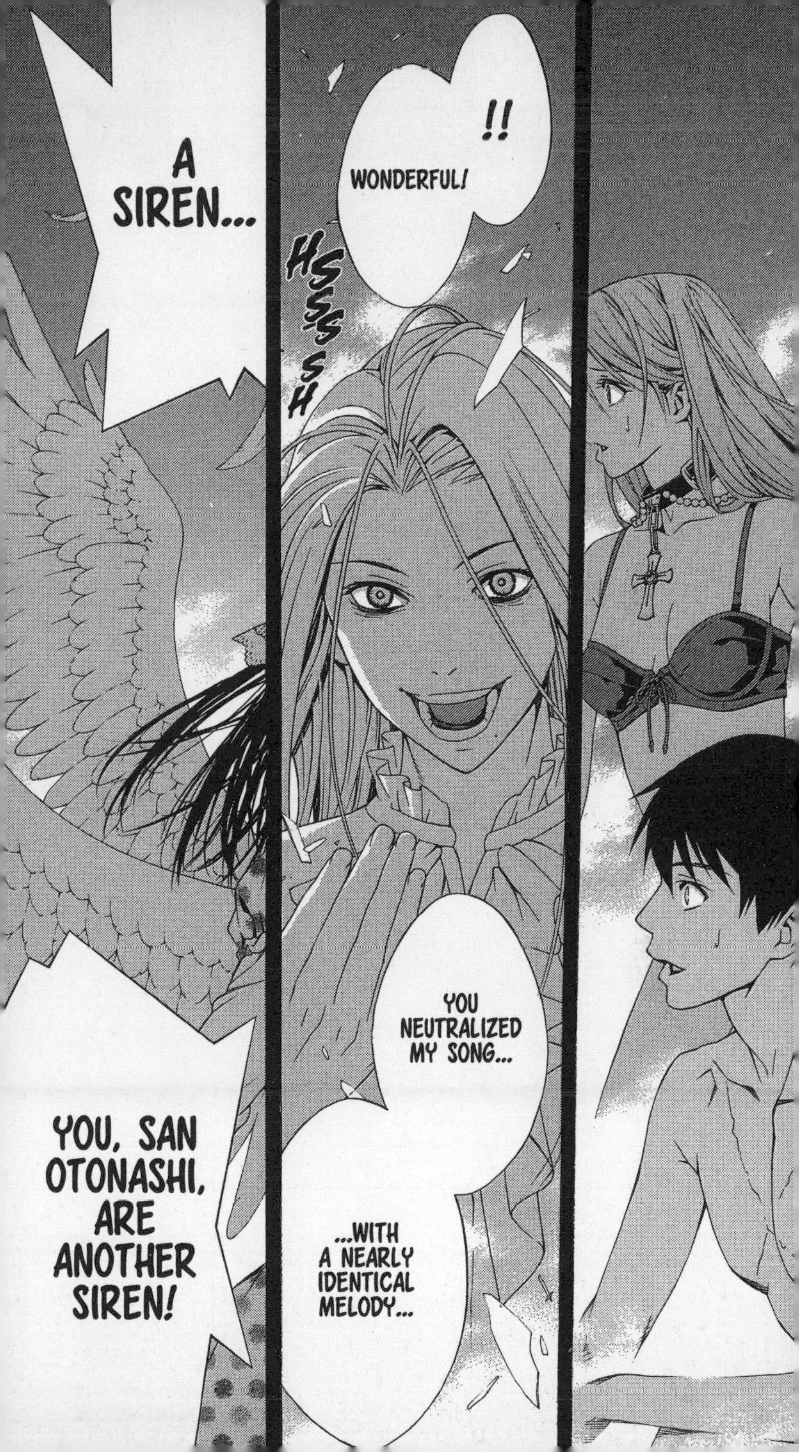
!!
WONDERFUL!
HSSSSH
YOU NEUTRALIZED MY SONG...
...WITH A NEARLY IDENTICAL MELODY...
A SIREN...
YOU, SAN OTONASHI, ARE ANOTHER SIREN!

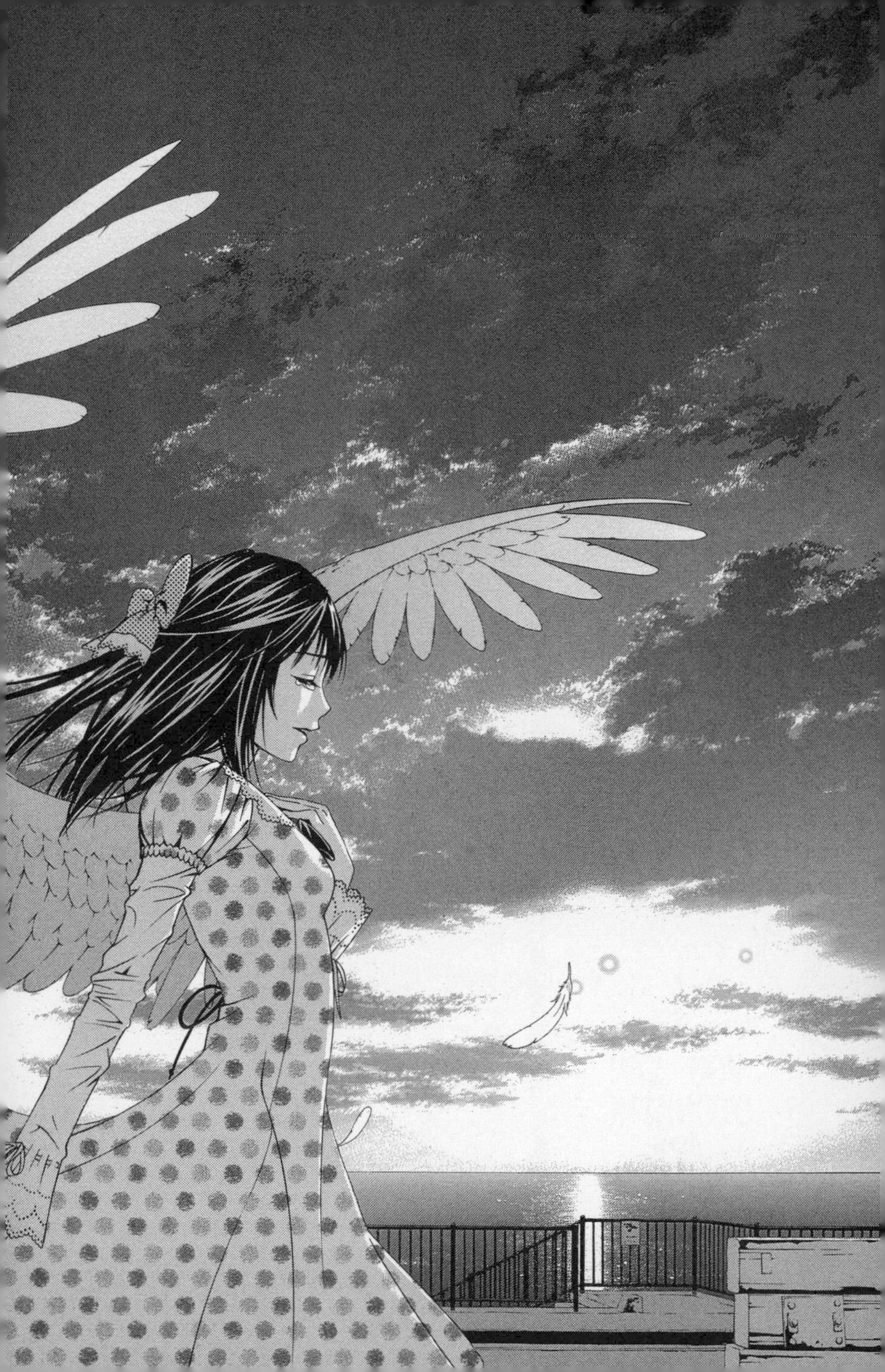

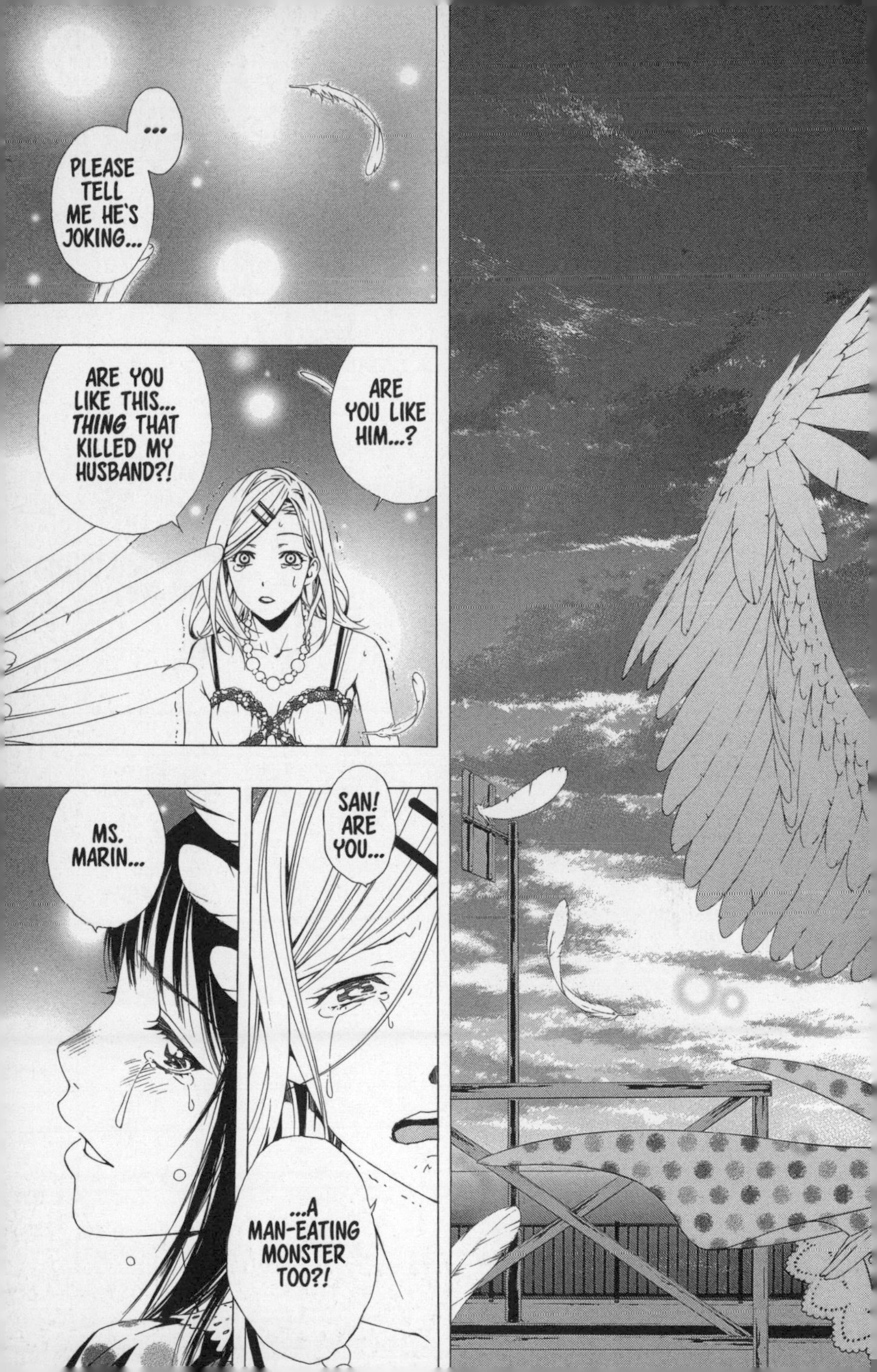
...
PLEASE TELL ME HE'S JOKING...
ARE YOU LIKE HIM...?
ARE YOU LIKE THIS... *THING* THAT KILLED MY HUSBAND?!
SAN! ARE YOU...
...A MAN-EATING MONSTER TOO?!
MS. MARIN...

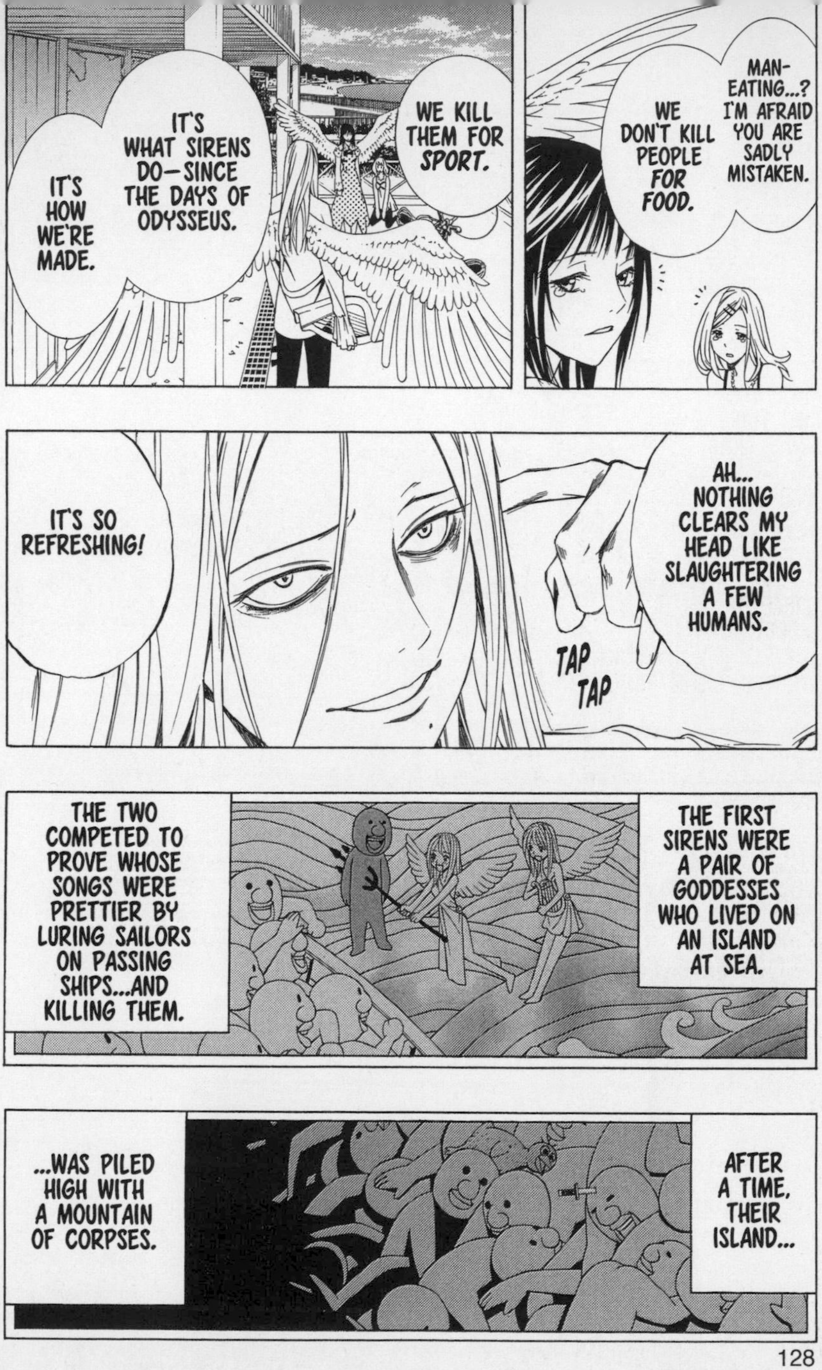
MAN-EATING...? I'M AFRAID YOU ARE SADLY MISTAKEN.
WE DON'T KILL PEOPLE FOR FOOD.
WE KILL THEM FOR SPORT.
IT'S WHAT SIRENS DO—SINCE THE DAYS OF ODYSSEUS.
IT'S HOW WE'RE MADE.
AH... NOTHING CLEARS MY HEAD LIKE SLAUGHTERING A FEW HUMANS.
TAP TAP
IT'S SO REFRESHING!
THE FIRST SIRENS WERE A PAIR OF GODDESSES WHO LIVED ON AN ISLAND AT SEA.
THE TWO COMPETED TO PROVE WHOSE SONGS WERE PRETTIER BY LURING SAILORS ON PASSING SHIPS...AND KILLING THEM.
AFTER A TIME, THEIR ISLAND...
...WAS PILED HIGH WITH A MOUNTAIN OF CORPSES.

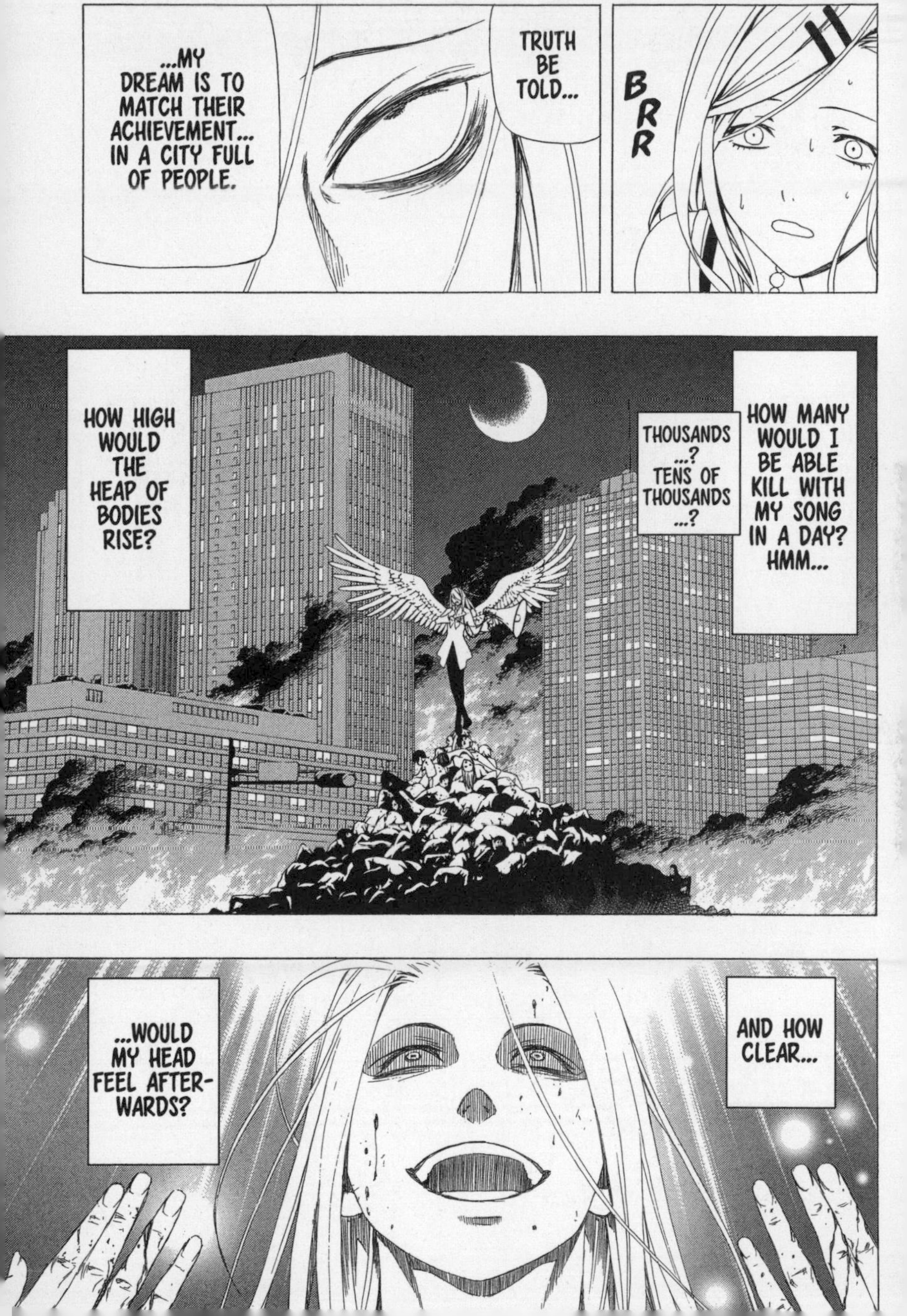
BRR
TRUTH BE TOLD...
...MY DREAM IS TO MATCH THEIR ACHIEVEMENT... IN A CITY FULL OF PEOPLE.
HOW MANY WOULD I BE ABLE KILL WITH MY SONG IN A DAY? HMM...
THOUSANDS...? TENS OF THOUSANDS...?
HOW HIGH WOULD THE HEAP OF BODIES RISE?
AND HOW CLEAR...
...WOULD MY HEAD FEEL AFTER-WARDS?

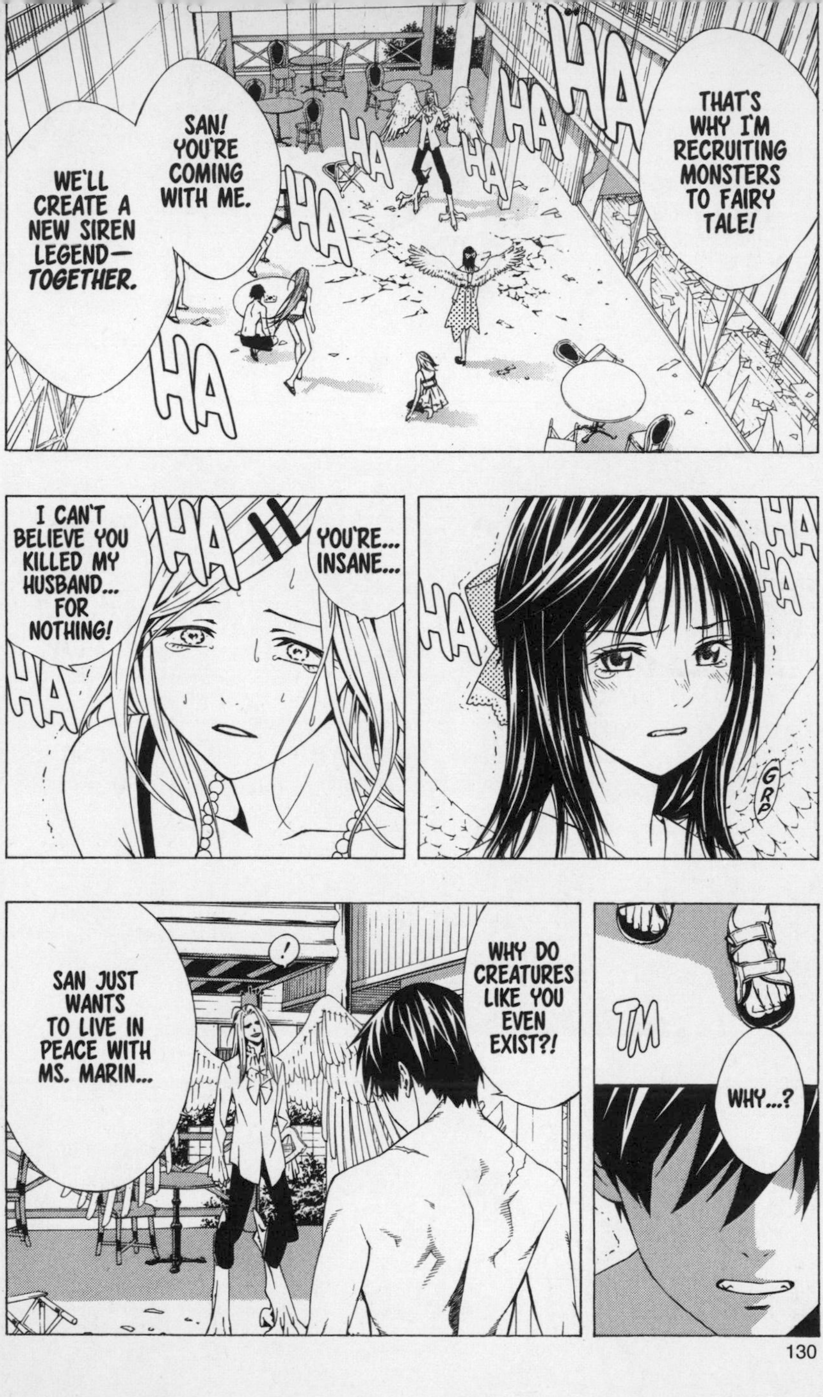
THAT'S WHY I'M RECRUITING MONSTERS TO FAIRY TALE!
HA HA HA HA HA HA HA HA
SAN! YOU'RE COMING WITH ME.
WE'LL CREATE A NEW SIREN LEGEND—TOGETHER.
HA
HA HA HA HA
GRP
YOU'RE... INSANE...
HA
I CAN'T BELIEVE YOU KILLED MY HUSBAND... FOR NOTHING!
HA
TM
WHY...?
WHY DO CREATURES LIKE YOU EVEN EXIST?!
!
SAN JUST WANTS TO LIVE IN PEACE WITH MS. MARIN...

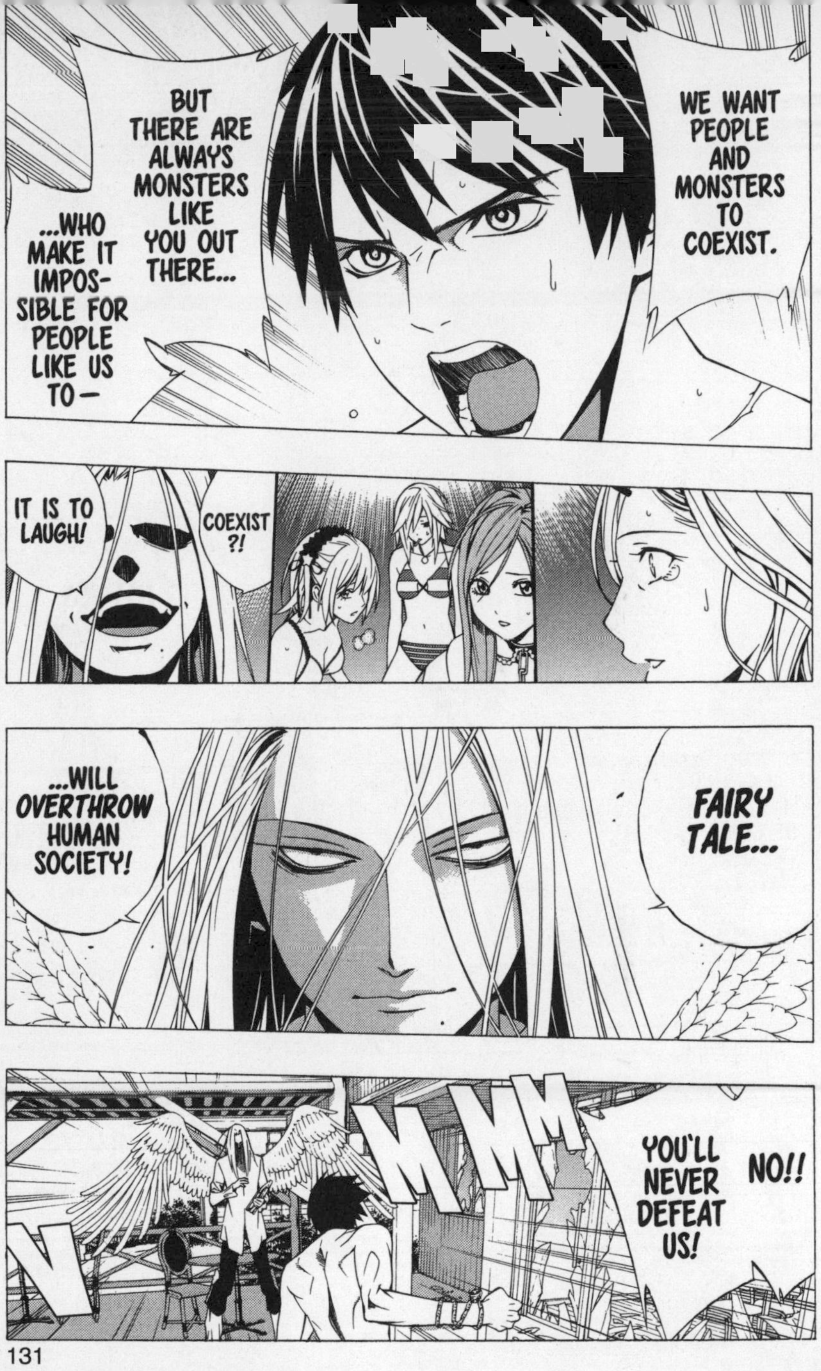
WE WANT PEOPLE AND MONSTERS TO COEXIST.
BUT THERE ARE ALWAYS MONSTERS LIKE YOU OUT THERE...
...WHO MAKE IT IMPOSSIBLE FOR PEOPLE LIKE US TO—
COEXIST ?!
IT IS TO LAUGH!
FAIRY TALE...
...WILL OVERTHROW HUMAN SOCIETY!
NO!!
YOU'LL NEVER DEFEAT US!
MMM
N

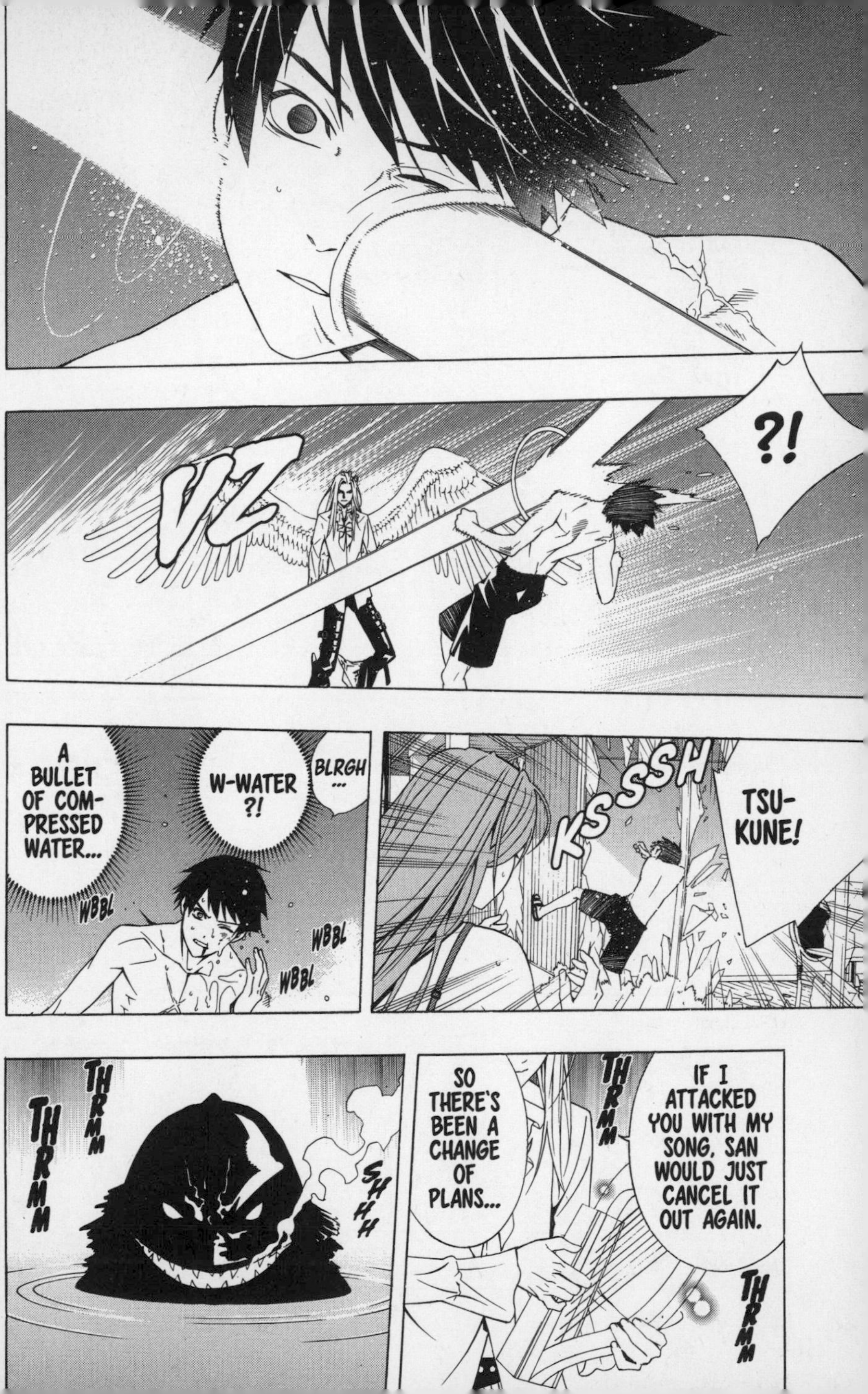
?!
VZ
TSU-KUNE!
KSSSH
BLRGH...
W-WATER?!
A BULLET OF COM-PRESSED WATER...
WBBL
WBBL
WBBL
IF I ATTACKED YOU WITH MY SONG, SAN WOULD JUST CANCEL IT OUT AGAIN.
THRMM
SO THERE'S BEEN A CHANGE OF PLANS...
THRMM
THRMM
SHHH
THRMM
THRMM

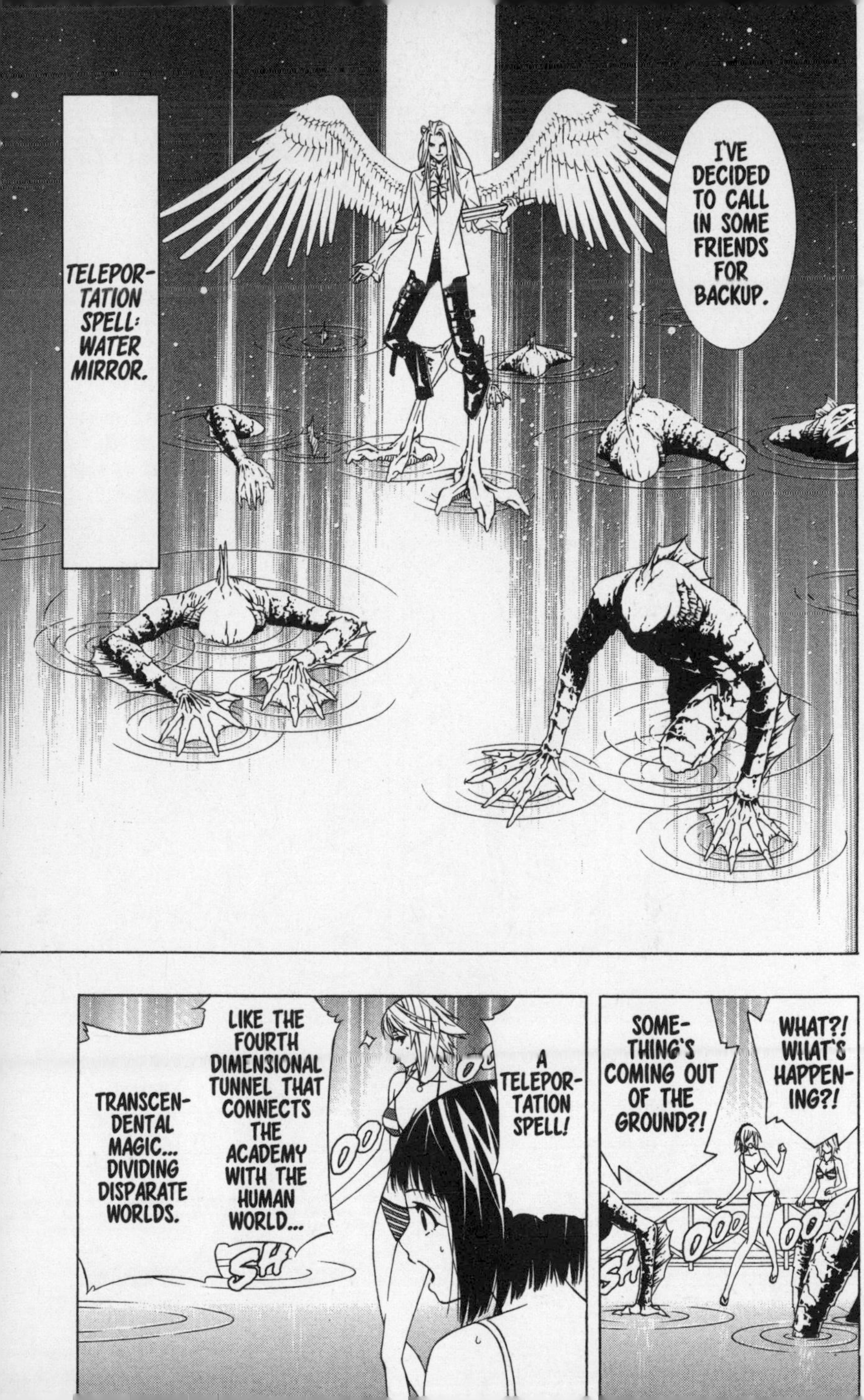
I'VE DECIDED TO CALL IN SOME FRIENDS FOR BACKUP.
TELEPORTATION SPELL: WATER MIRROR.
WHAT?! WHAT'S HAPPENING?!
SOMETHING'S COMING OUT OF THE GROUND?!
OOO
OO
SH
A TELEPORTATION SPELL!
LIKE THE FOURTH DIMENSIONAL TUNNEL THAT CONNECTS THE ACADEMY WITH THE HUMAN WORLD...
TRANSCENDENTAL MAGIC... DIVIDING DISPARATE WORLDS.
OO
SH

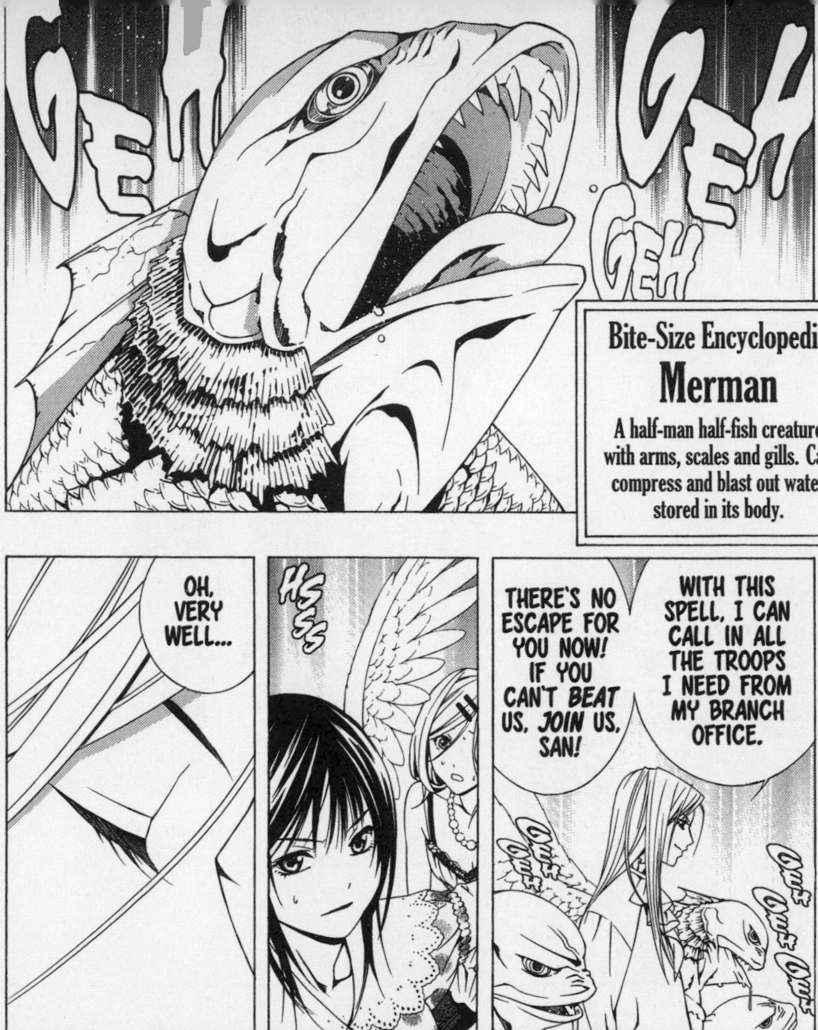
GEH
GEH
GEH
Bite-Size Encyclopedia
Merman
A half-man half-fish creature with arms, scales and gills. Can compress and blast out water stored in its body.
GEH
WITH THIS SPELL, I CAN CALL IN ALL THE TROOPS I NEED FROM MY BRANCH OFFICE.
THERE'S NO ESCAPE FOR YOU NOW! IF YOU CAN'T *BEAT* US, *JOIN* US, SAN!
HSSS
OH, VERY WELL...
I SUPPOSE I'LL JUST HAVE TO TAKE YOU BY FORCE AND BRAINWASH YOU. *SIGH...*

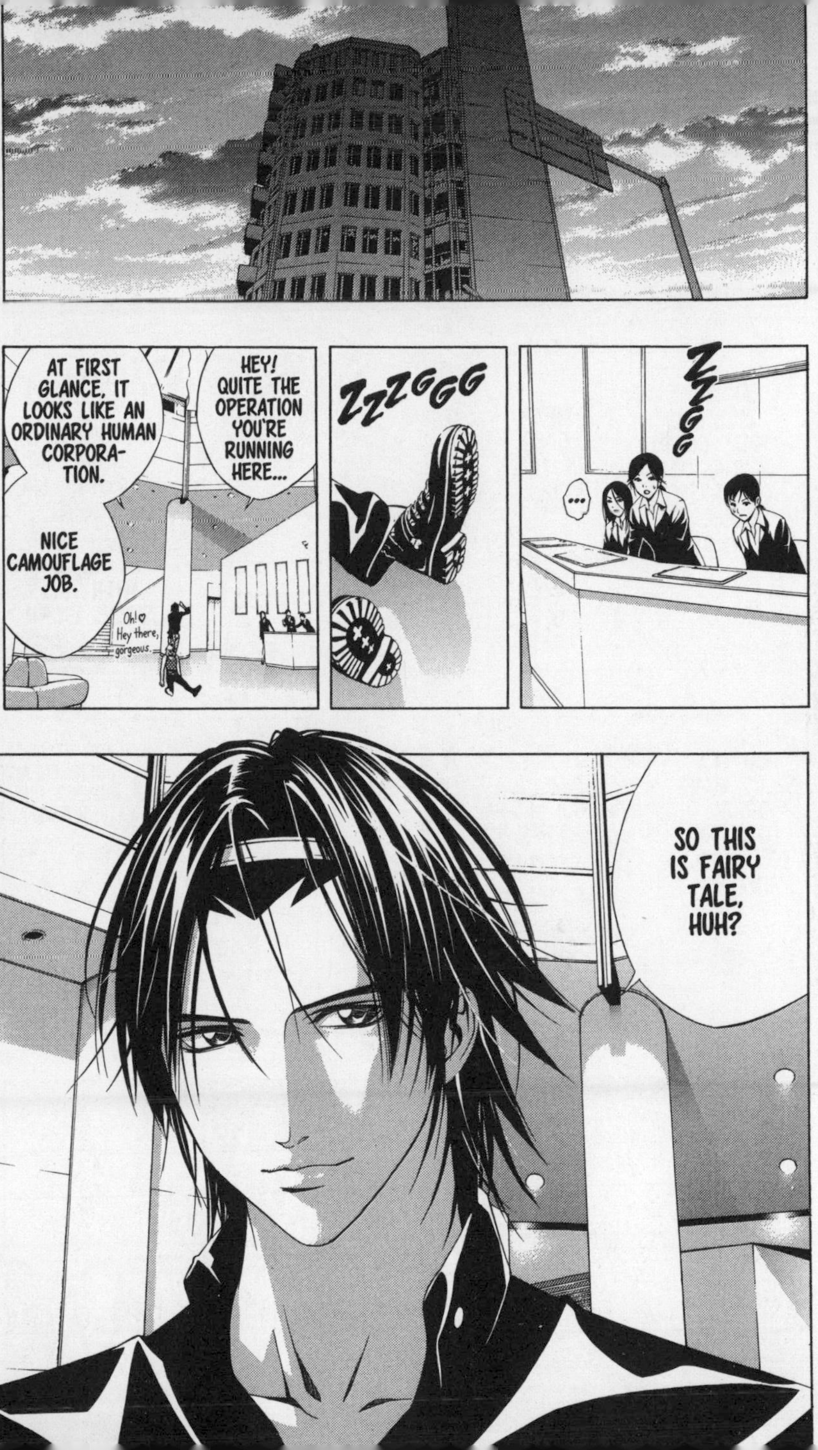
…
ZZGGG
ZZZGGG
HEY! QUITE THE OPERATION YOU'RE RUNNING HERE...
AT FIRST GLANCE, IT LOOKS LIKE AN ORDINARY HUMAN CORPORATION.
NICE CAMOUFLAGE JOB.
Oh!♡ Hey there, gorgeous.
SO THIS IS FAIRY TALE, HUH?

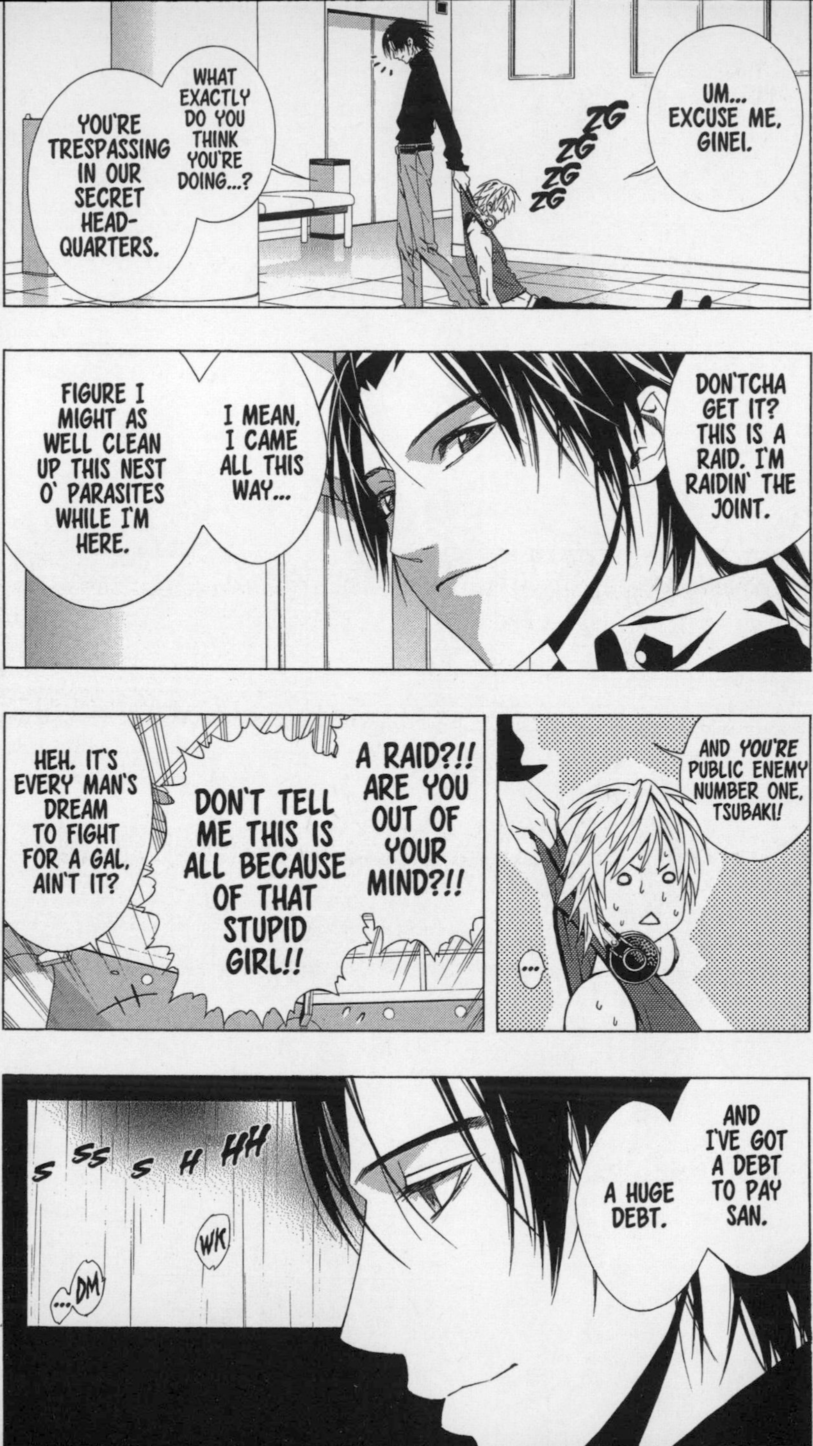
UM... EXCUSE ME, GINEI.
ZG ZG ZG ZG
WHAT EXACTLY DO YOU THINK YOU'RE DOING...?
YOU'RE TRESPASSING IN OUR SECRET HEAD-QUARTERS.
DON'TCHA GET IT? THIS IS A RAID. I'M RAIDIN' THE JOINT.
I MEAN, I CAME ALL THIS WAY...
FIGURE I MIGHT AS WELL CLEAN UP THIS NEST O' PARASITES WHILE I'M HERE.
AND YOU'RE PUBLIC ENEMY NUMBER ONE, TSUBAKI!
...
A RAID?!! ARE YOU OUT OF YOUR MIND?!!
DON'T TELL ME THIS IS ALL BECAUSE OF THAT STUPID GIRL!!
HEH. IT'S EVERY MAN'S DREAM TO FIGHT FOR A GAL, AIN'T IT?
AND I'VE GOT A DEBT TO PAY SAN.
A HUGE DEBT.
S SS S H HH
WK
...DM

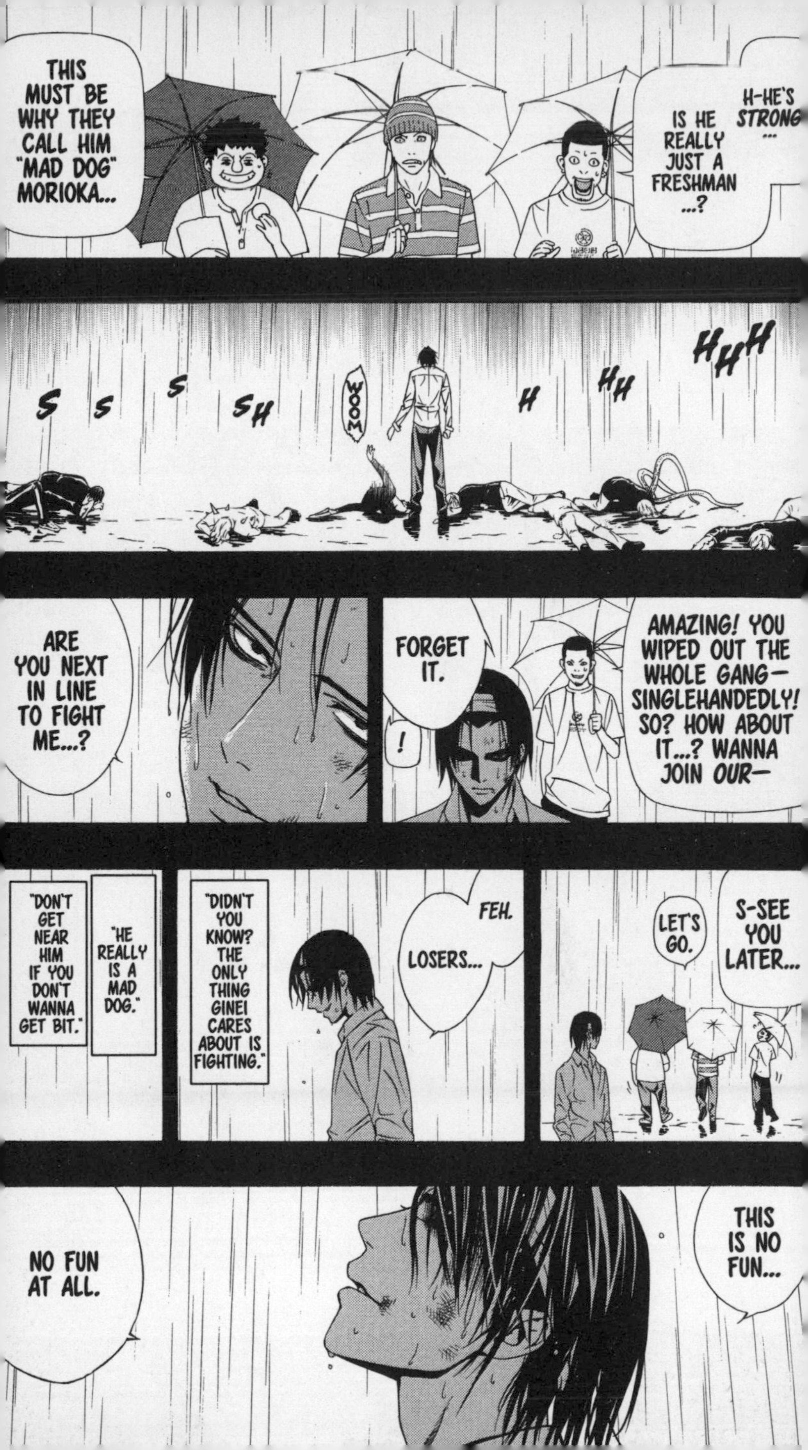
H-HE'S STRONG...
IS HE REALLY JUST A FRESHMAN...?
THIS MUST BE WHY THEY CALL HIM "MAD DOG" MORIOKA...
HHH
HH
H
WOOM
SH
S
S
S
AMAZING! YOU WIPED OUT THE WHOLE GANG— SINGLEHANDEDLY! SO? HOW ABOUT IT...? WANNA JOIN OUR—
FORGET IT.
!
ARE YOU NEXT IN LINE TO FIGHT ME...?
S-SEE YOU LATER...
LET'S GO.
FEH.
LOSERS...
"DIDN'T YOU KNOW? THE ONLY THING GINEI CARES ABOUT IS FIGHTING."
"HE REALLY IS A MAD DOG."
"DON'T GET NEAR HIM IF YOU DON'T WANNA GET BIT."
THIS IS NO FUN...
NO FUN AT ALL.

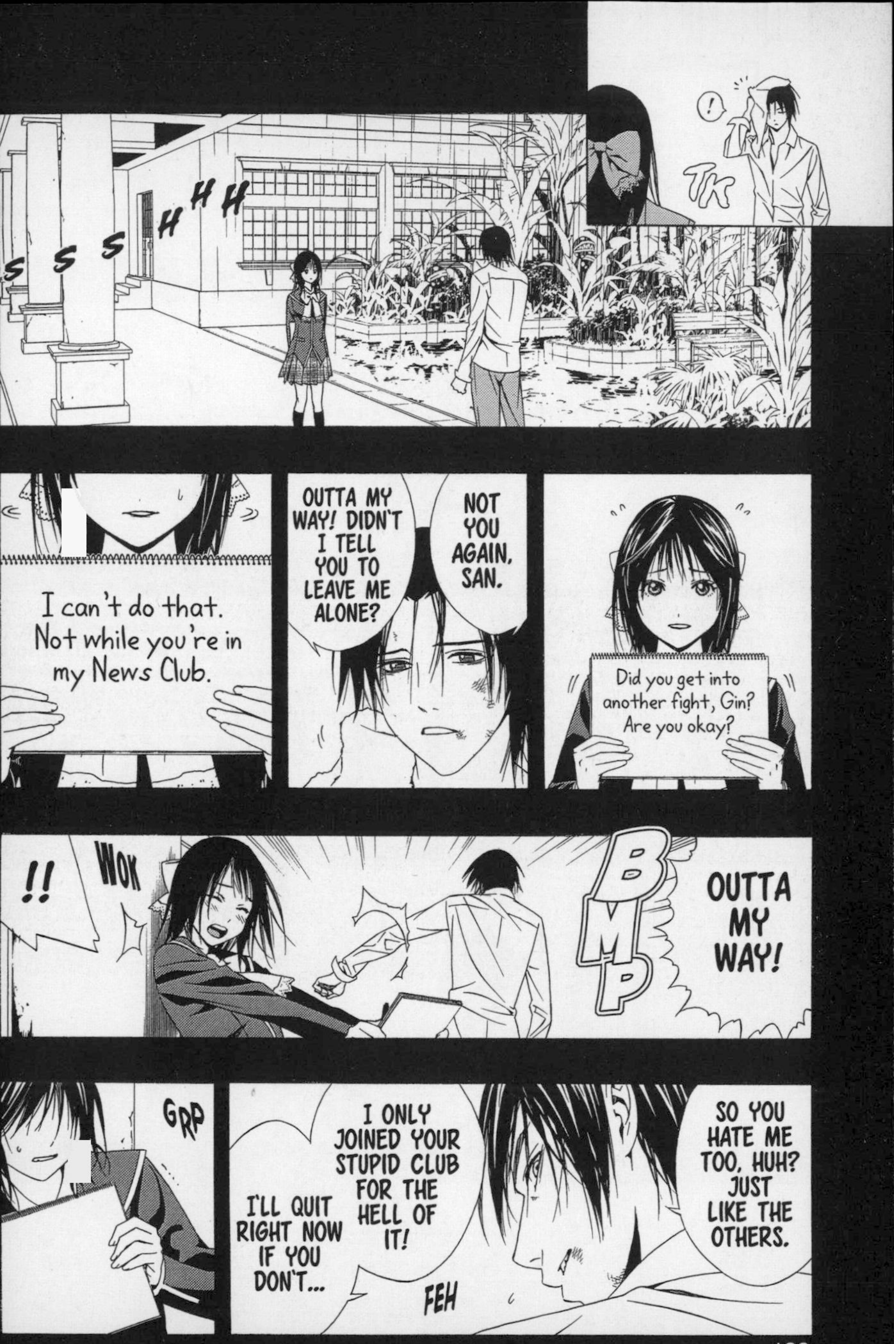
!
TK
SSSHHHH
Did you get into another fight, Gin? Are you okay?
NOT YOU AGAIN, SAN.
OUTTA MY WAY! DIDN'T I TELL YOU TO LEAVE ME ALONE?
I can't do that. Not while you're in my News Club.
OUTTA MY WAY!
BMP
WOK
!!
SO YOU HATE ME TOO, HUH? JUST LIKE THE OTHERS.
I ONLY JOINED YOUR STUPID CLUB FOR THE HELL OF IT!
I'LL QUIT RIGHT NOW IF YOU DON'T...
FEH
GRP

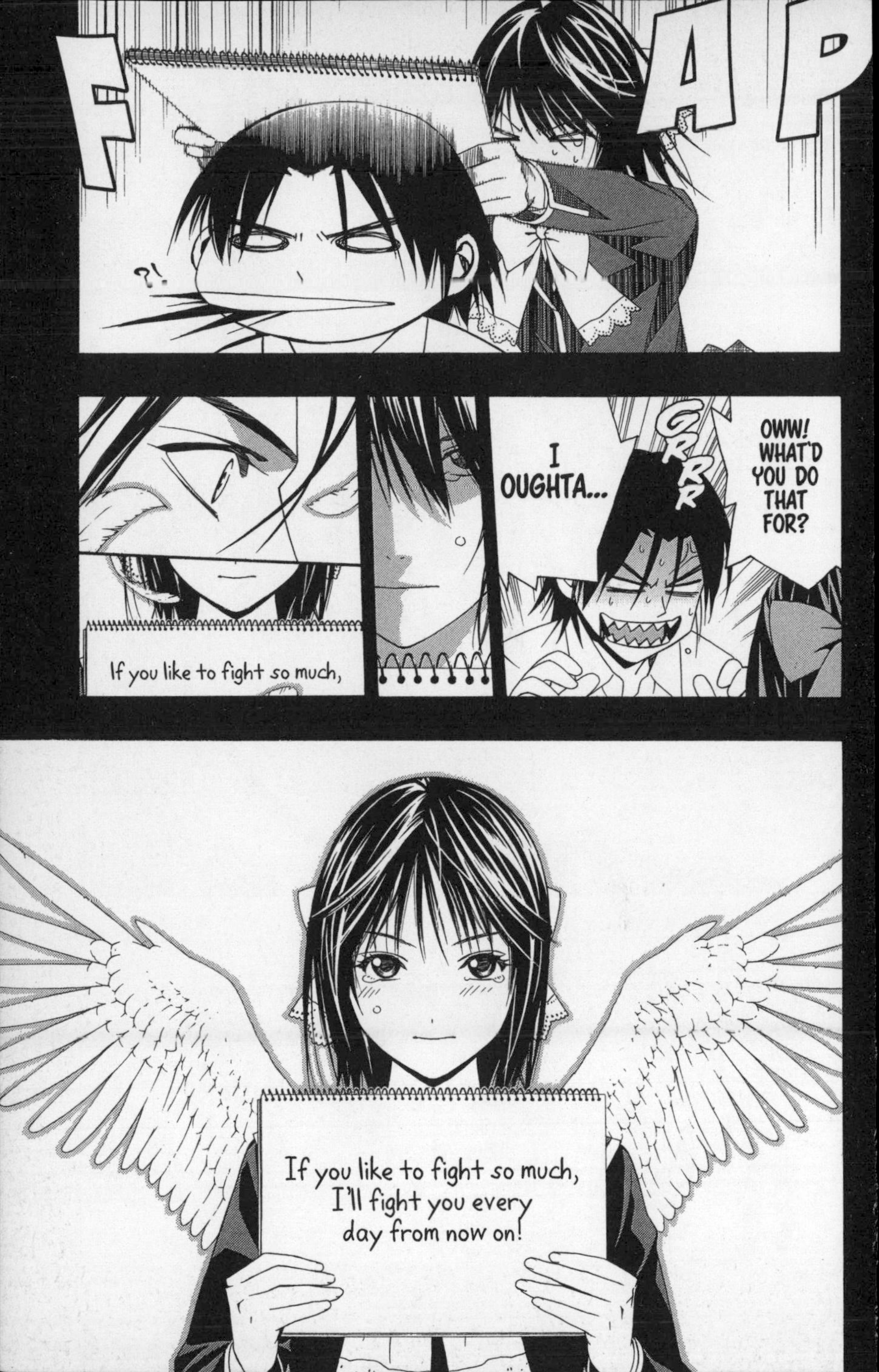
AP
F
?!
OWW! WHAT'D YOU DO THAT FOR?
GRRR
I OUGHTA...
If you like to fight so much,
If you like to fight so much, I'll fight you every day from now on!

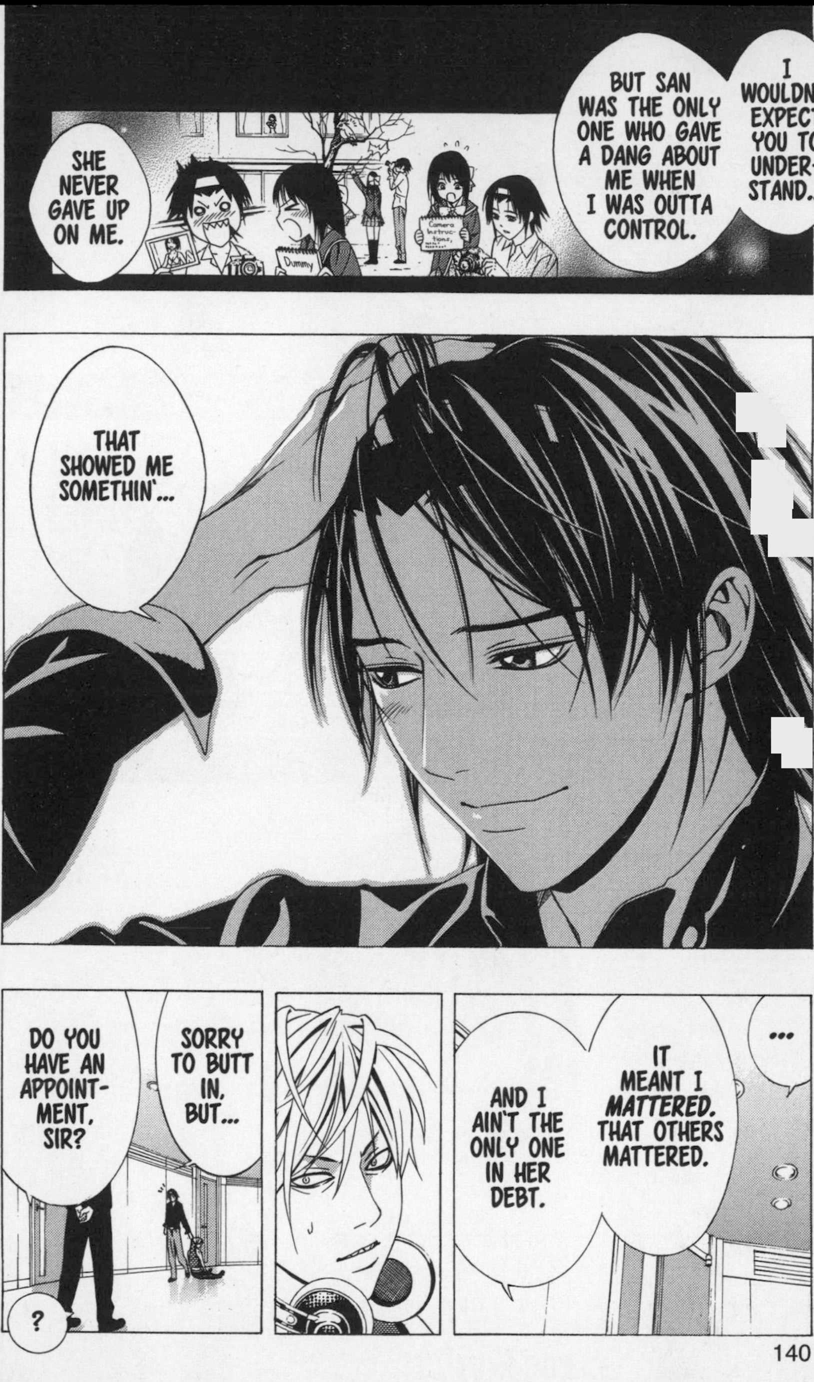
I WOULDN'T EXPECT YOU TO UNDERSTAND...
BUT SAN WAS THE ONLY ONE WHO GAVE A DANG ABOUT ME WHEN I WAS OUTTA CONTROL.
Camera Instructions,
Dummy
SHE NEVER GAVE UP ON ME.
THAT SHOWED ME SOMETHIN'...
...
IT MEANT I *MATTERED*. THAT OTHERS MATTERED.
AND I AIN'T THE ONLY ONE IN HER DEBT.
SORRY TO BUTT IN, BUT...
DO YOU HAVE AN APPOINTMENT, SIR?
?

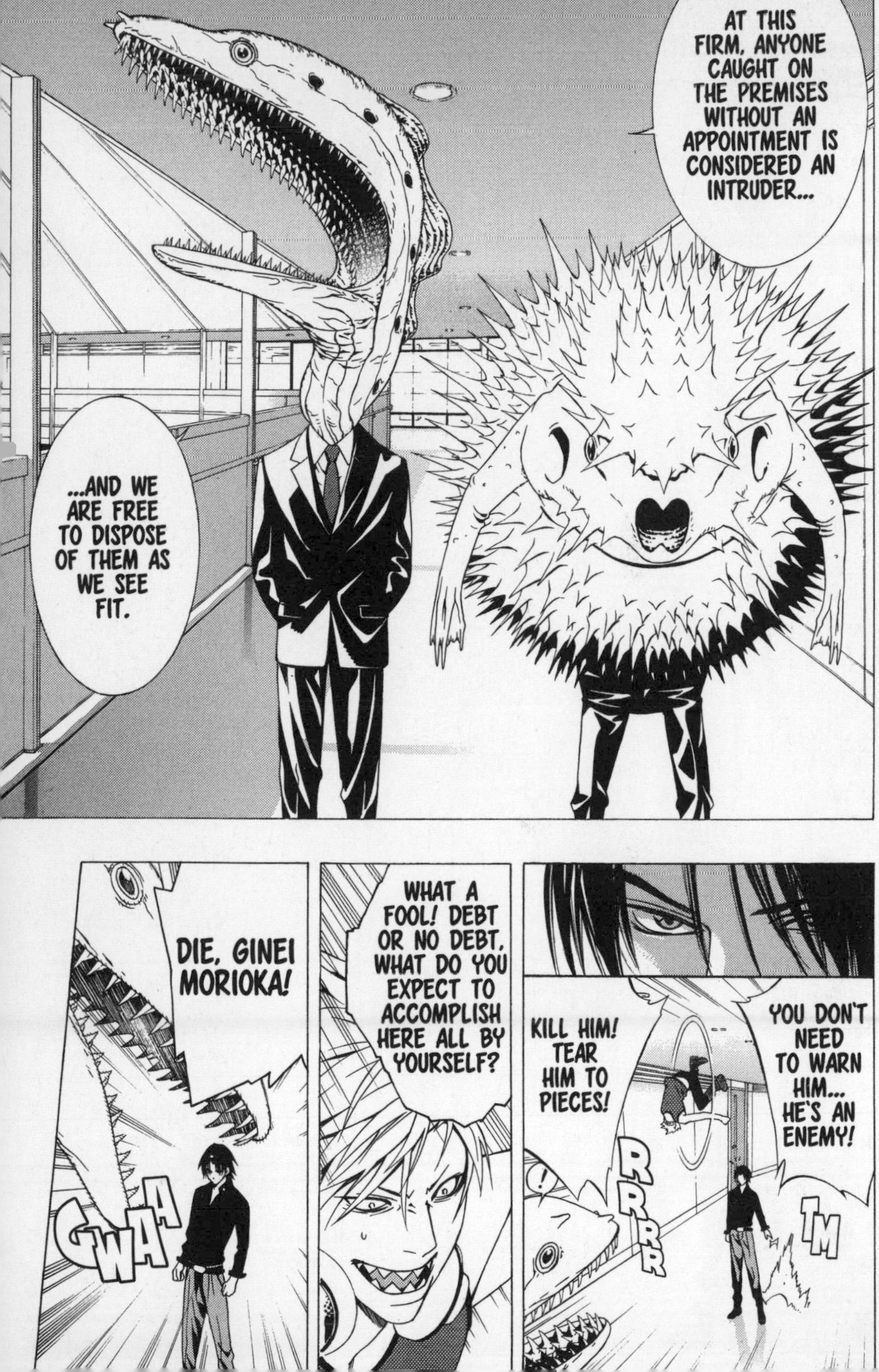
AT THIS FIRM, ANYONE CAUGHT ON THE PREMISES WITHOUT AN APPOINTMENT IS CONSIDERED AN INTRUDER...
...AND WE ARE FREE TO DISPOSE OF THEM AS WE SEE FIT.
YOU DON'T NEED TO WARN HIM... HE'S AN ENEMY!
KILL HIM! TEAR HIM TO PIECES!
!
RRRR
TM
WHAT A FOOL! DEBT OR NO DEBT, WHAT DO YOU EXPECT TO ACCOMPLISH HERE ALL BY YOURSELF?
DIE, GINEI MORIOKA!
GWAAA

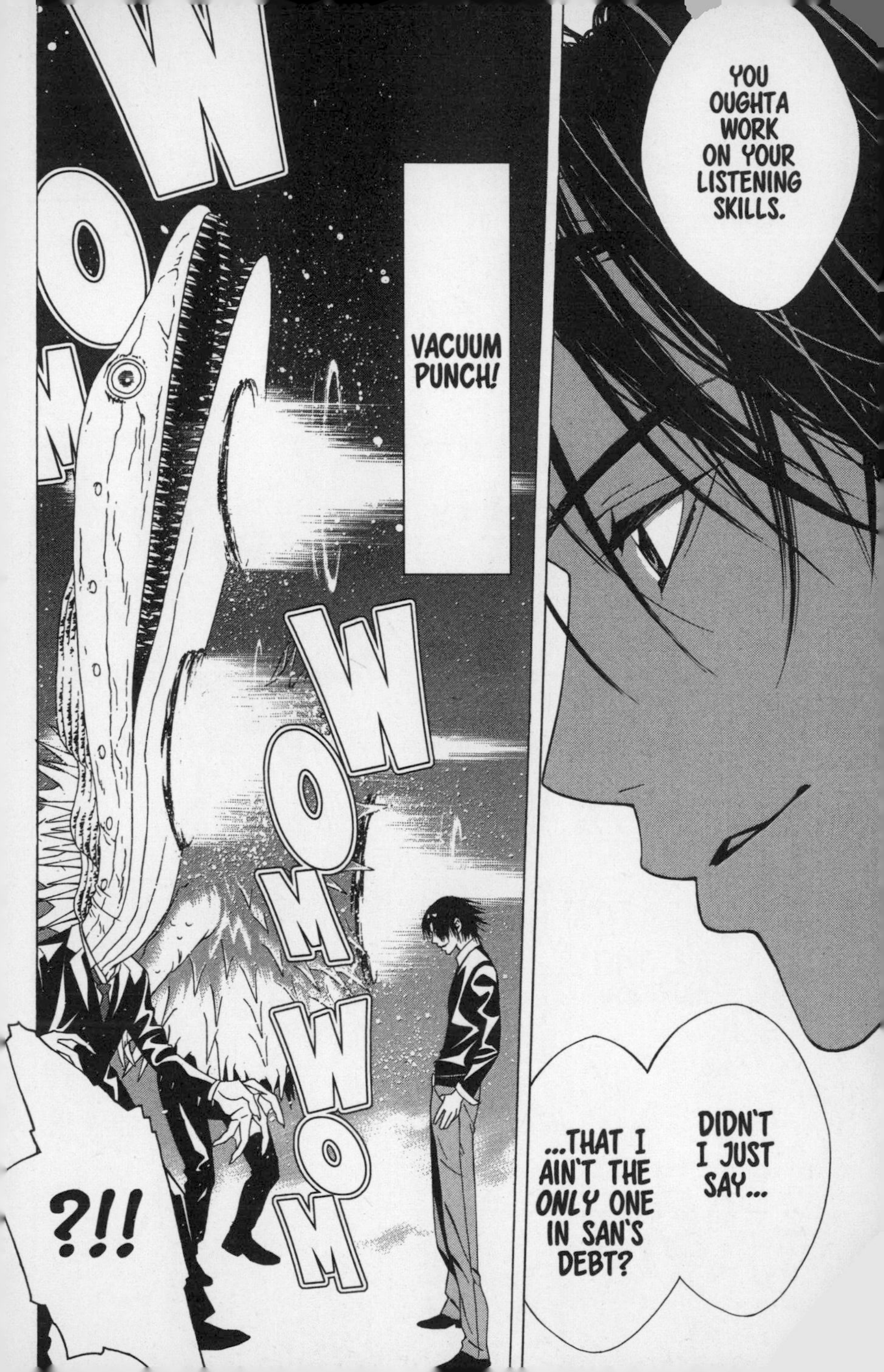
YOU OUGHTA WORK ON YOUR LISTENING SKILLS.
DIDN'T I JUST SAY...
...THAT I AIN'T THE ONLY ONE IN SAN'S DEBT?
VACUUM PUNCH!
WOM
WOMWOM
?!!

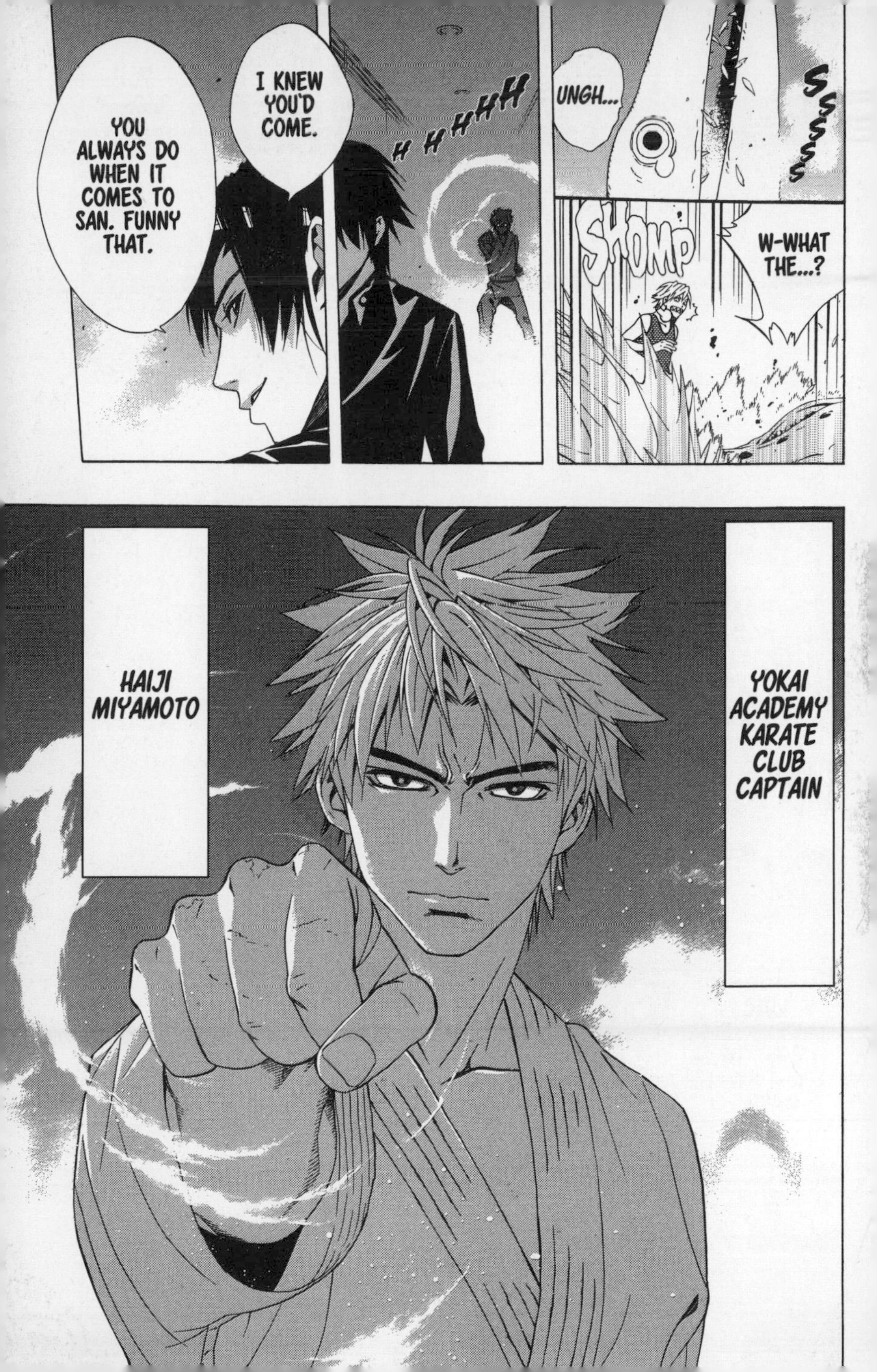
SSSSSS
UNGH...
SHOMP
W-WHAT THE...?
I KNEW YOU'D COME.
HHHHHH
YOU ALWAYS DO WHEN IT COMES TO SAN. FUNNY THAT.
YOKAI ACADEMY KARATE CLUB CAPTAIN
HAIJI MIYAMOTO

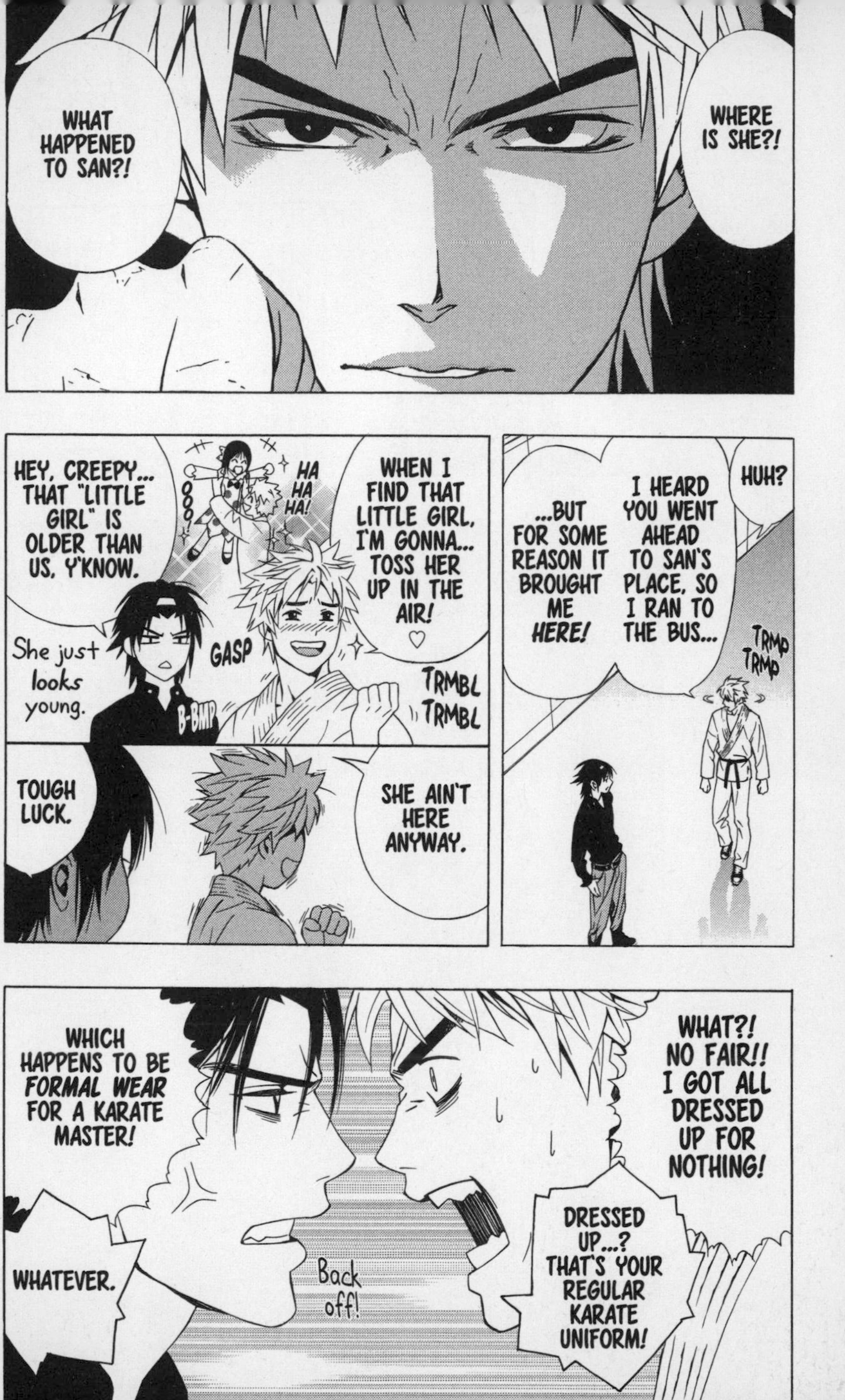
WHERE IS SHE?!
WHAT HAPPENED TO SAN?!
HUH?
I HEARD YOU WENT AHEAD TO SAN'S PLACE, SO I RAN TO THE BUS...
...BUT FOR SOME REASON IT BROUGHT ME HERE!
TRMP TRMP
WHEN I FIND THAT LITTLE GIRL, I'M GONNA... TOSS HER UP IN THE AIR! ♡
HA HA HA!
OOO!
TRMBL TRMBL
GASP
HEY, CREEPY... THAT "LITTLE GIRL" IS OLDER THAN US, Y'KNOW.
She just looks young.
B-BMP
SHE AIN'T HERE ANYWAY.
TOUGH LUCK.
WHAT?! NO FAIR!! I GOT ALL DRESSED UP FOR NOTHING!
DRESSED UP...? THAT'S YOUR REGULAR KARATE UNIFORM!
WHICH HAPPENS TO BE FORMAL WEAR FOR A KARATE MASTER!
Back off!
WHATEVER.

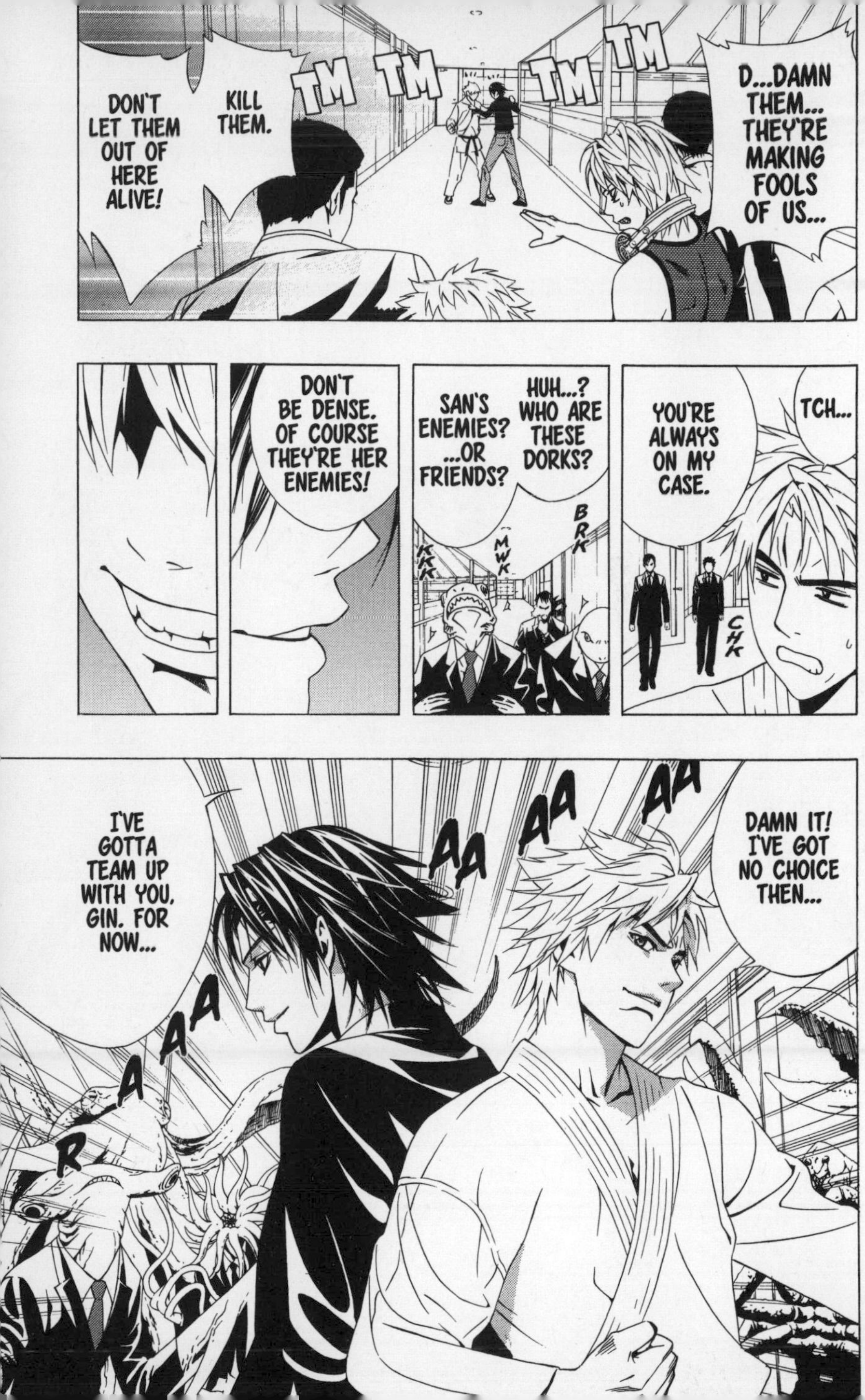
D...DAMN THEM... THEY'RE MAKING FOOLS OF US...
TM TM
TM TM
KILL THEM.
DON'T LET THEM OUT OF HERE ALIVE!
TCH...
YOU'RE ALWAYS ON MY CASE.
CHK
HUH...? WHO ARE THESE DORKS?
SAN'S ENEMIES? ...OR FRIENDS?
BRK
MWK
KKK
DON'T BE DENSE. OF COURSE THEY'RE HER ENEMIES!
DAMN IT! I'VE GOT NO CHOICE THEN...
AA AA AA
I'VE GOTTA TEAM UP WITH YOU, GIN. FOR NOW...
AA A R

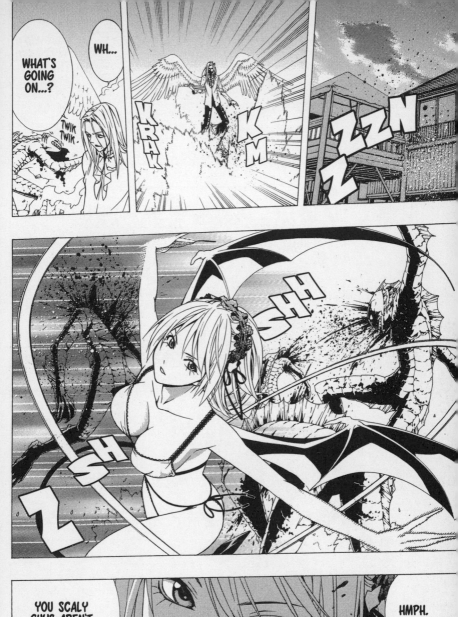

WHAT'S GOING ON...?

WH...

TWIK TWIK

KRAK

KM

ZZN

Z

SHH

ZSH

Z

YOU SCALY GUYS AREN'T AS TOUGH AS I THOUGHT.

HMPH.

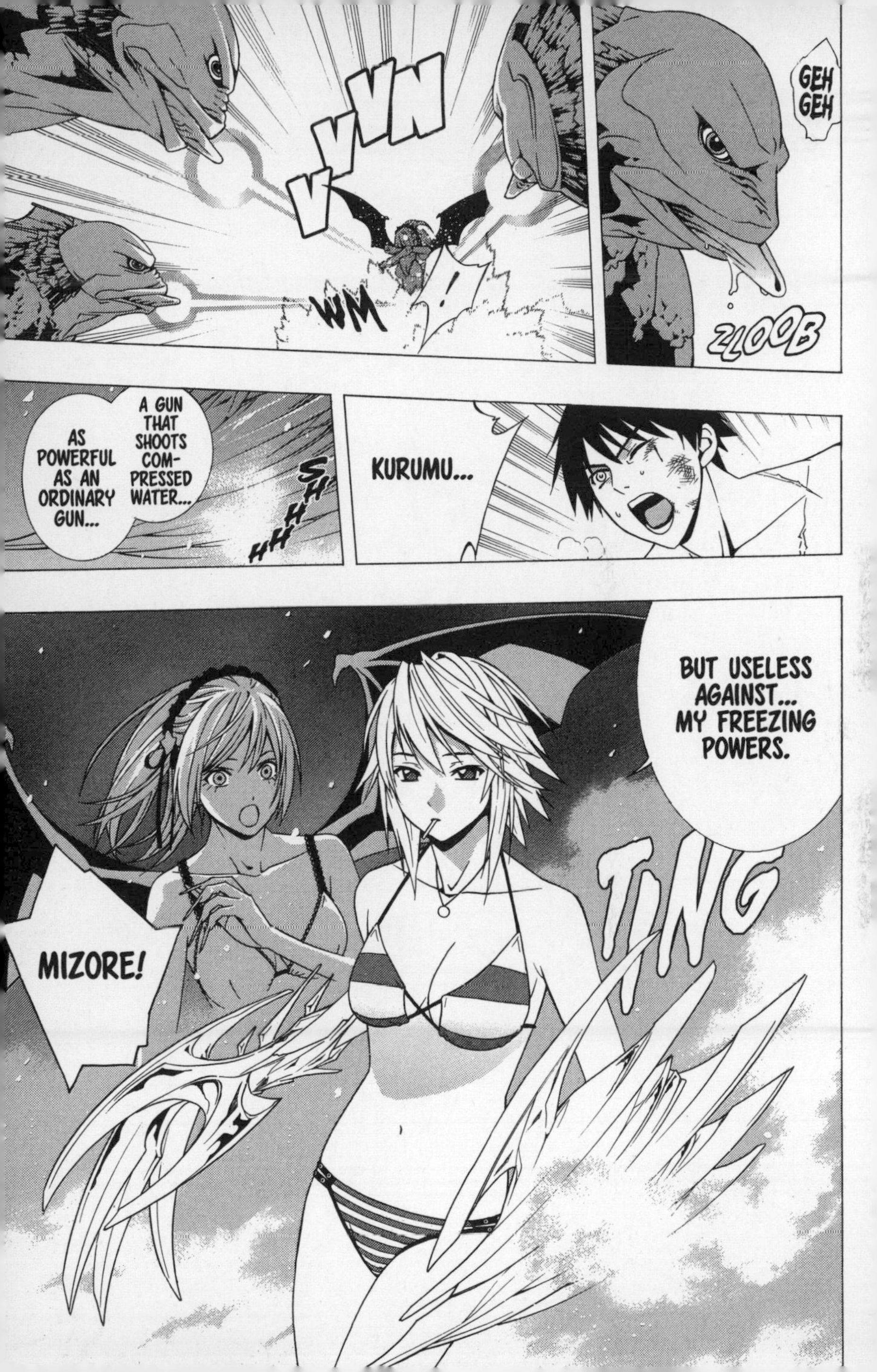
GEH GEH
ZLOOB
VVVN
!
WM
KURUMU...
A GUN THAT SHOOTS COM-PRESSED WATER...
AS POWERFUL AS AN ORDINARY GUN...
SHHHHH
BUT USELESS AGAINST... MY FREEZING POWERS.
TING
MIZORE!

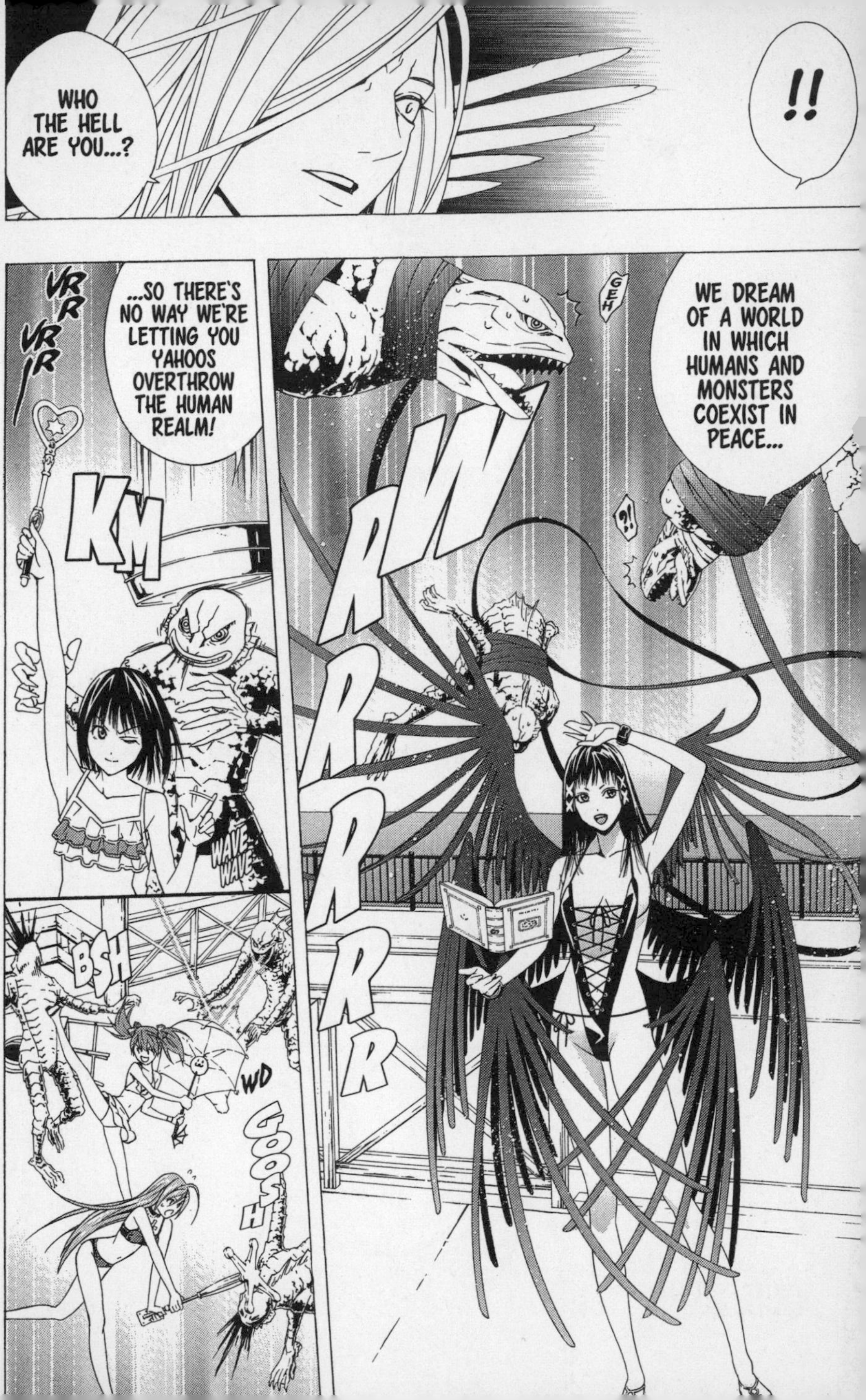
!!
WHO THE HELL ARE YOU...?
GEH
WE DREAM OF A WORLD IN WHICH HUMANS AND MONSTERS COEXIST IN PEACE...
?!
...SO THERE'S NO WAY WE'RE LETTING YOU YAHOOS OVERTHROW THE HUMAN REALM!
VRR VRR
KM
WAVE WAVE
BSH
WD
GOOSH

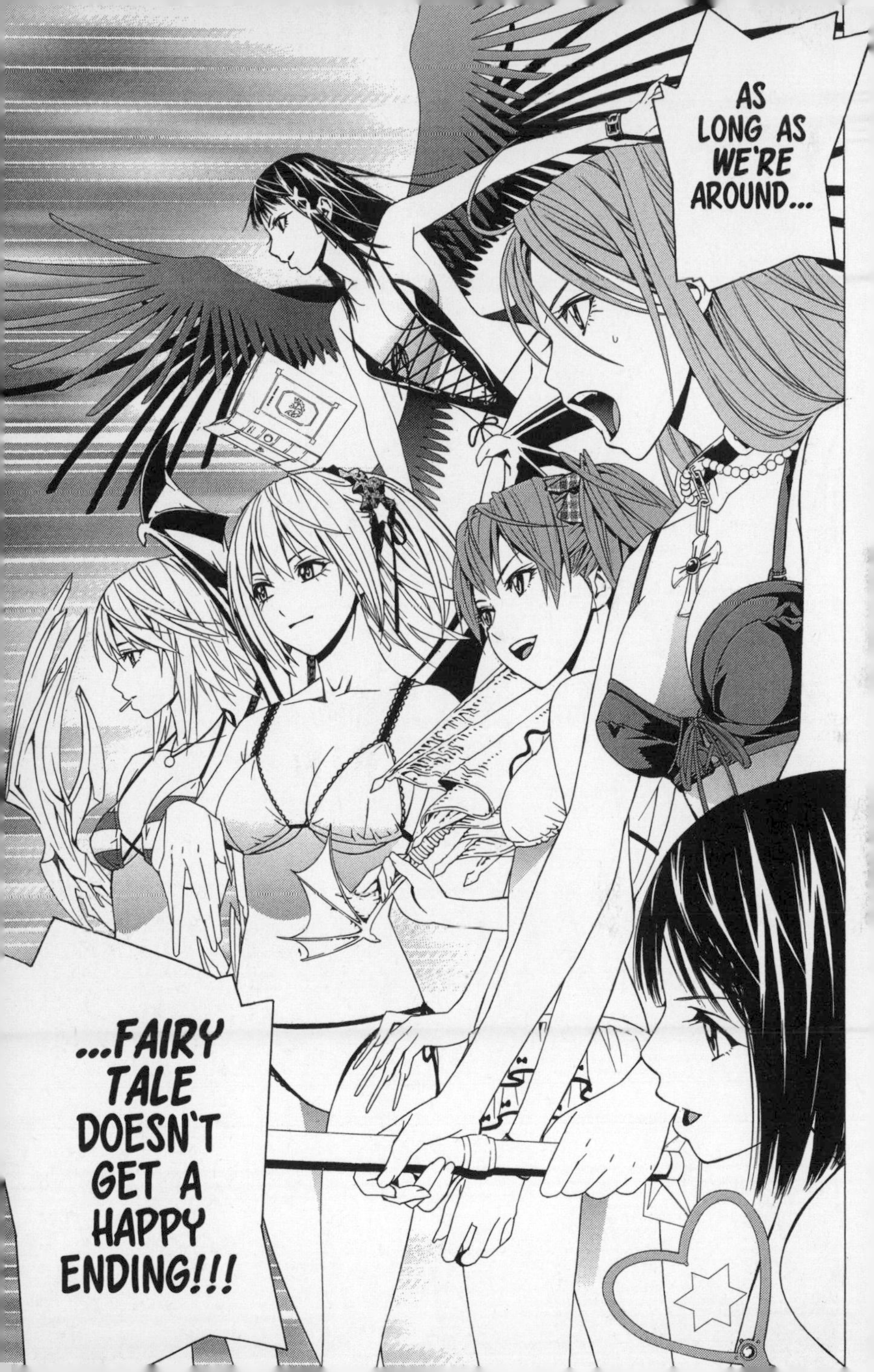
AS LONG AS WE'RE AROUND...
...FAIRY TALE DOESN'T GET A HAPPY ENDING!!!

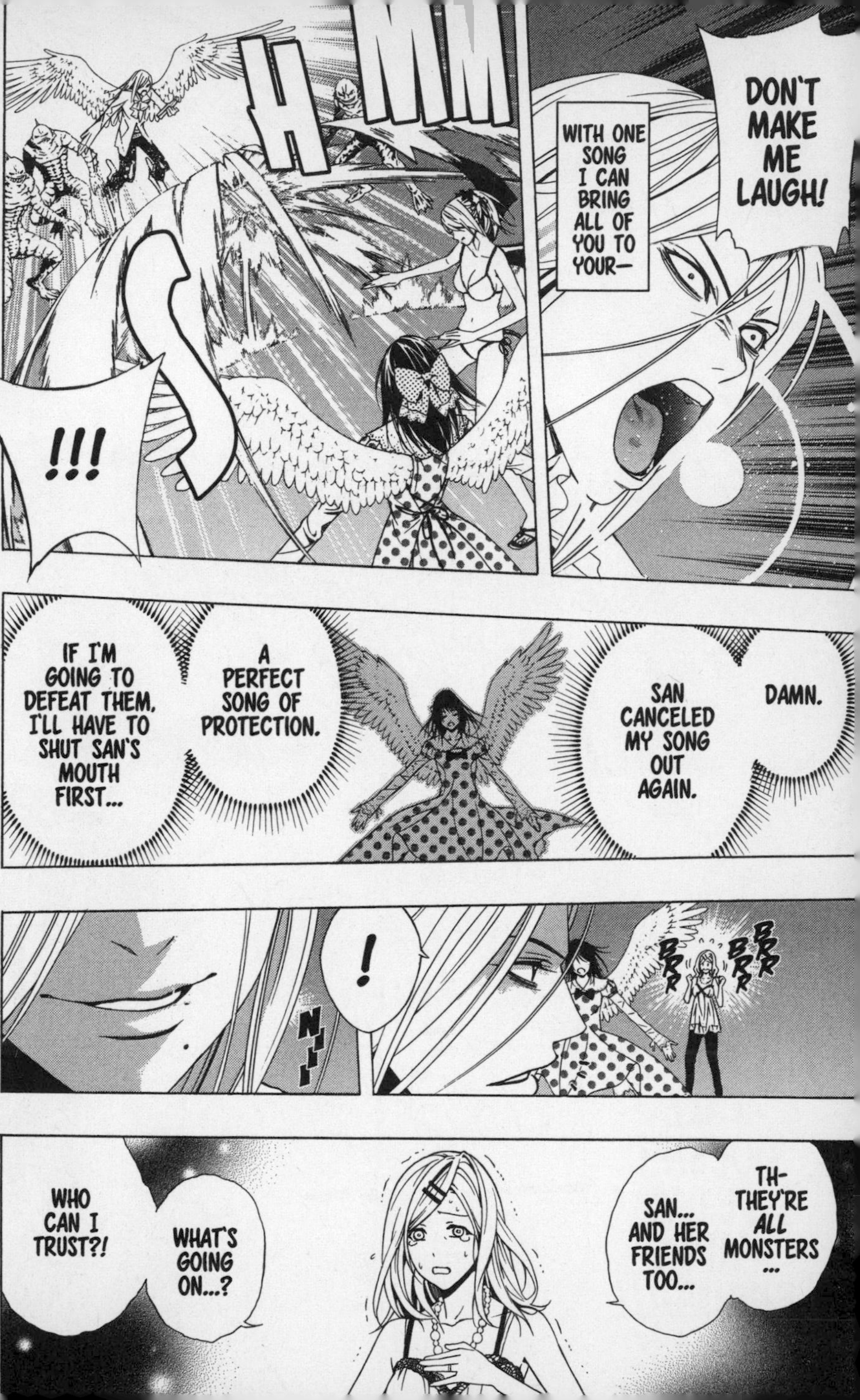
DON'T MAKE ME LAUGH!
WITH ONE SONG I CAN BRING ALL OF YOU TO YOUR—
HMM
!!!
DAMN.
SAN CANCELED MY SONG OUT AGAIN.
A PERFECT SONG OF PROTECTION.
IF I'M GOING TO DEFEAT THEM, I'LL HAVE TO SHUT SAN'S MOUTH FIRST...
BRR
BRR
BRR
!
NII
TH- THEY'RE ALL MONSTERS...
SAN... AND HER FRIENDS TOO...
WHAT'S GOING ON...?
WHO CAN I TRUST?!

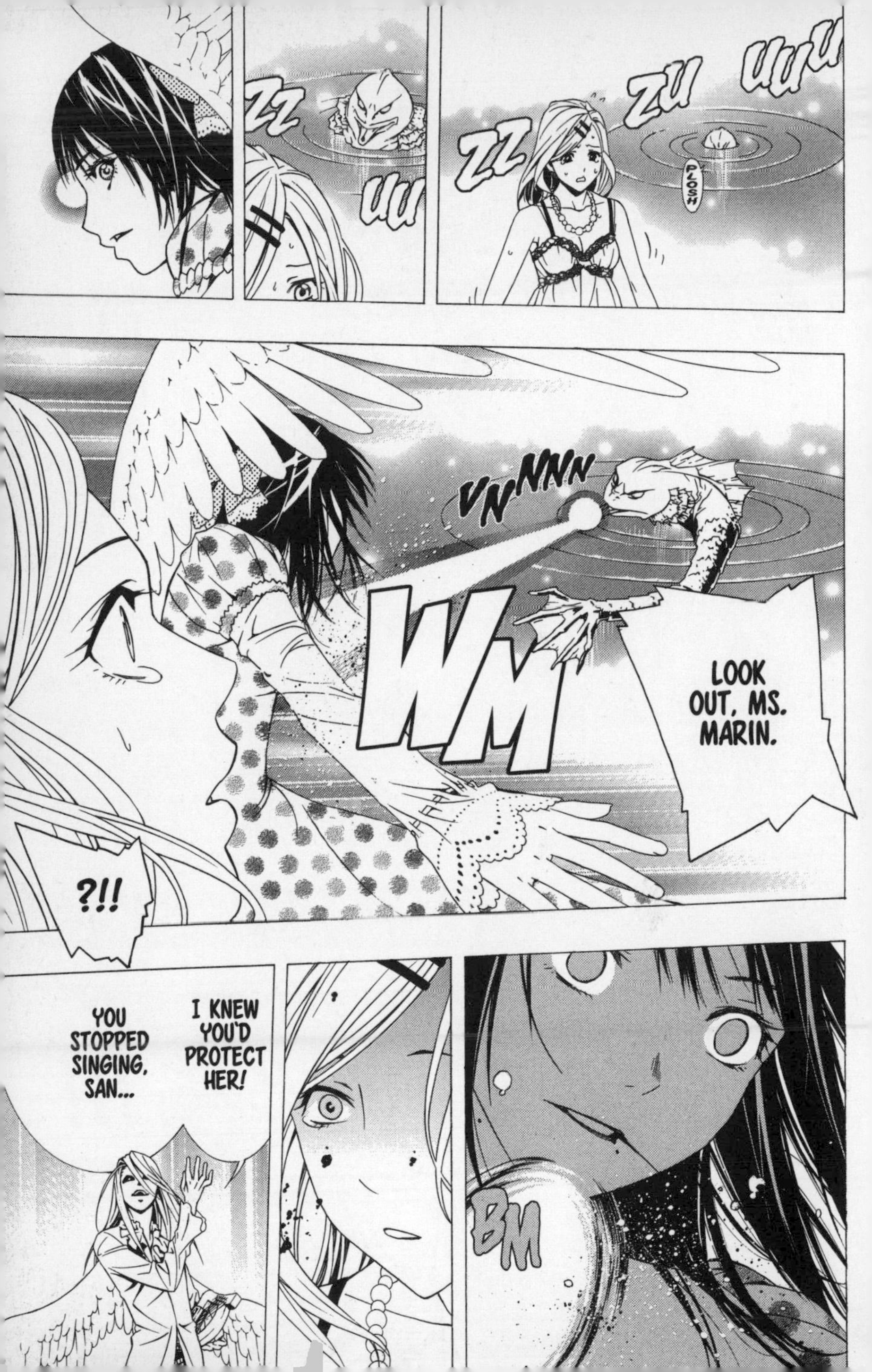
ZZ
ZU
UUUU
PLOSH
ZZ
UU
VNNNN
WM
LOOK OUT, MS. MARIN.
?!!
BM
I KNEW YOU'D PROTECT HER!
YOU STOPPED SINGING, SAN...

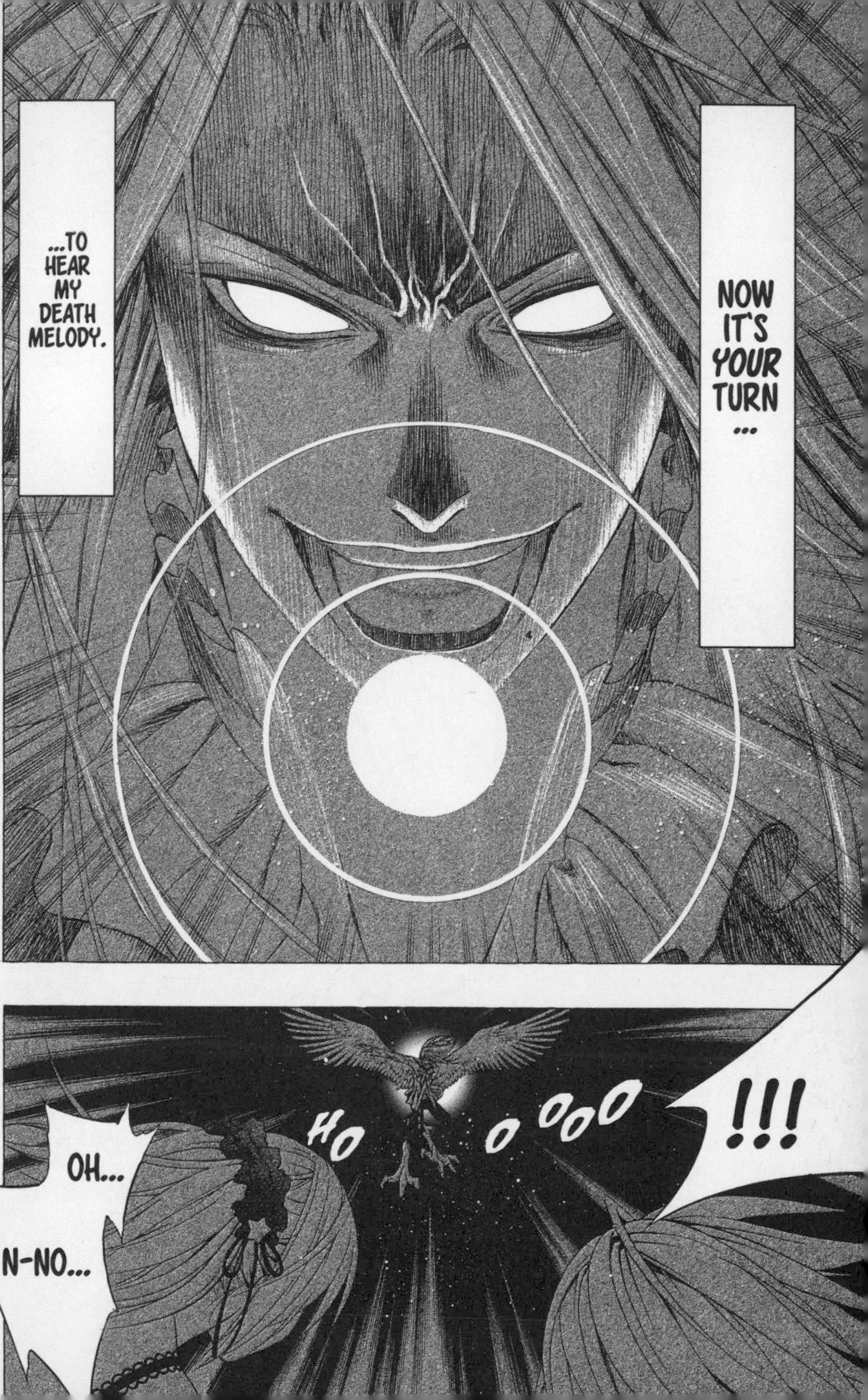
NOW IT'S YOUR TURN...
...TO HEAR MY DEATH MELODY.
!!!
HO O OOO
OH...
N-NO...

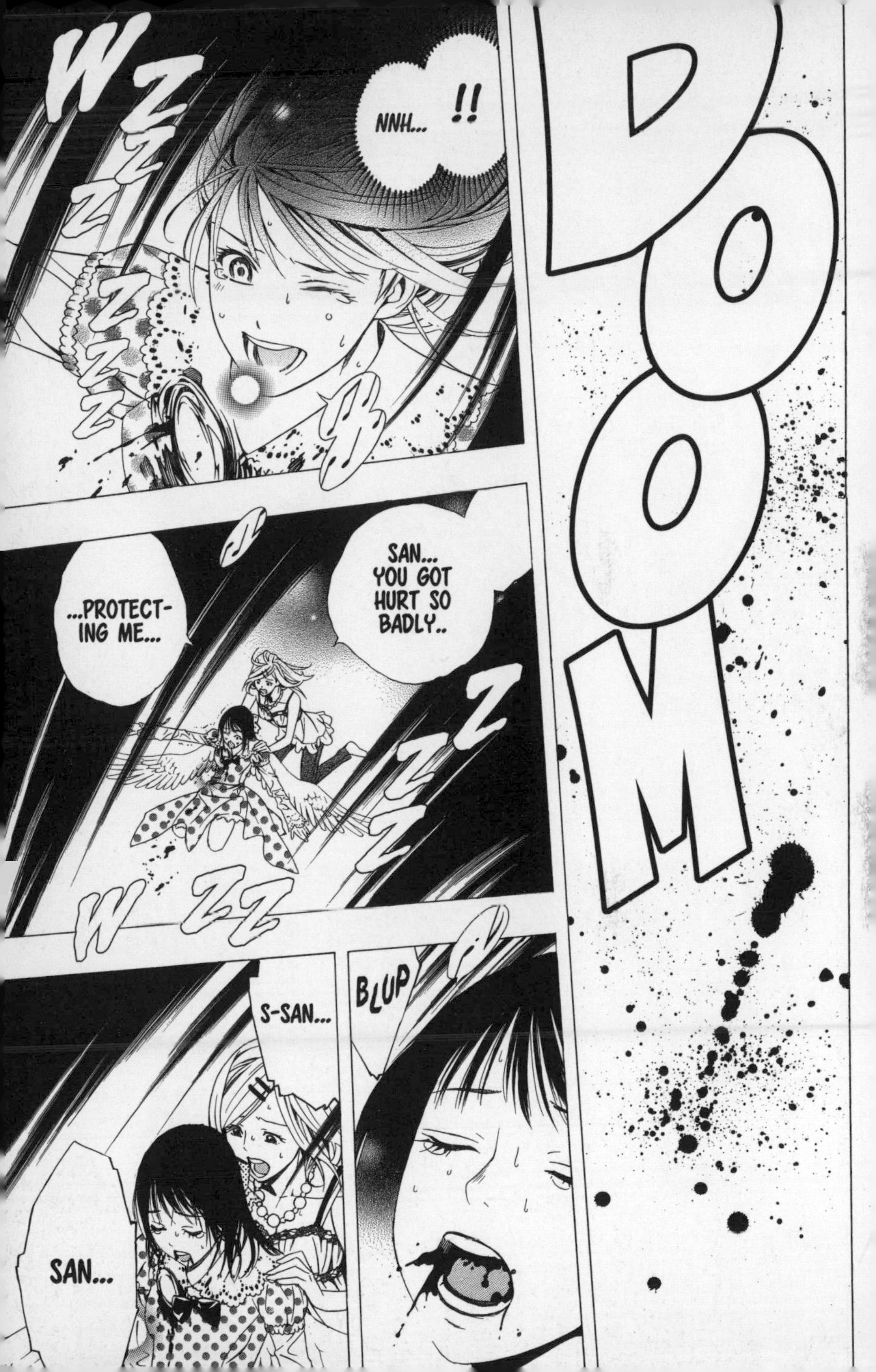
DOOM
NNH... !!
WZZZZZZZZZ
SAN... YOU GOT HURT SO BADLY..
...PROTECT-ING ME...
WZZZZZ
BLUP
S-SAN...
SAN...

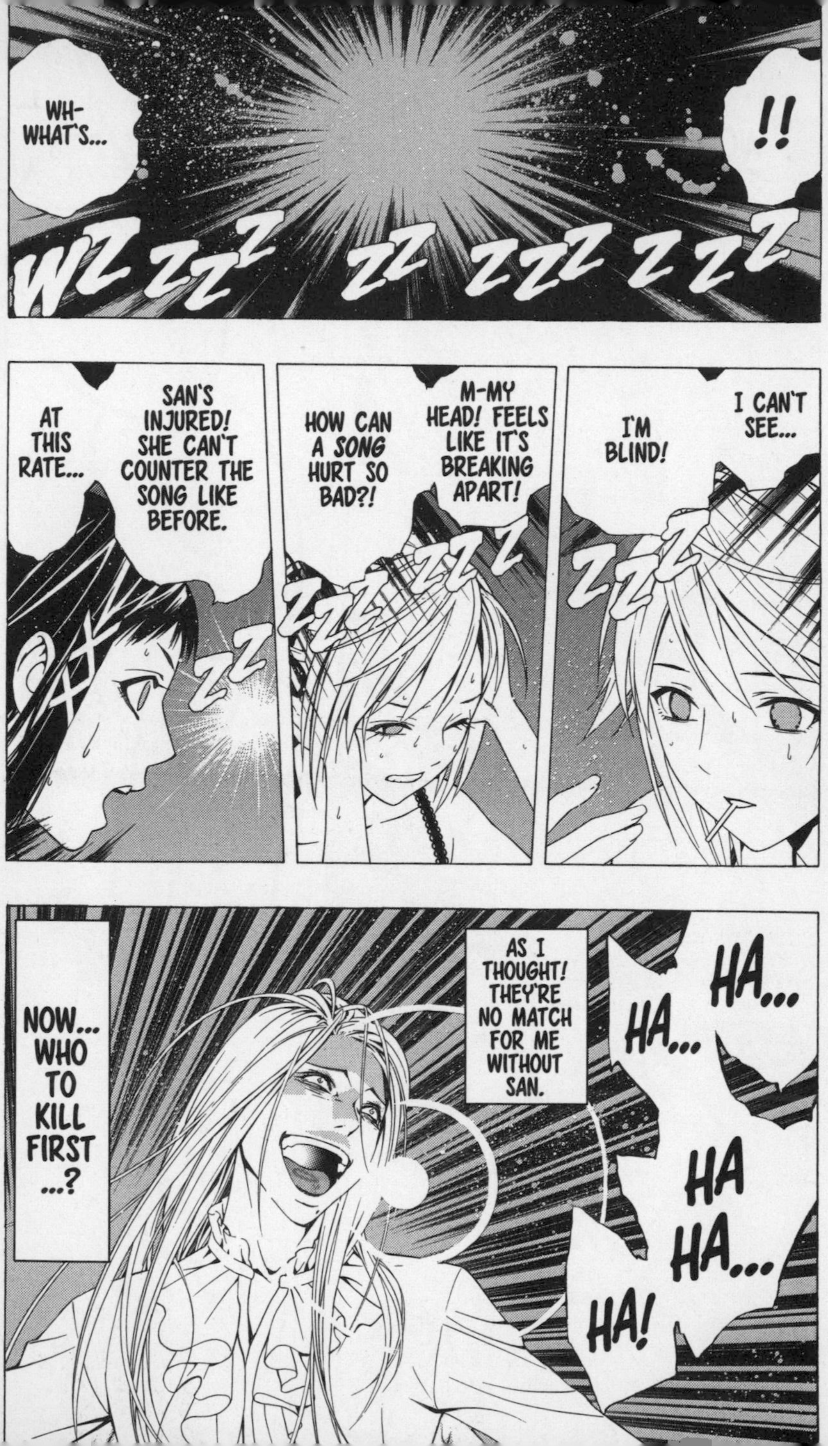
!!
WH- WHAT'S...
WZZ ZZZ ZZ ZZZZ ZZZ
I CAN'T SEE...
I'M BLIND!
ZZZ
M-MY HEAD! FEELS LIKE IT'S BREAKING APART!
HOW CAN A SONG HURT SO BAD?!
ZZZZZZZ
SAN'S INJURED! SHE CAN'T COUNTER THE SONG LIKE BEFORE.
AT THIS RATE...
ZZ
HA... HA...
HA HA... HA!
AS I THOUGHT! THEY'RE NO MATCH FOR ME WITHOUT SAN.
NOW... WHO TO KILL FIRST...?

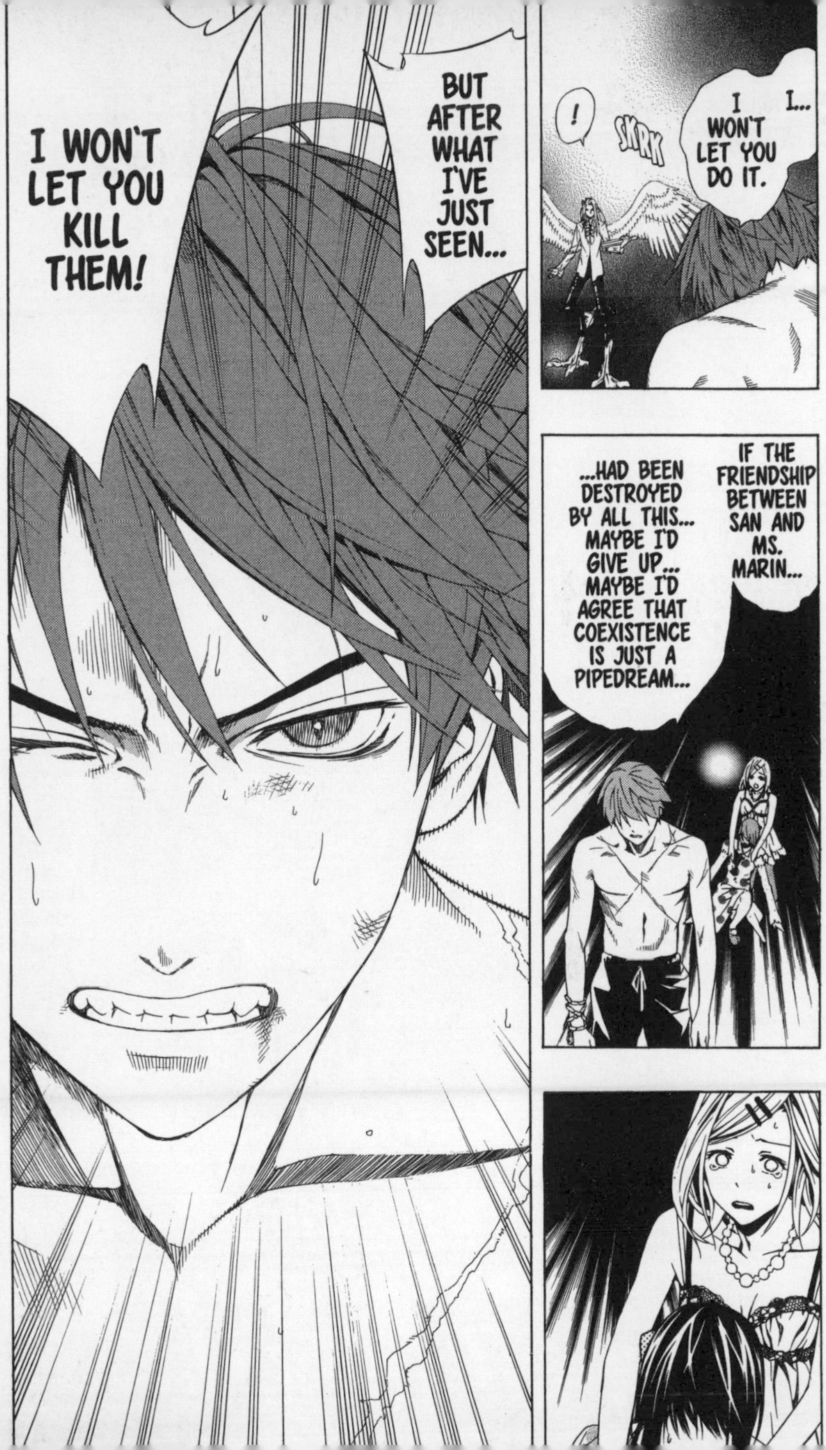
I...
I WON'T LET YOU DO IT.
!
SKRK
IF THE FRIENDSHIP BETWEEN SAN AND MS. MARIN...
...HAD BEEN DESTROYED BY ALL THIS... MAYBE I'D GIVE UP... MAYBE I'D AGREE THAT COEXISTENCE IS JUST A PIPEDREAM...
BUT AFTER WHAT I'VE JUST SEEN...
I WON'T LET YOU KILL THEM!

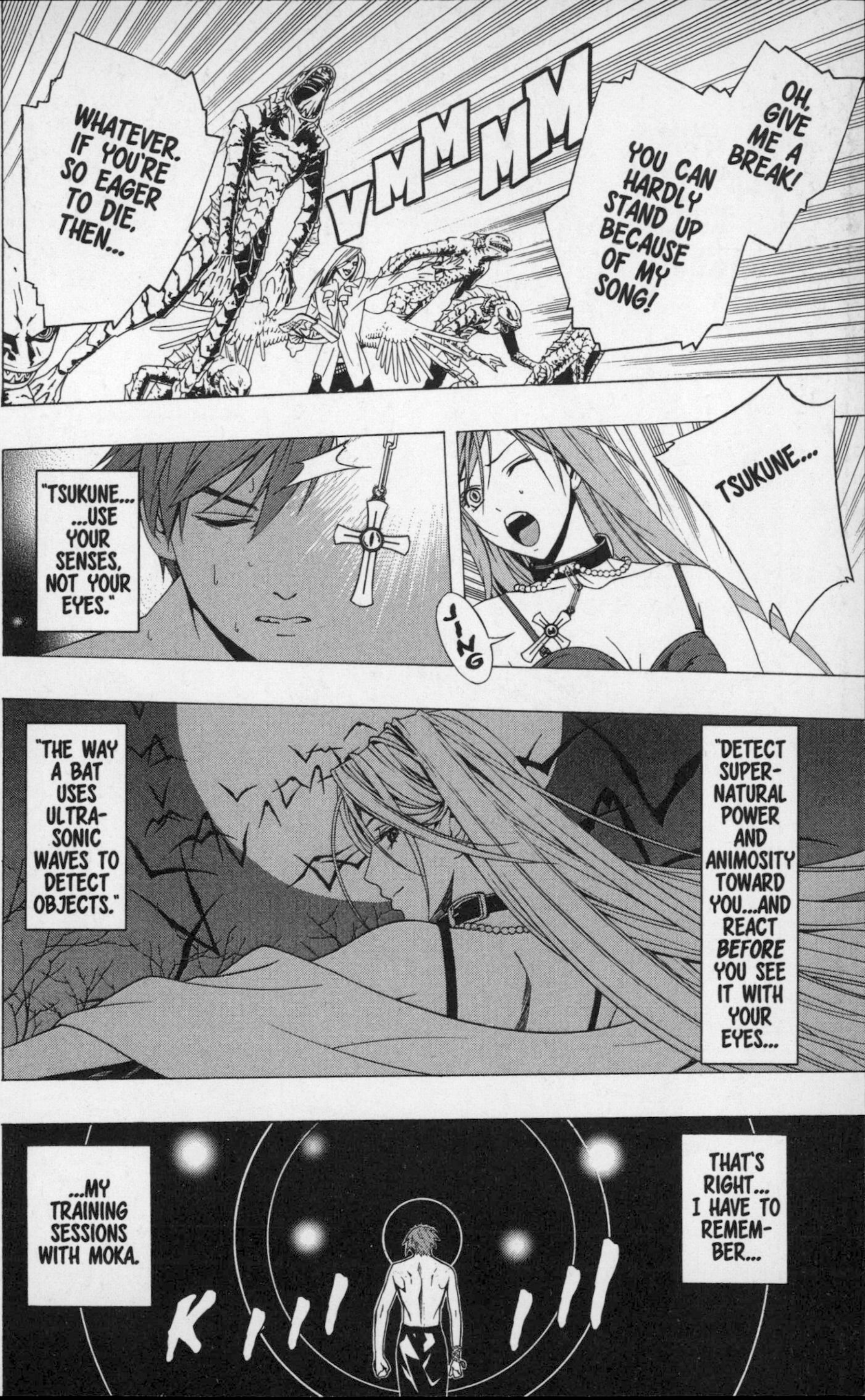
OH, GIVE ME A BREAK!
YOU CAN HARDLY STAND UP BECAUSE OF MY SONG!
VMMMMM
WHATEVER. IF YOU'RE SO EAGER TO DIE, THEN...
TSUKUNE...
JING
"TSUKUNE... ...USE YOUR SENSES, NOT YOUR EYES."
"DETECT SUPER-NATURAL POWER AND ANIMOSITY TOWARD YOU...AND REACT BEFORE YOU SEE IT WITH YOUR EYES...
"THE WAY A BAT USES ULTRA-SONIC WAVES TO DETECT OBJECTS."
THAT'S RIGHT... I HAVE TO REMEM-BER...
...MY TRAINING SESSIONS WITH MOKA.
KIIIIIII

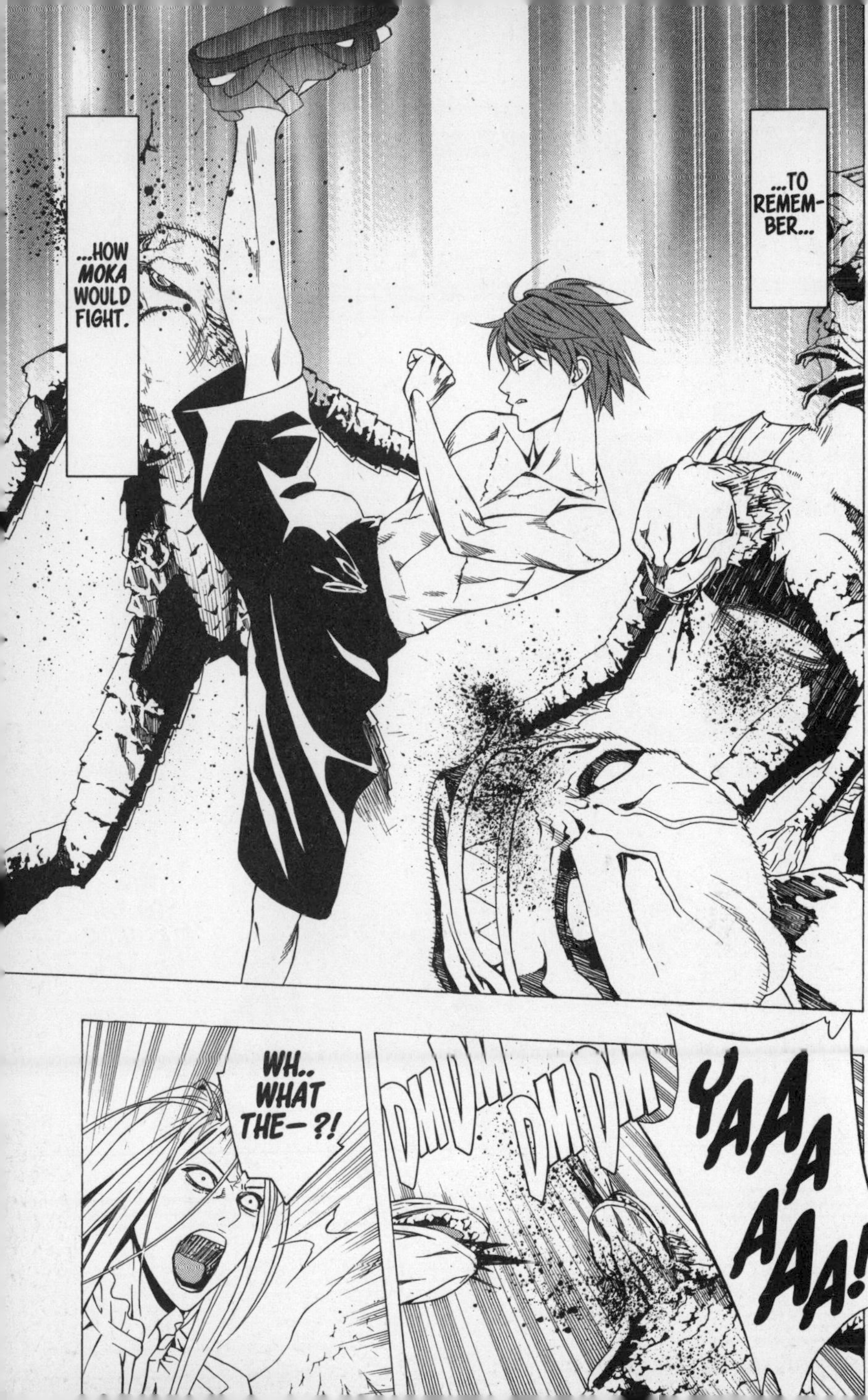
...TO REMEMBER...
...HOW MOKA WOULD FIGHT.
YAAAAAAAA!
DMDM
DMDM
WH.. WHAT THE-?!

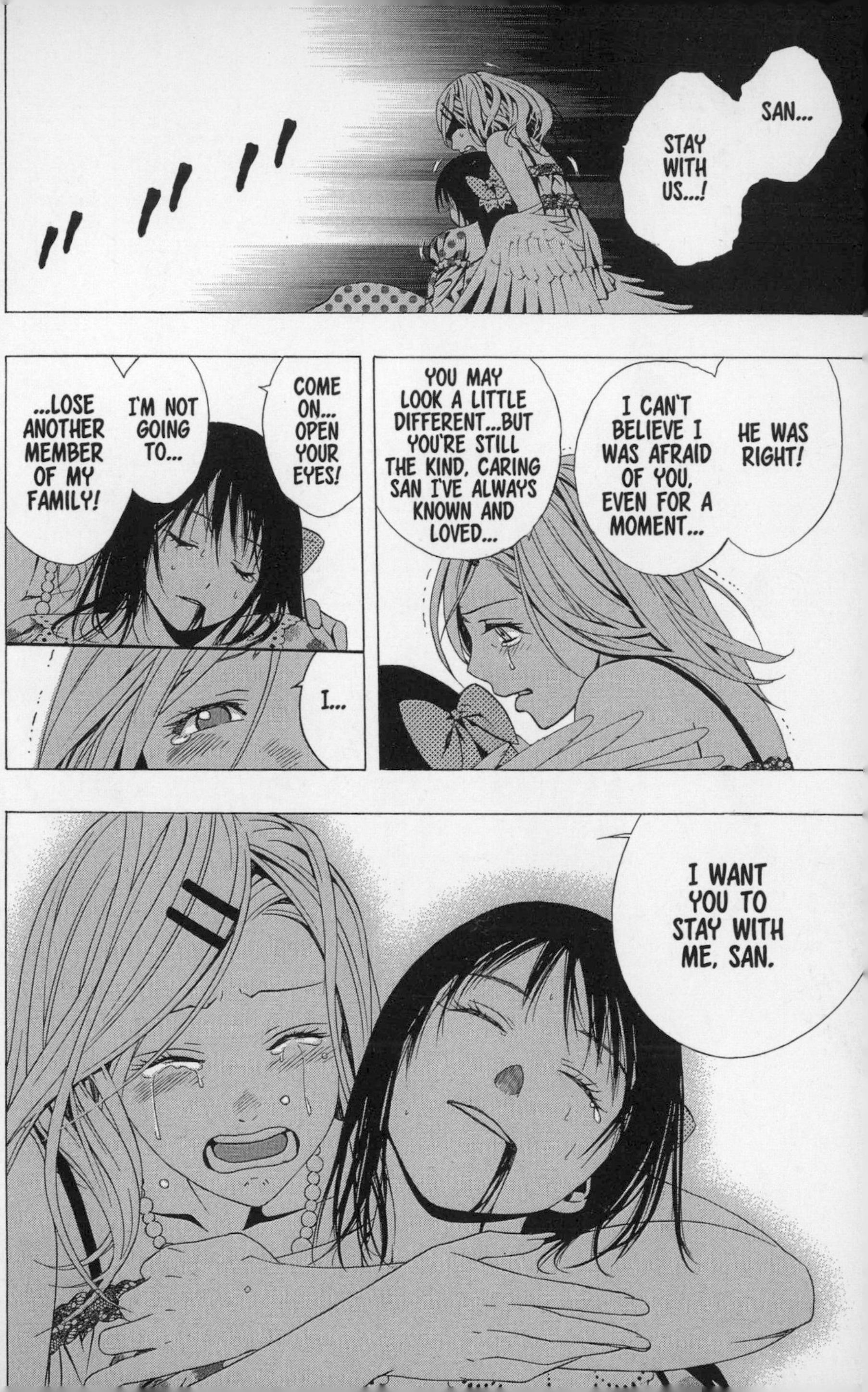
SAN...
STAY WITH US...!
HE WAS RIGHT!
I CAN'T BELIEVE I WAS AFRAID OF YOU, EVEN FOR A MOMENT...
YOU MAY LOOK A LITTLE DIFFERENT...BUT YOU'RE STILL THE KIND, CARING SAN I'VE ALWAYS KNOWN AND LOVED...
COME ON... OPEN YOUR EYES!
I'M NOT GOING TO...
...LOSE ANOTHER MEMBER OF MY FAMILY!
I...
I WANT YOU TO STAY WITH ME, SAN.

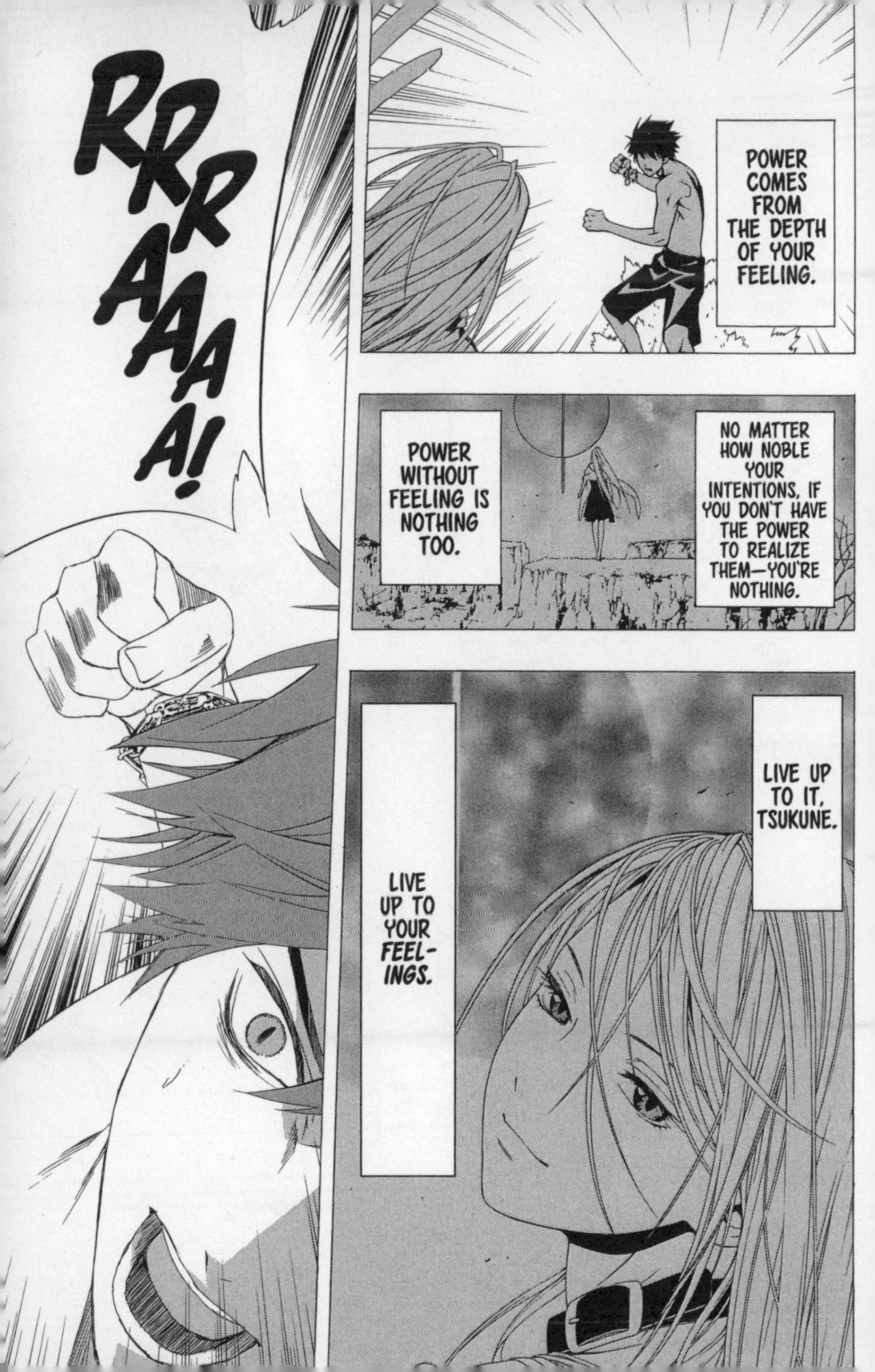
POWER COMES FROM THE DEPTH OF YOUR FEELING.
NO MATTER HOW NOBLE YOUR INTENTIONS, IF YOU DON'T HAVE THE POWER TO REALIZE THEM—YOU'RE NOTHING.
POWER WITHOUT FEELING IS NOTHING TOO.
LIVE UP TO IT, TSUKUNE.
LIVE UP TO YOUR FEEL-INGS.
RRRAAAAA!

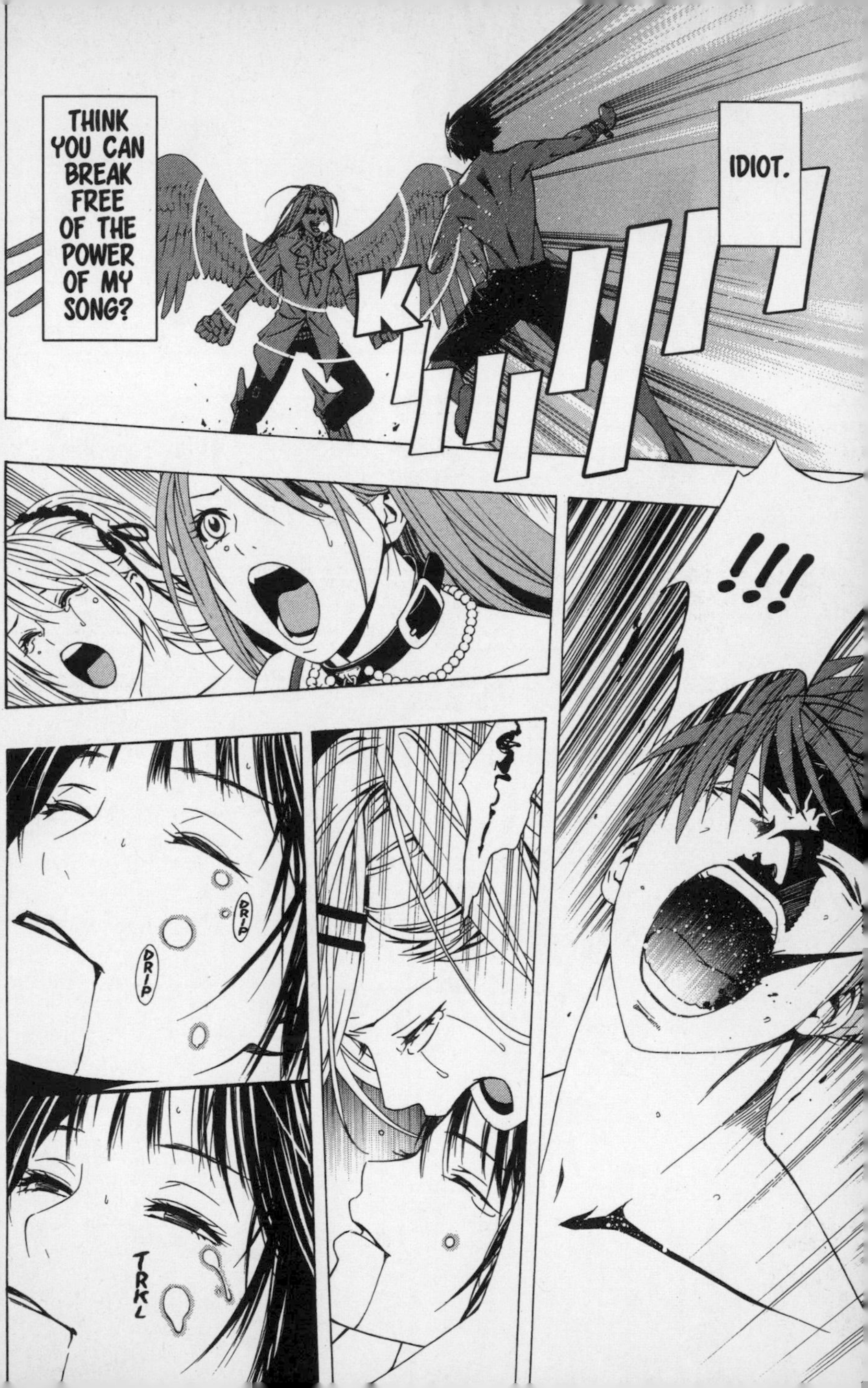
IDIOT.
KLIIIIIIII
THINK YOU CAN BREAK FREE OF THE POWER OF MY SONG?
!!!
DRIP
DRIP
TRKL

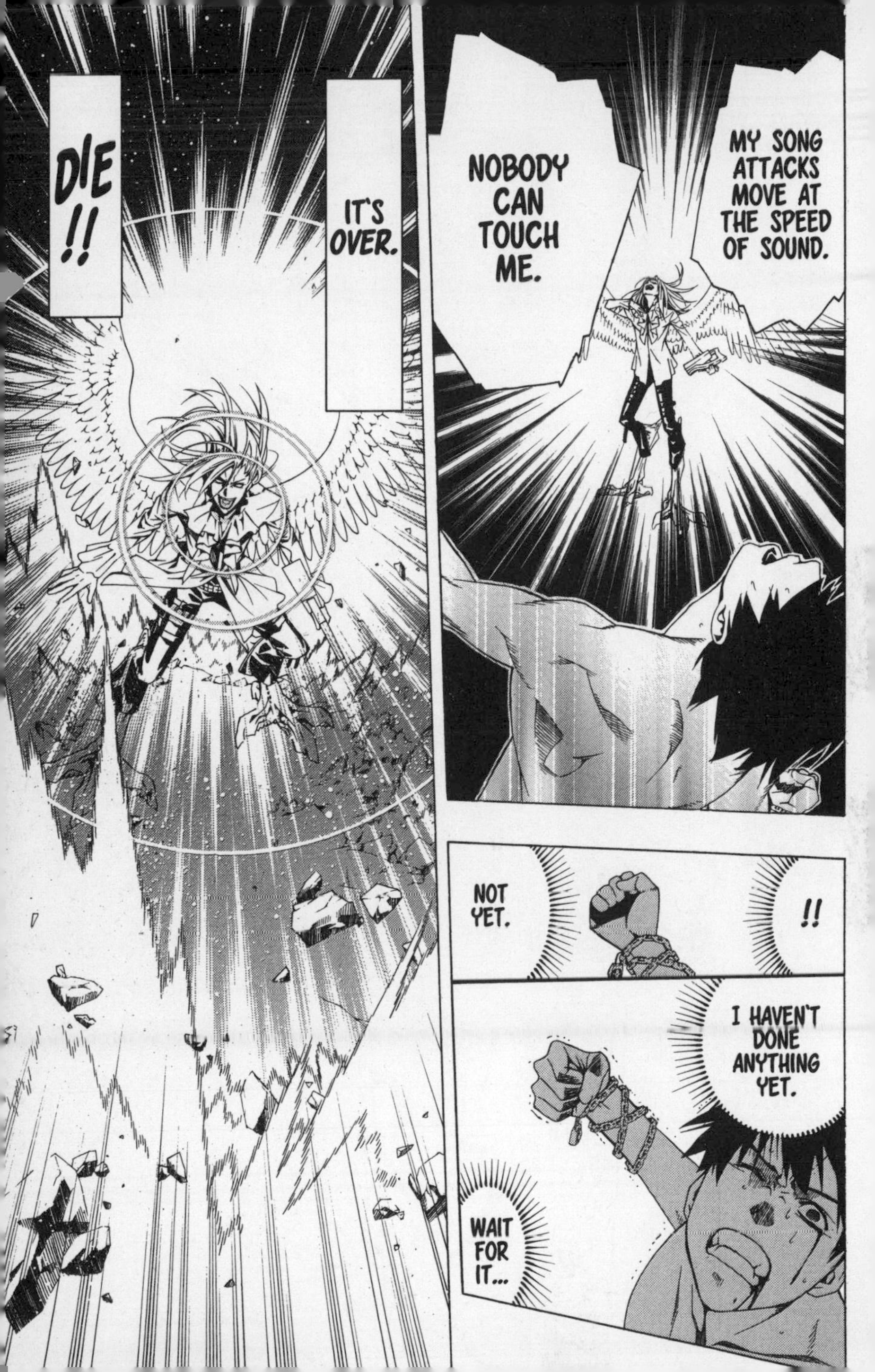
MY SONG ATTACKS MOVE AT THE SPEED OF SOUND.
NOBODY CAN TOUCH ME.
!!
NOT YET.
I HAVEN'T DONE ANYTHING YET.
WAIT FOR IT...
IT'S OVER.
DIE!!

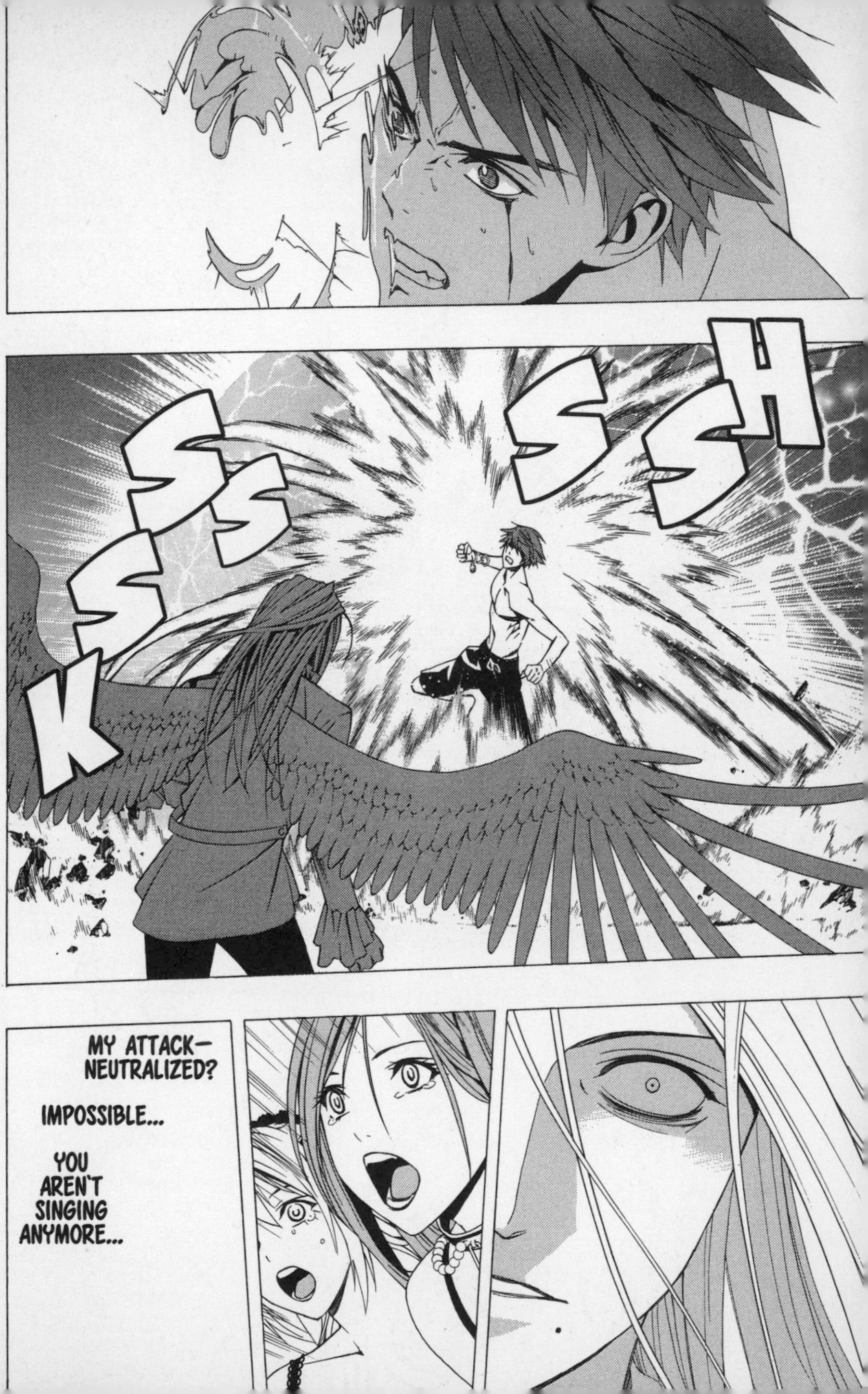
SSH
SSSK
MY ATTACK—NEUTRALIZED?
IMPOSSIBLE...
YOU AREN'T SINGING ANYMORE...

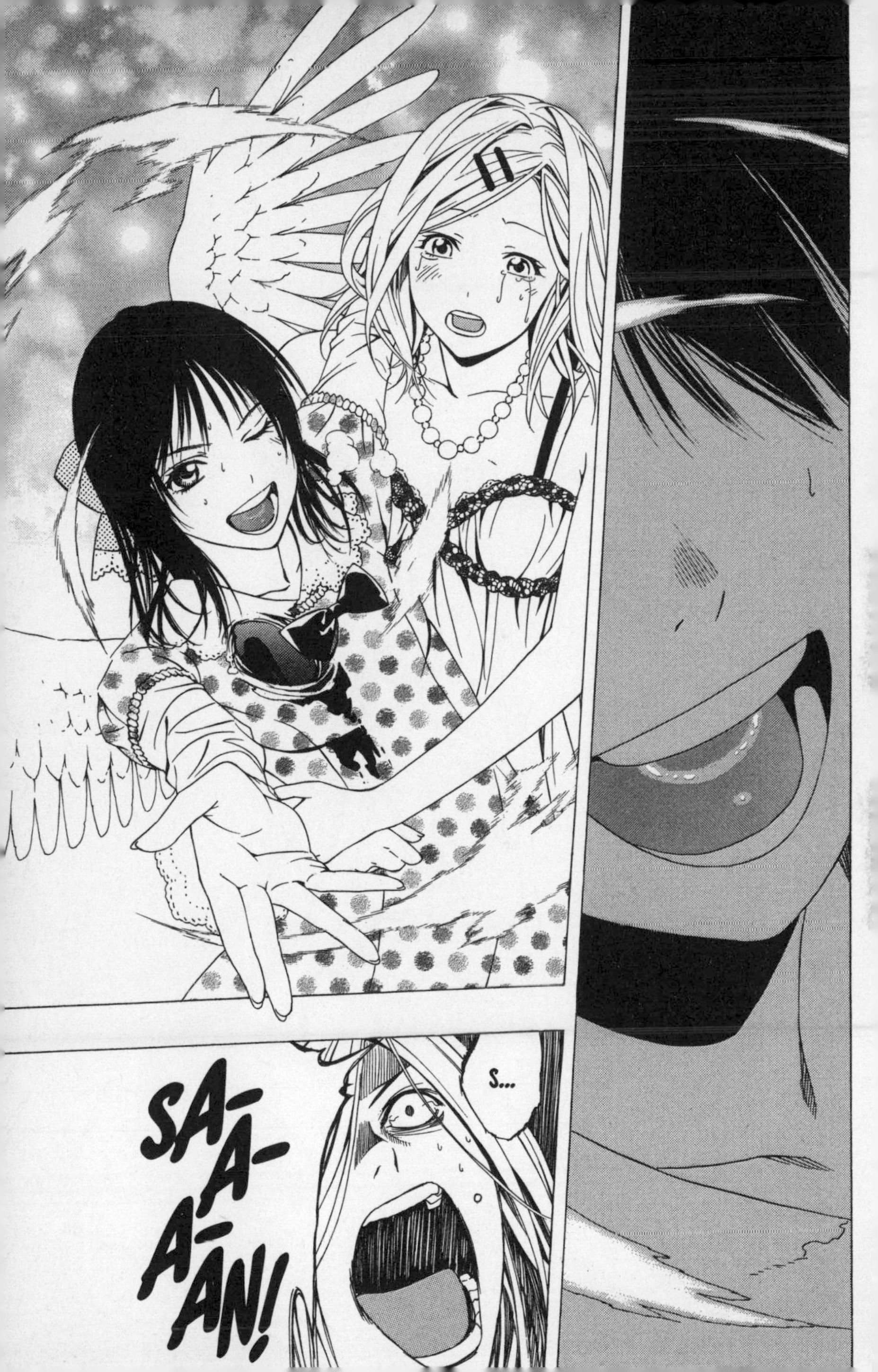
S...
SA-A-A-AN!

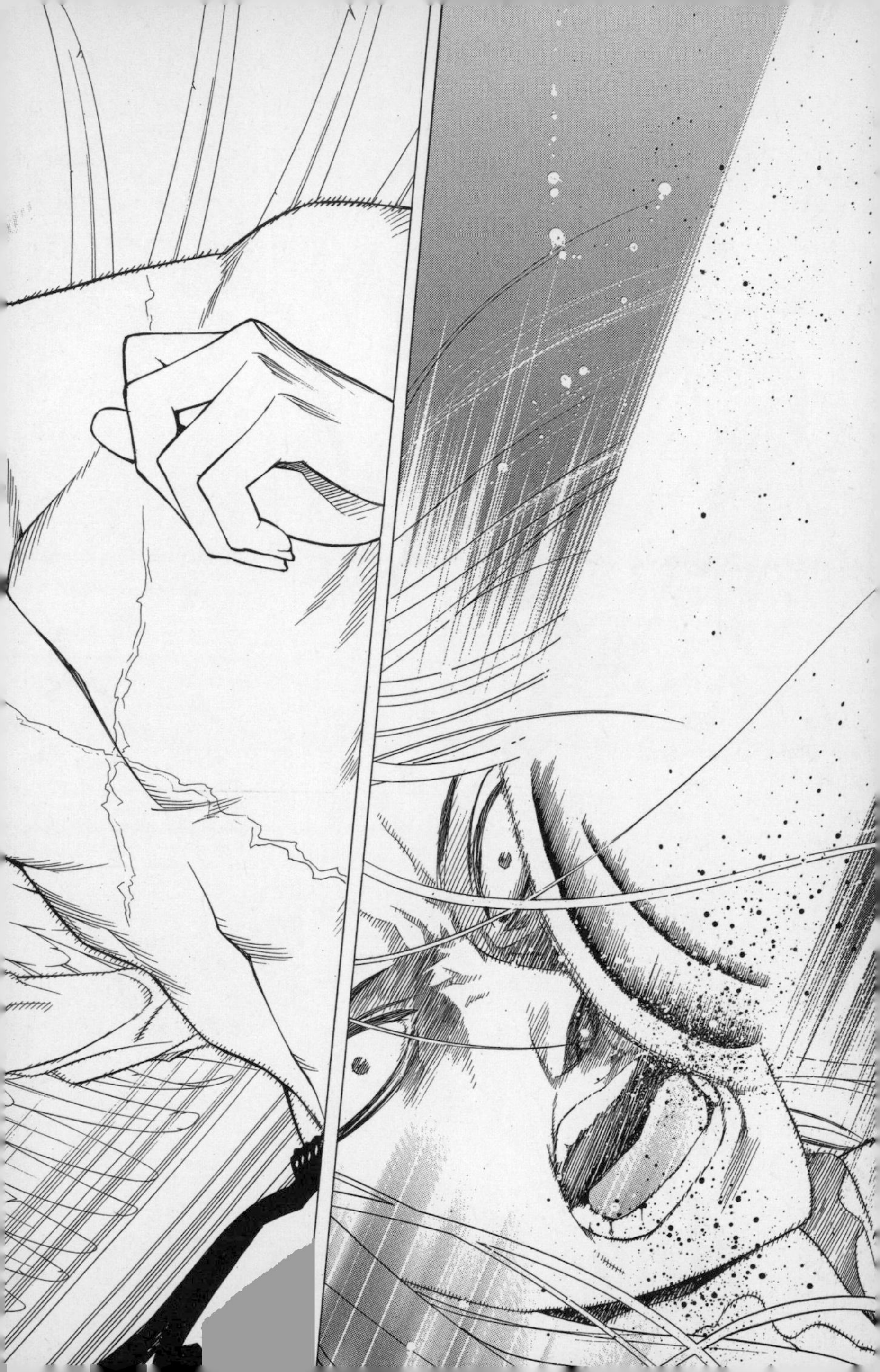

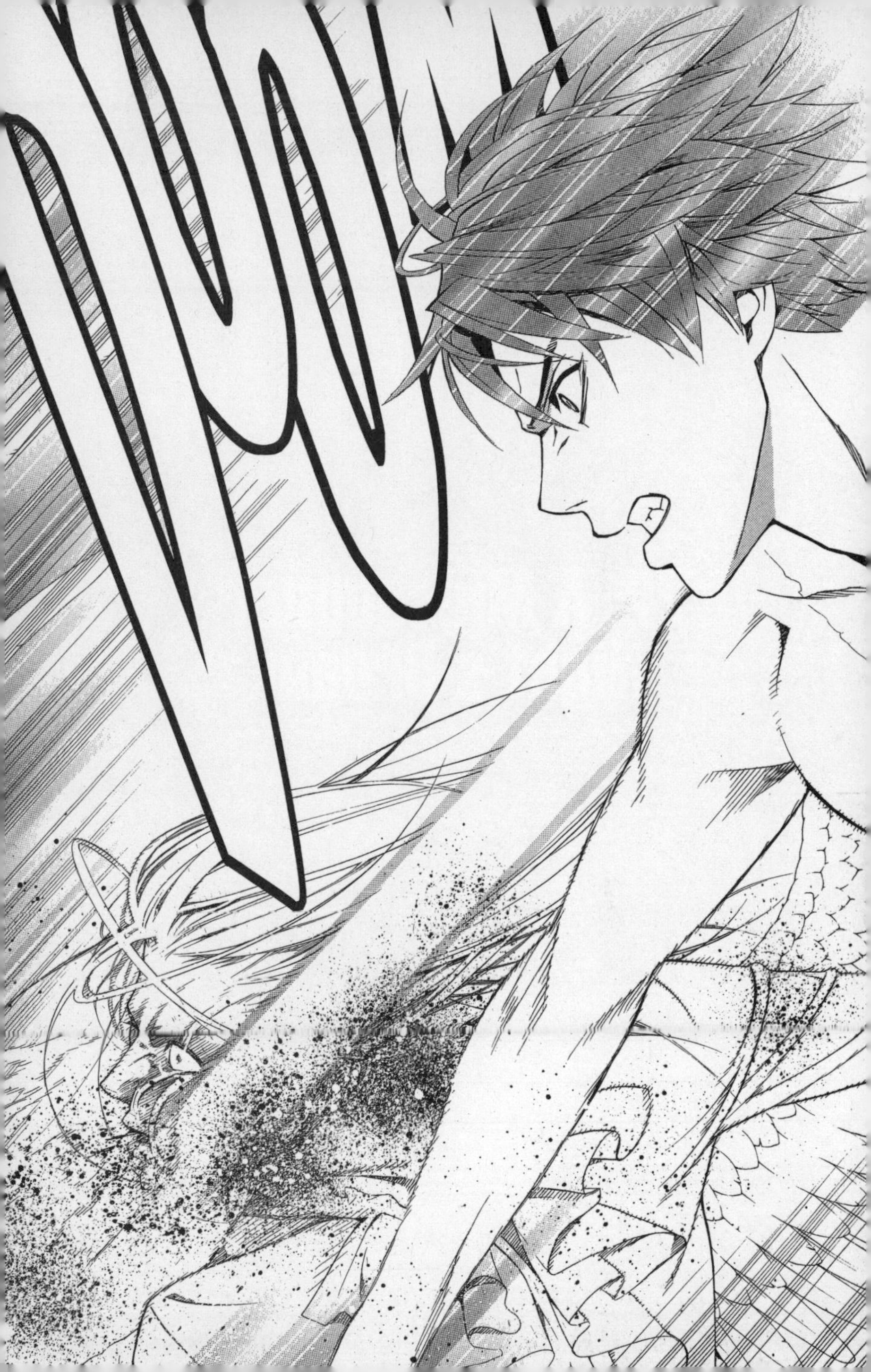

22: A Midsummer Night's Dream

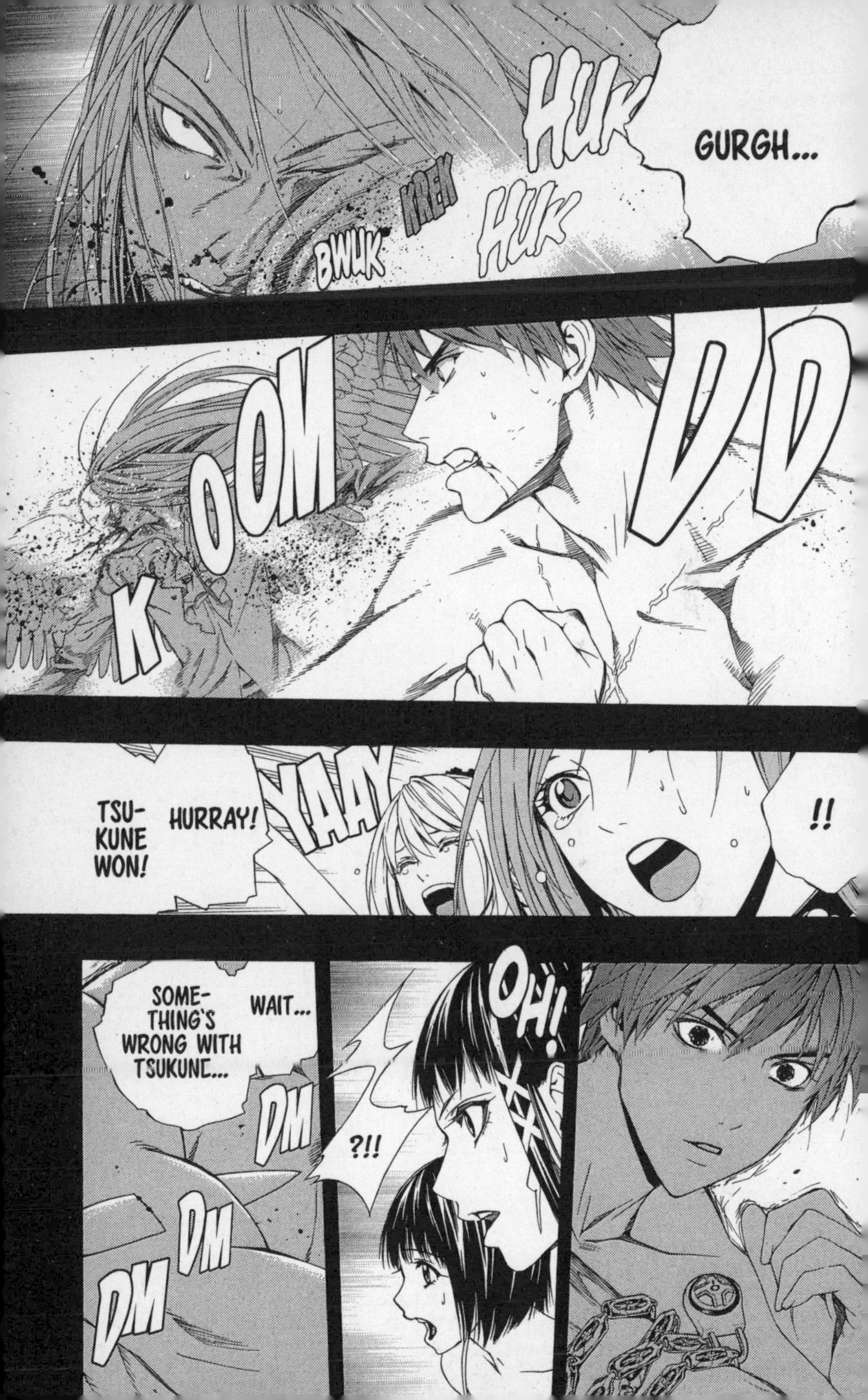
GURGH...
HUK
HUK
KREK
BWUK
DD
OOM
K
!!
YAAY
HURRAY!
TSU-
KUNE
WON!
OH!
?!!
WAIT...
SOME-
THING'S
WRONG WITH
TSUKUNE...
DM
DM
DM

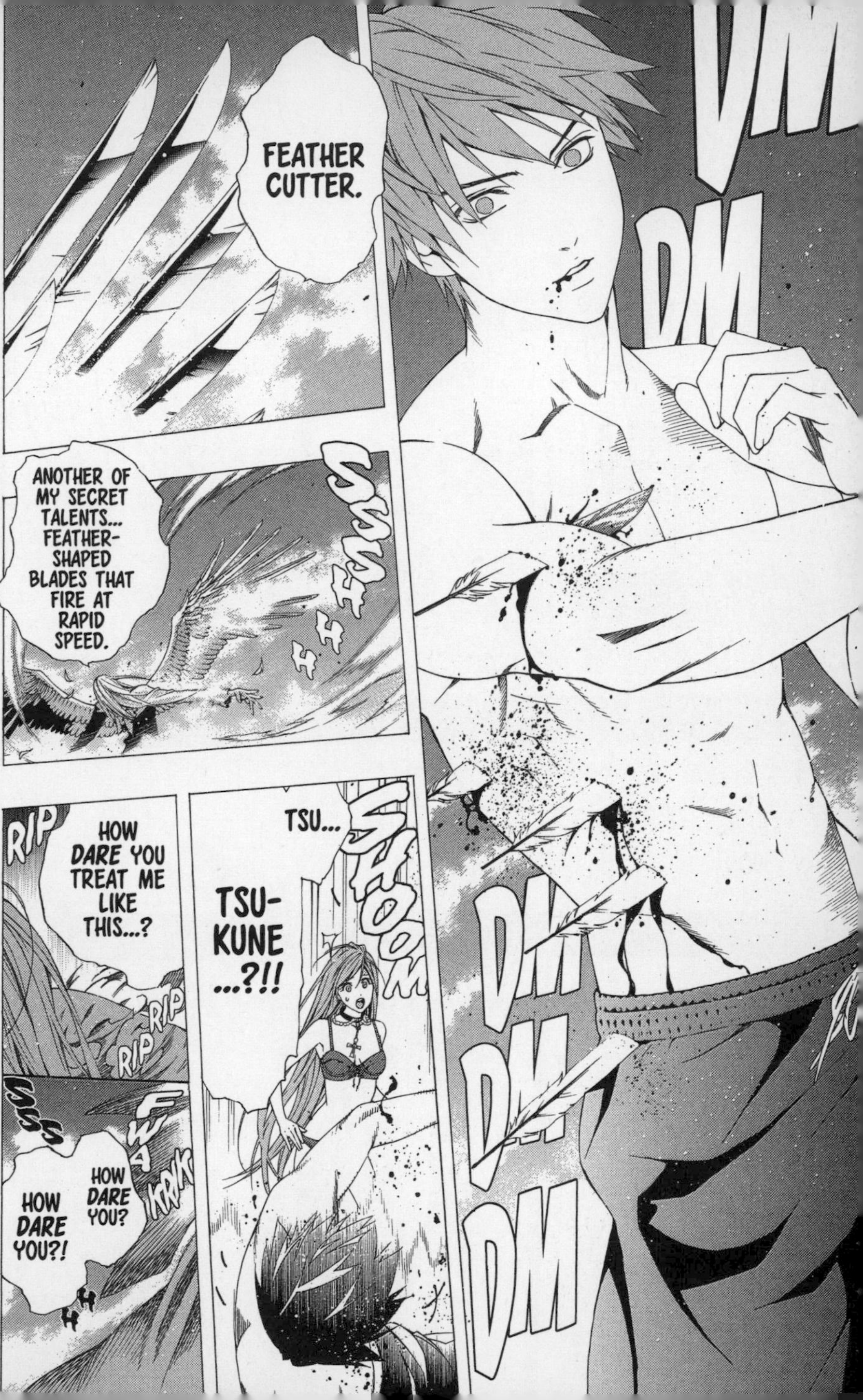
VM
DM
DM
DM
DM
DM
FEATHER CUTTER.
ANOTHER OF MY SECRET TALENTS... FEATHER-SHAPED BLADES THAT FIRE AT RAPID SPEED.
SSSHHHH
TSU...
TSU-KUNE ...?!!
SHOOOM
RIP
HOW DARE YOU TREAT ME LIKE THIS...?
RIP
RIP
SSS
FWA
KRIK
HOW DARE YOU?
HOW DARE YOU?!
HHH

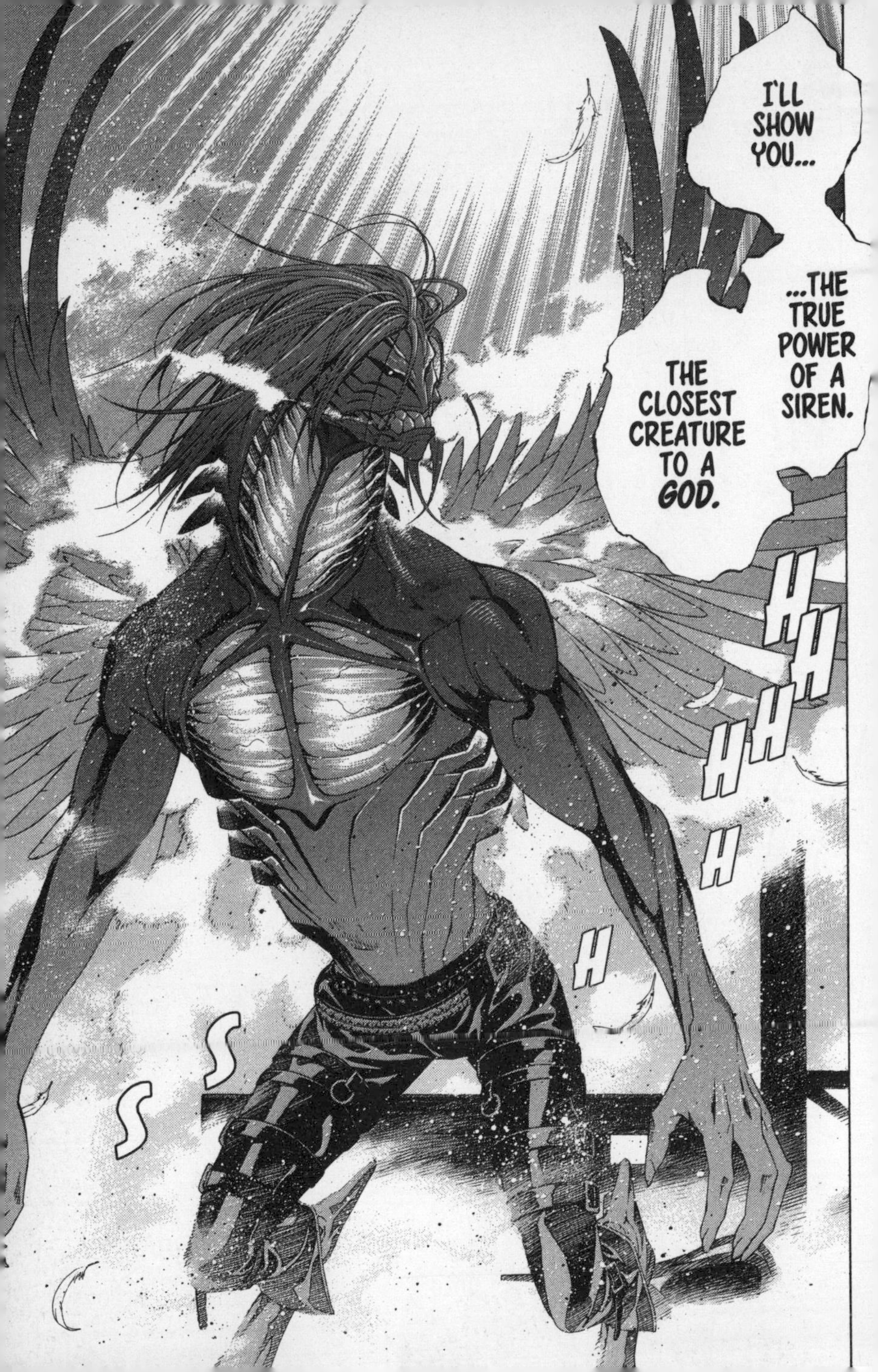
I'LL SHOW YOU...
...THE TRUE POWER OF A SIREN.
THE CLOSEST CREATURE TO A GOD.
HHHHHHH
SSS

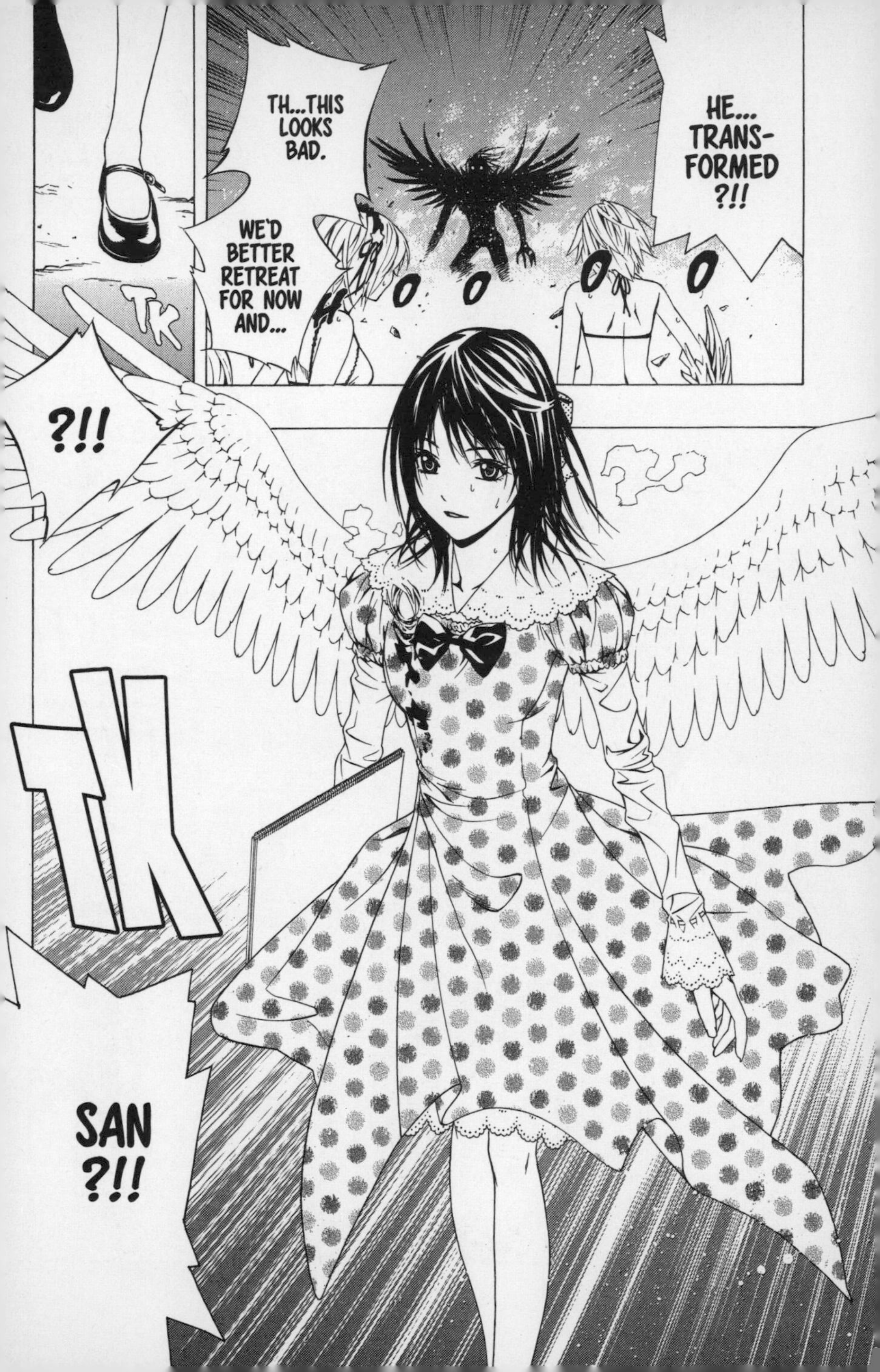
HE... TRANS-FORMED ?!!
HOOOOO
TH...THIS LOOKS BAD.
WE'D BETTER RETREAT FOR NOW AND...
TK
?!!
TK
SAN ?!!

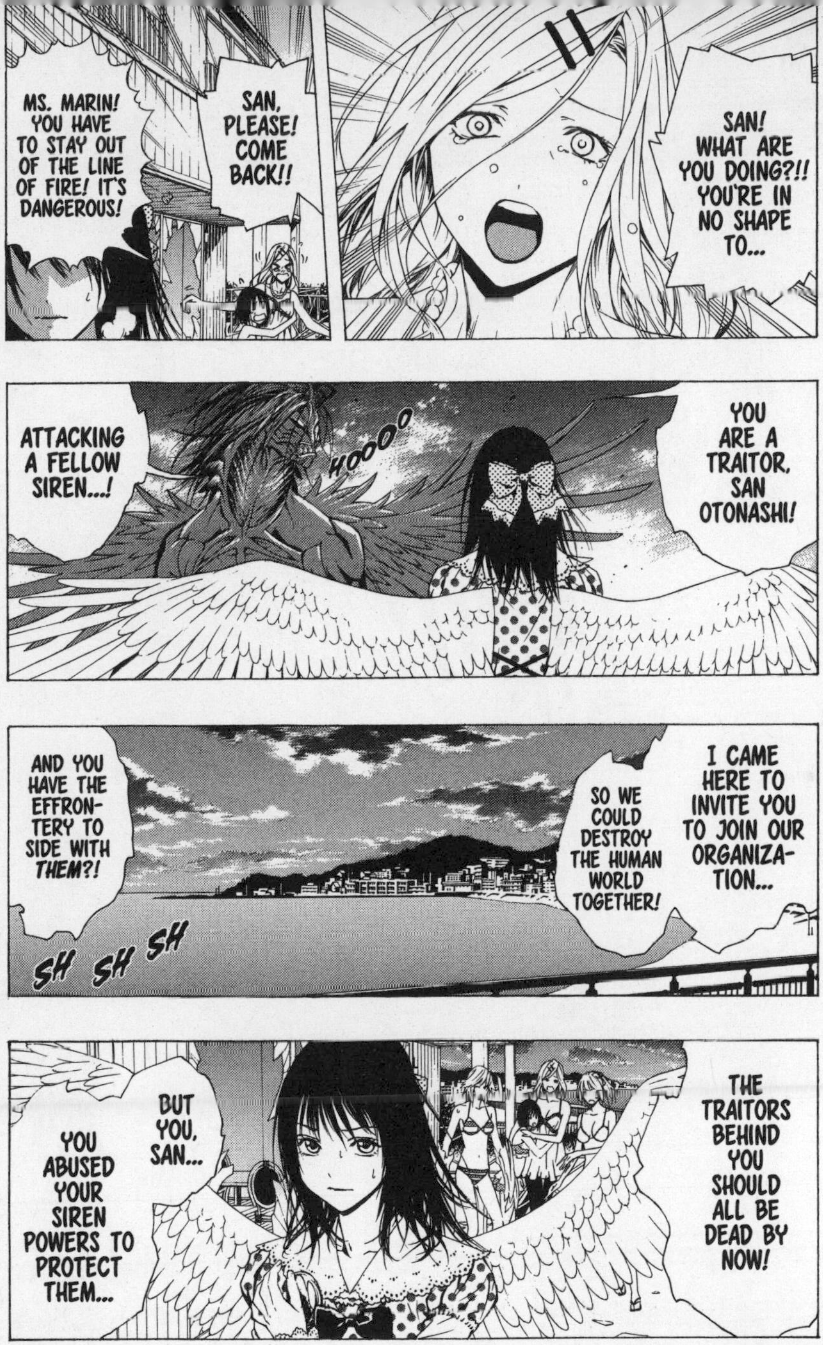
SAN! WHAT ARE YOU DOING?!! YOU'RE IN NO SHAPE TO...
SAN, PLEASE! COME BACK!!
MS. MARIN! YOU HAVE TO STAY OUT OF THE LINE OF FIRE! IT'S DANGEROUS!
YOU ARE A TRAITOR, SAN OTONASHI!
HOOOO
ATTACKING A FELLOW SIREN...!
I CAME HERE TO INVITE YOU TO JOIN OUR ORGANIZATION...
SO WE COULD DESTROY THE HUMAN WORLD TOGETHER!
AND YOU HAVE THE EFFRONTERY TO SIDE WITH *THEM*?!
SH SH SH
THE TRAITORS BEHIND YOU SHOULD ALL BE DEAD BY NOW!
BUT YOU, SAN...
YOU ABUSED YOUR SIREN POWERS TO PROTECT THEM...

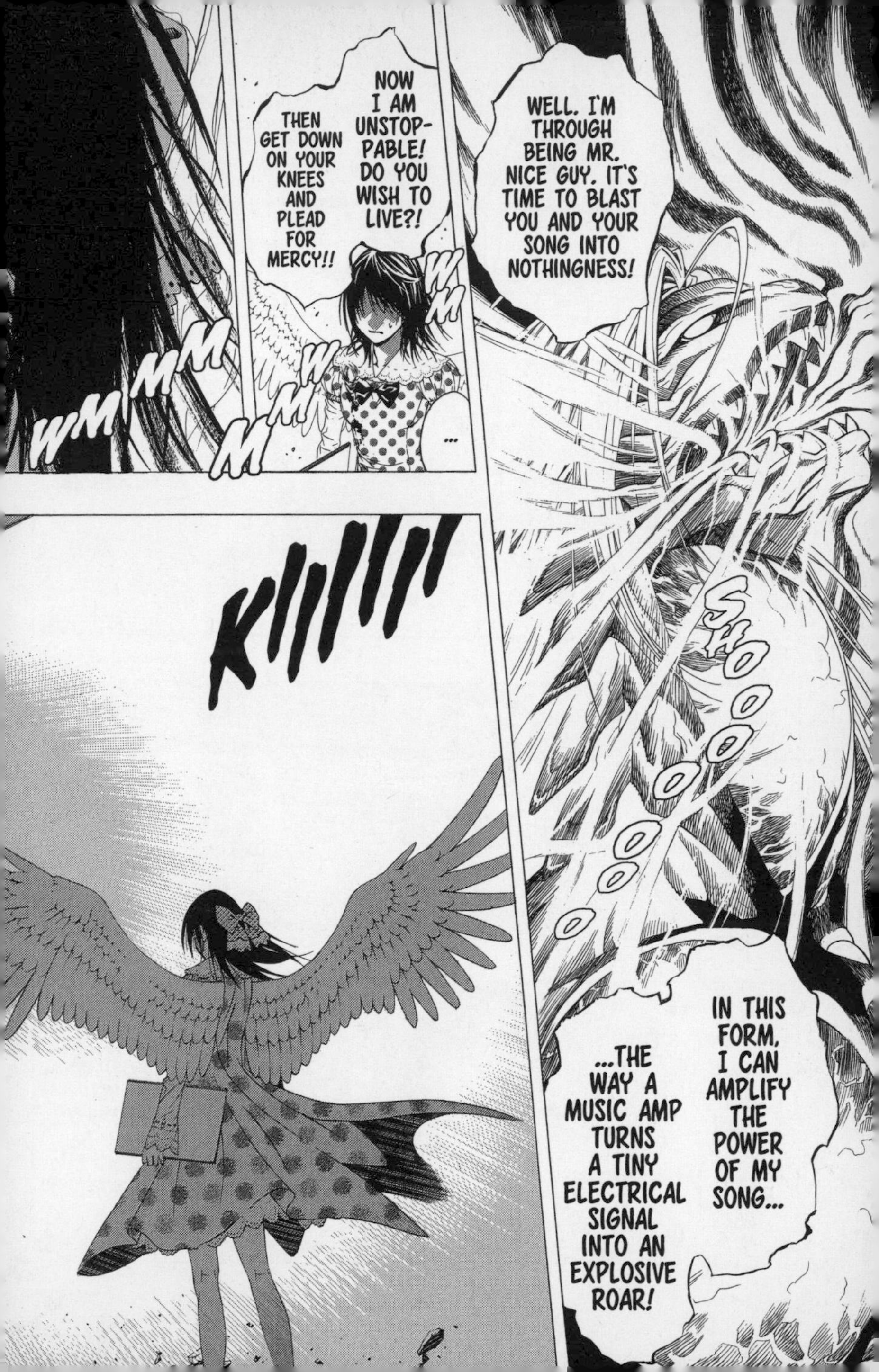
WELL. I'M THROUGH BEING MR. NICE GUY. IT'S TIME TO BLAST YOU AND YOUR SONG INTO NOTHINGNESS!
SHOOOOOOOOOO
IN THIS FORM, I CAN AMPLIFY THE POWER OF MY SONG...
...THE WAY A MUSIC AMP TURNS A TINY ELECTRICAL SIGNAL INTO AN EXPLOSIVE ROAR!
NOW I AM UNSTOP-PABLE! DO YOU WISH TO LIVE?!
THEN GET DOWN ON YOUR KNEES AND PLEAD FOR MERCY!!
WMMMM
WMMMWM
...
KIIIIII

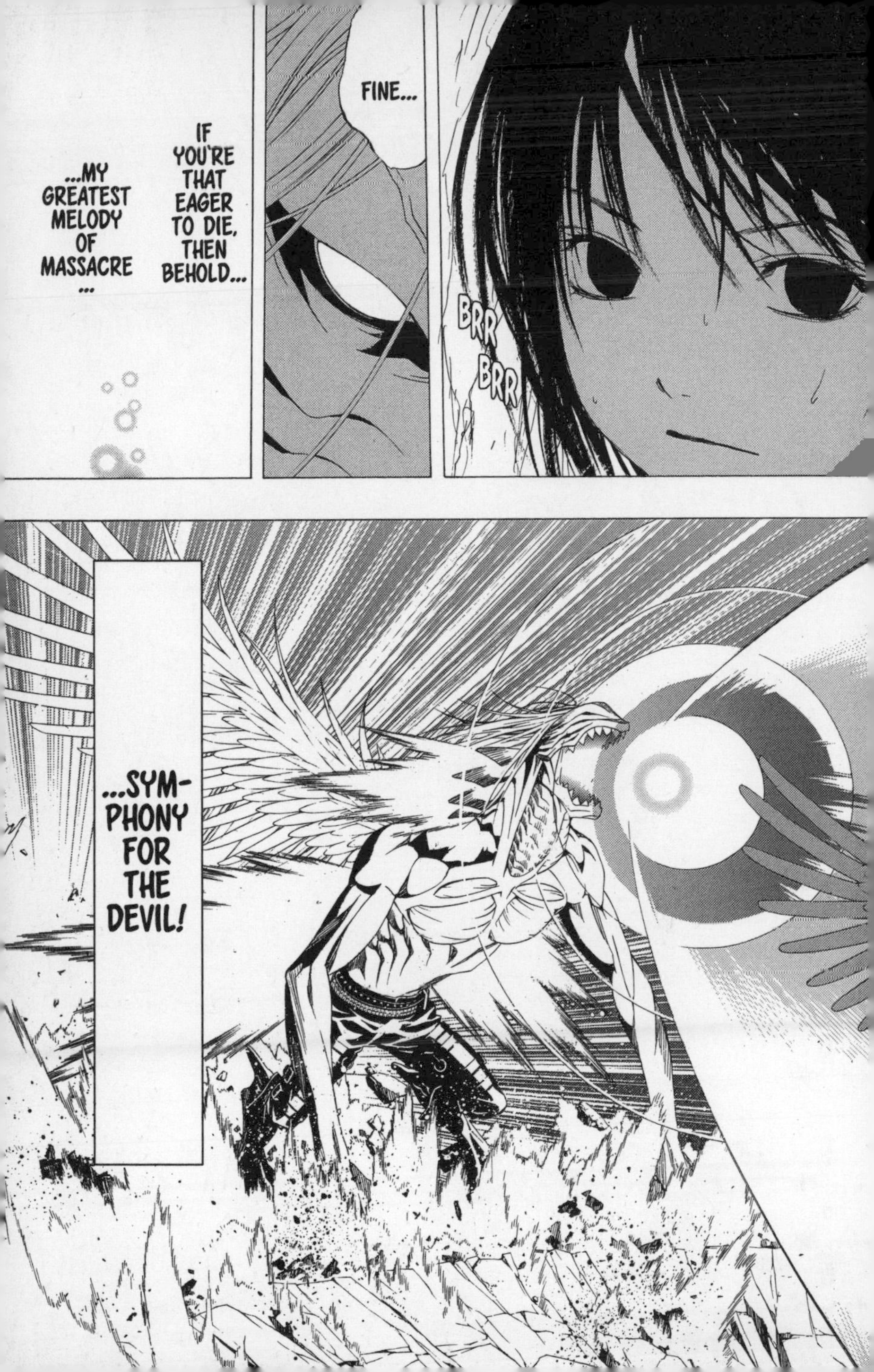
BRR
BRR
FINE...
IF YOU'RE THAT EAGER TO DIE, THEN BEHOLD...
...MY GREATEST MELODY OF MASSACRE...
...SYM-PHONY FOR THE DEVIL!

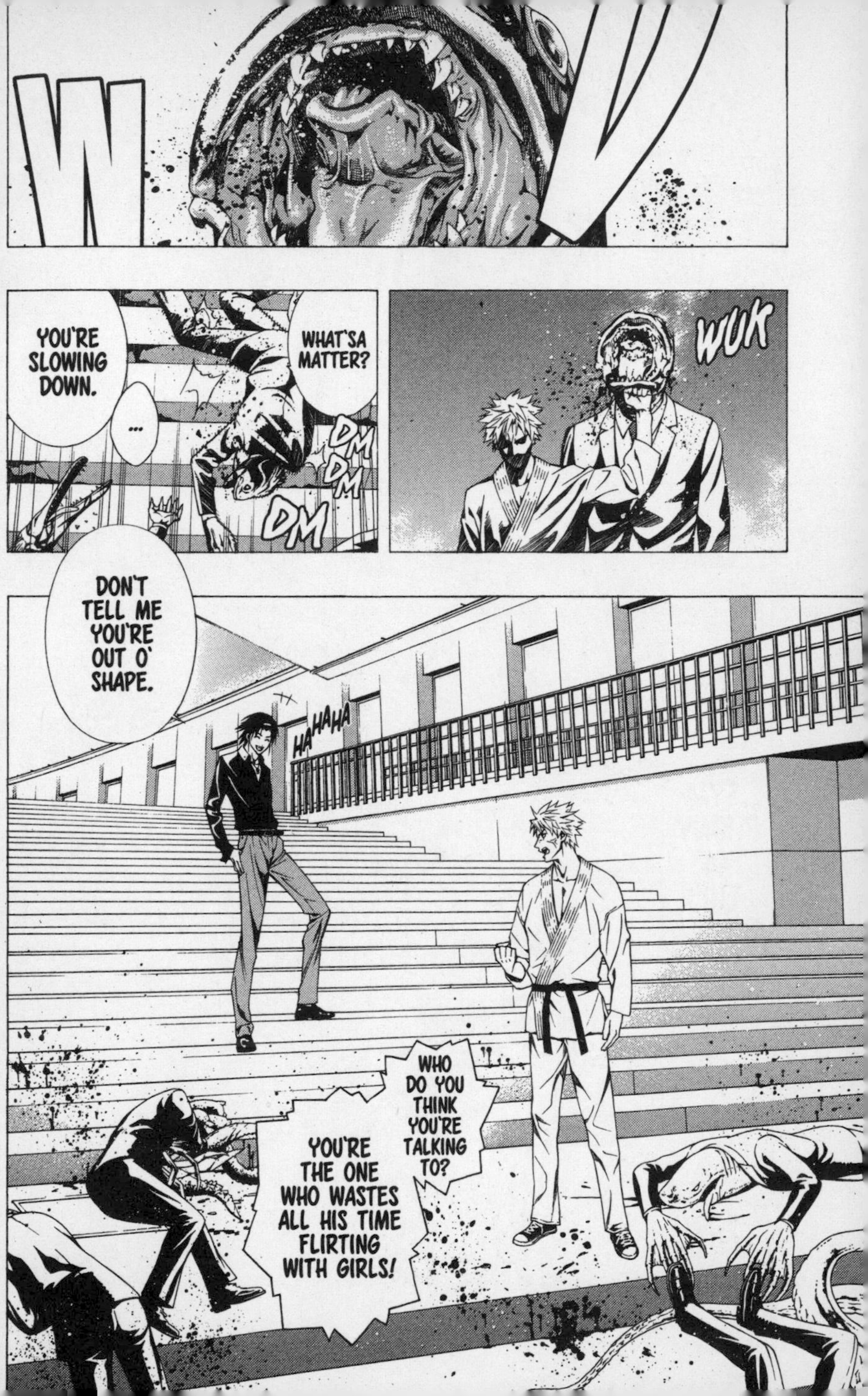
WUK
WHAT'SA MATTER?
YOU'RE SLOWING DOWN.
...
DM DM DM
DON'T TELL ME YOU'RE OUT O' SHAPE.
HAHAHA
WHO DO YOU THINK YOU'RE TALKING TO?
YOU'RE THE ONE WHO WASTES ALL HIS TIME FLIRTING WITH GIRLS!

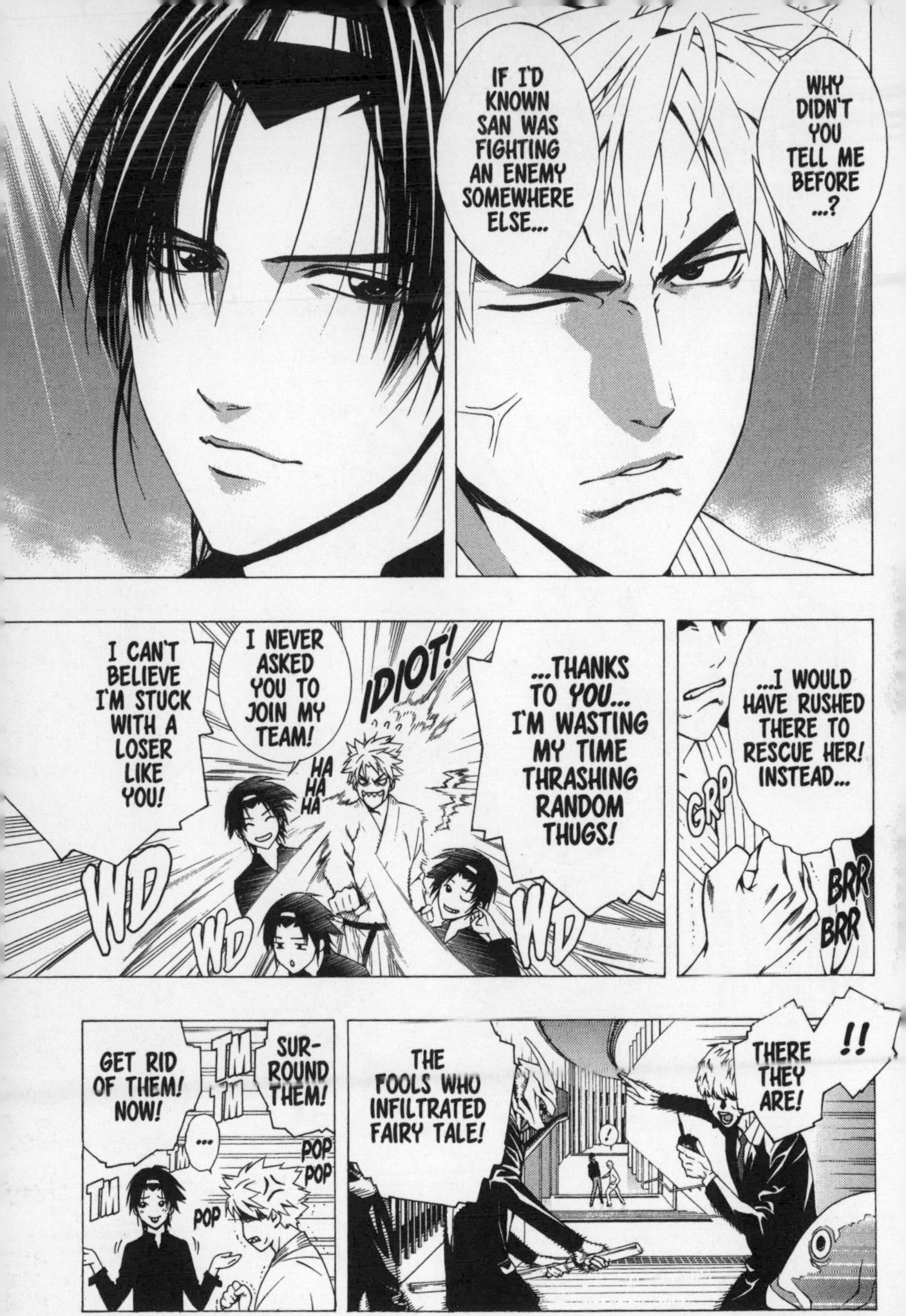
WHY DIDN'T YOU TELL ME BEFORE ...?
IF I'D KNOWN SAN WAS FIGHTING AN ENEMY SOMEWHERE ELSE...
...I WOULD HAVE RUSHED THERE TO RESCUE HER! INSTEAD...
GRP
BRR BRR
...THANKS TO YOU... I'M WASTING MY TIME THRASHING RANDOM THUGS!
IDIOT!
I NEVER ASKED YOU TO JOIN MY TEAM!
HA HA HA
I CAN'T BELIEVE I'M STUCK WITH A LOSER LIKE YOU!
WD
WD
WD
!!
THERE THEY ARE!
THE FOOLS WHO INFILTRATED FAIRY TALE!
!
SUR-ROUND THEM!
GET RID OF THEM! NOW!
TM TM
TM
...
POP POP
POP
TM

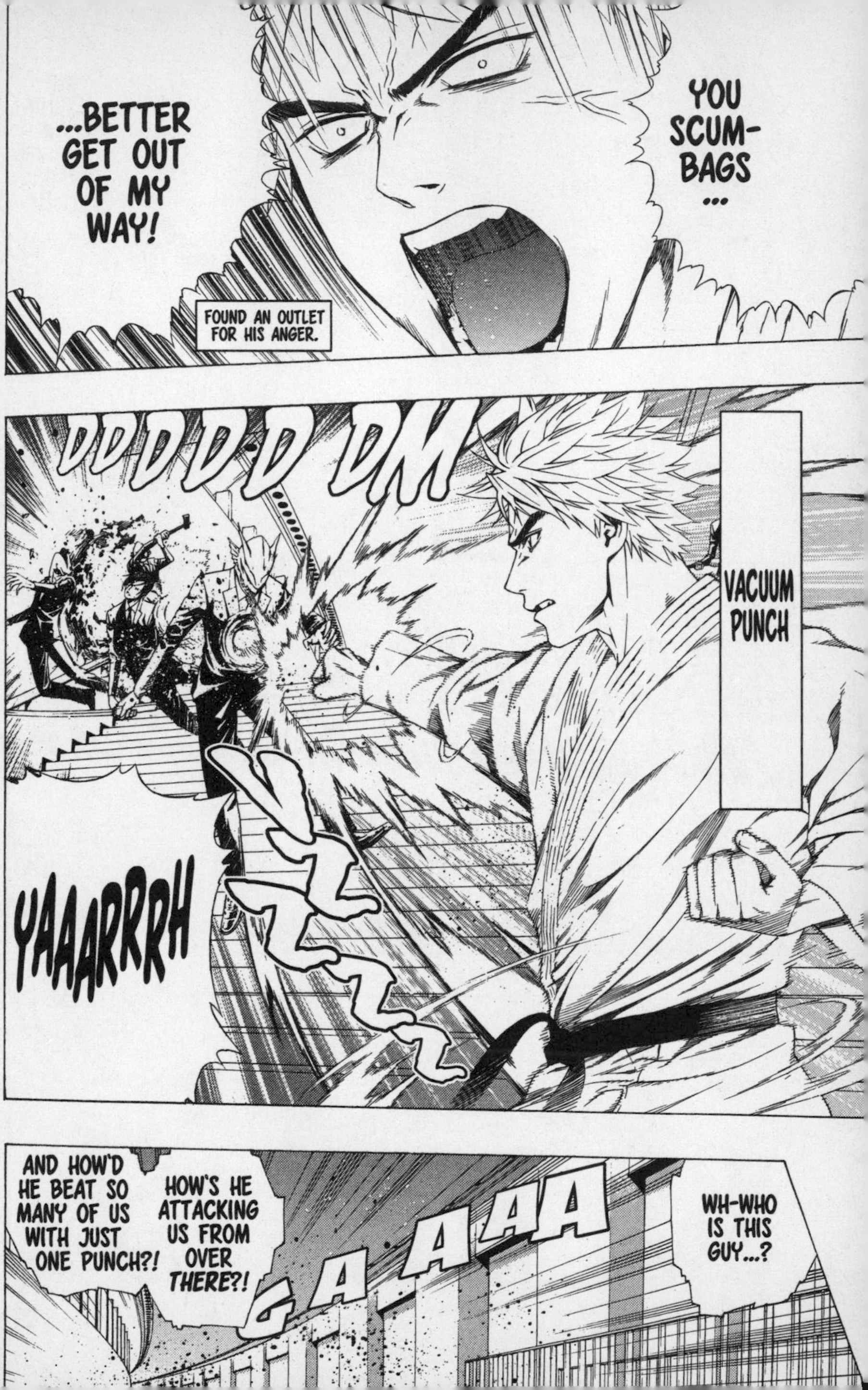
YOU SCUM-BAGS...
...BETTER GET OUT OF MY WAY!
FOUND AN OUTLET FOR HIS ANGER.
VACUUM PUNCH
DDDDD DM
YAAARRRH
WH-WHO IS THIS GUY...?
GAAAAA
HOW'S HE ATTACKING US FROM OVER THERE?!
AND HOW'D HE BEAT SO MANY OF US WITH JUST ONE PUNCH?!

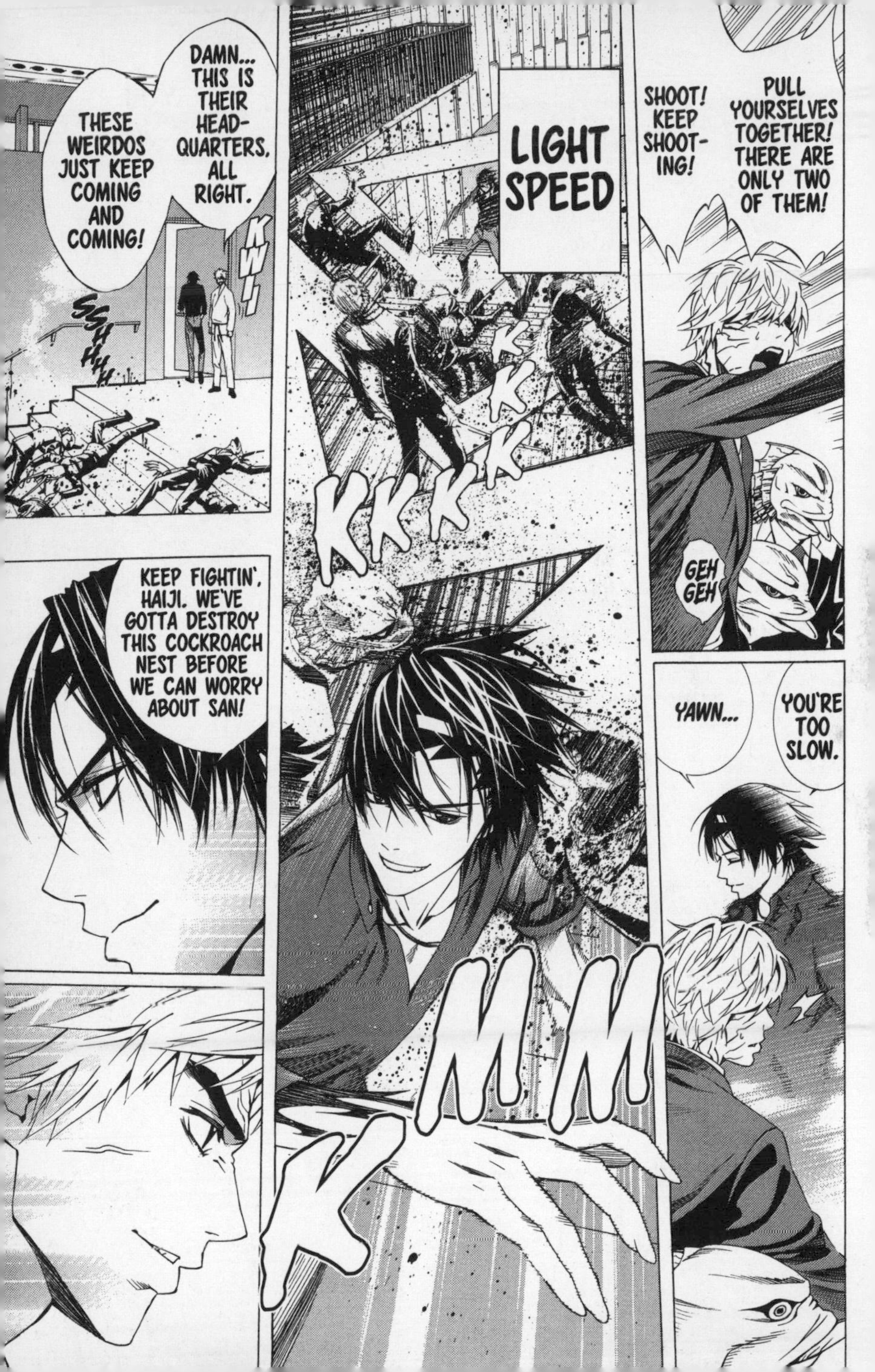
PULL YOURSELVES TOGETHER! THERE ARE ONLY TWO OF THEM!
SHOOT! KEEP SHOOT-ING!
GEH GEH
YOU'RE TOO SLOW.
YAWN...
LIGHT SPEED
KKKKKK
MM
DAMN... THIS IS THEIR HEAD-QUARTERS, ALL RIGHT.
KWIII
THESE WEIRDOS JUST KEEP COMING AND COMING!
SSHHHH
KEEP FIGHTIN', HAIJI. WE'VE GOTTA DESTROY THIS COCKROACH NEST BEFORE WE CAN WORRY ABOUT SAN!

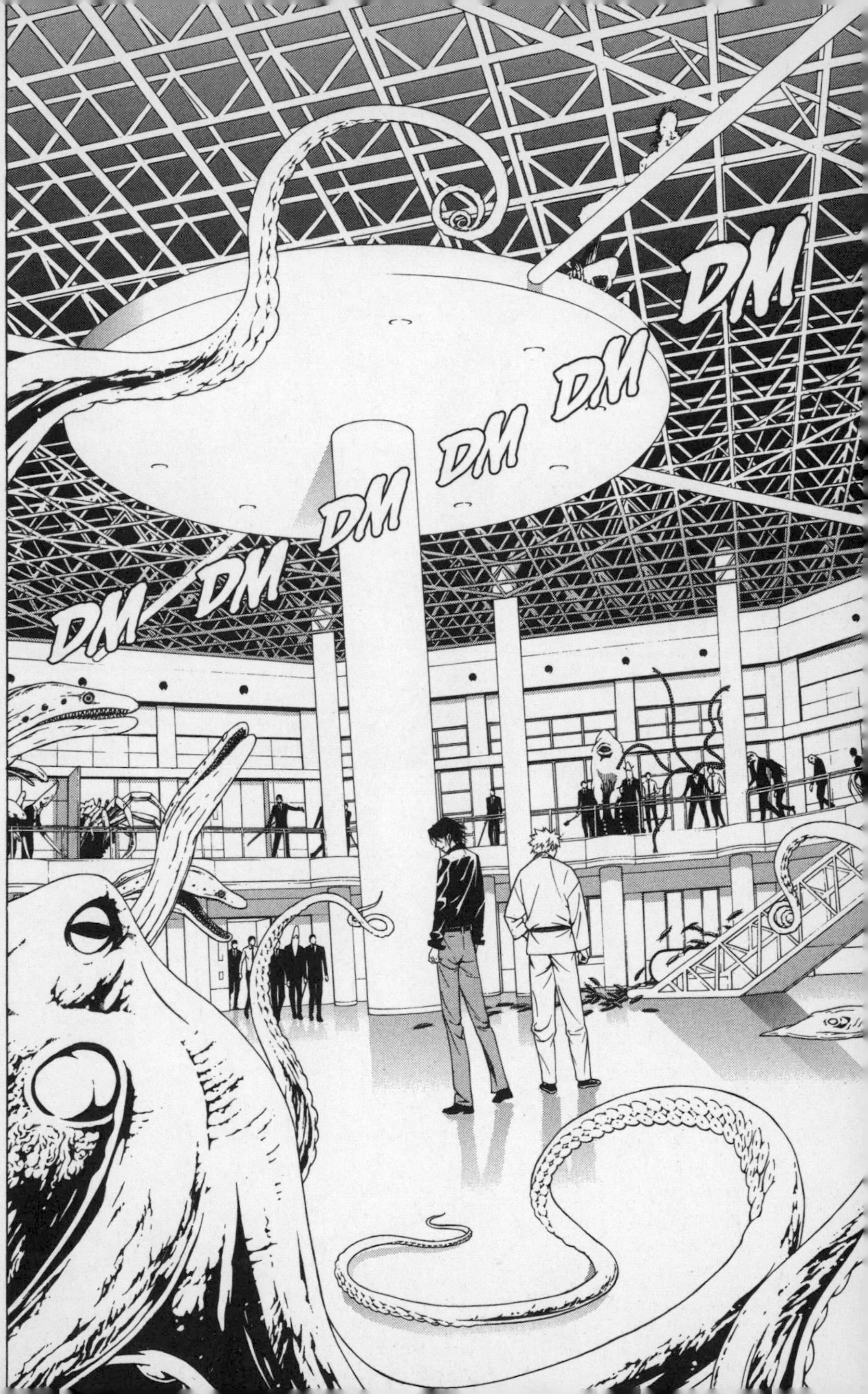
DM DM DM DM DM DM

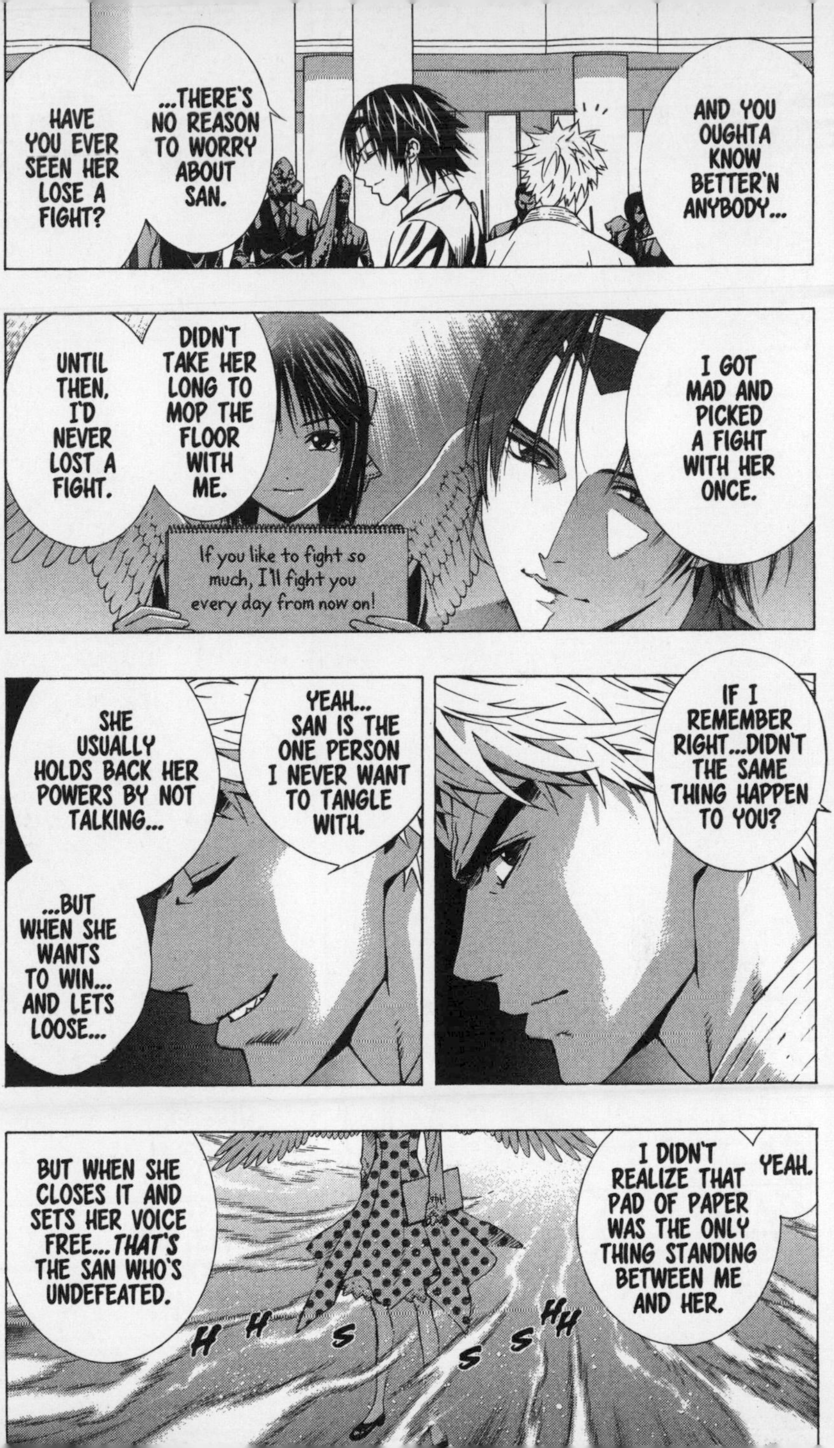
AND YOU OUGHTA KNOW BETTER'N ANYBODY...
...THERE'S NO REASON TO WORRY ABOUT SAN.
HAVE YOU EVER SEEN HER LOSE A FIGHT?
I GOT MAD AND PICKED A FIGHT WITH HER ONCE.
DIDN'T TAKE HER LONG TO MOP THE FLOOR WITH ME.
UNTIL THEN, I'D NEVER LOST A FIGHT.
If you like to fight so much, I'll fight you every day from now on!
IF I REMEMBER RIGHT...DIDN'T THE SAME THING HAPPEN TO YOU?
YEAH... SAN IS THE ONE PERSON I NEVER WANT TO TANGLE WITH.
SHE USUALLY HOLDS BACK HER POWERS BY NOT TALKING...
...BUT WHEN SHE WANTS TO WIN... AND LETS LOOSE...
YEAH.
I DIDN'T REALIZE THAT PAD OF PAPER WAS THE ONLY THING STANDING BETWEEN ME AND HER.
BUT WHEN SHE CLOSES IT AND SETS HER VOICE FREE...*THAT'S* THE SAN WHO'S UNDEFEATED.
HHSSSHH

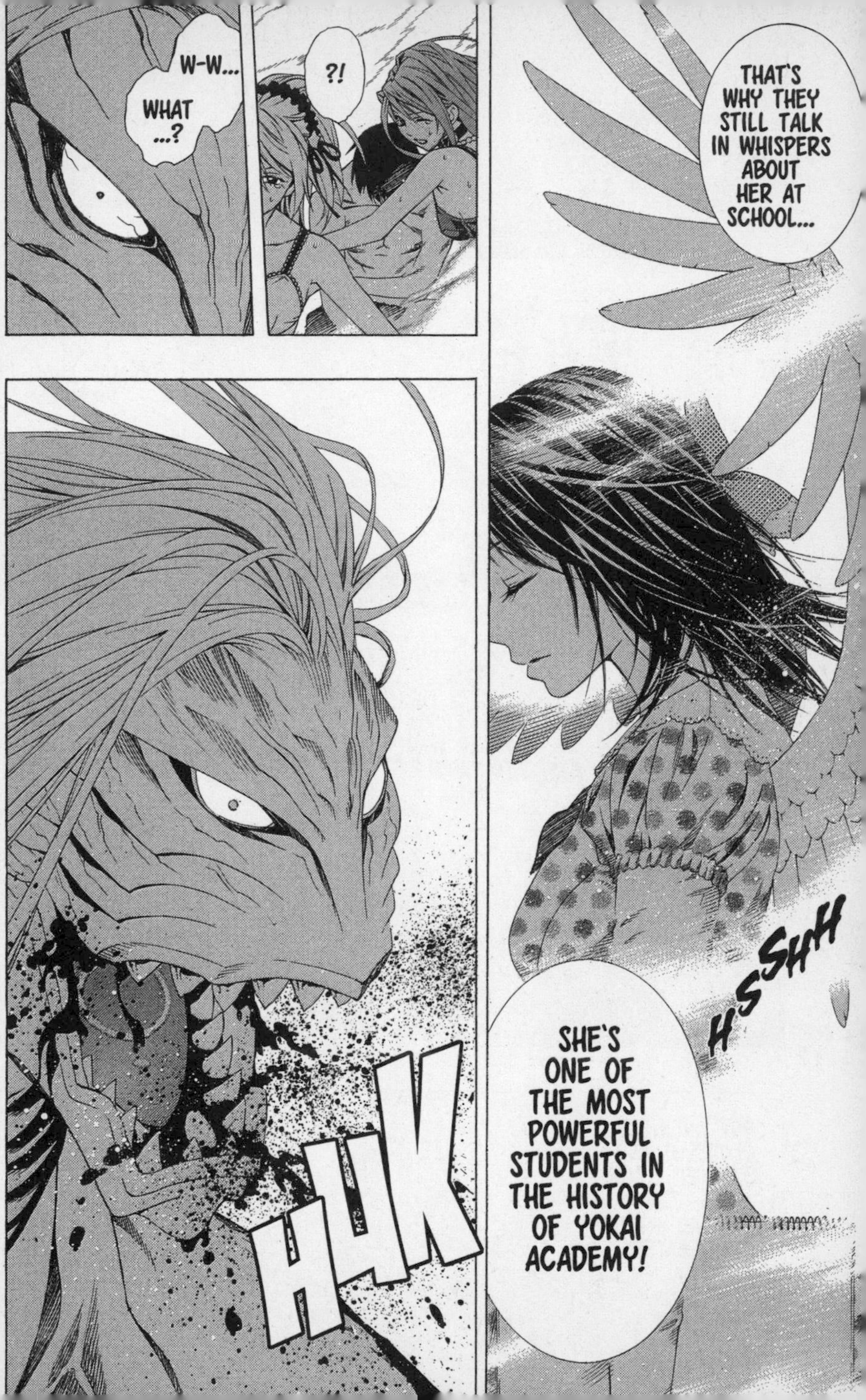
THAT'S WHY THEY STILL TALK IN WHISPERS ABOUT HER AT SCHOOL...
HSSHH
SHE'S ONE OF THE MOST POWERFUL STUDENTS IN THE HISTORY OF YOKAI ACADEMY!
?!
W-W...
WHAT ...?
HUK

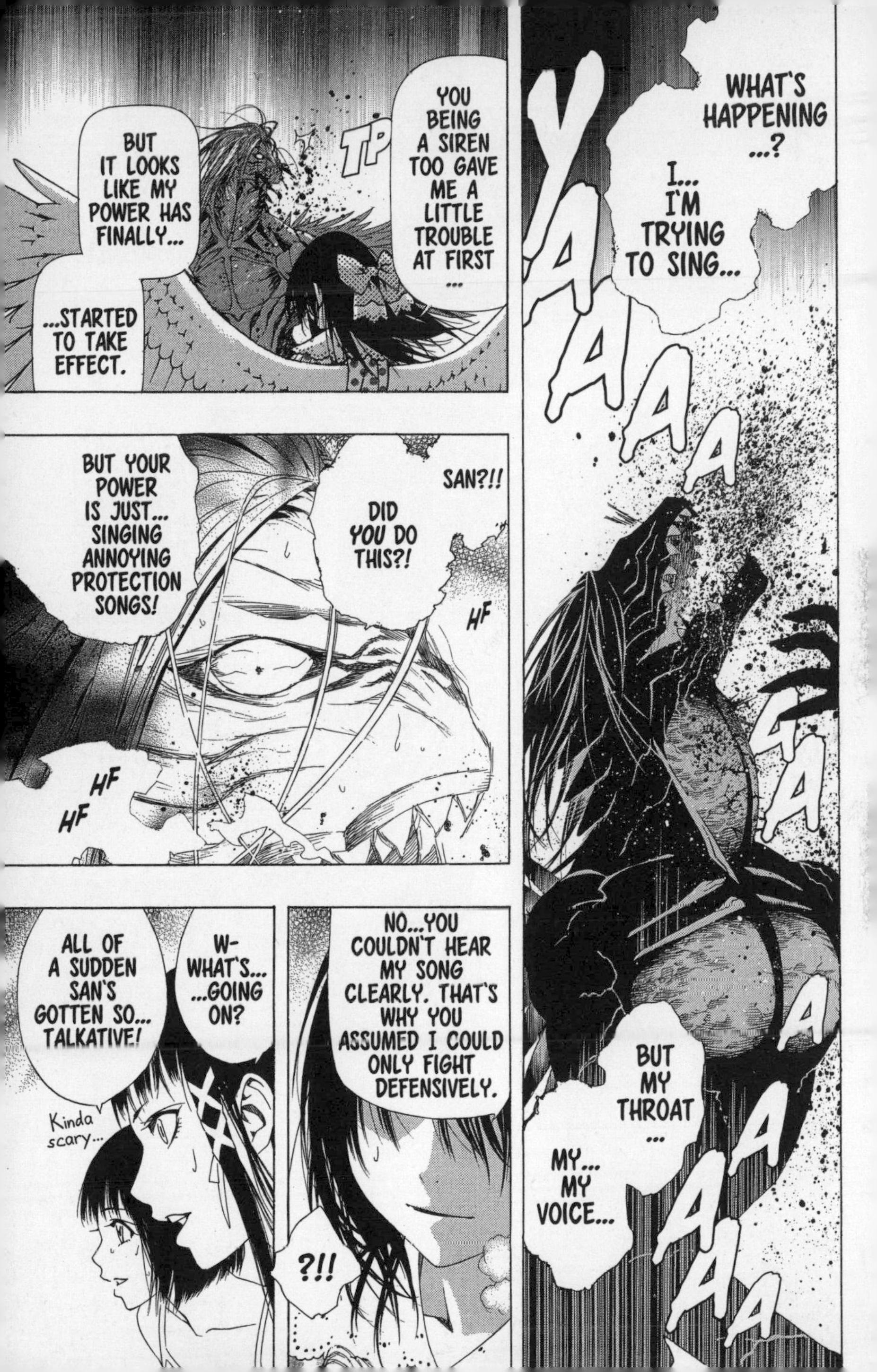
YAAAAA
WHAT'S HAPPENING...?
I... I'M TRYING TO SING...
GAA
BUT MY THROAT...
MY... MY VOICE...
AAAAAA
YOU BEING A SIREN TOO GAVE ME A LITTLE TROUBLE AT FIRST...
TP
BUT IT LOOKS LIKE MY POWER HAS FINALLY...
...STARTED TO TAKE EFFECT.
SAN?!!
DID YOU DO THIS?!
HF
BUT YOUR POWER IS JUST... SINGING ANNOYING PROTECTION SONGS!
HF HF
NO...YOU COULDN'T HEAR MY SONG CLEARLY. THAT'S WHY YOU ASSUMED I COULD ONLY FIGHT DEFENSIVELY.
?!!
W-WHAT'S... ...GOING ON?
ALL OF A SUDDEN SAN'S GOTTEN SO... TALKATIVE!
Kinda scary...

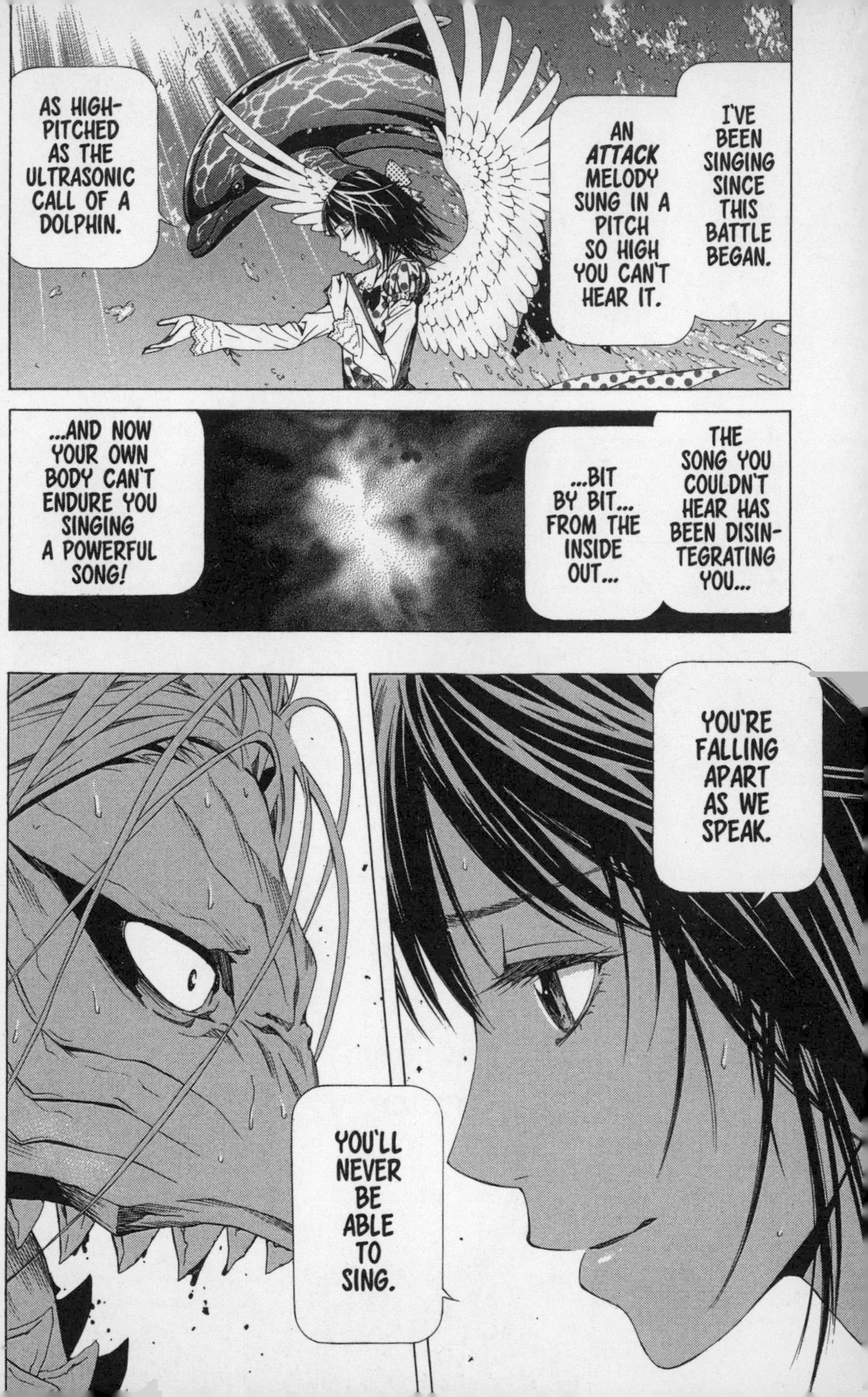
I'VE BEEN SINGING SINCE THIS BATTLE BEGAN.
AN *ATTACK* MELODY SUNG IN A PITCH SO HIGH YOU CAN'T HEAR IT.
AS HIGH-PITCHED AS THE ULTRASONIC CALL OF A DOLPHIN.
THE SONG YOU COULDN'T HEAR HAS BEEN DISINTEGRATING YOU...
...BIT BY BIT... FROM THE INSIDE OUT...
...AND NOW YOUR OWN BODY CAN'T ENDURE YOU SINGING A POWERFUL SONG!
YOU'RE FALLING APART AS WE SPEAK.
YOU'LL NEVER BE ABLE TO SING.

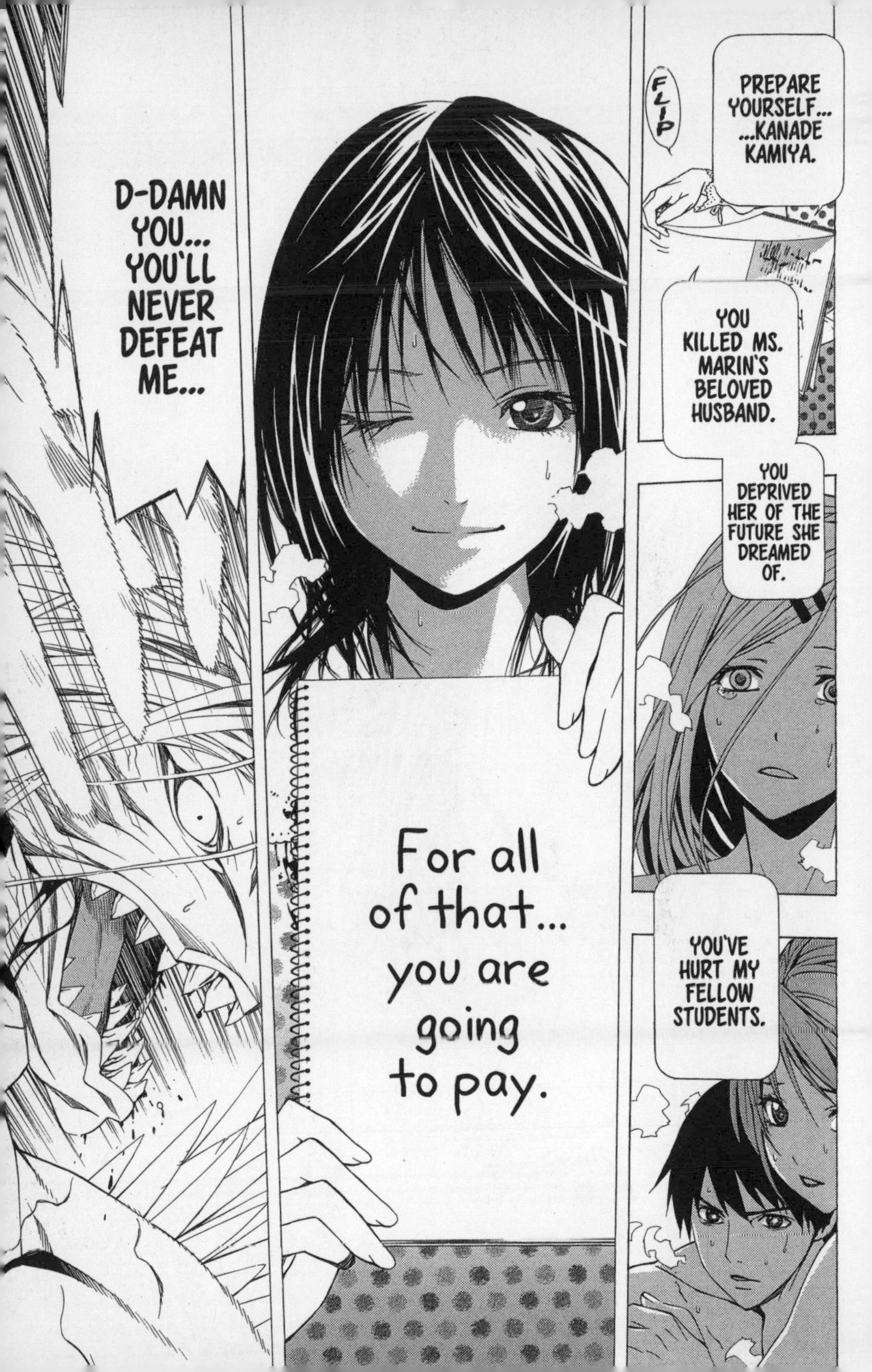
PREPARE YOURSELF... ...KANADE KAMIYA.
FLIP
YOU KILLED MS. MARIN'S BELOVED HUSBAND.
YOU DEPRIVED HER OF THE FUTURE SHE DREAMED OF.
YOU'VE HURT MY FELLOW STUDENTS.
For all of that... you are going to pay.
D-DAMN YOU... YOU'LL NEVER DEFEAT ME...

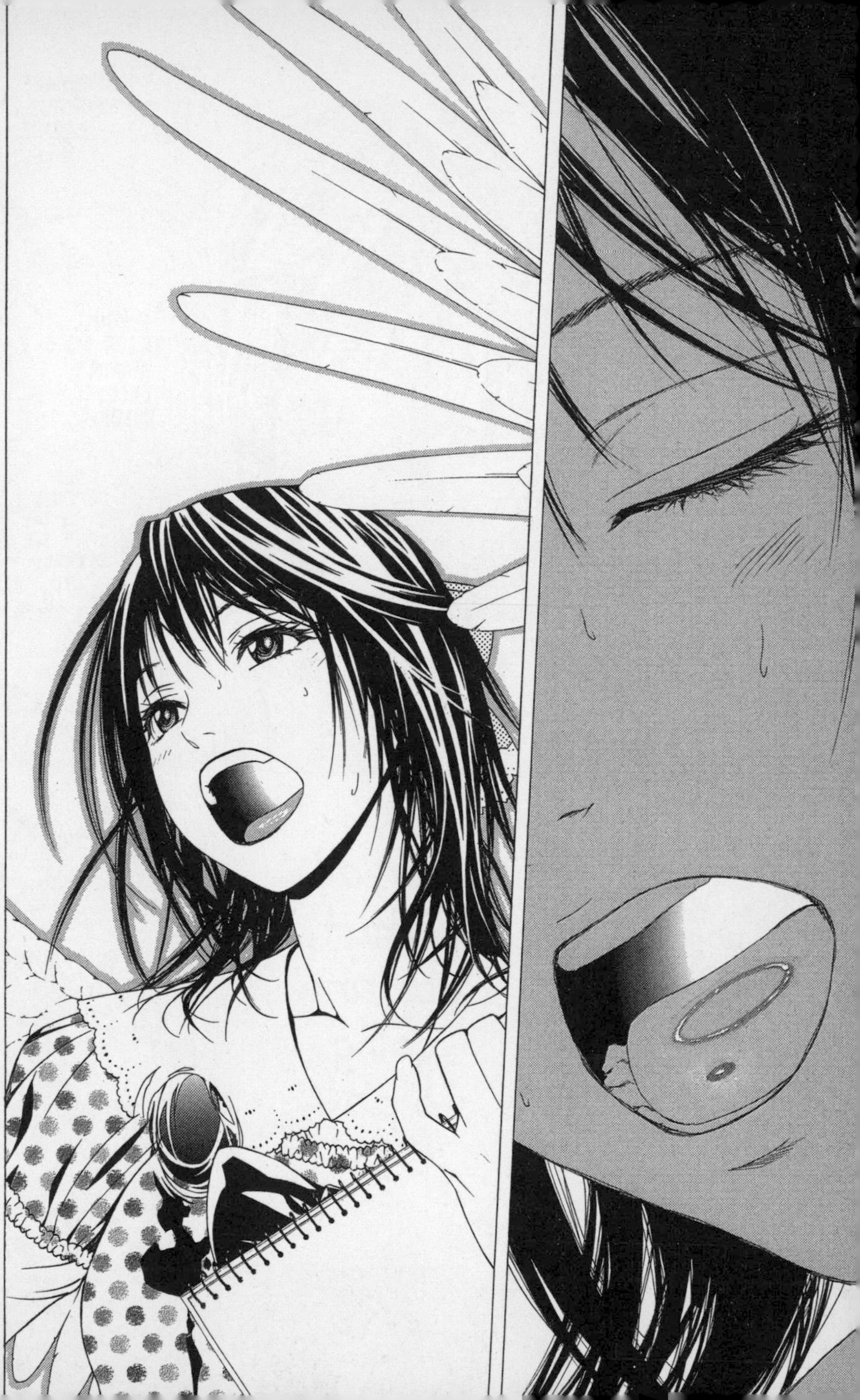

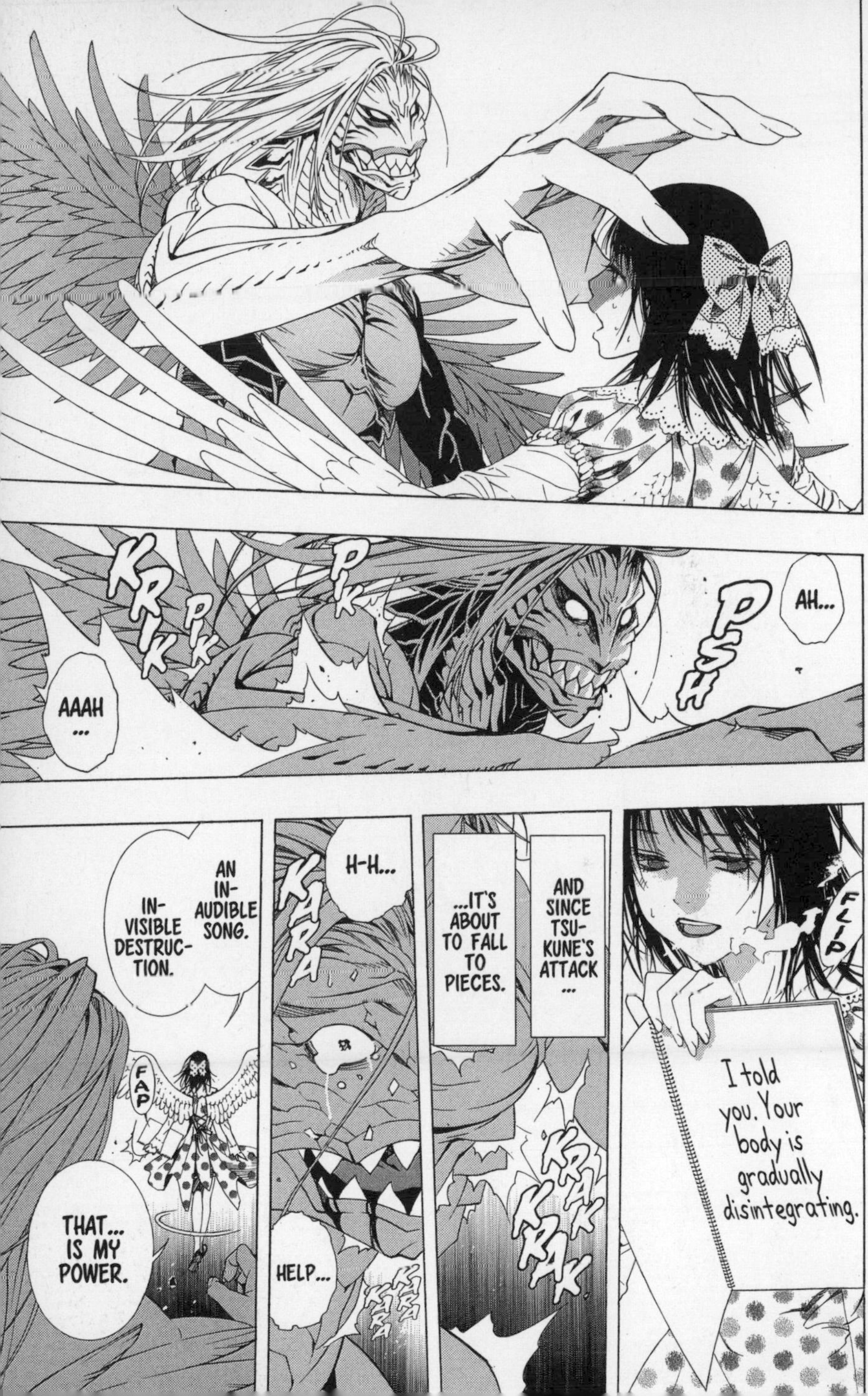
AH...
PSH
PIK
KRIK
PIK
AAAH ...
FLIP
I told you. Your body is gradually disintegrating.
AND SINCE TSU-KUNE'S ATTACK ...
...IT'S ABOUT TO FALL TO PIECES.
KRAK
KRAK
H-H...
KARA
HELP...
KARA
KARA
AN IN-AUDIBLE SONG.
IN-VISIBLE DESTRUC-TION.
FAP
THAT... IS MY POWER.

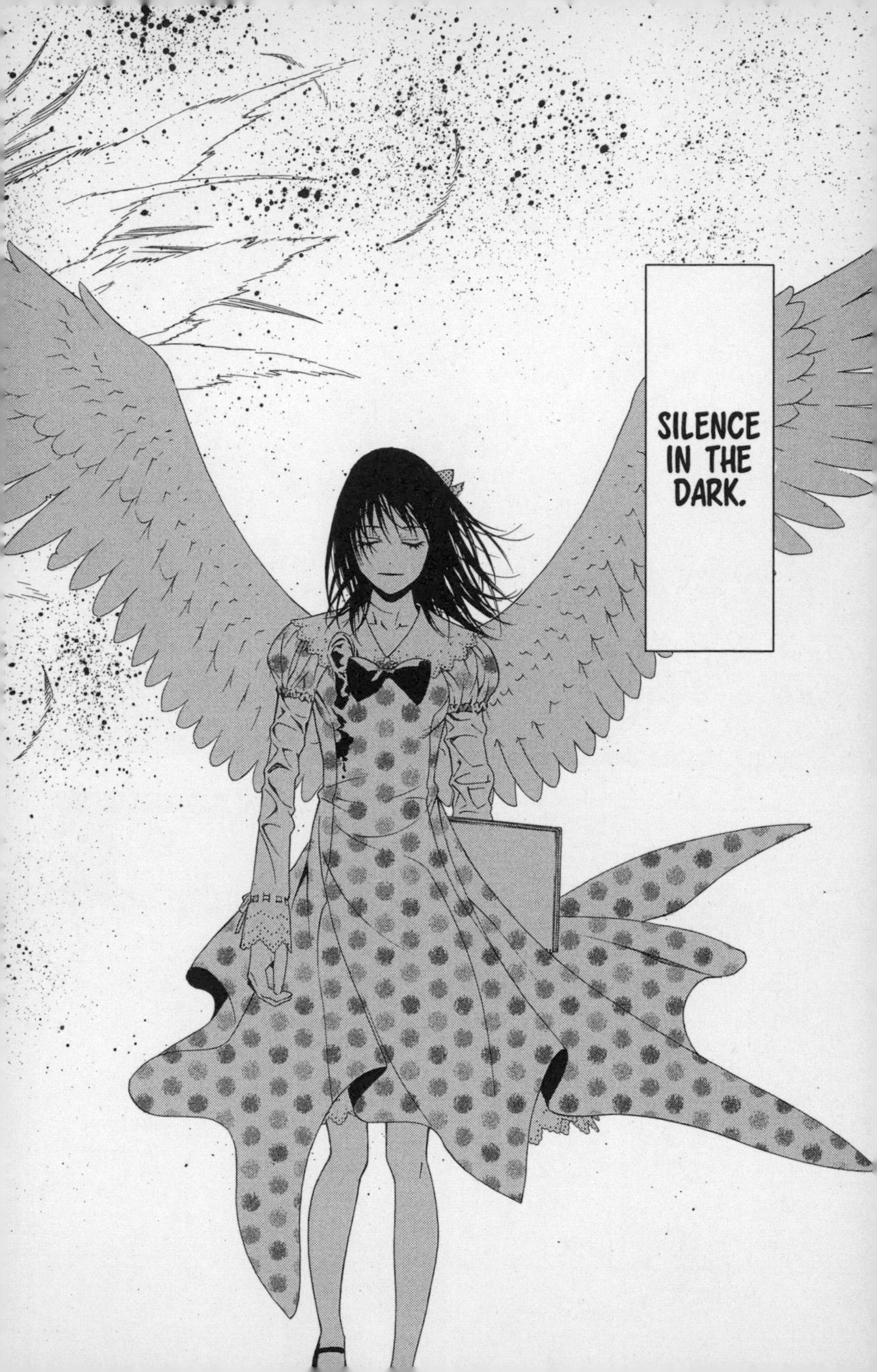
SILENCE IN THE DARK.

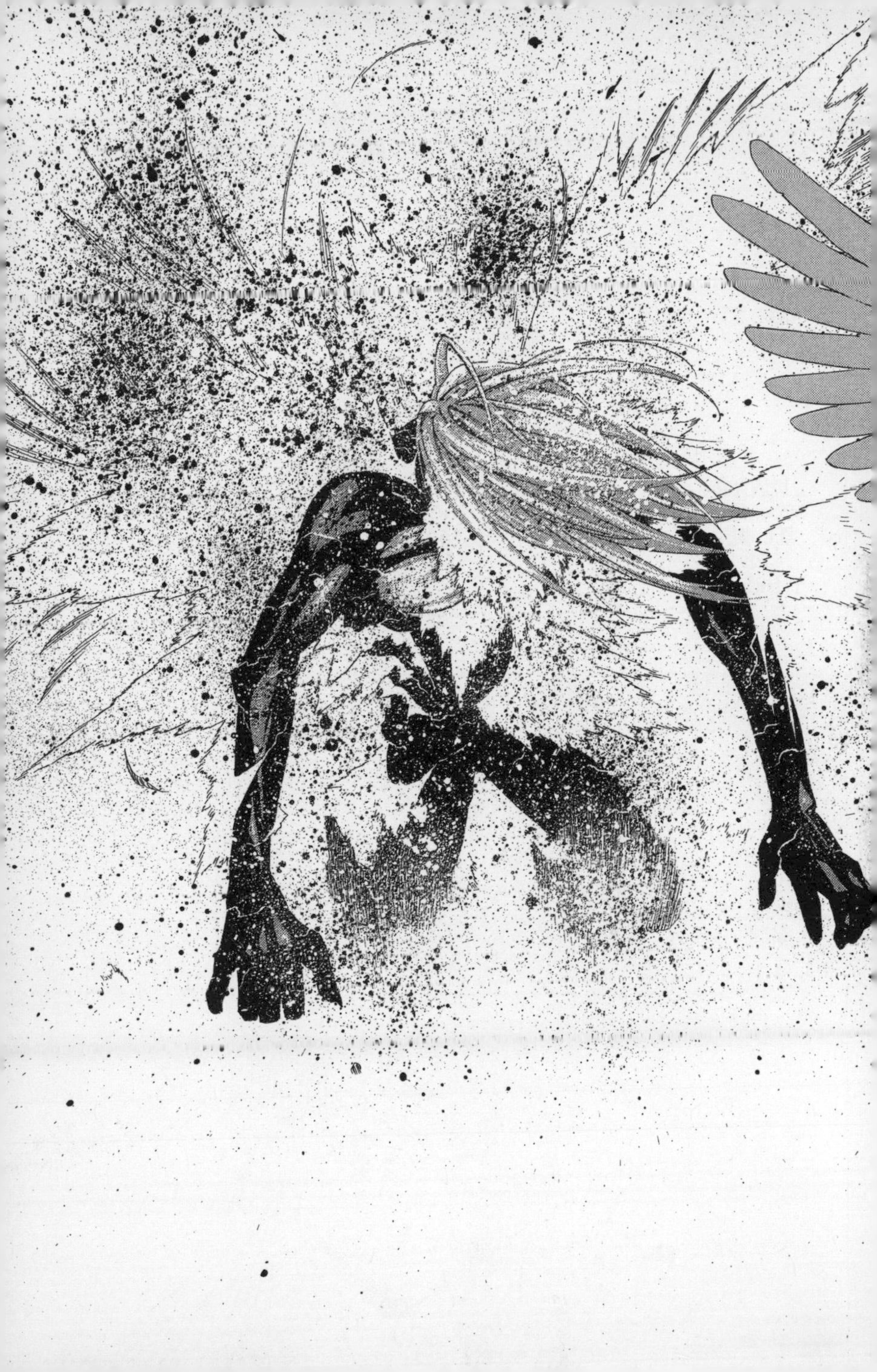

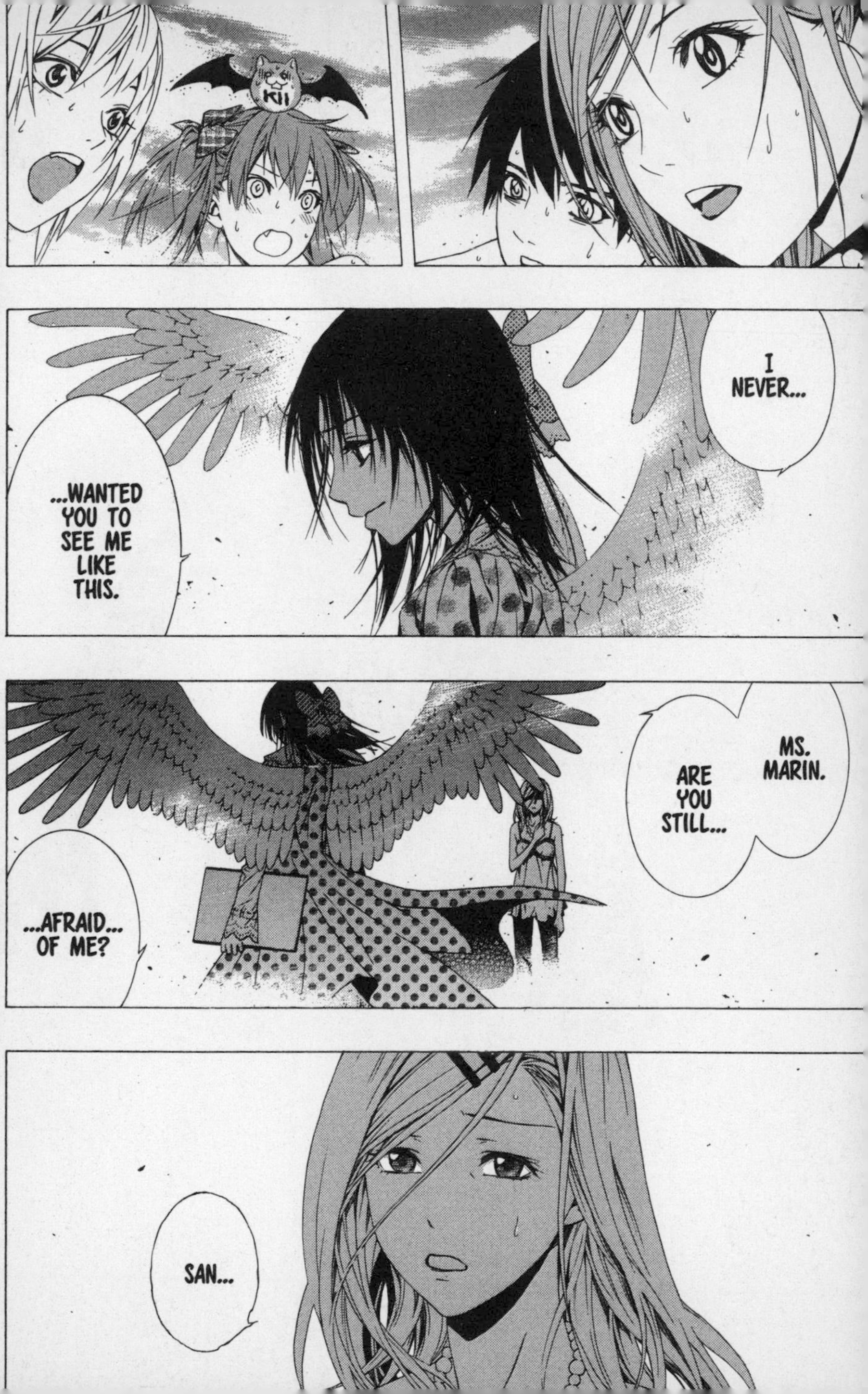
KII
I NEVER...
...WANTED YOU TO SEE ME LIKE THIS.
MS. MARIN.
ARE YOU STILL...
...AFRAID... OF ME?
SAN...

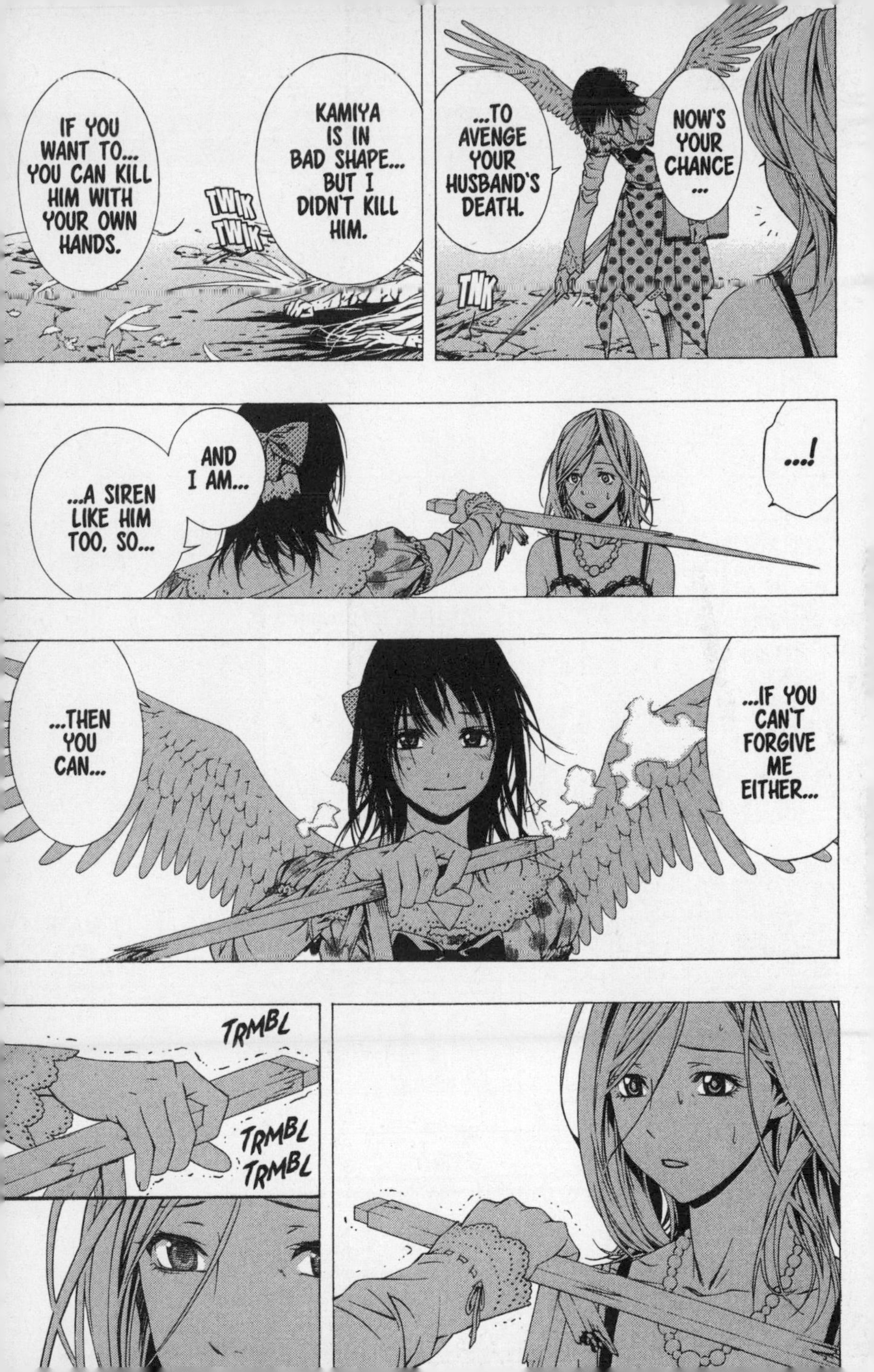
NOW'S YOUR CHANCE ...
...TO AVENGE YOUR HUSBAND'S DEATH.
TNK
KAMIYA IS IN BAD SHAPE... BUT I DIDN'T KILL HIM.
TWIK TWIK
IF YOU WANT TO... YOU CAN KILL HIM WITH YOUR OWN HANDS.
...!
AND I AM...
...A SIREN LIKE HIM TOO, SO...
...IF YOU CAN'T FORGIVE ME EITHER...
...THEN YOU CAN...
TRMBL
TRMBL TRMBL

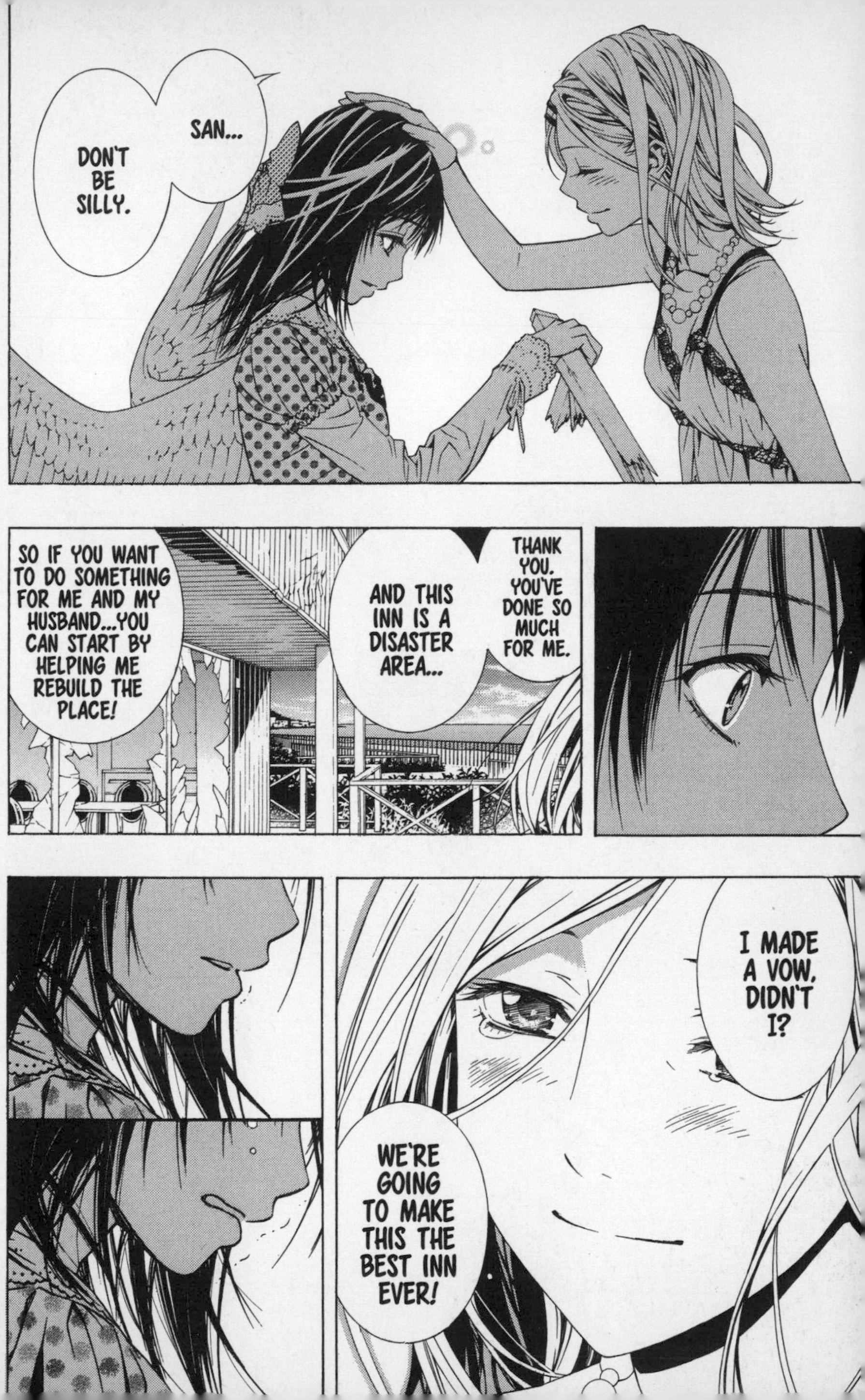
SAN...
DON'T BE SILLY.
THANK YOU. YOU'VE DONE SO MUCH FOR ME.
AND THIS INN IS A DISASTER AREA...
SO IF YOU WANT TO DO SOMETHING FOR ME AND MY HUSBAND...YOU CAN START BY HELPING ME REBUILD THE PLACE!
I MADE A VOW, DIDN'T I?
WE'RE GOING TO MAKE THIS THE BEST INN EVER!

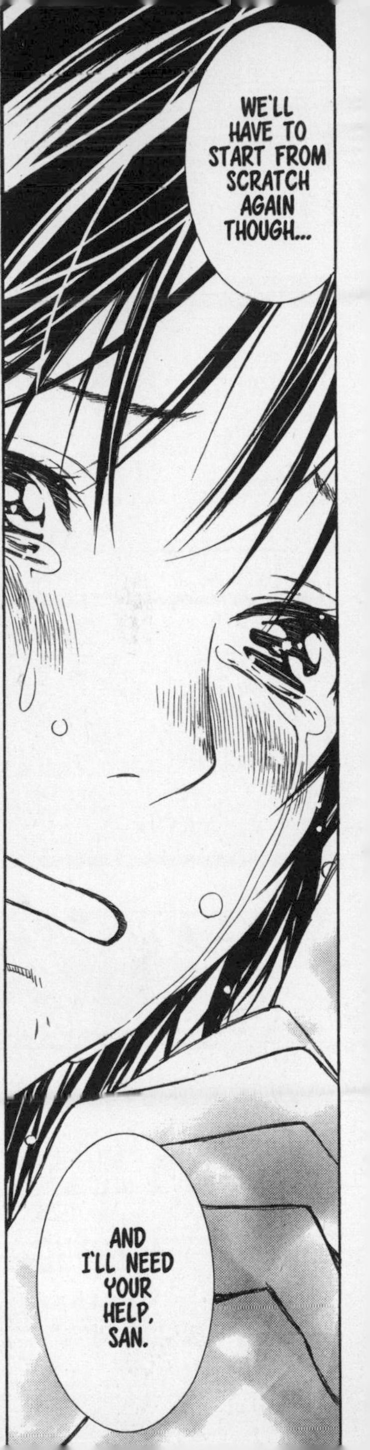
WE'LL HAVE TO START FROM SCRATCH AGAIN THOUGH...
AND I'LL NEED YOUR HELP, SAN.

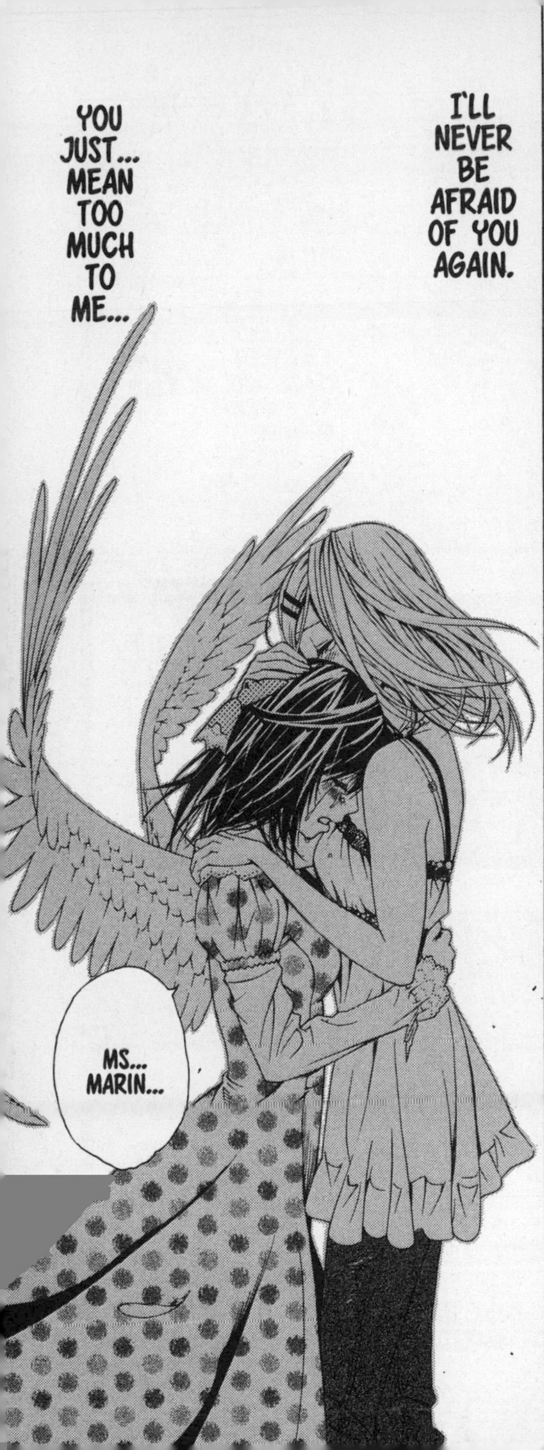
I'LL NEVER BE AFRAID OF YOU AGAIN.
YOU JUST... MEAN TOO MUCH TO ME...
MS... MARIN...

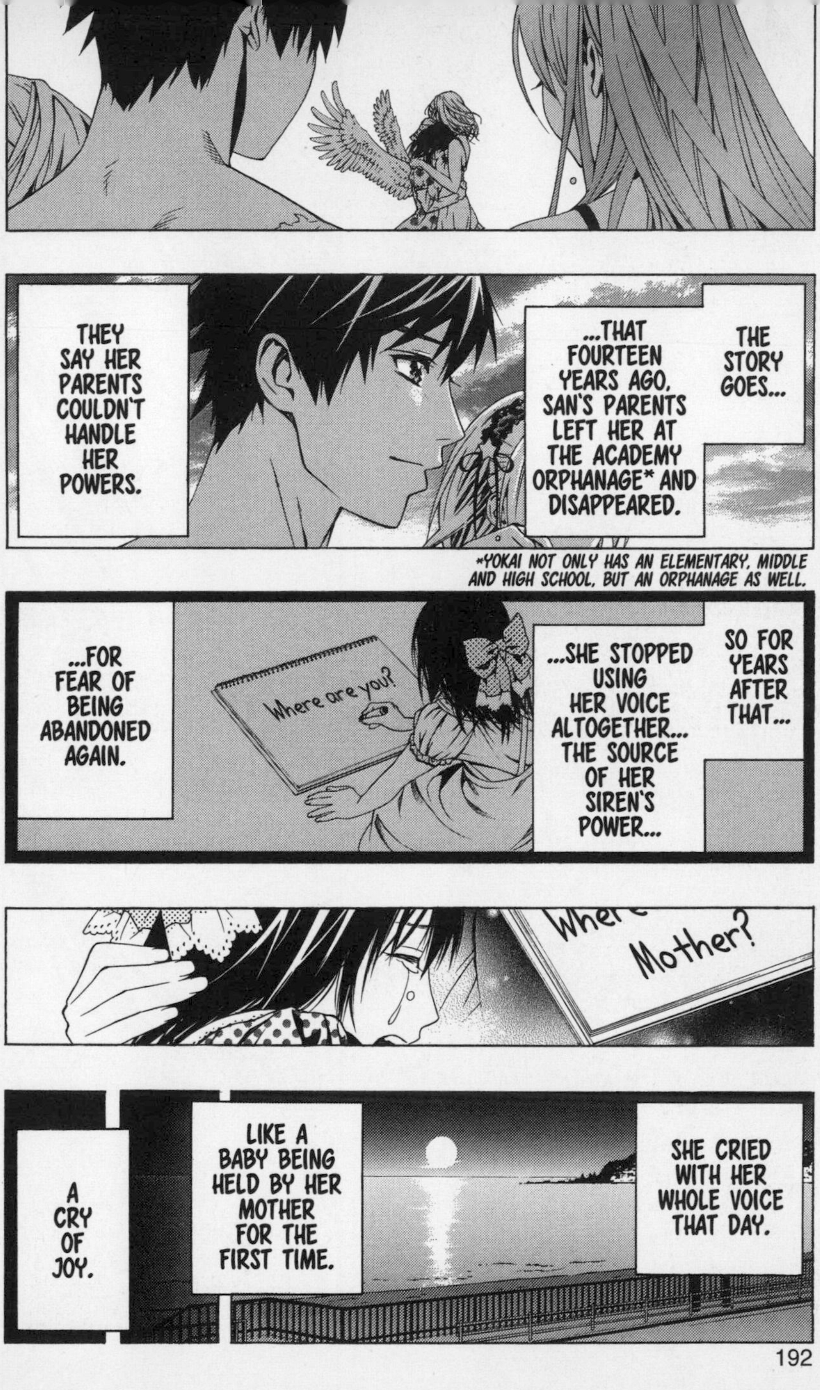
THE STORY GOES...
...THAT FOURTEEN YEARS AGO, SAN'S PARENTS LEFT HER AT THE ACADEMY ORPHANAGE* AND DISAPPEARED.
THEY SAY HER PARENTS COULDN'T HANDLE HER POWERS.
*YOKAI NOT ONLY HAS AN ELEMENTARY, MIDDLE AND HIGH SCHOOL, BUT AN ORPHANAGE AS WELL.
SO FOR YEARS AFTER THAT...
...SHE STOPPED USING HER VOICE ALTOGETHER... THE SOURCE OF HER SIREN'S POWER...
...FOR FEAR OF BEING ABANDONED AGAIN.
Where are you?
Mother?
SHE CRIED WITH HER WHOLE VOICE THAT DAY.
LIKE A BABY BEING HELD BY HER MOTHER FOR THE FIRST TIME.
A CRY OF JOY.

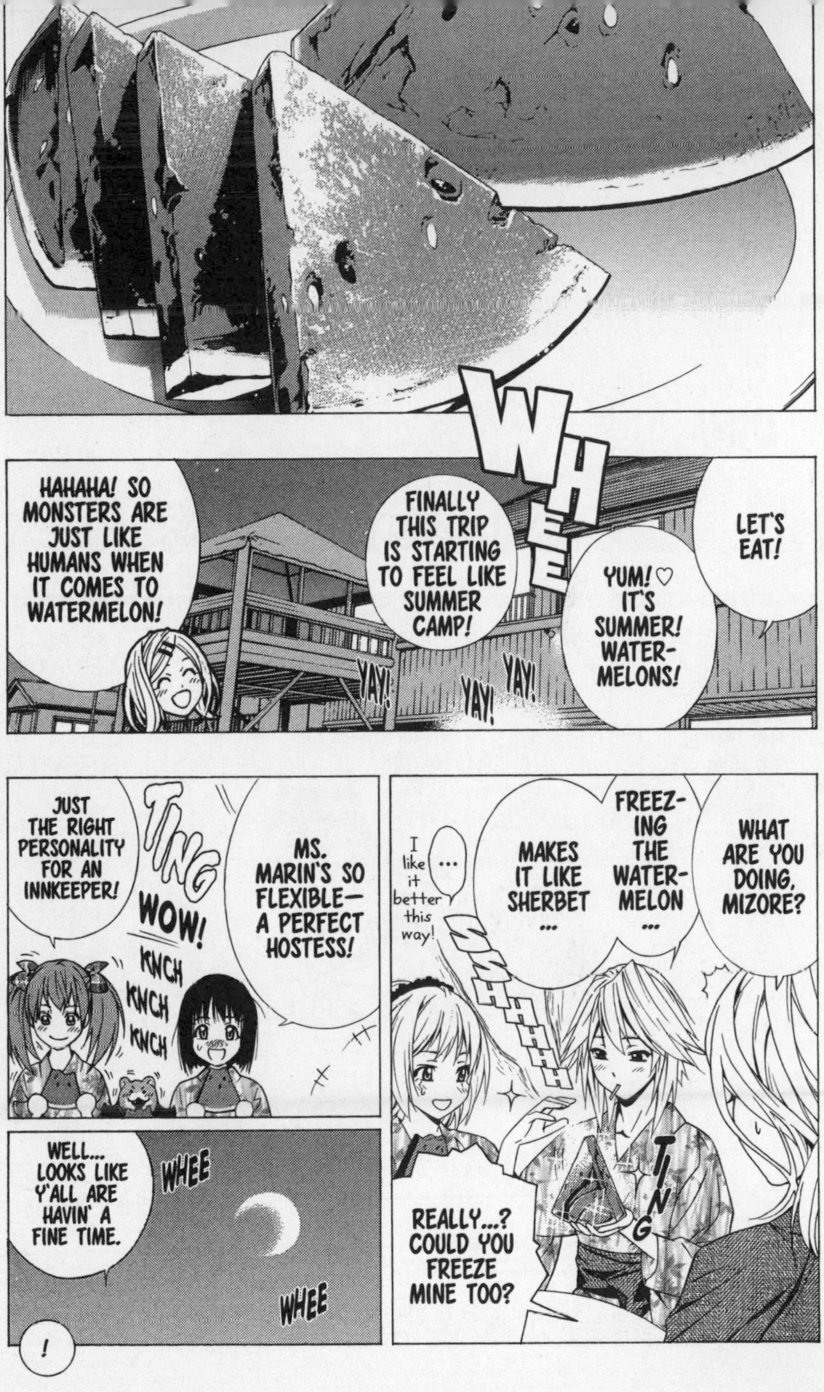
WHEE
LET'S EAT!
YUM! ♡ IT'S SUMMER! WATER-MELONS!
FINALLY THIS TRIP IS STARTING TO FEEL LIKE SUMMER CAMP!
YAY!
YAY!
YAY!
HAHAHA! SO MONSTERS ARE JUST LIKE HUMANS WHEN IT COMES TO WATERMELON!
WHAT ARE YOU DOING, MIZORE?
FREEZ-ING THE WATER-MELON ...
MAKES IT LIKE SHERBET ...
...
I like it better this way!
SHHHHHH
TING
REALLY...? COULD YOU FREEZE MINE TOO?
MS. MARIN'S SO FLEXIBLE— A PERFECT HOSTESS!
TING
JUST THE RIGHT PERSONALITY FOR AN INNKEEPER!
WOW!
KNCH
KNCH
KNCH
WHEE
WELL... LOOKS LIKE Y'ALL ARE HAVIN' A FINE TIME.
WHEE
!

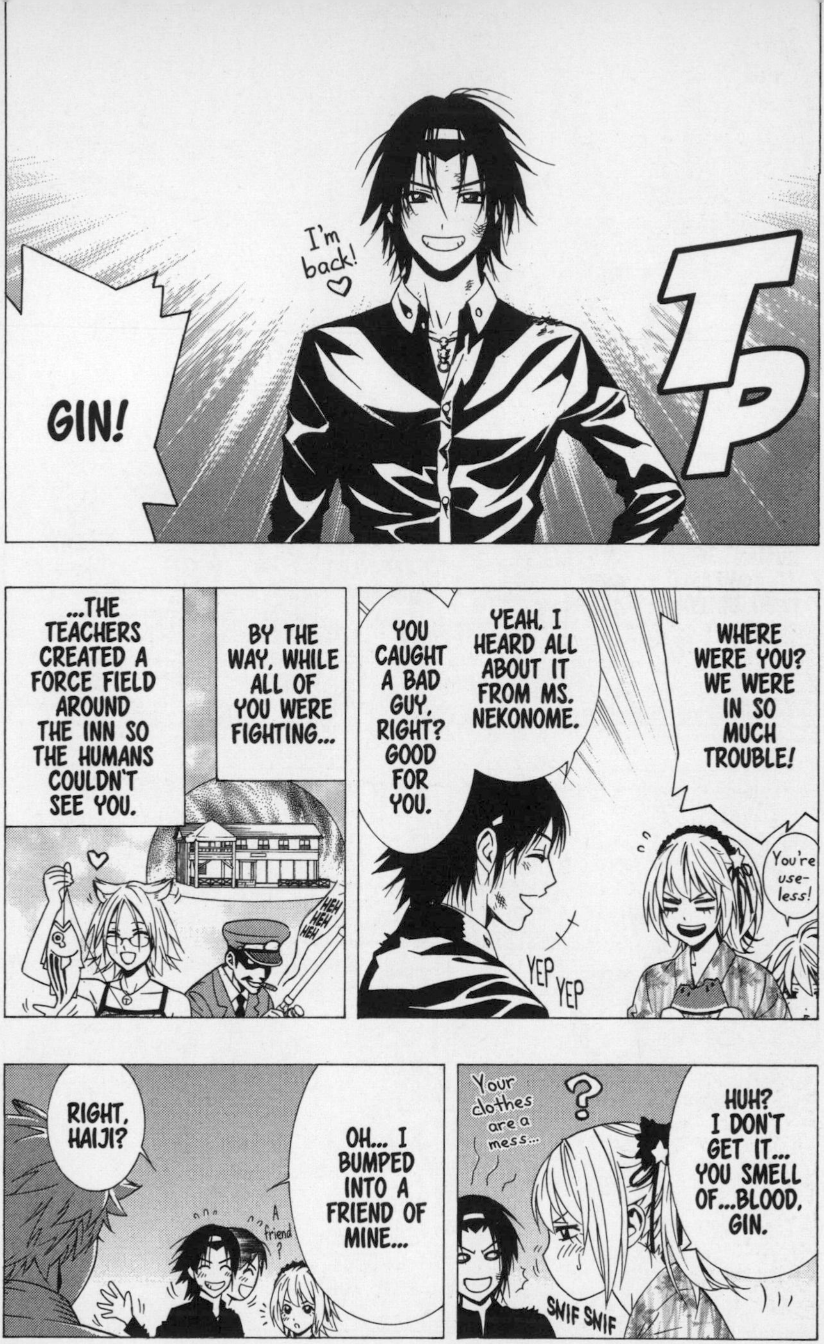
TP
I'm back! ♥
GIN!
WHERE WERE YOU? WE WERE IN SO MUCH TROUBLE!
You're useless!
YEAH, I HEARD ALL ABOUT IT FROM MS. NEKONOME.
YOU CAUGHT A BAD GUY, RIGHT? GOOD FOR YOU.
YEP YEP
BY THE WAY, WHILE ALL OF YOU WERE FIGHTING...
...THE TEACHERS CREATED A FORCE FIELD AROUND THE INN SO THE HUMANS COULDN'T SEE YOU.
HEH HEH HEH
HUH? I DON'T GET IT... YOU SMELL OF...BLOOD, GIN.
?
Your clothes are a mess...
SNIF SNIF
OH... I BUMPED INTO A FRIEND OF MINE...
A friend?
RIGHT, HAIJI?

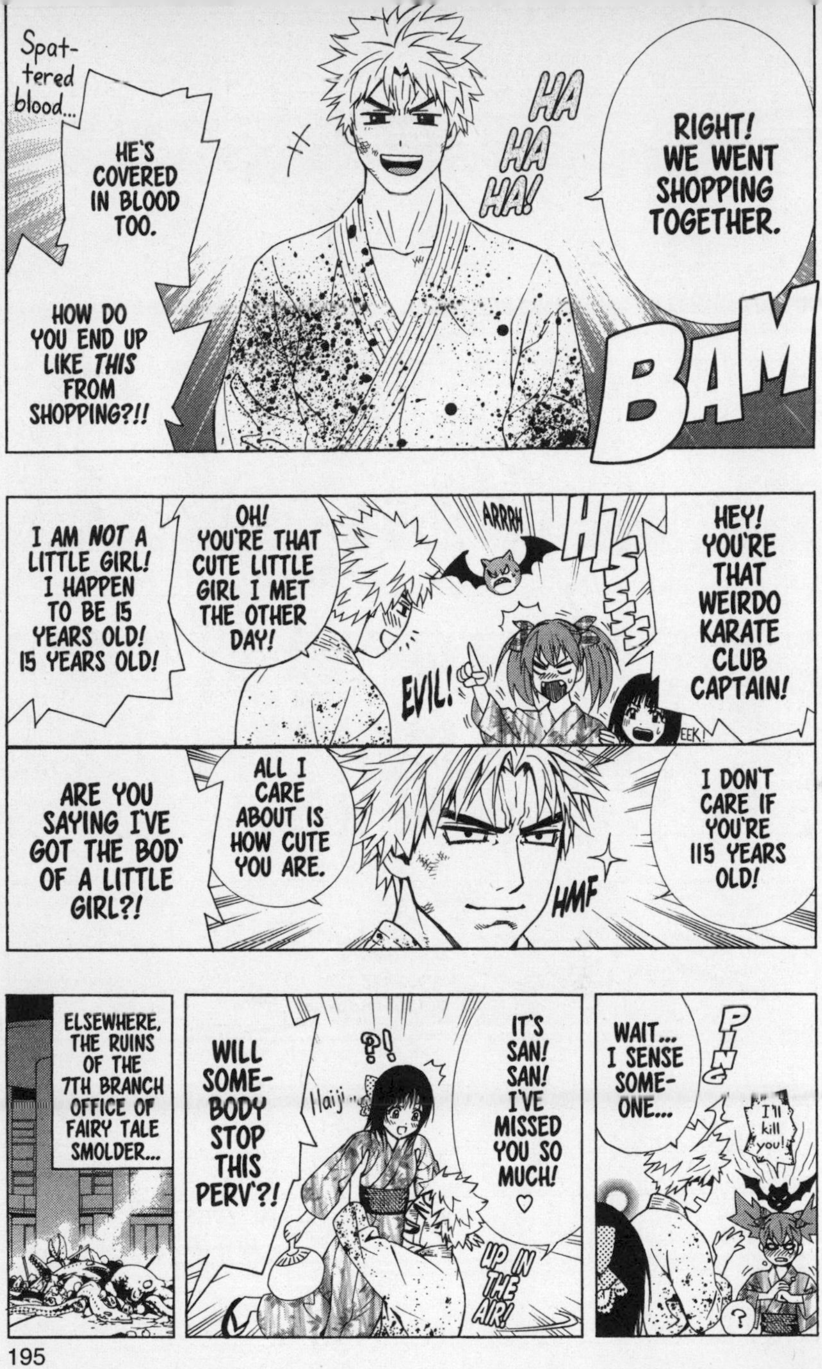
RIGHT! WE WENT SHOPPING TOGETHER.
HA HA HA!
BAM
Spat-tered blood...
HE'S COVERED IN BLOOD TOO.
HOW DO YOU END UP LIKE *THIS* FROM SHOPPING?!!
HEY! YOU'RE THAT WEIRDO KARATE CLUB CAPTAIN!
HISSSS
ARRRH
EVIL!
EEK!
OH! YOU'RE THAT CUTE LITTLE GIRL I MET THE OTHER DAY!
I AM *NOT* A LITTLE GIRL! I HAPPEN TO BE 15 YEARS OLD! 15 YEARS OLD!
I DON'T CARE IF YOU'RE 115 YEARS OLD!
HMF
ALL I CARE ABOUT IS HOW CUTE YOU ARE.
ARE YOU SAYING I'VE GOT THE BOD' OF A LITTLE GIRL?!
PING
WAIT... I SENSE SOME-ONE...
I'll kill you!
?
IT'S SAN! SAN! I'VE MISSED YOU SO MUCH! ♡
?!
Haiji...
WILL SOME-BODY STOP THIS PERV'?!
UP IN THE AIR!
ELSEWHERE, THE RUINS OF THE 7TH BRANCH OFFICE OF FAIRY TALE SMOLDER...

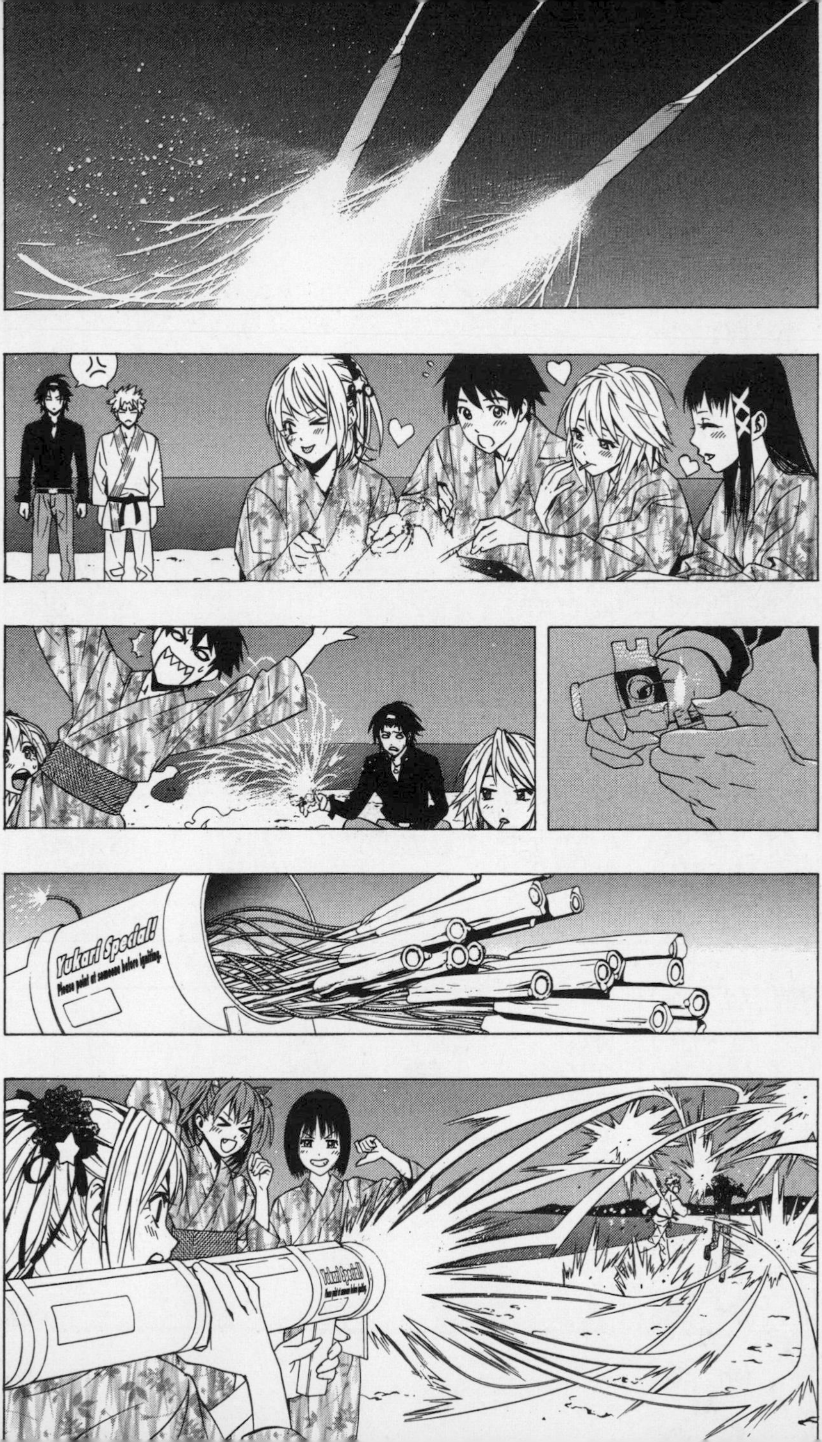
Yukari Special!
Please point at someone before igniting.

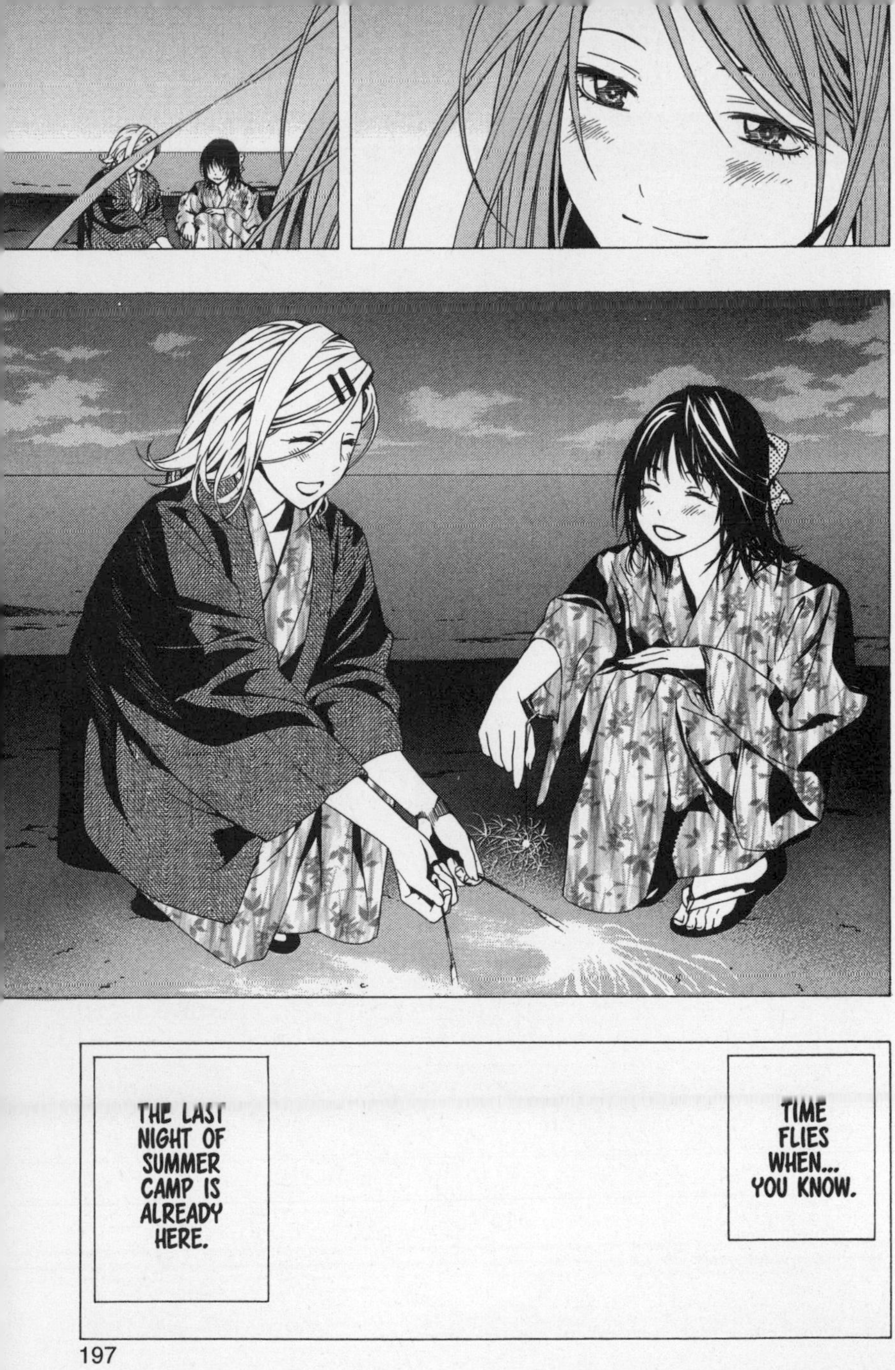
TIME FLIES WHEN... YOU KNOW.
THE LAST NIGHT OF SUMMER CAMP IS ALREADY HERE.

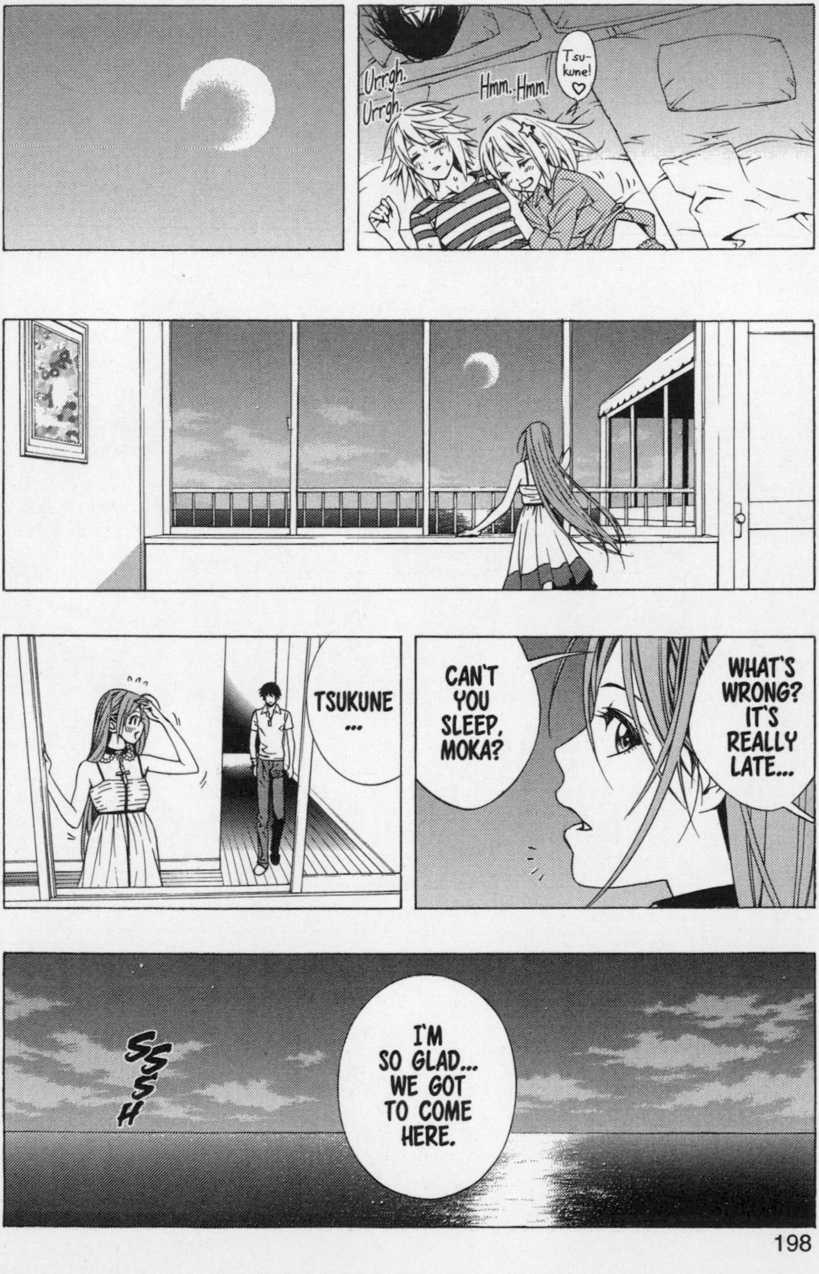
Tsu-kune! ♡
Hmm. Hmm.
Urrgh. Urrgh.
WHAT'S WRONG? IT'S REALLY LATE...
CAN'T YOU SLEEP, MOKA?
TSUKUNE ...
I'M SO GLAD... WE GOT TO COME HERE.
SSSH

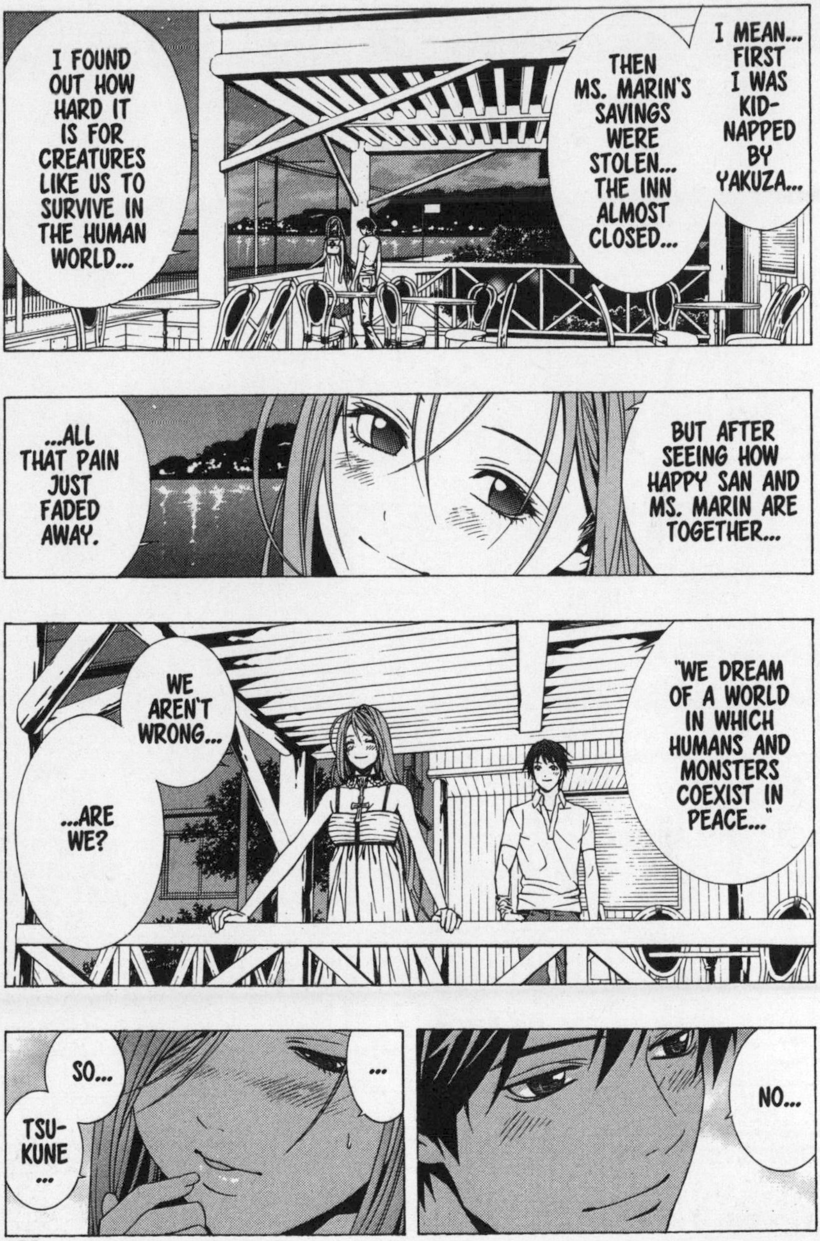
I MEAN... FIRST I WAS KID-NAPPED BY YAKUZA...
THEN MS. MARIN'S SAVINGS WERE STOLEN... THE INN ALMOST CLOSED...
I FOUND OUT HOW HARD IT IS FOR CREATURES LIKE US TO SURVIVE IN THE HUMAN WORLD...
BUT AFTER SEEING HOW HAPPY SAN AND MS. MARIN ARE TOGETHER...
...ALL THAT PAIN JUST FADED AWAY.
"WE DREAM OF A WORLD IN WHICH HUMANS AND MONSTERS COEXIST IN PEACE..."
WE AREN'T WRONG...
...ARE WE?
NO...
...
SO...
TSU-KUNE ...

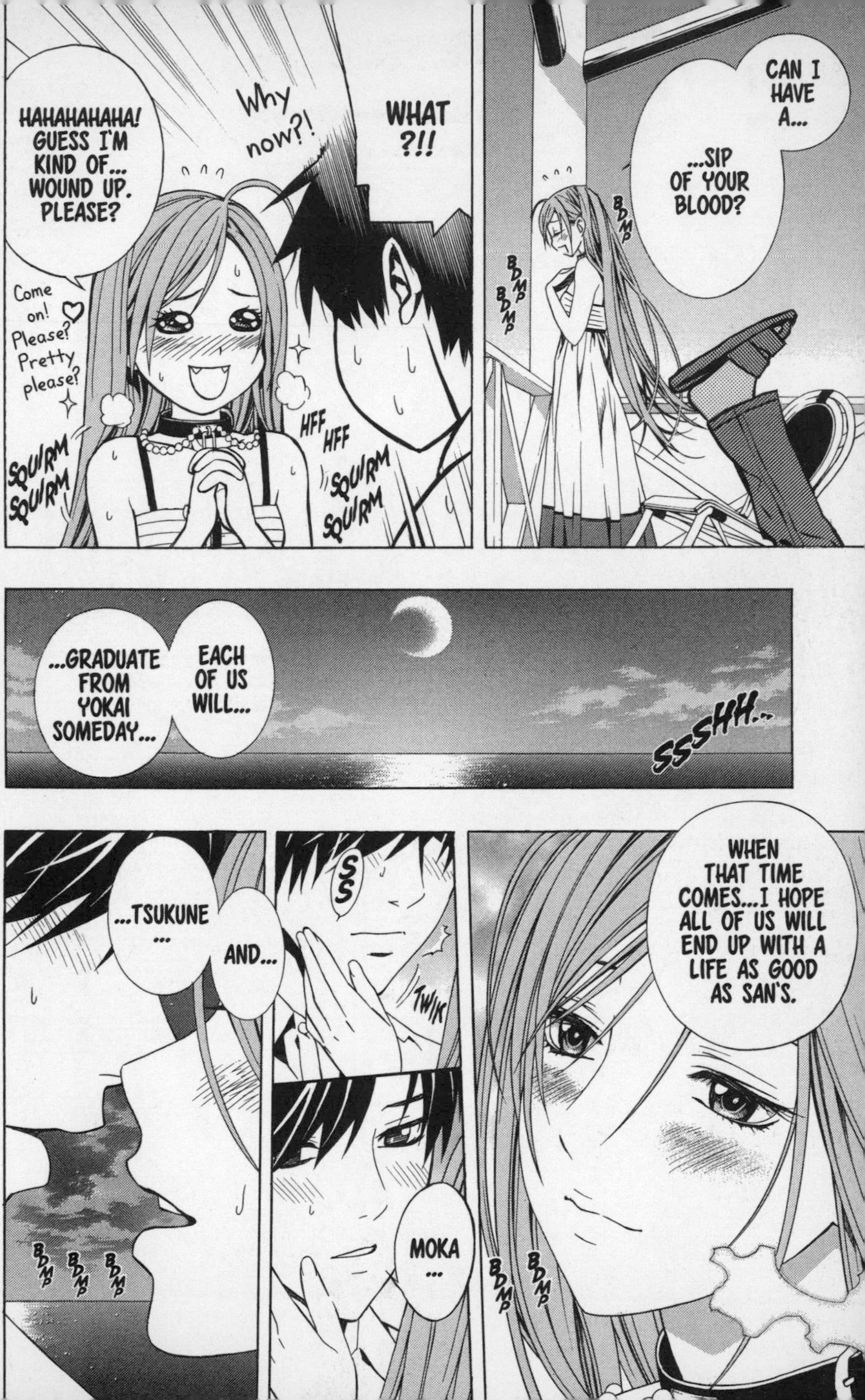
CAN I HAVE A...
...SIP OF YOUR BLOOD?
BDMP
BDMP BDMP
WHAT ?!!
Why now?!
HAHAHAHAHA! GUESS I'M KIND OF... WOUND UP. PLEASE?
Come on! Please? Pretty please?
HFF HFF
SQUIRM SQUIRM
SQUIRM SQUIRM
EACH OF US WILL...
...GRADUATE FROM YOKAI SOMEDAY...
SSSHH...
WHEN THAT TIME COMES...I HOPE ALL OF US WILL END UP WITH A LIFE AS GOOD AS SAN'S.
BDMP BDMP
SS
TWIK
AND...
MOKA ...
...TSUKUNE ...
BDMP BDMP BDMP

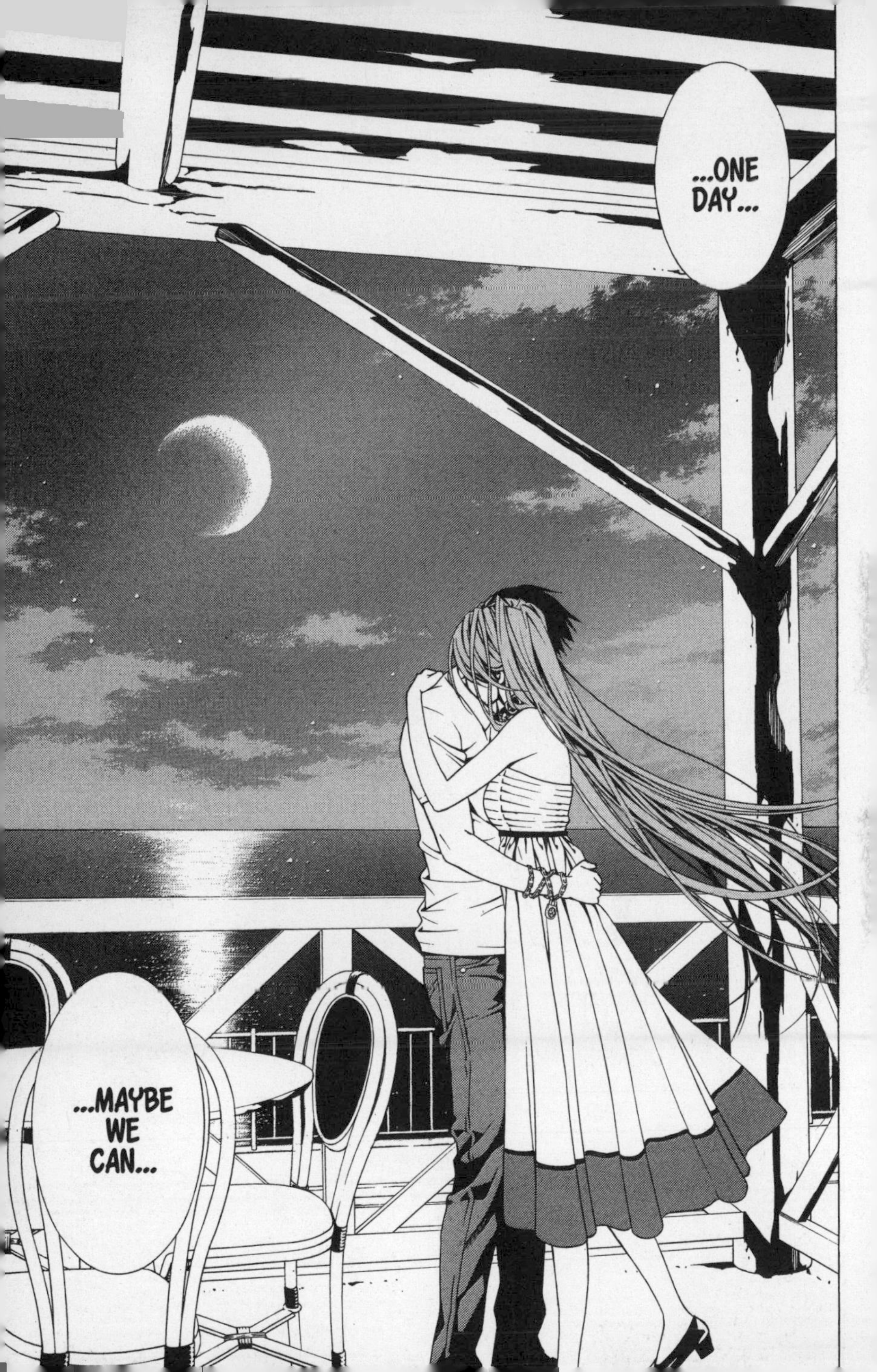
...ONE DAY...
...MAYBE WE CAN...

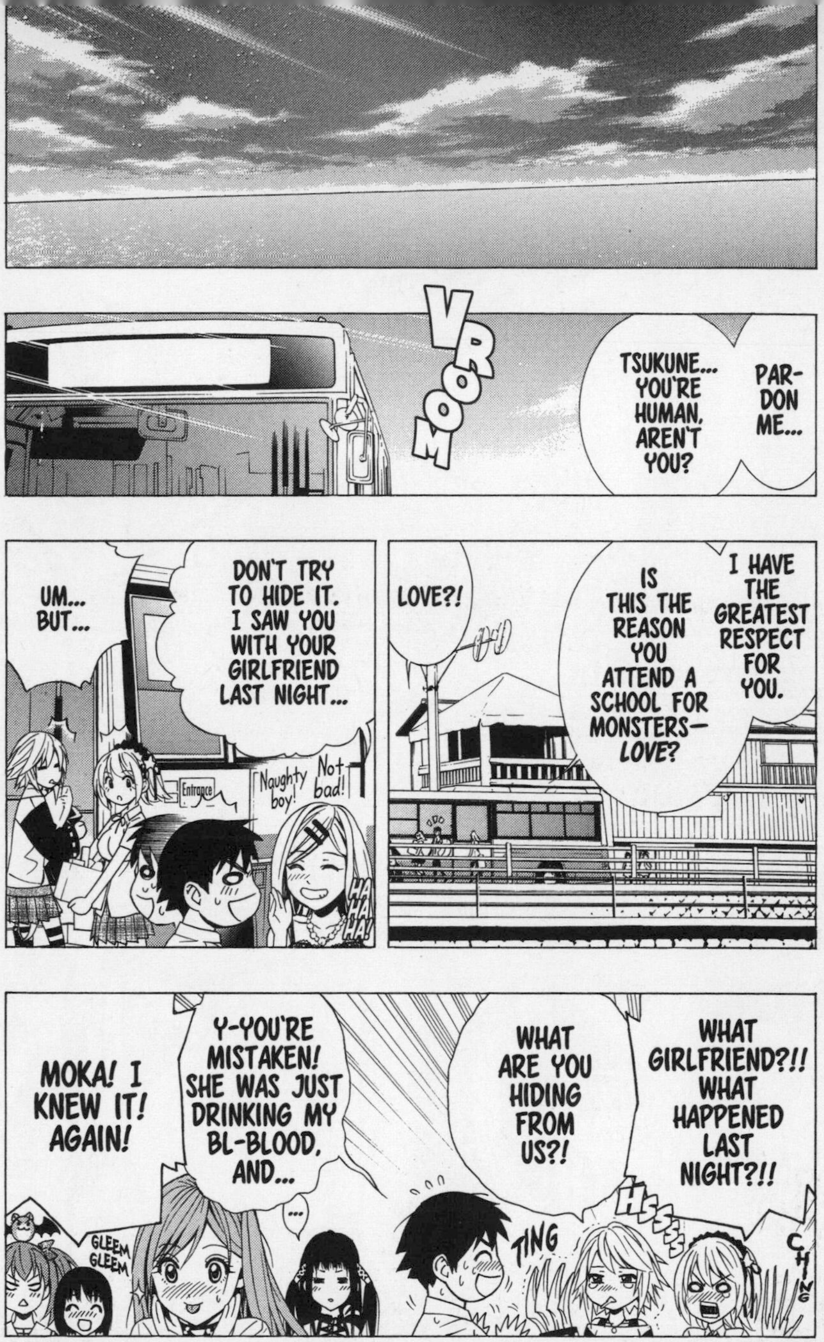
PARDON ME...
TSUKUNE... YOU'RE HUMAN, AREN'T YOU?
VROOM
I HAVE THE GREATEST RESPECT FOR YOU.
IS THIS THE REASON YOU ATTEND A SCHOOL FOR MONSTERS— LOVE?
LOVE?!
DON'T TRY TO HIDE IT. I SAW YOU WITH YOUR GIRLFRIEND LAST NIGHT...
UM... BUT...
Not bad!
Naughty boy!
Entrance
HA HA HA!
WHAT GIRLFRIEND?!! WHAT HAPPENED LAST NIGHT?!!
CHING
HSSSS
WHAT ARE YOU HIDING FROM US?!
TING
Y-YOU'RE MISTAKEN! SHE WAS JUST DRINKING MY BL-BLOOD, AND...
...
MOKA! I KNEW IT! AGAIN!
GLEEM GLEEM

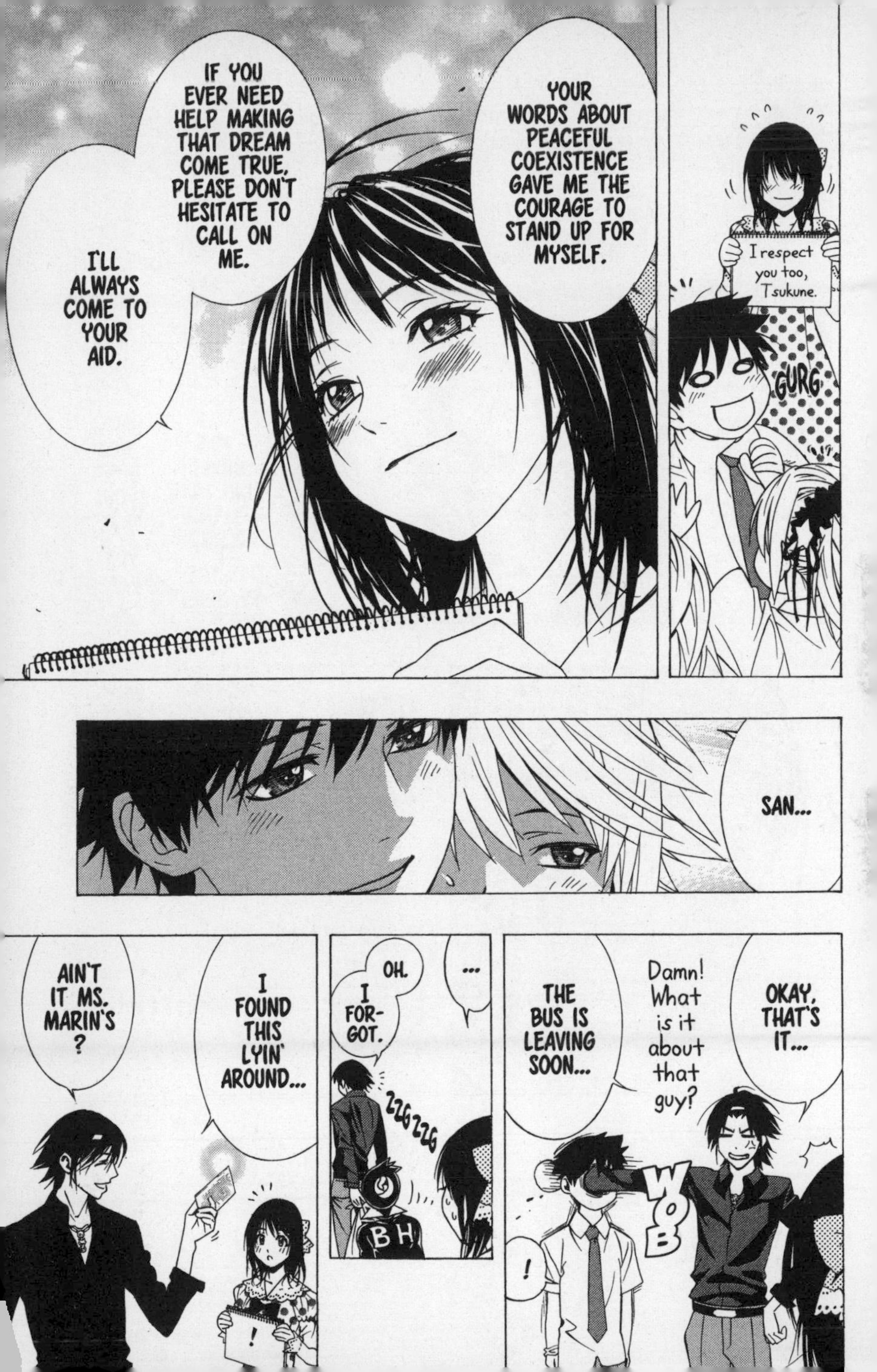

I respect you too, Tsukune.
GURG
YOUR WORDS ABOUT PEACEFUL COEXISTENCE GAVE ME THE COURAGE TO STAND UP FOR MYSELF.
IF YOU EVER NEED HELP MAKING THAT DREAM COME TRUE, PLEASE DON'T HESITATE TO CALL ON ME.
I'LL ALWAYS COME TO YOUR AID.
SAN...
OKAY, THAT'S IT...
Damn! What is it about that guy?
THE BUS IS LEAVING SOON...
WOB
!
...
OH.
I FOR-GOT.
ZZG ZZG
BH
I FOUND THIS LYIN' AROUND...
AIN'T IT MS. MARIN'S ?
!

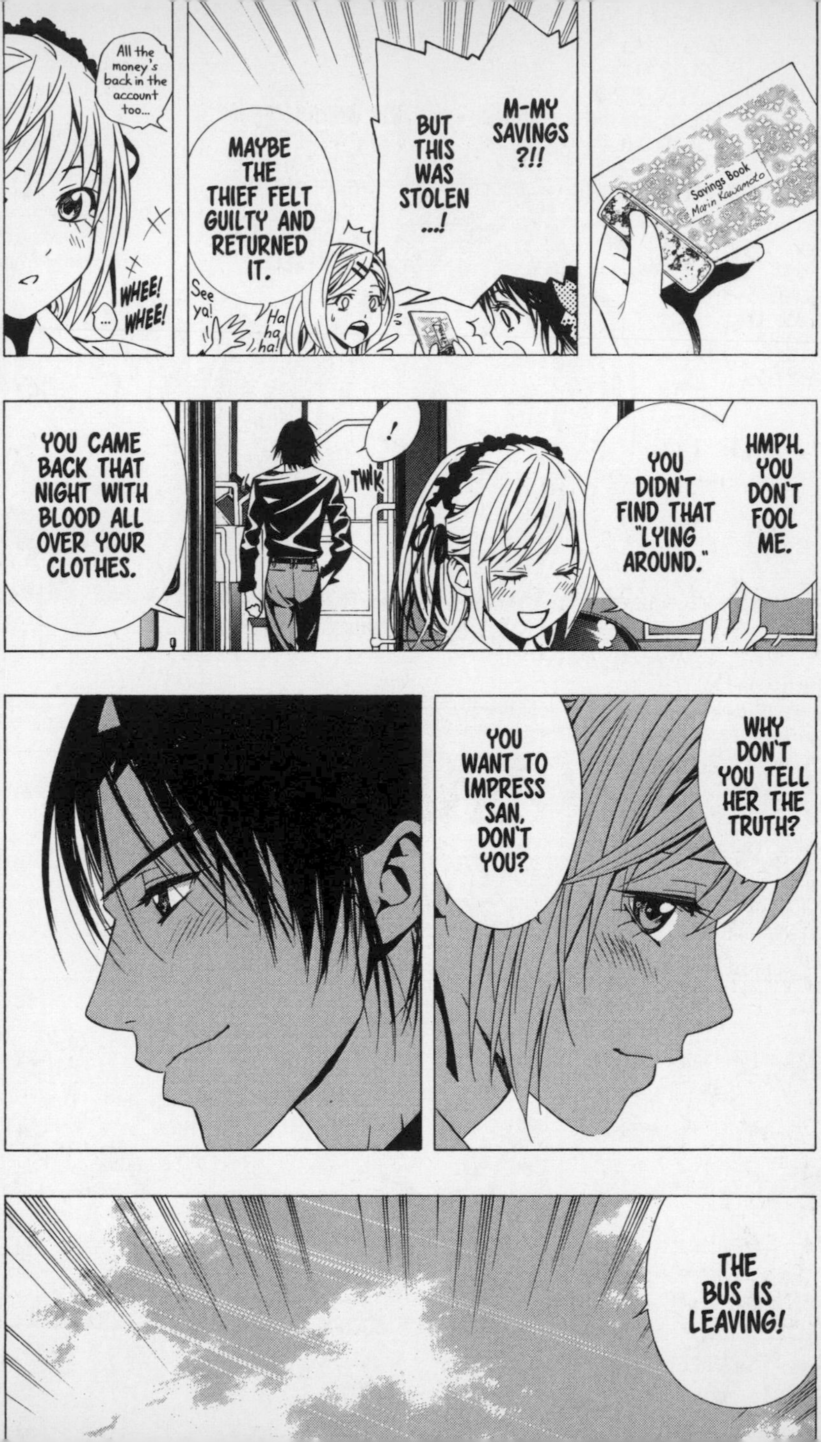
Savings Book
Marin Kawamoto
M-MY SAVINGS ?!!
BUT THIS WAS STOLEN ...!
MAYBE THE THIEF FELT GUILTY AND RETURNED IT.
Ha ha ha!
See ya!
All the money's back in the account too...
WHEE! WHEE!
...
HMPH. YOU DON'T FOOL ME.
YOU DIDN'T FIND THAT "LYING AROUND."
TWK
!
YOU CAME BACK THAT NIGHT WITH BLOOD ALL OVER YOUR CLOTHES.
WHY DON'T YOU TELL HER THE TRUTH?
YOU WANT TO IMPRESS SAN, DON'T YOU?
THE BUS IS LEAVING!

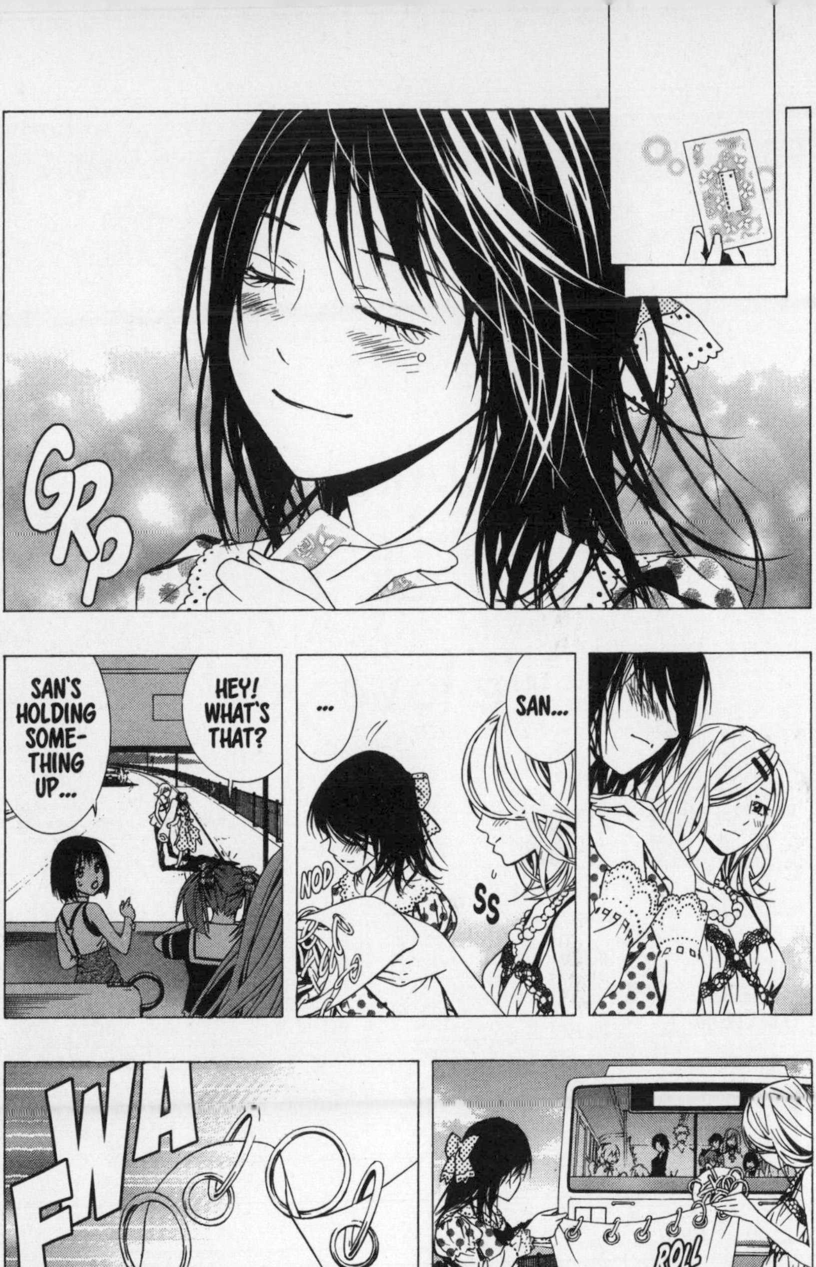
GRP
SAN...
...
NOD
SS
HEY! WHAT'S THAT?
SAN'S HOLDING SOME-THING UP...
ROLL
ROLL
FWA

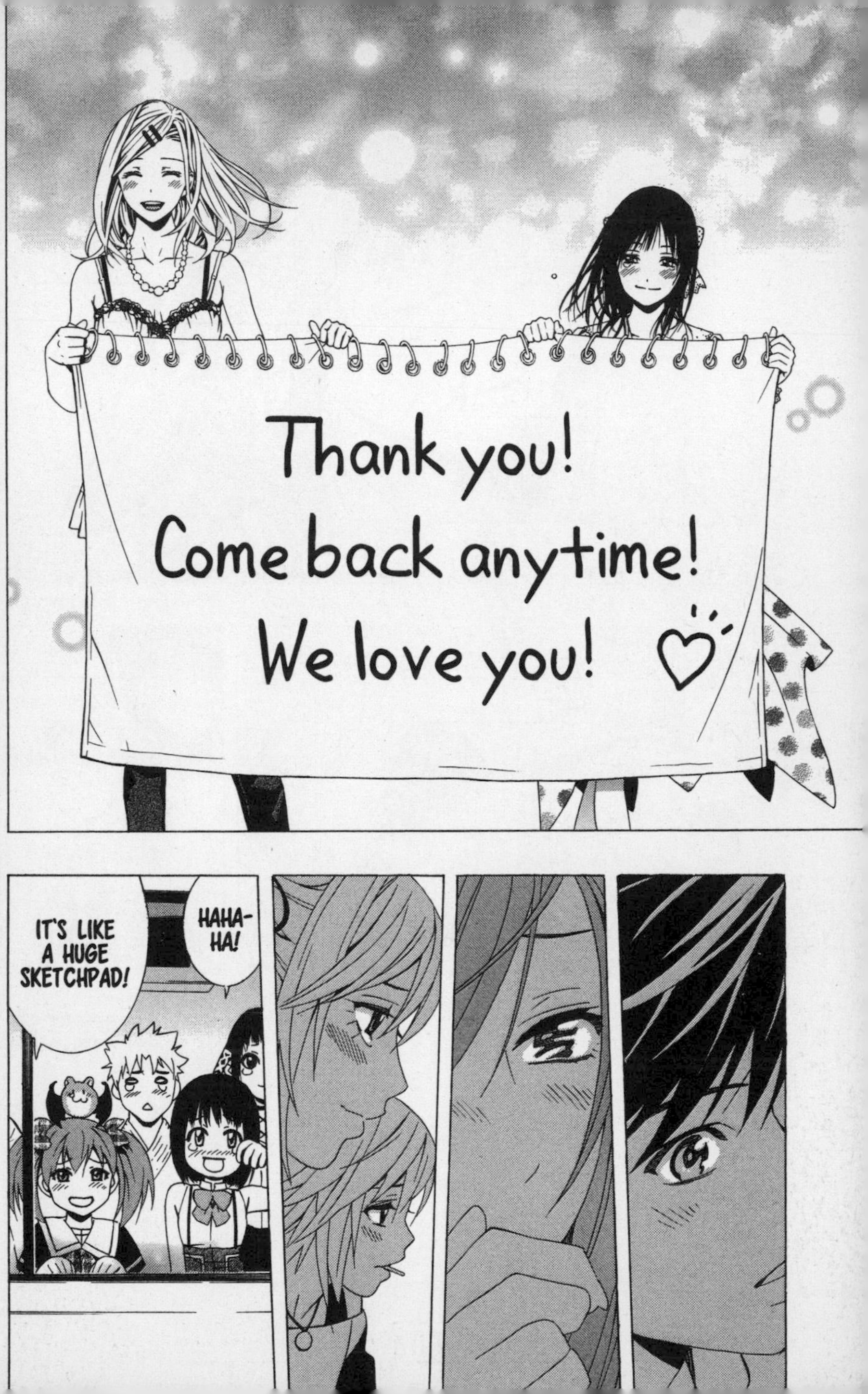
Thank you!
Come back anytime!
We love you!
HAHAHA!
IT'S LIKE A HUGE SKETCHPAD!

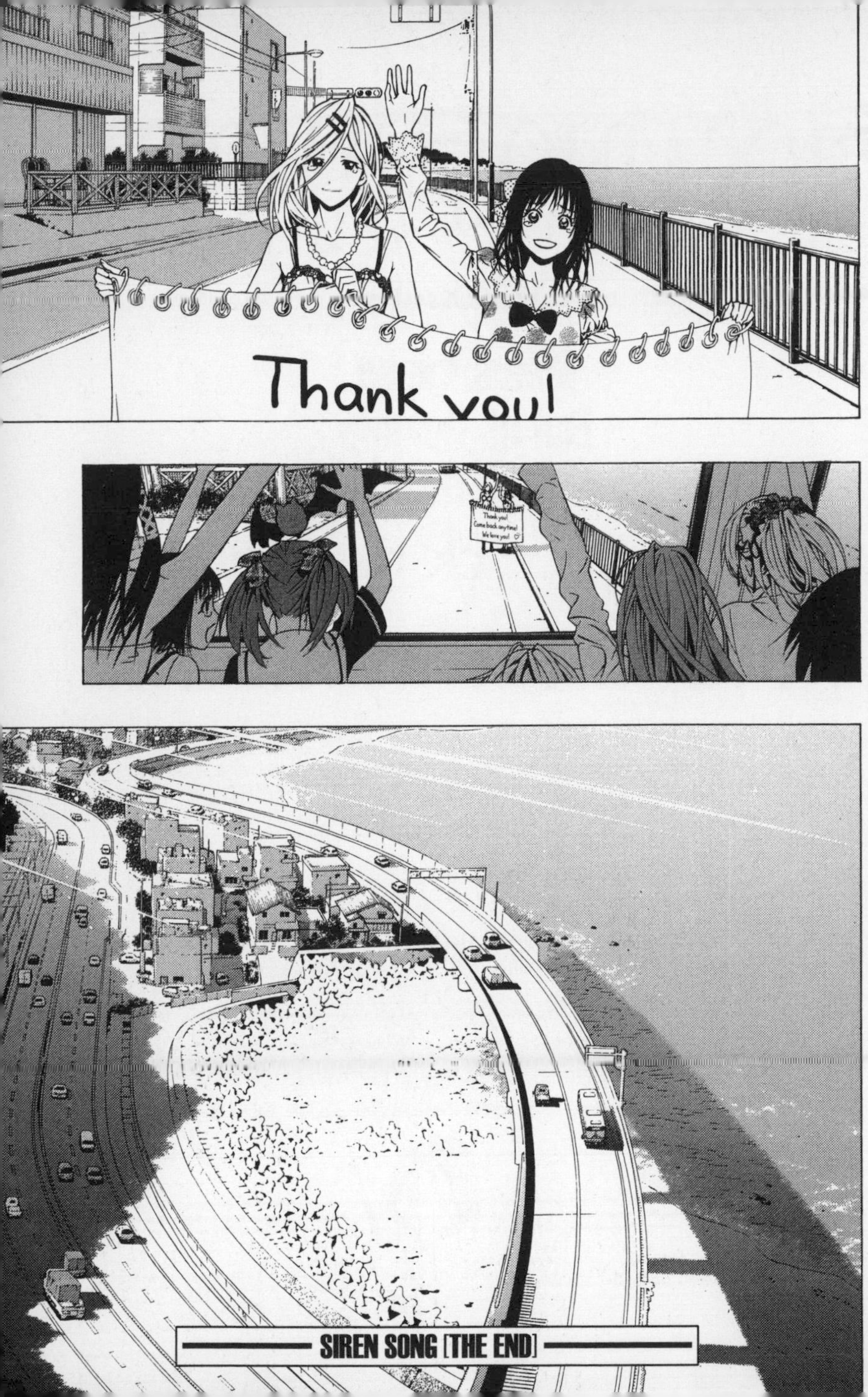
Thank you!
Thank you! Come back anytime! We love you! ♡
SIREN SONG [THE END]

ROSARIO+VAMPIRE
Season II

Meaningless End-of-Volume Theater
V

Spring
- Gin enters the academy. He joins the News Club. So happy! ♪
- Gin still gets into fights, but participates in club activities. So happy! ♪ (I got into a fight with him too.)

Summer
- I meet Haiji. Cheerful! ♪
- Haiji starts Karate. He's hooked on it and seems to be having fun. ♪ He makes a great duo with Gin.

Autumn
- 3rd Year Students start to think about their future. I retire from the News Club. I work part-time jobs in the human world. Hard work.

Winter
- While I'm gone, the Student Security Enforcement Committee attack the News Club. All the members except Gin leave the club. How could they...?!

Spring
- Tsukune and his friends join the News Club. Take care of Gin for me! ♪
- Ms. Marin finds me wandering around jobless and takes me in. So happy!

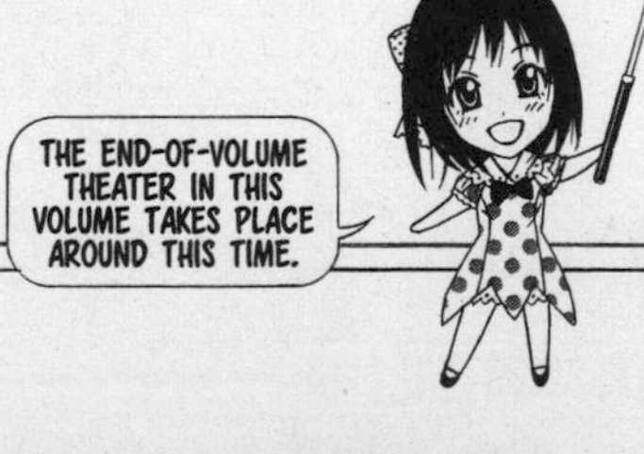
THE END-OF-VOLUME THEATER IN THIS VOLUME TAKES PLACE AROUND THIS TIME.

• Rumored Leader •

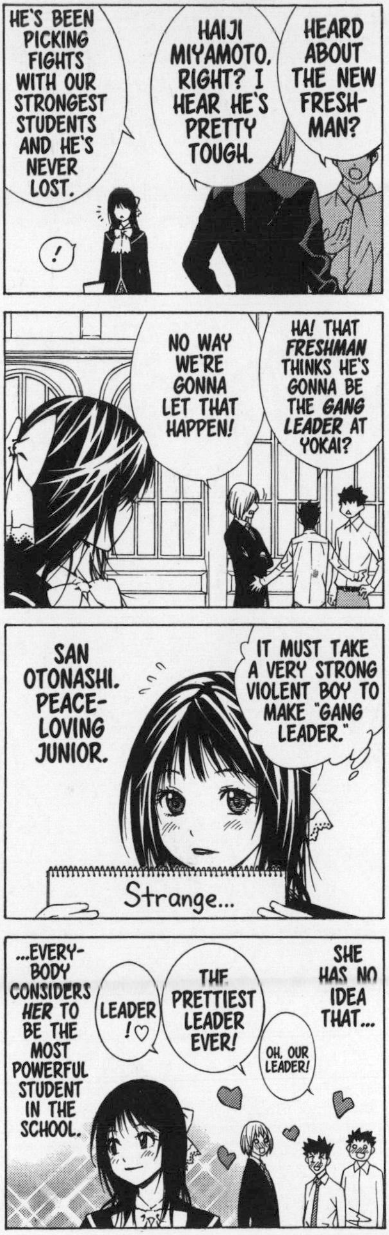
HEARD ABOUT THE NEW FRESH-MAN?
HAIJI MIYAMOTO, RIGHT? I HEAR HE'S PRETTY TOUGH.
HE'S BEEN PICKING FIGHTS WITH OUR STRONGEST STUDENTS AND HE'S NEVER LOST.
!
HA! THAT *FRESHMAN* THINKS HE'S GONNA BE THE *GANG LEADER* AT YOKAI?
NO WAY WE'RE GONNA LET THAT HAPPEN!
IT MUST TAKE A VERY STRONG VIOLENT BOY TO MAKE "GANG LEADER."
SAN OTONASHI. PEACE-LOVING JUNIOR.
Strange...
SHE HAS NO IDEA THAT...
OH, OUR LEADER!
THE PRETTIEST LEADER EVER!
LEADER!♡
...EVERY-BODY CONSIDERS *HER* TO BE THE MOST POWERFUL STUDENT IN THE SCHOOL.

• San's Invincible Legend, Part 1 •

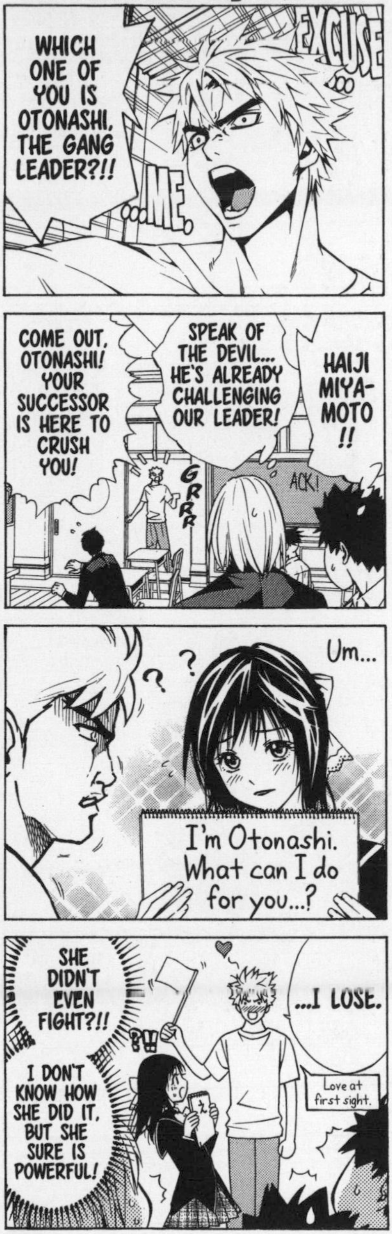
EXCUSE ...ME.
WHICH ONE OF YOU IS OTONASHI, THE GANG LEADER?!!
HAIJI MIYA-MOTO!!
SPEAK OF THE DEVIL... HE'S ALREADY CHALLENGING OUR LEADER!
ACK!
COME OUT, OTONASHI! YOUR SUCCESSOR IS HERE TO CRUSH YOU!
GRRR
Um...
? ?
I'm Otonashi. What can I do for you...?
...I LOSE.
Love at first sight.
SHE DIDN'T EVEN FIGHT?!!
?!!
I DON'T KNOW HOW SHE DID IT, BUT SHE SURE IS POWERFUL!

• Birth of a Lolita Complex •

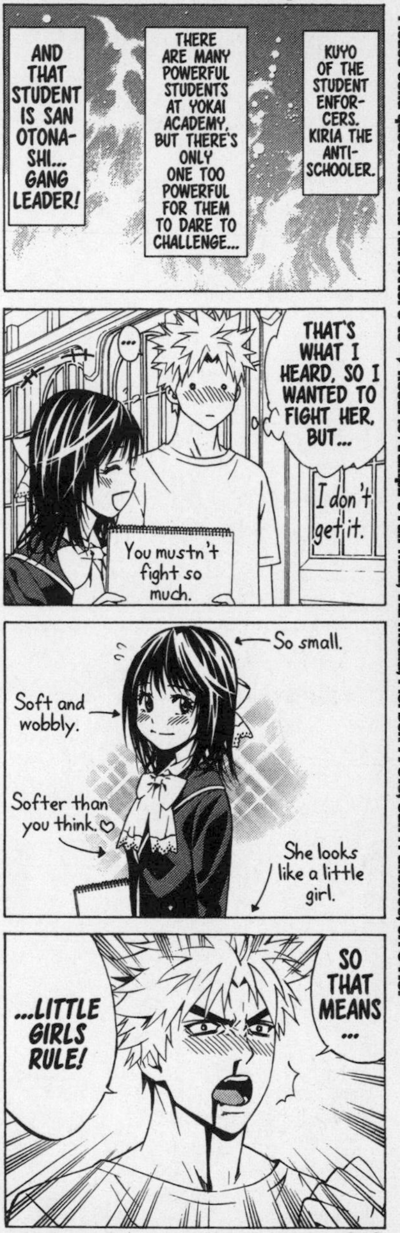
KUYO OF THE STUDENT ENFORCERS. KIRIA THE ANTI-SCHOOLER.
THERE ARE MANY POWERFUL STUDENTS AT YOKAI ACADEMY, BUT THERE'S ONLY ONE TOO POWERFUL FOR THEM TO DARE TO CHALLENGE...
AND THAT STUDENT IS SAN OTONASHI... GANG LEADER!
THAT'S WHAT I HEARD, SO I WANTED TO FIGHT HER. BUT...
I don't get it.
...
You mustn't fight so much.
So small.
Soft and wobbly.
She looks like a little girl.
Softer than you think. ♡
SO THAT MEANS...
...LITTLE GIRLS RULE!

• San's Invincible Legend, Part 2 •

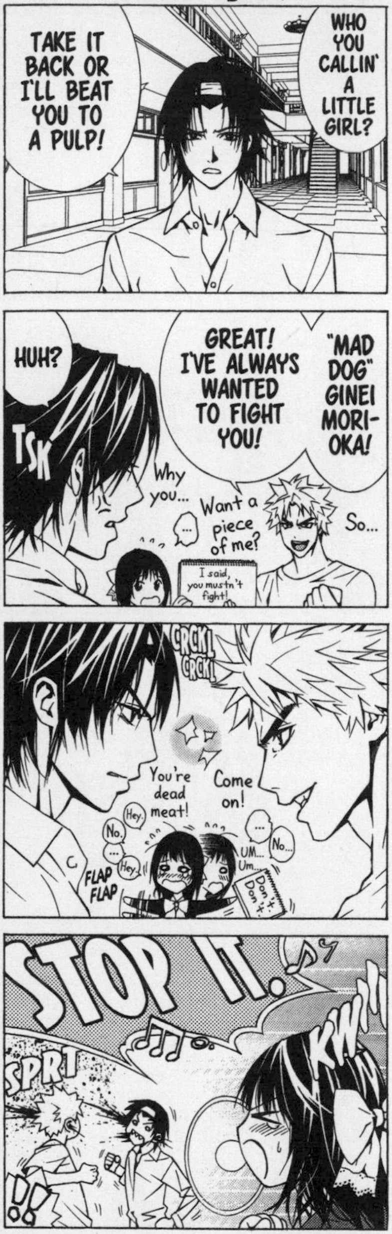
WHO YOU CALLIN' A LITTLE GIRL?
TAKE IT BACK OR I'LL BEAT YOU TO A PULP!
"MAD DOG" GINEI MORIOKA!
GREAT! I'VE ALWAYS WANTED TO FIGHT YOU!
HUH?
TSK
So...
Want a piece of me?
Why you...
...
I said, you mustn't fight!
CRCKL CRCKL
Come on!
You're dead meat!
...
No...
UM... Um...
Don't. Don't.
Hey.
No.
...
Hey.
FLAP FLAP
STOP IT.
SPRT
!!

Please send questions and fan letters to ➡ Rosario+Vampire Fan Mail, VIZ Media, P.O. Box 77010, San Francisco, CA 94107

Rosario+Vampire

Akihisa Ikeda

• Staff •

Makoto Saito
Kenji Tashiro
Nobuyuki Hayashi

• Help •

Hajime Maeda
Kumiko Yamamoto

• 3DCG •

Takaharu Yoshizawa

• Editors •

Makoto Watanabe
Takanori Asada

• Comic •

Kenju Noro

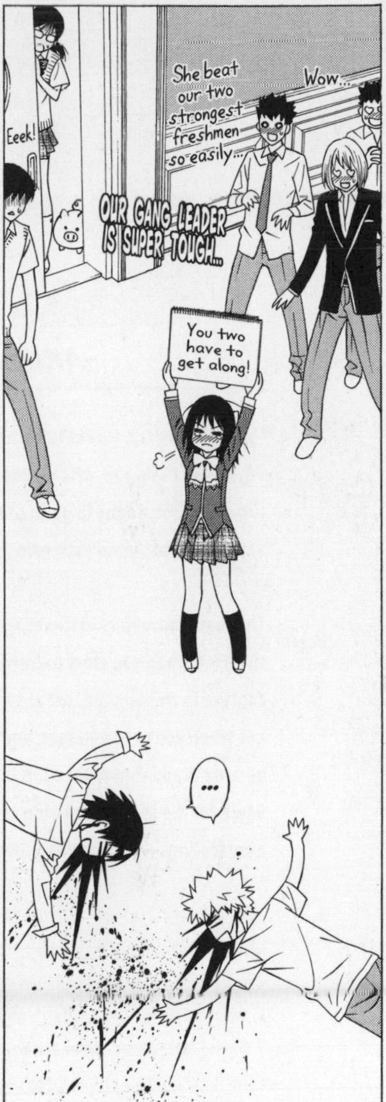
Wow...
She beat our two strongest freshmen so easily...
OUR GANG LEADER IS SUPER TOUGH...
Eeek!
You two have to get along!
...

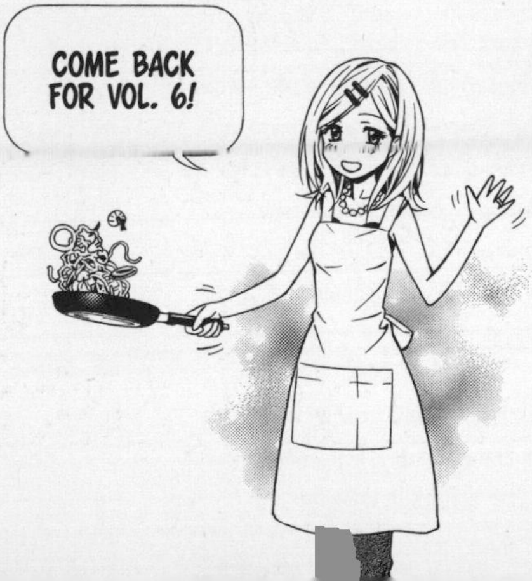
COME BACK FOR VOL. 6!

AKIHISA IKEDA

"When I grow up, I want to be a manga artist!"
Whenever I said this when I was a student, my teachers would gently
urge me, "You ought to go to college and find a career first." Thank you
very much, but mind your own business! *(laugh)*

The main characters in this story are sophomores in high school. This is
the time when you start to think about your future. What I wanted to
capture in this volume, set at summer camp, was that uneasy feeling you
get when you're a teenager, and the envy you feel for those who have
already graduated and begun their adult lives. All those feelings came up
again for me as I was drawing this story. My student life was full of uneasy feelings—and nothing else. Anyway... I hope you enjoy this volume!

Akihisa Ikeda was born in 1976 in Miyazaki. He debuted as a mangaka
with the four-volume magical warrior fantasy series *Kiruto* in 2002, which
was serialized in *Monthly Shonen Jump*. *Rosario+Vampire* debuted in
Monthly Shonen Jump in March of 2004 and is continuing in the magazine
Jump Square (Jump SQ) as *Rosario+Vampire: Season II*. In Japan,
Rosario+Vampire is also available as a drama CD. In 2008, the story was
released as an anime. Season II is also available as an anime now. And in
Japan, there is a Nintendo DS game based on the series.

Ikeda has been a huge fan of vampires and monsters since he was a little
kid. He says one of the perks of being a manga artist is being able to go for
walks during the day when everybody else is stuck in the office.

ROSARIO+VAMPIRE: Season II
5
SHONEN JUMP ADVANCED Manga Edition

STORY & ART BY AKIHISA IKEDA

Translation/Tetsuichiro Miyaki
English Adaptation/Gerard Jones
Touch-up Art & Lettering/Stephen Dutro
Cover & Interior Design/Ronnie Casson
Editor/Annette Roman

ROSARIO TO VAMPIRE SEASON II © 2007 by Akihisa Ikeda
All rights reserved. First published in Japan in 2007 by SHUEISHA Inc.,
Tokyo. English translation rights arranged by SHUEISHA Inc.

The rights of the author(s) of the work(s) in this publication to be so
identified have been asserted in accordance with the Copyright, Designs
and Patents Act 1988. A CIP catalogue record for this book is available
from the British Library.

Printed in the U.S.A.

Published by VIZ Media, LLC
P.O. Box 77010
San Francisco, CA 94107

10 9 8 7 6 5 4 3 2
First printing, July 2011
Second printing, February 2013

www.viz.com
www.shonenjump.com

CRYPT SHEET FOR

ROSARIO+VAMPIRE: SEASON II, VOL. 6

GANGSTAH

TEST 6

WHEN A SUPERNATURAL CLAN OF GANGSTERS MAKES YOU AN OFFER YOU CAN'T REFUSE...

a. refuse

b. gang up on them

c. take the Rosario (off)

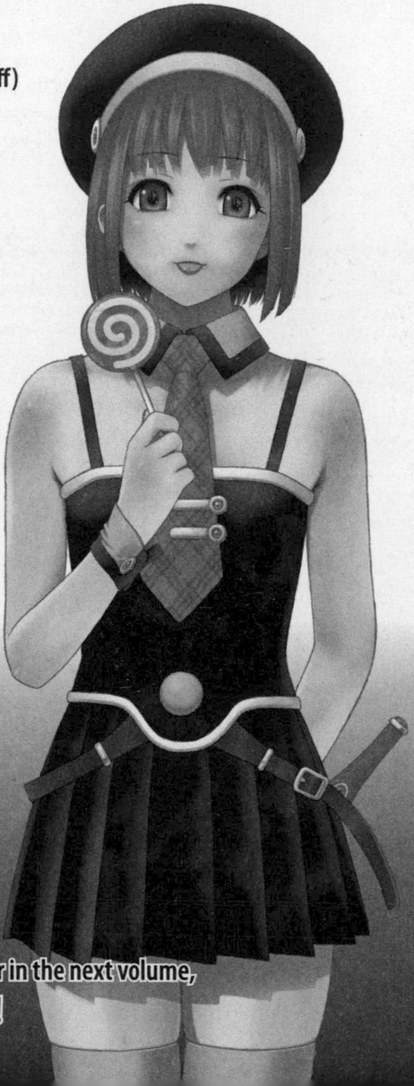

Find out the answer in the next volume,

available now!

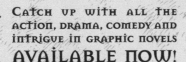